Vulnerability, Marginalization and Culture

About the Editors

Rashmi Pramanik is an Assistant Professor in the Department of Anthropology, Sambalpur University, Odisha. Dr. Pramanik was awarded the degree in Doctor of Philosophy in Anthropology by Sambalpur University in 2005. In 1999, she topped the merit list in M. Phil., Anthropology. She was the University Gold Medallist in Anthropology in the year 1998. She was awarded the best graduate medal in Arts in 1996 for obtaining First Class First position in Anthropology (Honours). She is broadly interested in the Anthropology of Children and Childhood and Tribal Studies. Dr. Pramanik has to her credit twenty research articles; published in peer-reviewed journals and has authored two books. Besides that she has participated in more than forty national and International conferences within and beyond India.

Uwe Skoda is Associate Professor in India and South Asia Studies at the Department of Global Studies, Aarhus University, Denmark. Currently, he is working on transformations of kingship in Odisha/Middle India and is broadly interested in the fields of political anthropology and visual culture especially photography. He recently co-edited two volumes titled "India and Its Visual Cultures. Community, Class and Gender in a Symbolic Landscape" (together with B. Lettmann, New Delhi: Sage, 2017) and "Highland Odisha: Life and Society beyond the Coastal World" (together with P. Pati, New Delhi: Primus, 2017).

Lidia Guzy, Dr. Hab., is a Social Anthropologist, Anthropologist of Religions, South Asia Expert and Global Educator, specialising in the anthropology of marginalisation and global indigenous studies. She is Head of Study of Religions Department, Lecturer in Contemporary South Asian Religions, a Director of the Marginalised and Endangered Worldviews Study Centre (MEWSC), Member of Latin American Strategy Group, and Board member of the India Study Centre Cork (ISCC) at University College Cork (UCC), National University of Ireland. Her recent publications include: Special Journal Issues Emerging Adivasi and Indigenous Studies in Ireland & II (2015 & 2017), Irish Journal of Anthropology; co-editor Special Issue Contemporary Indigeneity and Religion (2015), in International Quarterly for Asian Studies; 2013 Marginalised Music. Music, Religion and Politics from the Bora Sambar Region of Western Odisha, Lit.; co-editor 2012 Voices from the periphery. Subalternity and Empowerment in India. New Delhi: Routledge India.

VULNERABILITY, MARGINALIZATION AND CULTURE

(Felicitation Volume for Prof. Deepak Kumar Behera)

Editors

RASHMI PRAMANIK

UWE SKODA

LIDIA GUZY

CONCEPT PUBLISHING COMPANY PVT. LTD.

NEW DELHI-110059

ISBN-13: 978-93-86682-55-0

First Published 2018

Published and Printed by

Since 1974

Concept Publishing Company Pvt. Ltd.
A/15-16, Commercial Block, Mohan Garden,
New Delhi-110059 (India)
T: 91 11 25351460, 91 11 25351794
E: publishing@conceptpub.com, *W*: www.conceptpub.com

Cataloging in Publication Data--Courtesy: D.K. Agencies (P) Ltd. <docinfo@dkagencies.com>

Vulnerability, marginalization and culture : felicitation volume for Prof. Deepak Kumar Behera / editors, Rashmi Pramanik, Uwe Skoda, Lidia Guzy.
pages cm
Includes bibliographical references and index.
ISBN 9789386682550 (hardback)

1. Ethnology—India. 2. Tribes—India. 3. Marginality, Social—India. 4. India—Social life and customs. 5. India—Social conditions. 6. Odisha (India)—Social conditions. I. Behera, Deepak Kumar, honouree. II. Pramanik, Rashmi, 1975- editor. III. Skoda, Uwe, 1973- editor. IV. Guzy, Lidia, editor.

LCC GN635.I4V85 2018 DDC 305.800954 23

FOREWORD

Professor Deepak Kumar Behera is one of the few internationally renowned anthropologists in India. He is also a fine administrator and last not least a human being of immaculate integrity. I have closely cooperated with him over the last 20 years and could count on his word in every minute during this long period of time.

I first met Dr. Behera in 1981, when he was an assistant of Professor S.N. Ratha and a dynamic young man full of energy and drive. He had been an excellent Cricket player before he made up his mind to hit a century in the game of anthropology. His doctoral research had taken him into the very heterogeneous Christian community of a good number of denominations, tribes and castes. Very early it was an indicator of his independent and analytical mind. Thereafter, he engaged himself in the study of *Ashram* schools in the tribal areas with the result, that he did not hesitate to denounce the callousness of officials, the corruption of staff members and the very obvious fact that the tribal pupils were badly exploited. Perhaps in the course of this research he found the topic of his career and of his life, the protection of the most vulnerable among us, the cause of the children against the brutalities of the world of adults. Professor Behera did not advocate certain educational improvements. He was a revolutionary. He wanted and wants children to decide, what is good and right for them. Perhaps the confident young humans among the Kisan tribe had impressed him, when he spent another long spree of ethnographic research among them.

Many of us preach water and drink wine, but not Deepak Kumar Behera. No discrepancy can be discovered between his words and his actions. His child, young Titli, grew up as a fully self-determined young human. Mrs.

Rita Behera, a wonderful educationalist, along with Titli's father included the girl, whenever a decision had to be taken. It also goes without saying that the eminent anthropologist makes no difference between females and males in matters of politeness and respect, opportunities and positions of power. His behaviour is equally decent to rich and poor, man and woman, old and young, or Hindu and Christian. I could feel this in a very personal experience which is unusual for Europeans.

Whenever I came to India, Professor Behera made me stay at his house, so I met his mother who had long conversations with me, or his father, who treated patients as a homoeopathic doctor free of any charges. Like many other Indian and non-Indian colleagues I was immediately included into his entire family, perhaps because he did not know, what was in store for him. In fact, I exploited this situation beyond treasonable measure. From the late 1990s onward, one German scholar after the other came and stayed at the Beheras' house. Since that time seven or eight major contributions to the anthropological research of Odisha were completed and all of these authors had lived in the Professor's house and were guided or even personally placed in the field by their host himself. Clearly this important stage of tribal research could not have been achieved without our splendid and absolutely responsible Indian counterpart.

The innumerable international contacts were one obvious result of this combination of academic competence and personal integrity. Dr. Behera toured the globe several times, having friends on all continents. In Germany, he cooperated with the Free University of Berlin and the University of Tübingen and I personally had the honour to edit ten different volumes of *Tribal Studies* together with him. All members of the *International Union of Anthropological and Ethnological Sciences* elected him for ten years as one of the five leaders and only recently he could host a conference of this renowned body in Bhubaneswar.

Personally, I was a bit sad to lose this scholar to the field of administration, when he became Vice-Chancellor of Berhampur University, but now I am happy that he has returned to academic research and will once again engage himself in writing and thinking anthropology. Today, I am proud to say: Deepak Kumar Behera is my esteemed colleague and my close friend.

Free University, Berlin
(7.8.2017)

Professor (Dr.) Georg Pfeffer
Professor Emeritus
Department of Social and
Cultural Anthropology

ACKNOWLEDGEMENTS

This volume brings together a range of renowned international scholars from India, Latin America, North America and Europe, who — as experienced fieldworkers — have approached Vulnerability, Marginalization and Culture from various angles including anthropology, sociology or cultural studies. The chapters result from long-term international collaborations with Professor Deepak Kumar Behera and the Department of Anthropology of Sambalpur University which he successfully headed for many years. During this time, he was instrumental in promoting a wide range of scholarly activities such as workshops, international conferences, field-work and excursions, various joint research as well as publications projects in which all of the contributors participated in multiple ways.

Professor Behera's intellectual, academic and institutional support was invaluable for the advancement of *Adivasi*/Tribal Studies, for the study of children and childhoods and for the understanding of marginalized and vulnerable communities from an anthropological and cultural perspective. The editors and authors assembled in this volume gratefully acknowledge Professor Behera's outstanding contributions to these fields.

As editors we would also like to thank the *Irish Journal of Anthropology* (IJA) for the generous permission to reprint the article *Cockfights and Champa Bird Fights: Adivasis, Farmers and Popular Pastimes in North-western Odisha* by Uwe Skoda published in IJA 2015, vol. 18 (2), pp. 48-64. Moreover, we would like to express our gratitude to Concept Publishing Co. (P.) Ltd. for taking up this volume and for the constant encouragement and support throughout the publication process.

CONTENTS

BIO-NOTE OF THE CONTRIBUTORS

Alfred Toppo, is currently undertaking a research on Kodaku Tribe of Surguja, Chhattisgarh. Before this he was the Director of Xavier Institute of Development Action and Studies (XIDAS), Jabalpur, Madhya Pradesh where taught Post Graduate students who perused Post Graduate Diploma in Management (Rural Management). He also served the Institute as the Assistant Director before he took over as the Director. Before he joined XIDAS, Jabalpur he worked as Development Professional for tribal and rural development for more than 10 years in rural areas of Chhattisgarh. His main focus of development initiatives was on Kodaku, Oraon and Gond tribes of Chhattisgarh. During his stint as Development Professional, he also served as the Director of Xavier Institute of Social Action, Raipur, Chhattisgarh, and Jeevan VikasMaitri, Pathalgaon, Jashpur, Chhattisgarh and as the Coordinator of Kodaku Community Development Programme, Dhanwarkala, Balrampur, Chhattisgarh. His interest is in tribal studies and he keeps writing for various journals and edited volumes on tribal issues.

Mailing Address: Loyola Niketan, Rajeev Vihar, SECL Sub Post, Bilaspur-495 006, Chhattisgarh.

E-mail: *alfredtoppo@gmail.com*

Armando Moctezuma Suàrez is currently pursuing his Ph.D. study at Autonomous University of Nuevo Leon, Monterrey, Mexico. He has completed his master degree in Social Sciences. His areas of interest are human trafficking, Public Policies and discourse Analysis.

E-mail: *ras.moctezeuma@gmail.com*

Dr. Arun Kumar Acharya, is Professor at Institute of Social Science Research, Autonomous University of Nuevo Leon, Monterrey, Mexico. He is founder of Mexican Centre for Migration and Human Trafficking Studies, Monterrey. Prof. Acharya has actively participated on drafting of human trafficking law in Mexico in 2012 and 2014. His book *Perspectives of Human Trafficking in Mexico* led most of the states of Mexico to reformulate their local trafficking law. He has also published more than 50 research papers in various international journals on issues of Migration, Human Trafficking, Gender Violence and Human Rights, also 6 books on Migration and Human Trafficking in Mexico. Recently, World Bank, Washington DC has invited him to deliver a lecture on "The Fragility of the Mexican State and Gender Inequality: The Case of Trafficking in Women". He is also member of National Council on Science and Technology (CONACYT) level III.

E-mail: *acharya_77@yahoo.com*

Dr. Christine Finnan is a Professor in the Department of Sociology and Anthropology and the Department of Teacher Education at the College of Charleston in Charleston, South Carolina, USA. Her research focuses on the role of schools in children's lives and futures. She teaches courses that explore the intersection of culture, language, and education. In 2014-2015, she was a Fulbright-Nehru Research Scholar.

E-mail: *finnanc@cofc.edu*

Francisco de Jesús Gómez Ontiveros completed his master degree in Social Sciences from Autonomous University of Nuevo Leon. Currently, he is working in an organization as a project coordinator. His areas of interest are: human trafficking, Gender analysis.

E-mail: *jgentiveras@hotmail.com*

Georg Pfeffer is a former Professor of Social Anthropology in the Institute of Ethnology at Freie Universität, Berlin since 1985. He studied ethnology, sociology and history of religions at Freiburg University, Germany, where he obtained his doctoral degree in 1970. He did his postdoctoral research at the University of Heidelberg, where he taught afterwards. He has conducted fieldwork for several years in various parts of India and Pakistan and is an active member of several national and international academic societies as well as being on the editorial board of the German Zeitschrift für Ethnologie. Religious cults and kinship structures of the Scheduled Tribes in the Koraput and Phulbani districts of Odisha (India) are his key areas of interest. Recently, he published "Verwandtschaft als Verfassung. Unbürokratische Muster öffentlicher Ordnung" (Baden-Baden: NOMOS, 2016) and "Hunters, Tribes, Peasants: Cultural Crisis and Comparison" (Bhubaneswar: NISWASS, 2003).

E-mail: *gpfeffer*@gmx.com

Dr. Harald Tambs-Lyche is Professor Emeritus of Ethnology at the University of Picardie-Jules Verne, Amiens. He has written widely on the history, society and religion of Saurashtra, Gujarat ("Power, Profit and Poetry", Delhi, 1997: "The Good Country", Delhi, 2004) and, more recently, on the Gauda Saraswat Brahmins of coastal Karnataka ("Business Brahmins", Delhi, 2011). A theoretical essay on caste is currently in press (Transaction and Hierarchy: Elements for a Theory of Caste). With Marine Carrin he wrote "An Encounter of Peripheries" (Delhi, 2008) on the Scandinavian Mission to the Santals. He has edited "The Feminine Sacred in South Asia", (Delhi, 1999), and co-edited "People of the Jangal" (Delhi, 2008) with Marine Carrin. With Nikita Sud he edited a special number of the Journal "South Asia", on the theme "Religion in the Making of a Region" (2011).

E-mail: *htambslyche4@gmail.com*

Jens Seeberg, Ph.D., is a Professor of Medical Anthropology. He has worked with WHO and with the TB control programme in India, in addition to his academic work. His research has included international projects on HIV/AIDS, Tuberculosis, health systems in poor urban neighbourhoods, migration, and health ethics. He has worked extensively with poor and marginalised people in India, especially in the State of Odisha.

E-mail: *jseeberg@cas.au.dk*

Lidia Guzy is Head of Study of Religions Department and Lecturer in Contemporary South Asian Religions, UCC. She is a social anthropologist and scientist of religions, specialising in the anthropology of religions and global indigenous studies. She is a Director of the Marginalised and Endangered Worldviews Study Centre (MEWSC).

Lidia was born in Poland from where she started her international academic journey between Poland, Germany, France, India and Brazil.

Lidia holds a bi-national Ph.D. (2002) in Ethnology/Social Anthropology from Freie Universität Berlin, Germany and the École des Hautes Études en Sciences Sociales (EHESS), Paris (thèse en co-tutelle). In 2011 Lidia obtained her Habilitation (post-doctoral thesis and professorial qualification) at the Faculty of Cultural and Historical Studies at Freie Universität Berlin with a work based on extensive ethnography and documentation of hitherto unknown and endangered traditions of sacred music of rural India. She came to Ireland in 2011 and joined UCC as Lecturer in Contemporary South Asian Religions, UCC.

Dr. Guzy worked throughout her academic career in international cooperation with École des Hautes Études en Sciences Sociales (EHESS) in Paris, Freie Universität Berlin, Germany; Utkal University in Bhubaneshwar (India) (visiting Ph.D. scholar), Sambalpur University (India) (visiting Ph.D. scholar), the Centre d'Anthropologie in Toulouse (Visiting Professor in Anthropology March, 2016), the India Study Centre Aarhus University (CISCA), Denmark, with the Anthropological Survey of India in Kolkata, the National Museum of Mankind/ Indira Gandhi Rashtriya Manav Sangrahalaya in Bhopal, India and Universidade Federal de Piauí in Teresina, and Universidade Federal Fluminense–UFF, in Rio de Janeiro, Brazil.

Over the past 17 years, Lidia has specialised in comparative anthropology with special interest in indigenous worldviews, eco-cosmologies, indigeneity, cultural heritage, cultural minorities, the politics of representation and the arts.

Her recent publications include: Special Journal Issues Emerging Adivasi and Indigenous Studies in Ireland I & II (2015 & 2017), Irish Journal of Anthropology; co-editor Special Issue Contemporary Indigeneity and Religion (2015), in International Quarterly for Asian Studies; 2013 Marginalised Music. Music,

Religion and Politics from the Bora Sambar Region of Western Odisha, Lit; co-editor 2012 Voices from the Periphery. Subalternity and Empowerment in India. New Delhi: Routledge India.

E-mail: *l.guzy@ucc.ie*

Lucia Rabello de Castro, Ph.D. (Univ. London). Professor of Childhood and Youth, Institute of Psychology, Universidade Federal do Rio de Janeiro, Brazil. Founder and Chair from 1998 to 2011, and present Scientific Director of the Centre for Interdisciplinary Research and Exchange on Contemporary Childhood and Youth (NIPIAC/UFRJ/Brazil). Senior Researcher of the Brazilian Council of Science and Technological Development (CNPQ). Officer at Large of RC 53/ISA 1994-1998; 1998-2002. Co-editor of ISA RC53 Newsletter (2014-18). Executive Board Member of the Child and Youth Committee of IUAES (International Union of Anthropological and Ethnological Sciences). Chief Editor of DESidades, an electronic scientific journal in the area of childhood and youth www.desidades.ufrj.br Research interests: children's and youth's social and political participation; research methodologies with children and youth; theories of childhood; intergenerational relationships.

E-mail: *lrcastro@infalink.com.br*

Marcela Rabello de C. Centelhas is graduated in Social Sciences by the Federal University of Rio de Janeiro, Master in Social Anthropology by the National Museum of the Federal University of Rio de Janeiro and Ph.D. student of Social Anthropology in the same institution. Presently, she is conducting a research on social movements in the rural North-east of Brazil.

E-mail: *marcelarabelo91@gmail.com*

Marine Carrin, Anthropologist, is Director of Research Emeritus (CNRS) at the Centre d'Anthropologie Sociale, Toulouse. She is the author of *La Fleur et l'Os :symbolisme et rituel chez les Santal,* 1986) ; *Enfants de la Déesse : prêtrise et dévotion féminine au Bengal* (1997) and co-author of *A Peripheral Encounter, Santals, Missionaries and their Changing Worlds* (with H. Tambs-Lyche, 2008). She is the co-author of *From Fire Rain to Rebellion Reasserting Identity through Narratives* (Santal Texts edited and translated by P. Andersen, M. Carrin and S. Soren, 2011). She has edited *Managing Distress :Therapeutic Cults in South Asia,* (1999*).*She has co-edited *Tribus et Basses Castes: Resistance et Autonomie dans la société indienne*, Purusartha, (with Ch. Jaffrelot, 2002) and *People of the Jangal: Reformulating Identities and Adaptations in Crisis* (with H. Tambs-Lyche, 2008) *Voices from the Periphery: Subalternity and Empowerment*, (with L. Guzy), 2012 and the *Politics of Ethnicity in India* Nepal and China [co-edited with G. Toffin and Pralay Kanung,) Delhi, Primus (2014)]. She has a book (*in press*) on Santal Ritual Discourse (*Société d'Ethnologie, 2016)* and is currently working on indigenous knowledge and related issues in Central India. She is also co-editing *Re-making Knowledge: The Agency of Youth* with H. Tambs-Lyche and D. Blanc (*in press*) Delhi, Primus.

Marine Carrin, anthropologue, est Directrice de Recherche (CNRS) au Centre d'Anthropologie Sociale, Toulouse. Elle est l'auteur de *La Fleur et l'Os: symbolisme et rituel chez les Santal,* 1986) ; *Enfants de la Déesse : prêtrise et dévotion féminine au Bengal* (1997) et co-auteur de *A Peripheral Encounter, Santals, Missionaries and their Changing Worlds* (with H. Tambs-Lyche, 2008). Elle est le co-auteur de *From Fire Rain to Rebellion Reasserting Identity through Narratives* (Santal Texts édités et traduits par P. Andersen, M. Carrin and S. Soren, 2011). Elle a édité *Managing Distress :Therapeutic Cults in South Asia* (1999). Elle a co-édité *Tribus et Basses Castes: Resistance et Autonomie dans la société indienne*, Purusartha, (avec Ch. Jaffrelot, 2002) et *People of the Jangal: Reformulating Identities and Adaptations in Crisis* (avec H. Tambs-Lyche, 2008) et *Voices from the Periphery: Subalternity and Empowerment*, (with L. Guzy), 2012 et la Politique de l'Ethnicité en Inde, au Népal et en Chine, Delhi, Primus (sous presse). Elle a aussi co-edité *Transfer of Knowledge and Children Agency: Reconstructing the Paradigms of Socialization, A Cross-cultural Perspective* (eds.), D. Blanc, M. Carrin H. Tambs-Lyche (*in press*) Delhi, Primus. Elle publie un ouvrage en français sur le *Discours Rituel Santal* (*Société d'Ethnologie, Nanterre, sous presse)* et travaille actuellement à un livre sur la connaissance indigène et son contexte politique en Inde Centrale.

E-mail: *marinecarrin@hotmail.fr*

M.C. Behera, M.A., Ph.D. (Economics) from Utkal University, Bhubaneswar, Odisha, has been pursuing researches on Tribal Studies and Rural Economics from mid-1980s. He has authored/edited/co-edited 30 volumes on socio-economic and cultural life of tribal and rural people from diverse theoretical and cultural perspectives, primarily, in the context of globalisation. To his credit, he has about sixty research papers on national and international topics published in various national and international journals/periodicals. He has presented about fifty five papers in national and international seminars/conferences in the country and abroad. He is a member of many professional bodies. Dr. Behera was a Professor of Indigenous Culture Studies and Dean, School of Cultural Studies, Central University of Jharkhand before he joined as Director of Arunachal Institute of Tribal Studies, Rajiv Gandhi University, Itanagar, Arunachal Pradesh.

E-mail: *mcbeheral959@gmail.com*

Dr. Mehul Chauhan is currently the Executive Director of Gramodyog Sansthan, Madhya Pradesh, India. He has also served as Dean of Xavier Institute of Development Action and Studies and has got around 10 years of experience in economic and social research, evaluation and assessment, institutional strengthening and capacity building in development, reforms and restructuring projects in India. He has been involved with social impact assessment of sectoral reform projects and evaluation of public services in both rural and urban areas. He has worked with organizations like CASA, XIDAS and has lead the assignments supported by NTPC Ltd., Reliance Energy Ltd., Power Grid, Mahan Coal Field Ltd., CAPART, Moser Baer Power Pvt. Ltd., Society of Jesus Darjeeling and

Madhya Pradesh Province, CASA, NABARD, TATA Trust and Asian Development Bank. He is professionally trained in Entrepreneurship at EDII, Ahmedabad and Management Research Methods at IIM, Calicut. He has presented papers at various national and international conferences. He has visited countries like Nepal, Denmark, Portugal and Germany for various academic and social programmes.

E-mail: *mehsbpods@gmail.com*, Mobile: 91 9977064882

Dr. Ranju Hasini Sahoo is an M.A., M.Phil. and Ph.D. from Sambalpur University, Odisha and at present she is an Associate Professor of Sociology and Head of Department of Sociology and Social Anthropology, Indira Gandhi National Tribal University. Before joining as a teacher in the University she was working in Anthropological Survey of India, Government of India, as an Anthropologist and most of her research work was related to tribes of Bastar and South Chhattisgarh. However, she has vast field exposure to the tribal dominated villages of Odisha, Chhattisgarh and Madhya Pradesh.

Her field of Specialization is Inter-Ethnic Relation, Tribal Development, Displacement and Rehabilitation, Disaster Management, Anthropology of Health and Museum, Traditional Knowledge and Resource Management, Visual Anthropology and Ethnographic Film.

Hence, her representative publications varies from Inter-ethnic relations, tribal issues, displacement and rehabilitation, disaster management, gender issues, Anthropology of Museum, health and children issues.

She has received R.K. Padhee Memorial Scholarship in Graduation and qualified for ICSSR Institute Doctoral Fellow-ship and received P.G. Research Scholar Scheme.

She was the Principal Investigator and Co-project Director of two major projects "Study of Folk Narrative of Human Origin" and "An Interdisciplinary Study of Baiga: To Develop a Data Base to be Used for inputs for Sustainable Development." An ICSSR Sponsored major research project in Anthropological Survey of India and Indira Gandhi National Tribal University respectively.

Presented papers in eight and 34 international seminars and national seminars respectively, besides organizing a good number of national seminar and workshops.

She is a compassionate supporter of Tribal Issues and has been working for the protection of the Constitutional Rights of the tribes since last one decade.

She is the team leader of the evaluation work of Implementation of Forest Rights Act, 2006 and carried on extensive fieldwork with the tribes in interior parts of Rajasthan, Odisha, Karnataka and Kerala.

Awarded and honoured for best story and poetry. Her literary works are published in Oriya, English and Hindi. At present, she is working on the biopic of her revered teacher Prof. Satya Narayan Ratha who has taught her Anthropology and Sociology.

E-mail: *sahoo.ranju@gmail.com*

Dr. Rashmi Pramanik is an Assistant Professor in the Department of Anthropology, Sambalpur University. Dr. Pramanik was awarded Ph.D. in

Anthropology in 2005 and was the University Gold Medalist in Anthropology. She has to her credit 20 articles; published in peer-reviewed journals and has authored two books. She has participated in more than 40 National and International Conferences. She was invited at the National University of Singapore and also at Aarhus University, Denmark for academic purposes.

E-mail: *rashmipramanik@yahoo.co.in*

Rikke Aarhus, Ph.D., is currently working on her Ph.D. study on the organization and experience of cancer control initiatives in Denmark. She holds a master's degree in anthropology and is positioned at University Research Clinic for Innovative Patient Pathways, Silkeborg Regional Hospital. Her academic interest lies within medical anthropology with a current focus on time, organization, and standardization.

E-mail: *rikke.aarhus@ph.au.dk*

Dr. Satyendra C. Pandey is a Fellow (Ph.D.) of Xavier Institute of Management Bhubaneswar, Odisha. He is currently working as Assistant Professor in OB-HR Area at Institute of Rural Management Anand (IRMA). Before joining IRMA he was associated with Centre for Management Studies at NALSAR University of Law, Hyderabad. During his association with NALSAR he has carried out training and consulting for Department of Justice, Ministry of Law and Justice under the scheme on measuring and upgrading efficiency of Court Managers at High Courts and Subordinate Courts. His research interest is in knowledge management, entrepreneurship, and CSR in emerging economies. Dr. Pandey has over 20 publications in Journals of International repute like Journal of Knowledge Management, Journal of Knowledge Based Development, International Journal of Law and Management among others. At IRMA he is associated with Centre for Social Entrepreneurship and Enterprises and Centre for Public Policy and Governance.

E-mail: *satyendra@irma.ac.in*, Mobile: 8106745488

Prof. Satya Narayana Ratha born in 1936 in a tribal village in forest clad Koraput district of Odisha, had his primary education in the village school and passed matriculation from H.E. School, Titlagarh. Prof. Ratha studied Anthropology under the fostering care of Prof. A. Aiyappan and began his career with a teaching assignment at Gauhati University in 1962. Then he moved on Sambalpur University, Odisha in 1976 as the youngest Professor and Head of the Department of Anthropology and Sociology. He has written a number of papers on all branches of Anthropology though his primary interest has always been to tribal studies.

E-mail: *satyanratha@gmail.com*

Shreyasi, Bhattacharya is pursuing her doctoral research under Sambalpur University, Odisha as SRF-(UGC) since March 2011. She completed her Masters in Anthropology from Calcutta University in the year 2008. Ms. Bhattacharya has to her credit a couple of publications in peer-reviewed journals. She has participated in seven national and two international conferences. Ms. Bhattacharya is a life member in (INCAA) and member of (IUAES). Her areas of interest are: Anthropology of Children and Childhood, Tribal Anthropology and Gender Studies.

E-mail: *shreyasibhattacharya@gmal.com*

Dr. Suresh Chandra Murmu is an Assistant Professor in the Department of Anthropology, Sambalpur University. Mr. Murmu qualified UGC-JRF in Anthropology in 2009. He was the University Gold Medalist in Anthropology from Utkal University in 2007. He has to his credit a couple of articles published in peer-reviewed journals. He has participated in more than half a dozen of national level conferences. He is a life member of INCAA. Dr. Murmu's current interest in research is tribal ethnicity and religious studies.

E-mail: *smurmul0@gmail.com*

Dr. Uwe Skoda is Associate Professor in India and South Asia Studies at the Department of Global Studies, Aarhus University. Currently, he is working on transformations of kingship in Odisha and is broadly interested in the fields of political anthropology and visual culture. He recently co-edited a volume on "Highland Odisha: Life and Society Beyond the Coastal World" (New Delhi: Primus, 2017).

E-mail: *oustus@cas.au.dk*

ONE

INTRODUCTION
Vulnerability, Marginalization and Culture

RASHMI PRAMANIK, UWE SKODA AND LIDIA GUZY

Introduction

This volume honours Professor Deepak Kumar Behera's social anthropological and especially fieldwork orientated approach. Prof. Behera's research work focuses primarily on Odisha, but his findings go much beyond this region. One of his great contributions has been a sensitization of the academic community as well as the wider society on the issues of cultural and socio-economic vulnerability and marginalization of communities commonly classified as "tribal" in India—particularly by Government agencies. Thus, Prof. Behera's studies and interrogations furthered a deeper understanding of these communities in eastern India and thus contributed to a new engagement with vulnerable, frequently marginalized communities called tribal, indigenous, *Adivasi* etc. and especially their culture and world views—leading to and reflected in the renaming of the derogative colonially—inspired administrative appellation "Primitive Tribal Group" (PTG) into "Particularly Vulnerable Tribal Group" (PVTG).

While his extensive work as listed in his bibliography (*see* Appendix) overlaps with and includes other areas of interests such as indigenous knowledge and practices concerning primary production, health, resource conservation and utilization, and particularly children and childhoods, this *Festschrift* highlights the intersecting aspects of vulnerability, marginalization and culture.

Vulnerability

Though perhaps still undertheorized as a concept, as Mackenzie, Rogers and Dodds (2013) argued, of late vulnerability has received more scholarly attention (*see* Butler, 2004; Butler, Gambetti & Sabsay, 2016 *et al.*) and Professor Behera's interventions need to be mentioned in this regard. Derived from the Latin word "vulnus" for "wound" debates around vulnerability stressed two different directions: on the one hand, the universal side of, i.e. the idea that human life is always linked to vulnerability, and on the other hand to the situation of groups in need of protective measures, care or support in order to reduce their specific vulnerability.

The former highlights the broader human and bodily dimension, i.e. as humans we have physical, mental and material needs (food, shelter etc.) while being exposed to risks, fears, more tangible diseases, to accidents and in the worst case death. Vulnerability as ontological condition of all human existence is in this sense, also as frailty and potential suffering, opposed to health and well-being. The former approach focuses on individual needs, psychological and emotional vulnerability, without denying a social or collective dimension, i.e. as individual or community humans are involved in interactions with other humans or agents which have a direct impact on their lives such as exposure to violence, social exclusion, marginalization, state actions in a wider sense. This relational aspect of vulnerability is even more emphasized in the latter usage with a focus on communities in need of additional care, experiencing threats to their autonomy, with a limited capacity to protect themselves and their interests *vis-à-vis* other communities or groups more likely to experience conditions of poverty or powerlessness or living under conditions diametrically opposed to contextually defined standards of a self-determined, dignified "good life".

While these two understandings of vulnerability highlight either more universal, ontological conditions or specific, collective dimensions of fragility, suffering and wounding, they are mutually exclusive as Butler (Butler, 2004: 29) argued, i.e.:

> "*... we all live with ... a vulnerability to the other that is part of bodily life, a vulnerability to a sudden address from elsewhere that we cannot preempt. This vulnerability, however, becomes highly exacerbated under certain social and political conditions,*

especially those in which violence is a way of life and the means to secure self-defense are limited."

Keeping the overlaps and contextual dimension in mind, Mackenzie, Rogers and Dodds (2013: 9ff) tried to sharpen an conceptual understanding of vulnerability by developing a taxonomy that distinguishes between an inherent vulnerability (as tied to corporeality) as against a situational one (as linked to disasters, environmental issues etc., though mediated through social contexts); between "dispositional" (or potential) and "occurent" (or actual) states of vulnerability, while considering an additional form of pathogenic vulnerability, i.e. when policies to reduce or limit risks or conditions turn out to be counter-productive.

Such pathogenic vulnerability is visible in the Indian context, in which attempts by the post-colonial state and its variety of institutions to address and subsequently reduce blatant inequalities and to redress historical injustices led to exercises in creating categories and identifying groups various described as, for example, "tribal", "primitive", "backward" etc. – and more recently as "vulnerable". However, the idea of recognizing and mitigating historical wrongdoings by introducing reservations for Scheduled Tribes in the Indian Constitution as redistributive measures included a darker side in the sense that such a paternalistic labelling also entailed and indirectly fostered a continuing stereotyping and discrimination of communities. The renaming of so-called "Primitive Tribal Groups", identified by the state as the most needy groups, among the Scheduled Tribes as "Particularly Vulnerable Tribal Groups" in 2006, thereby shedding partially a colonial legacy, exemplifies the dynamics, complexity and politics of classificatory processes that aim at supporting disadvantaged groups while simultaneously being implicated in their stigmatizing – often also as passive victims. Arguing forcefully against any such notion of vulnerable populations as lacking agency, Butler, Gambetti & Sabsey (2016: 1) rather ask whether vulnerability is imaginable as "one of the conditions of the very possibility of resistance?"

Marginalization

Marginalization as a concept is often equated with social exclusion and the social position at the margins, a dynamic which relates to the systematic association of someone or some groups to an inferior, less powerful and less influential position in society. Marginalization results not only from any direct and straightforward or total social exclusion, it may equally arise from what Amartya Sen termed "unfavourable inclusion" (Sen, 2000; see also Skoda, Nielsen & Fibiger, 2013) or social disadvantage.

Indigenous people are among the most disadvantaged social groups worldwide. According to the UN Permanent Forum on Indigenous Issues:

> "*The situation of indigenous peoples in many parts of the world continues to be critical: indigenous peoples face systemic discrimination and exclusion from political and economic power; they continue to be over-Irepresented among the poorest, the illiterate, the destitute; they are displaced by wars and environmental disasters; the weapon of rape and sexual humiliation is also turned against indigenous women for the ethnic cleansing and demoralization of indigenous communities; indigenous peoples are dispossessed of their ancestral lands and deprived of their resources for survival, both physical and cultural; they are even robbed of their very right to life. In more modern versions of market exploitation, indigenous peoples see their traditional knowledge and culture marketed and patented without their consent or participation. Of the some 7,000 languages today, it is estimated that more than 4,000 are spoken by indigenous peoples. Language specialists predict that up to 90 per cent of the world's languages are likely to become extinct or threatened with extinction by the end of the century. This statistic illustrates the grave danger faced by indigenous peoples*" (State of the World's Indigenous Peoples, United Nations, 2009:1).

India is the country with the largest number of indigenous peoples in the world. The indigenous people of India as crucial focal point of Professor Behera's work, are generally known as *ādivāsīs*, "tribals". Legal discourse in India often identifies them as members of "Scheduled Tribes" and "Particularly Vulnerable Tribal Groups" which enjoy sophisticated constitutional provisions for their protection and preservation. These groups constitute, according to the 2011 Census, 8.6 per cent of the population: 10,45,45,716 out of 1,21,08,54,977 (1.21 billion) of the Indian population. The People of India project (1985-1995) conducted by the Anthropological Survey of India identified and located 635 distinct tribes in India, identifying among them 461 main tribes and 172 minor segments

(Singh, 1994) with over 700 languages belonging to language families of Austro-Asiatic, Dravidian and Tibeto-Burman (Das, 2015: 16). *Adivasis* have their own cultural and religious traditions, observances, stories, and ideas which in recent years have gained rising academic attention [(Behera/Pfeffer, Vols. I-X), Guzy, Alles and Skoda 2015a: 12-20; Guzy, Alles, Skoda and Valk, 2015b: 5-15; Carrin and Guzy (eds.) 2012)].

The distinctive languages, cultures, worldviews, life-worlds and livelihoods of indigenous groups in India have been preserved since ancient times while co-existing with the Hindu majority society, for example a historical co-existence based on the cultural institution of "jungle kingdoms" (*see* Schnepel, 2002) which exerted a strong cultural interdependence with local tribal groups. This historical interdependency and cross-fertilization created interrelated but diversified cultural entities.

With few exceptions such as kingdom ruled by "Adivasi"—dynasties and a small emerging middle class, *Adivasi* groups have been persistently marginalised (*see* Carrin and Jaffrelot, 2002: 21-24) in pre- and post-Independence India. Marginalisation within the British colonial system was related to the establishment of the *zamindari* system (the Bengal Permanent Settlement Act) in 1793. Since then, the *Adivasi* territories were conferred to feudal lords for the purpose of revenue collection (Bijoi, 2007:15-27; Munda, 2002). This territorial taxation incited *Adivasi* rebellions (*see* Hardiman, 1987) and increased their impoverishment. Sociologically, the marginalisation of indigenous peoples can be seen in relation to the differences between *Adivasi* cultures, religions and kinship systems and the hegemonic Hindu caste system. Paradoxically, the post-Independence governmental purpose of positive discrimination through administratively constructed categories of "Social Backwardness", such as "Scheduled Tribes" or "Primitive Tribal Groups", continued to marginalise *Adivasi* cultures stigmatised as tribal, primitive, non-sedentary and non-urban, with a pre-industrial way of life.

Adivasi cultures continued to be measured by an evolutionary model of urban modernity, sedentariness and industrial development. Especially, the lack of script has become a socio-cultural pattern in the sociological and ideological marginalisation of societies dominated by orality and aurality. In short, societies and cultures relying on non-scriptural systems of meaning tend to be considered as inferior, devoid of possibilities to gain a complex intellectual – theoretical – hold of the world.

Culture

Prof. Behera's perhaps most sustainable contribution to anthropological scholarship is the understanding of the interrelatedness between vulnerability, marginalization and culture. Culture in Behera's approach refers to a classical anthropological understanding of culture as cumulative deposit of knowledge, experience, beliefs, values, attitudes, meanings, hierarchies, religion, notions of time, roles, spatial relations, concepts of the universe, material objects and possessions acquired by a group of people in the course of generations through individual and group striving. Culture is expressed by the external symbols that a society uses rather than being locked inside people's heads. Geertz defines culture as "an historically transmitted pattern of meanings embodied in symbols, a system of inherited conceptions expressed in symbolic forms by means of which men communicate, perpetuate, and develop their knowledge about and their attitudes toward life" (Geertz, 1973e:89). Societies use these symbols to express their "worldview, value-orientation, ethos, [and other aspects of their culture]", seen as "vehicles of 'culture'" (Ortner, 1983:129), meaning that symbols should not be studied in and of themselves, but for what they can reveal about culture.

Professor Behera's anthropological work contributes to the celebration of the rich diversity of cultures which is increasingly recognized as a source of mutual enrichment and innovation in our present-day world. With the persistent anthropological work of revaluation and recognition of marginalized and vulnerable knowledge systems—such as with the exemplary work of Professor Behera—it is broadly recognised in India and beyond that the respect for the values and the history of other cultures and societies are essential in our struggle for peace, reconciliation and harmony. Particularly in today's world of globalization, more and more people in India express their worries about the extinction of their own cultural heritage. Cultural heritage is interrelated with indigenous knowledge systems which are on the one hand keeping up a specific tradition as a custom or as meaningful practices in collective and individual life. On the other hand, they are always situational, variable and changing. Therefore, indigenous knowledge and practice always needs to be understood contextually, as multiple volumes of Professor Behera exemplify.

Keeping the above perspective in mind, the present volume attempts to uncover those valuable but endangered tangible and intangible cultural traditions and indigenous practices, which are fast disappearing in India and beyond. We need to emphasize what indigenous people know about their resources and how they use them by distinguishing the techniques of knowledge systems and their formal applications. We need to study the various aspects of the rich cultural heritage across cultures in relation to its immediate environment in terms of hills, rivers, streams and groves, their locations in time and space and the perception of place within local communities and cosmologies. Struggling along and against other than human elements (i.e. nature), indigenous people in their "little worlds" largely depend upon its bounty for subsistence. Indigenous knowledge generated within tribal communities is locational and culture specific. Such knowledge is the basis for their survival strategies as it covers critical issues such as primary production, craftsmanship and natural resources conservation and management.

The UNESCO, 2003 Convention for the Safeguarding of the Intangible Cultural Heritage (ICH) is a major landmark in the history of Mankind. As many as 59 States (including India) have already ratified this important Convention. The Convention states that the safeguarding of intangible cultural heritage is of general interest to humanity and underlines its invaluable role in bringing human beings closer together and ensuring exchange and understanding among them. The 2003 Convention underlies the urgency to safeguard the important, but fragile intangible heritage in a spirit of mutual understanding and through international cooperation. The Convention has now come into effect and a UNESCO-based international effort to safeguard ICH is starting to get underway in a full-fledged manner. It is extremely important for regions across the globe to hand down their cultural heritage, and, at the same time, respect and appreciate the cultural heritage of other regions. This deepens the mutual understanding of each other's histories and cultures.

Culture is transmitted from generation to generation—an aspect Professor Behera constantly stressed in his research on children and their processes of learning. It is constantly recreated by communities and groups, in response to their environment, their interaction with nature, and their history. Culture provides communities and groups with a sense of identity and continuity. It promotes respect for cultural diversity and human creativity. Culture is compatible with international human rights instruments and it complies with the requirements of mutual respect among communities, and of sustainable development. The knowledge and skills are shared within a community, and manifestations of cultural heritage are performed collectively. Many elements of the intangible cultural heritage are endangered, due to effects of globalization, uniformization policies, and lack of means, appreciation and understanding which—taken together—may lead to the erosion of functions and values of such elements and to lack of interest among younger generations.

Conclusion

Touching upon various aspects of vulnerability, marginalization and culture—using these frameworks sometimes explicitly, sometimes implicitly—, Professor Deepak Kumar Behera's work built-up over many years as documented in his extensive bibliography (*see* Appendix). It also relates to other fields which should be mentioned here, namely (1) the ethnography of *Adivasi* groups and tribal society in Odisha and beyond; (2) forms and processes of marginalization as social exclusion, *e.g.* in the context of development; and (3) promoting an anthropology of children and childhoods based on in-depth research. While all of them are closely interwoven with the three guiding concepts of this volume – for example, children are "paradigm examples of persons who are vulnerable to harm or exploitation by virtue of the asymmetrical relations of dependency, power, and authority in which they stand to parents or other caregivers" (Mackenzie, Rogers and Dodds, 2013: 18). In many ways, children are often experiencing multiple forms of vulnerability, not only as children, but also as persons of marginalized or socially excluded communities, i.e. belonging to *Adivasi* communities or families displaced by dam projects etc. and thus being the more vulnerable among the vulnerable. And it was D.K. Behera's constant credo to take the children's point of view seriously, to understand their agency in and ways of negotiating processes of socio-cultural in- and exclusion.

Similarly, the authors of this volume who all collaborated with Professor Behera, often over decades were engaged with notions of culture, marginalization and vulnerability. Working intensively with Prof. Behera either in long-term projects or through other forms of collaboration they have gained invaluable inspiration from their academic and personal interaction which in turn is reflected in their ethnographic analysis.

References

Alles, G. ; Guzy, L. ; Skoda, U. and Ü. Valk (eds.) 2015b. Contemporary Indigeneity and Religion in India. (Special Issue) In: *International Quarterly for Asian Studies*, Vol. 46, Nos. 1-2.

Bijoi, C.R., 2007. Adivasis of India. A history of discrimination, conflict and resistance. In: Chanchani, Aditi; Dash, Mamata; Viswanath, Rosemary; Ananthkrishnan, Sinduja; Ragan, Vidhya (eds.), *This is our homeland. A collection of essays on the betrayal of Adivasi rights in India*. Bangalore, 15-27.

Butler, J., Gambetti, Z., Sabsay, L., 2016. Introduction, in: *ibid.* (eds.) Vulnerability in Resistance, Durham: Duke University Press.

Butler, J., 2004. *Precarious Life: The Powers of Mourning and Violence*, London: Verso.

Carrin, Marine/Jaffrelot, Christophe (eds.) 2002. Tribuset Basses Castes. Résistance et Autonomiedans la sociétéIndienne, *Collection Purusartha*. Paris, 21-24.

Carrin, Marine / Guzy, Lidia (eds.) 2012. Voices from the periphery. *Subalternity and Empowerment in India*. New Delhi: Routledge India.

Das, N.K., 2015. Indigeneity, Anthropology and the Indian Tribes: *A Critique Journal of Adivasi and Indigenous Studies* (JAIS). Vol. II, No. 1, February 2015: 11-34.

Geertz, Clifford. 1973. Religion as a Cultural System. In *The Interpretation of Cultures*. pp. 87-125. New York: Basic Books, Inc.

Guzy, Lidia (Guest editor) 2015. Special Issue Emerging Adivasi and Indigenous Studies Irish Journal of Anthropology, Guest editor Lidia Guzy, General Editor: J.B. Cuffe, *Irish Journal of Anthropology*, Volume 18(2), 2015, ISSN: 1393-8592. http://anthropologyireland.org/index.php/ija-journal/journal-archives/81-2015/106-2015-2.

Hardiman, David, 1987. The coming of the Devi: *Adivasi Assertion in Western India*. Delhi.

Mackenzie, C., Rogers, W., Dodds, S., 2013. Introduction. What is Vulnerability, and Why Does it Matter for Moral Theory?, in: *ibid.* (eds.) *Vulnerability: New Essays in Ethics and Feminist Philosophy*, Oxford: Oxford University Press.

Munda, Ram Dayal, 2002. India's Protection and Promotion of Tribal Rights: Obligations under ILO Convention on Indigenous and Tribal Peoples, 1957 (No. 107). Paper submitted at Indigenous Rights in the Commonwealth Project South and South Asia Regional Expert Meeting, 11th-13th March, 2002.

Ortner, Sherry B., 1983. Theory in anthropology since the Sixties. *Comparative Studies in Society and History*. 26:126-166.

Schnepel, Burkhard, 2002. *The Jungle Kings*. New Delhi: Manohar.

Sen, Amartya, 2000, Social Exclusion: Concept, Application, and Scrutiny. Social Development Papers No. 1, Office of Environment and Social Development Asian Development Bank. Manila: Asian Development Bank.

Singh, K.S., 1994. *People of India—The Scheduled Tribe*. National, Vol. III. Delhi: ASI and Oxford University Press.

Skoda, U.; Nielsen, K.B. and M. Qvortrup Fibiger, 2013. *Navigating Social Exclusion and Inclusion in Contemporary India and Beyond*, London: Anthem Press.

United Nations, 2009. State of the World's Indigenous Peoples. ST/ESA/328, New York.

TWO

SONDO DANCE OF KODAKU TRIBE
An Urgent Rethinking Required for Development

ALFRED TOPPO

Introduction

All tribes have some specificity in them. A tribe does not like to be compared with other tribes in any matter whatsoever. It tries to prove its definite identity rather than being grouped with other tribes. It has been experienced and noticed that some of the external facets of a tribe look similar to that of other tribes, but the close study proves their claims of distinctiveness. Even if the similarity index of two tribes is very high, but the two tribes would strongly prove their distinctiveness in a very simplistic way which other might find it absurd. Thus, it is clear that no two tribes are identical in socio-cultural practices and in their outlook to life. This adds to the beauty of tribal life, in fact, not only to tribal life, but beauty is added to the human society.

The multiplicity in socio-cultural practices among the tribes leads to a cross-fertilisation of tribal worldviews and the outcome is often positive. The best practices of one tribe, when clubbed together with the best practices of the other tribe, the obvious result is the best out of the bests. Promotion of mono-culture is an invitation to hatred and misunderstanding among tribes. The opportune time has come for all to respect and celebrate the socio-cultural diversities of one another.

However, all distinctive features of a particular tribe need not be all good for the development of the tribe. Some of the not-so-good practices might have been emerged over the years to cater to the selfish motives of a particular group within the tribal community, and eventually, it might have gained popularity and have become part and parcel of the tribe. The other possibilities also cannot be ignored that a good socio-cultural practice might have been diluted or diverted from the original practice. One needs to analyse that socio-cultural practices find relevance in the present context in which a particular community lives. This does not mean that the good practices are abandoned because of the undue pressures from the other neighbouring communities.

This chapter highlights one such dance, i.e. *sondo* dance and its implication for Kodaku tribe of Balrampur-Ramanujganj (formally part of Surguja) district of Chhattisgarh. The Kodakus enjoy the *sondo* dance. They love it and long for it, but they often do not look at it critically for holistic societal growth. The author strongly feels that the elders and well-wishers of the Kodaku community seriously look into the implication of *sondo* dance in the present context keeping in mind the various perspectives of holistic development.

1. Kodaku Tribe

Kodaku [also spelled as *Koṛaku* (Tirkey, 2008) and in Hindi कोड़ाकू] tribe is small and little known tribal community mostly concentrated in Balrampur (official name is Balrampur-Ramanujganj) district (formerly part of Surguja district) of Chhattisgarh. They are spread over a small geographical area adjoining the boarders of Jharkhand and Uttar Pradesh. They are always clubbed together with similar but better known tribe, i.e. Korwa for official documentation, i.e. Indian Census. They are also associated with Korku tribe of Madhya Pradesh because of their similarities in language. The Kodakus resemble the Korwas not only in language, but also in their economic patterns, i.e. both are primarily food gatherers; live in close proximity with the forest; poor and not able to secure the necessities of life. The Kodakus when asked about their tribal identity, they plainly say that they are 'Korwas'. But Kodakus are very clear about the differences between themselves and the Korwas and *vice versa* (Singh & Danda, 1986:1-2).

According to the *Koṛaku* oral tradition, *Koṛaku* is made-up of two words, i.e. *Koṛa* and *Ku*. The literal meaning of *Koṛa* is a boy and the derived meaning of the word can a man. The word *Ku* if added to *Koṛa,* the word becomes Koṛaku, which is plural form of *Koṛa* to mean boys and the derived meaning would be men. Therefore, the derived meaning of Koṛaku is thus human beings. According to the non-Koṛaku sources, the name Koṛaku is derived from *Kodwa* meaning digger of soil. The mother tongue is *Koṛwa* which belongs to the Munda branch of Austro-Asiatic family of languages. The principal livelihood is digging wild yams, roots and tubers in the jungle (Tirkey, 2008: 9-10).

The Kodaku tribe is divided into a number of exogamous clans (*gotra*) such as *Besra, chargat, Dumur, Edgi, Hadde, Hathlu, Kol, Kumharia, Murum, Nunihar, Palhe, Sadom, Sammat* etc. (Tirkey, 2008: 10; Singh, B., 1977: 75; Singh & Danda, 1986: 32). All clans are equal in status. There is neither hierarchy nor clustering among the clans. The clan is recognised for the purpose of regulating marriages (Singh, B., 1977: 75). Adult marriage is generally practiced among them though there are reports of child marriages. They practice monogamy. The bride price is paid to the girl's parents in cash or in kind. Divorce is permitted on the ground of barrenness, maladjustment and adultery. Remarriage is permissible for both men and women. Sons inherit the paternal property equally, but in the absence of sons, the son-in-law is permitted to inherit it as long as he stays with his wife's natal house (Tirkey, 2008:10).

The Indian Census always clubs the Kodakus with Korwas for its enumeration of demographic information. The official demographic details of Kodakus are not found. However, what is sometimes found is estimates of demographic details. According to the 1961 Census, the total population of the Kodakus was estimated to be 14,768 (Ahmad, 1977:9). Similarly, according to 1981 Census, the population of Korwas including Kodakus was 15,340 (Tirkey, 2008:9). Bageshwar Singh and Ajit Kumar Danda approximate 20 thousand Kodaku populations (Singh & Danda, 1986:2). No definitive official population is ascertained. However, it is clear that the Kodaku population is very small and if not preserved well, they will be wiped out completely in coming few decades.

Table 2.1 : Kodaku Population in Surguja

Tehsil	*Total Population*	*ST Population*	*Kodaku Population*	
			1961	*1970*
Pal	1,14,695	68,780	9,938	11,415
Surajpur	2,71,881	1,28,130	2,842	3,156
Samri	75,316	55,314	713	1,007

Source: The population figures were obtained from the Revenue Officials by Singh and Danda.

2. Kodaku Worships

Kodaku tribe, like other tribal tribes, has many socio-cultural similarities with the neighbouring tribes. The similarities with neighbouring tribes can easily be identified. However, there are some distinct socio-cultural features of the Kodakus which make them distinct from other tribes. These distinctions are worth noting while understanding the Kodaku life. These distinct cultural practices give them special identity as Kodakus apart from the language they speak.

Kodakus celebrate life through various feasts and festivals. They worship gods like Mahadeo, goddesses like Gauri, Parvati, Mahadani, yet they differ from other neighbouring tribes in their rituals and religious organisations. The Kodaku worships during the year are four in number, namely on *Mahadeosondo*, Gauri *Sondo*, *Karmc* and *Holi*. All these worships are officiated by the *Baiga* (village priest) and he fixes the day/date with the consultation of village *Mukhia* (head) for two *Sondos,* but the *Karma* and *Holi* festivals are ascertained by the lunar cycle. *Sondo* is a dance organised by the community to facilitate the selection of life partners. *Sondo* dances are always set either on Mondays or Fridays. Except in *Holi* all other worships are followed by dances. Mahadani is worshipped by Kodakus once in three years at a pre-fixed place in the village. The *Baiga* sacrifices pig to propitiate the deity. The other neighbouring tribal communities join this worship. This worship takes place either in the month of *Kartik* (October-November) or *Phagun* (February-March). The annual worship of Mahadeo and Gauri takes place in winter around December and in summer around May respectively. Mud figures of Mahadeo and Gauri are made to represent the deities on both the occasions. *Karma* is celebrated in the month of *Kuwar* (September- October) at the host Kodaku family. The villagers, relatives and people from neighbouring villages are invited for the occasion. The term Holi has been adopted by the Kodakus from neighbouring Hindus, but they have their own specific features. They sacrifice chicken on the occasion and the victim is roasted in the fire of Holi by the *Baiga* who prays for the welfare of all. Besides above worships, the spirits of ancestors are worshipped once a year. Even during the illness the spirits of ancestors are appeased and worshipped. The *Baiga* offers liquor to ancestral spirits and sacrifices chicken to appease them (Singh & Danda, 1986:87-91).

3. *Sondo* Dance

Sondo dance is the most important dance among the Kodakus. It is believed that it was started by Mahadeo and Gauri. The dance is organised twice a year in the month of *Aghan* (November-December) and *Baisakh* (April-May). The dance performed in *Aghan* is in honour of Gauri. The *Baiga* sacrifices a black chicken to Gauri. The dance in the month of *Baisakh* is performed in honour of Mahadeo. The *Baiga* sacrifices a pig to the deity. The village elders come together and decide in common when to begin the *Sondo* dance (Tirkey, 2008:118).

Vincent Ekka (2006) through his ethnographic study reports that the actual preparation of *sondo* begins with the finalisation of date for the same. It is danced strictly either on Mondays or Fridays. The *Baiga* and a few others keep vigil in the place where they plan to dance *Sondo*. This vigil is done to divine the place and to find out whether the deity is pleased with the place. The place is confirmed when somebody gets possessed by the deity on that particular place. Once this happens, they erect a pole known as *Chaura Khuta.*

The *Baiga* along with village elders checks still further whether all other deities and sprits are pleased. On the eve of the *sondo* (Sundays or Thursdays) in the *Baiga*'s house, a circle is made and rice grains are placed in four different places on the circle in the name of different village elders and people namely *Mukhiya* (village head), *Baiga* (village priest), *Dewar* (diviner) and *Assami* (public). The grains are covered with a basket for the whole night. The village elders come together in the morning and uncover the rice. They conclude that all deities and spirts are pleased if every one's share is intact. If they find that rice grains of particular elder or public is disappeared or dispersed or mixed with others he has to pacify the deity by offering sacrifice. The four have their own share of deity to pacify. The *Baiga* is responsible for three deities/ spirits namely *Khunt, Darha* and *Dihwarin*, *Dewar* is responsible for *Mahadani*, *Mukhiya* is responsible for *Machila Pat* and the general public is responsible for *Chordewan.*

The elders gather at the *Sondo* dancing ground in the afternoon on the actual day of *sondo* to purify the place. The ritual is known as *Akhra Bandhna* (Marking of the dancing ground). The *Mukhiya, Baiga, Alwa* (Baiga's assistant) and a few elders play important role. During this ritual someone from the elders gets possessed and goes to get a lump of soil from nearby place. Once lump of soil is brought, they make statues of

Mahadeo, Gauri and a horse. They place them in the winnowing basket. Mahadeo is made to sit on the house.

Once *Akhra Bandhna* rituals are over and statues are made and placed near *Chaura Khuta*, the *Baiga* offers scarifies in honour of deities. A pig is offered to Mahadeo and heifer to *Gauri*. Now, they normally offer pig and chicken only. It is also observed that *Baiga* offers *Mahuwa Daru* (liquor made of *Mahuwa* flowers) along with sacrificial victims. Once the sacrifice is over, boys and girls gather on the dancing ground and begin dancing. Some boys play the *Mandar* (cylindrical drum) and other boys and girls sing and dance. The dance is rhythmic, but movement is slow. The dance lasts for whole night. Boys and girls from neighbouring villages and even far off villages come to dance at night. It is an occasion for great fun and frolic, dance and enjoyment (Ekka, 2006:29-31).

The young boys and girls look for partners during the dance. The boys take the lead. If a boy likes a girl, he moves out of the circle and re-joins the circle where the girl is. Once the boy and girl consent, they go out of the dancing circle into the dark for spending their intimate time with each other. Other boys and girls continue dancing. If the boy is willing to take girl his home, he takes her after the dance and introduces her to his parents and villager elders. They in turn formalise their stay together. It is also observed that many couples agree to meet together in the next *Sondo* dance in the next village for similar fun and enjoyment.

The following morning the *Baiga* takes the basket with Mahadeo and Gauri round the village. Some village boys and girls join him. Every family offers them some money for drink and some food grains. The festivity continues till late morning (Singh & Danda, 1986:109). After going house to house dancing, they take statues to the place from where the lump of soil was brought in order to drown them in the river or pond. Some of the gifts are also thrown with them (Tirkey, 2008:121).

4. Detrimental Elements in *Sondo*

Celebration is part of human life. It breaks the monotony of life and adds beauty into human life. It brings people together on one platform breaking socio-economic barriers. Family members, relatives, friends and neighbours celebrate life together. It has innate unification character. Tribal life is a cycle of celebration throughout the year. There are celebrations for each season. There are celebrations when a person passes through one phase of life to the other. There are celebrations when people meet one another after a long period of time. In fact, celebration makes life more meaningful.

However, there are celebrations which lead the community backward rather than making them more futuristic. There are some socio-cultural practices and celebration, especially of tribals, which are being carried on till date in the name of preserving cultures. These practices, in reality, are detrimental to their own development. The elders of the tribe just want to keep them because they have inherited from their elders and it is coming down from generation to generation. On the other hand, some unhealthy elements have crept into the good socio-cultural practices of the community over the years. Today even these acquired unhealthy practices are considered as tradition and are preserved at the cost of the community development.

Sondo dance of Kodakus has many unhealthy practices attached to it today than perhaps initial understanding of it. It, in strict sense, is not a feast (Tirkey, 2008:119). Traditionally, it was organised to create an opportunity to the young unmarried boys and girls to meet and choose their mates. It becomes an occasion of a sort of momentary permissiveness with regard to sex (Singh & Danda, 1986:109). It is, in fact, a social system of Kodakus to facilitate choosing life partners. It is beautiful system and mechanism as far as it meets its end and orients the community towards development in the present sense of the term.

I was part of a Kodaku Community Development Programme implemented by Jeevan Vikas Mairi, Pathalgaon (Jashpur), Chhattisgarh for almost seven years (2005-2012). Along with this association with the community development programme, I was also the Manager of St. John Berchmans School, Dhanwarkala for three years (2005-2008) which is opened specifically to cater Kodaku children for their formal education. About 75 per cent students in the school were from Kodaku tribe and most of them were in the hostel attached to the school. My observation and experiences of working with the Kodakus over the years substantiates how *Sondo* dance is detrimental to Kodaku children.

Sondo dance, as stated above, is a social system to facilitate selection of life partners among the Kodakus. It is one of the traditional cultural practices which Kodakus cherish very much. Kodaku children have innate attraction to it. Once a boy or a girl decides to partake in *Sondo* dance of a particular village, he or she would go, come what may. Distance, classes, family responsibilities all become secondary. I realised that many Kodaku boys and girls from the hostel would quietly slip out during evening meals to join the *Sondo* dance. They came back early in the morning to continue their daily routine in the hostel and the school. They went up to 15-20 km on foot through the hilly path during night. A few teenage girls from the hostel dropped out from the school because of unwanted pregnancies. Eventually, even the boys dropped out those who were party to that. They started living together. Once Kodaku boys and girls reach puberty, *Sondo* dance becomes an occasion for sexual intimacy more than choosing a life partner. It is also observed today that sexual intimacy during the *Sondo* dance does not culminate to marriage, but just remains a momentary sexual pleasure.

I observed about 90 per cent of school drop-outs are Kodakus. St. John Berchmans School, Dhanwarkala admitted about 80 Kodaku children in KG section as part of special efforts for Kodaku education. It was very saddening to see only 5-6 students reaching up to class XII. One of the prominent reasons for excessive drop-out of Kodaku children from schools were tolerance and indirect promotion by the Kodaku community of the free sex among boys and girls during and outside *Sondo* dance along with failures and inability of parents to pay the fee. Parents shy away from guiding their children in this regard as they themselves has done the same in their youth. They do not seem to understand the importance of education.

Sondo dance is no more only of unmarried boys and girls to choose partners. The married couples also take undue advantages of the occasion. It has been reported that some married couples go for sexual satisfaction with others. A married women just tolerates her husband's adulterous behaviour during the *Sondo* dance and the *vice versa*. I once interacted with a man who openly told me that a particular child whom his wife gave birth was not his but it was result of *Sondo* dance. Similarly, a Kodaku woman confided to me that she just tolerates her husband's adulterous act to avoid quarrel at home and because of the grown up children they had. At times children see their parents' act in the *Sondo* ground and do like-wise as they grow up. In the long run with modern understanding, the institution of family may be get affected and eventually children will be at the receiving end.

Country liquor is ritually offered to Mahadeo and Gauri before the *Sondo* dance. The elders and others present for the rituals share liquor contributed from the villagers. Even a little child gets his share. It is observed that excessive drinking on the occasion is universal (Singh & Danda, 1986:109). Kodaku boys and girls start consuming liquor at a very early age. There are many boys who are addicted to liquor in their teenage. It was often observed in the hostel that a few Kodaku boys were drunk during evening time. One cannot expect a serious study hour in the evening after being drunk. I remember an incident. It was reported by the hostel warden that a few boys in the hostel were drinking regularly. I called the boys and told them to call their parents at the earliest. To my dismay, it was the last day of schooling for some of them. They did call parents but simply left the school once for all. The other boys called their parents only to tell me that students were drinking from their childhood.

Sondo dance is celebrated strictly on Mondays and Fridays (Ekka, 2006:28). It is not like other festivals we think of. *Holi* is universally celebrated on one particular day. Occasionally, due to lunar calendar one part of the country celebrates it one day and may be another part of the country may celebrate it on the following day. The celebration gets over within a day. It is not the same with *Sondo*. It is celebrated twice a year in one particular village, i.e. Mahadeo *Sondo* and Gauri *Sondo*. But some village organise *Sondo* dance more frequently (Ekka, 2006:31). It is important to notice that each village organises *Sondo* dances twice a year. This means that Kodaku boys and girls have the opportunity of joining of *Sondo* dance every Monday and Friday in other villages. As Kodakus are intrinsically attracted to it, most Kodaku boys and girls end up in dancing *sondo* every Monday and Friday in its seasons.

Yet another factor is observed during the *sondo* dance which is more dangerous for Kodakus themselves. As stated above, Kodakus like drinking and they go for excessive drinking. Many non-Kodakus take undue advantages of this reality. They sell liquor at *Sondo* dancing ground and the Kodakus have not any objection to this open sale of country liquor. The petty vendors occupy prominent places at *Sondo* dance grounds. The dancing grounds are becoming market places for sale of country liquor. This kind of arrangements at dancing grounds, tempt young boys and girls to consume liquor.

The prolonged period of *sondo* seasons with their prolonged celebration are affecting both livelihood and health of the Kodakus. First, Kodakus do not have their own traditional sustainable livelihood system as traditionally they were food gatherers. Neither do they have sufficient land for agriculture nor do they have any traditional occupation for regular source of income. The little pieces of land they have are often upper land with very little productivity. Second, their livelihood mostly depends on available daily wages in the locality. They often abstain from daily wage work because of the dance and drunkenness. The little savings they have is spent on liquor. They spoil their health on one side and their earning becomes meagre as they do not work for many days.

The ground reality of *Sondo* dance observed by a non-Kodaku concludes that it might have a value in it for the tribe in the past, but in the present-day context, a rethinking is the need of the hour. Of course, it brings Kodakus together for celebration of life. It facilitates procreation through making many life partners. On the other side, it facilitates child marriages and subsequent problems of health, livelihood and education. Is it feasible to continue dancing without really reflecting its implications in present-day life? Can they think of preserving good in it and doing away with what is not so good in it? Today life becomes more meaningful when every aspect of it is developed. People need to think of their own development first rather than expecting external agencies, including government, to do the thinking for them. It is a fact of life that a community which thinks for its development, develops much faster in every sphere of life. A critical thinking is a must for one's development. Are Kodakus capable of critical thinking?

5. Need for Urgent Rethinking

It has been observed that Kodakus love freedom from external controls in every place and every aspect of life. Kodaku parents love their children very much and try to provide their children whatever is possible. Children also love to be with their parents. Children run away from the hostel just to be with their parents even if facilities are more in the hostel than at home including food. They just run away to be with their parents. However, a sharp shift is observed in children's attitudes and behaviour as they step in to puberty. The familial bond between parents and children starts fading. Children start distancing themselves from their parents. Parents do not have a say when a child does not like to study. Parents do not have a say when a child often goes for *Sondo* dance and spoils his or her future life. Parents do not have a say when a teenage girl child elopes with a teenage boy leaving their schooling. Parent do not have a say when a teenage school going boy brings a teenage girl home as his spouse. They just tolerate it. The Kodaku community easily accommodates these facts of life. The tolerance, they show towards their children, in present-day context of development, is just at the cost of their own development and future.

The experiences during the implementation of Kodaku Community Development Programme is worth stating. The Kodaku social mechanism has become myopic in the present context. The Kodaku elders still hold on to traditional practices including *Sondo* dance in the name of preserving the tradition and culture. And without their attitudinal change, the development which government and many of us envisage for tribal communities will not take place. The elders' vision is myopic because of lack of exposure, progressive and critical thinking. The Kodaku neighbouring tribes, i.e. Cherwa, Gonds, Khairwars, Oraons are a little better off because their pace of attitudinal change is slightly better. The government with many development initiatives has managed to change even in Kodaku life and livelihood system, but the pace of change is slow and unsteady. The grip of tradition and culture on people is very strong. Critical thinking does not get initiated in them easily.

Education is a must for overall development of a society. An educated person with his knowledge is more capable to decide the right and wrong in the society (Singh, B.P., 2016: 311). The Kodaku Community Development Programme covered about 100 Kodaku villages working for their holistic development. One of the major thrust areas of the programme was the promotion of formal and non-formal education. Efforts were made to send all Kodaku children to schools. Parents were motivated. Children were encouraged. Kodaku children enrolment in schools shot up. However, over a period of time, it was realised that the many children did persevere long in schools. Most of them just dropped out. This phenomenon may be partially true to other tribes also as Dixit notes: "Many tribal schools are plagued by high dropout rates. Children attend for three to four years of primary school and gain smattering of knowledge, only to lapse into illiteracy later" (Dixit, 2006:46). The reasons for dropping out were mixed and overlapping for the Kodaku children. One of the major reasons was that they did not feel like studying. Schools demanded some discipline. Sitting in the classroom was a real tortuous task. The other reasons were excessive drinking and elopement. The alcoholics could not continue the study. The eloping couples settled in life in their teenage. The parents did not have a say in children's affairs. The Kodaku community is silent on the future of the children.

Sustainable livelihood for Kodakus is an issue to be explored amidst opportunities and possibilities. Kodakus cannot rely on forest roots and fibres today as forests are depleting and their harvest had been not in a sustainable manner. They are mostly engaged in wage labour in their own locality. "Due to lack of education and requisite skill, the tribals are not able to take advantage of the new economic opportunities which have been grabbed by outsiders migrated to the tribal areas" (Thakur, 2001:111). However, after the implementation of MGNREGA they receive better wages in the government run projects. They receive monthly share of ration from Public Distribution System (PDS). Life seems secured temporarily. But the drinking habits drain out the little money they save and a little ration they get from PDS. Sustainable livelihood is inevitable for better health care and education of children. The root cause of all these is unhealthy traditional practices which entrap the Kodaku mind-set is their outlook to life. The unhealthy practices attached to *Sondo* dance is just the tip of the iceberg.

6. Agents of Critical Rethinking

The cultural heritage of Kodakus is good in itself. They are tested and purified over the years to suite them. This heritage in terms of worships and sacrifices, songs and dances, way of life and thinking pattern has evolved when Kodakus were relatively isolated by themselves. This made much sense when their needs were limited. This governed the community well when their life was simple. Today interaction with other tribal and non-tribal communities has increased manifold. A tribe cannot isolate itself any more. It has to respond to the challenges faced, lest it perishes in the process of modernisation and globalisation. Kodakus are at the crossroad (Tirkey, 2008). They, as a community, need to give a direction to themselves for future. They need to embrace modernity keeping all the good in their own tradition.

The *Baigas* and *Mukhiyas* and other elders in the tribe have to pave ways for development. Kodakus still listen to them in social, religious and cultural matters. The wave of change has to emerge from them. Ordinary people will listen to them as they have done in the past. However, most of the *Baigas* and *Mukhiyas* are not educated and not exposed to world outside. Who then take initiatives to bring awareness among this group of people? The Government machinery has certainly can do something constructively as it has brought about changes in tribal life. All tribes are equal for the government and all need to be developed irrespective of present state of life. It does pay special attention if a particular tribe is categorised as Particularly Vulnerable Tribal Group

(PVTG). Kodakus do fall under this category. They are just one of the tribes in the list of the Scheduled Tribes.

There are a very few Kodakus who are really educated and capable of critical reflection on themselves. They are dispersed and not able to come together. The isolated new ideas are curbed harshly by traditionalists in the community. There are a few in local political leadership who are bold and capable of generating new tides of change. But the party politics does not allow them such a move.

The Kodaku Community Development Programme fostered village leadership. The result was positive. Many Kodakus were elected as *Sarpanches* in Panchayat election. A few *Sarpanches* genuinely worked for the tribe and its development, but many of them were succumbed to the party politics. They started uniting Kodakus in the district by organising *Kodaku Sammelan* at various places. There was a positive wave of change. People simply flocked together to these *Sammelans* to listen to them. Many well-wishers thought it was the beginning of systematic Kodaku development. The political parties closely observed their demographic strengths and organisational capabilities. Very soon *Sarpanches* became political party workers. The hope of the ordinary Kodakus shattered.

Various voluntary organisations do work for Kodakus in small pockets. They mostly work for livelihood promotion, health care and primary education on a project mode. They withdraw from the area once project is over. The core issue of people's attitudes governed by their tradition is seldom addressed. Some of the voluntary workers do recognise the core problems with them, but the demands of the project work do not allow them to focus on it. Thus, people come back to square one at the end of the project.

There is hardly anyone who seriously thinks of holistic development by doing away unhealthy socio-cultural and religious practices. Most of the Kodakus are poor, illiterate and unexposed to the world outside. Their worldview is myopic. Initiatives have to come from the people who know and understand their plight. The Kodaku intellectuals, though very few, have a great role to play in carving new outlook for the tribe as a whole. The core issue needs to be addressed by awareness building, education and exposures. Finally, it is the Kodakus themselves who have to take the lead for bringing the tribe out of clutches of evil practices and myopic vision.

Conclusion

Kodakus are vulnerable because of their state of life they are in. They have a rich tradition which keeps them moving in life amidst other tribals and non-tribals. The Census of India does not give their population clearly but clubs them with Korwa tribe which is also vulnerable but better known to the world. They distinguish themselves from Korwas and do not want to be clubbed with them. Their cultural heritage is unique, though with some unhealthy elements in them. *Sondo* dance, for example, is loved by all Kodakus. They love to participate in it, as it has been innately internalised by the Kodakus. However, over the years some unhealthy elements have crept in and these unhealthy elements have to be done away with. Similarly, other social evils needs to go to keep pace with other communities who are more prone to development.

The possibilities of critical thinking for change within the community is a distant reality. They are poor, illiterate and unexposed. They are often busy to secure their livelihoods. The relatively free atmosphere in the community clubbed with excessive alcoholism, child marriage and high rate of school drop-outs, is the stumbling block to their critical thinking. A critical thinking initiated with in the community is the best answer for their development. An open call from the Kodakus is that of helping them think for themselves. The material help will take them to a certain height but it has a limit. Once they think for themselves to do away with contained practices which are not progressive, they will be able preserve good in their traditions and work for their development.

Note

1. *Karma* is a famous autumnal festival of Kodakus like other neighbouring tribes.

References

Ahmad, S.H. (1977). An Anthropometric Study of Four Tribes of Chhattisgarh. In A.K. Danda, *Chhattisgarh: An Area Study* (pp. 7-19). Calcutta: Anthropological Survey of India.

Dixit, N.K. (2006). *Tribals in India.* Delhi: Vista International Publishing House.

Ekka, V. (2006). *Kodaku Experience of Jesus Christ (Unpublished Matter's Thesis).* Delhi : Vidyajyoti College of Theology.

Singh, B. (1977). Kodaku Kinship System. In A.K. Danda, *Chhattisgarh: An Area Study* (pp. 74-82). Calcutta: Anthropological Survey of India.

Singh, B.P. (2016). Predicament of Tribal Youth and Crises of Mainstreaming in Contemporary India. *Sociological Quest, 2*(4), 309-318.

Singh, B., and Danda, A.K. (1986). *The Kodaku of Surguja.* Calcutta: Anthropological Survey of India.

Thakur, A. (2001). *Tribal Development and its Paradoxes.* Delhi: Authors Press.

Tirkey, A. (2008). *Korakus at Crossroads.* Pathalgaon: Jeevan Vikas Maitri.

THREE

HUMAN TRAFFICKING DISCOURSE IN MEDIA AND ITS MISREPRESENTATIONS IN MEXICO

ARUN KUMAR ACHARYA, ARMANDO MOCTEZUMA SUÁREZ AND FRANCISCO DE JESÚS GÓMEZ ONTIVEROS

Introduction

Human trafficking has received attention over the past two decades in politics, academia as well as in media due to its multifaceted consequences (Burke, 2013). Initially, trafficking of women and girls forced into sex-work and, to a lesser extent, domestic servitude, were the sole focus of advocacy and assistance. Today, there is recognition that women, children and men are trafficked into many different forms of labour, and for sexual exploitation. It is estimated that between 8,00,000 and 40,00,000 people, mostly women and children are trafficked across international borders annually (USDS) and it is also the fastest growing crime, which has serious public health implications as well as a violation of human rights (Busza and Diarra, 2004; McClain and Garrity, 2011; Zimmerman, Hossain, Yun, Gajdadziev *et al.,* 2008).

Human trafficking or trafficking in persons and modern slavery are terms often used interchangeably to refer to a variety of crimes associated with economic exploitation of people (Burke, 2013). According to the Office for Democratic Institutions and Human Rights (ODIHR), human trafficking regarded as a modern form of slavery, is an affront to human dignity, often involving psychological terror and physical violence, which encompasses human rights issues and crime control, of inequality and discrimination, of corruption, economic deprivation and migration (ODIHR, 2004). Similarly, the Beijing Platform for Action identified trafficking for sexual exploitation as a form of violence against women. Trafficking for the purpose of sexual exploitation includes those women who have suffered intimidation and/or violence while being trafficked. Initial consent may not be relevant, as some enter the trafficking chain knowing they will work as prostitutes. However, they are then deprived of their basic human rights, in conditions akin to slavery (ASI, 2002).

The United Nations Protocol to Prevent, Suppress and Punish Trafficking in Persons, especially Women and Children (UNODC, 2004) defines human trafficking in Article 3 as:

> "The recruitment, transportation, transfer, harboring or receipt of persons, by means of threat or use of force or other forms of coercion, of abduction, of fraud, of deception, of the abuse of power or of a position of vulnerability or of the having control over another person, for the purpose of exploitation".

The protocol cites a list of acts such as recruitment, transportation and others, followed by the methods used to enforce those acts, for example threat, the use of force, or other abuses of power, or of a position of vulnerability. The definition further specifies that the term 'exploitation' shall include, at a minimum, the exploitation of the prostitution of others or other forms of sexual exploitation, forced labour or services, slavery or practices similar to slavery, servitude or the removal of organs (Skilbrei and Tveit, 2008).

The International Labour Organization (ILO) estimates that 2.5 million people worldwide are being trafficked at any given time, where, 43 per cent of trafficking victims are used for commercial sexual exploitation, while 32 per cent are used for forced economic exploitation, around 25 per cent of victims are used for a combination of forced exploitation and commercial sexual exploitation or for undetermined reasons (ILO, 2005). Furthermore, according to the latest ILO's Global Estimate of Forced Labour (2012), 20.9 million people worldwide are victims of forced labour, trapped in jobs into which they were coerced and cannot leave. Of the 9.1 million victims of forced labour, 44 per cent have moved either domestically or internationally. This indicates that migration can be an important vulnerability factor. In this context, it has also been shown that forced sexual exploitation is strongly associated with cross-border movement.

The Global Trafficking in Persons Report-2012 presented by the United Nations Office on Drugs and Crime states that: young girls and women who are being trafficked for the purpose of sexual exploitation and prostitution, often suffer from extreme sexual, physical and psychological abuses, associated with gender-based violence (UNODC, 2012). Trafficking of women for sexual exploitation has recently moved up on the international agenda due to growing concerns about violence against women, as well as its connection with the sex industry, forced and exploitative labour, sexually transmitted diseases (STDs) including HIV/AIDS and other forms of human rights violations (Huda, 2006).

Many international units such as the United Nations, IOM, ILO, GAATW, CATW and ECPAT-International and Stop-Traffic, in order to fight against the trafficking problem, have drawn the governments' attention through their reports, articles and publications, offering shelter and assistance to victims, however, it is perceived that there is a lack of government responsiveness on this issue especially in a country such as Mexico, which constitutes an origin, transit and destination country for human trafficking. Thus, the purpose of our paper is to examine how Mexican mass media has represented the human trafficking issue in the country for the past decade, and we have also made an effort to describe how this misrepresentation is affecting the law enforcement process in Mexico.

A Brief History of Human Trafficking in Mexico

Human trafficking is not a new problem in Mexico, in fact, it is considered as old as human society (Acharya, 2015). During the prehispanic period the trafficking of human beings was associated with buying and selling indigenous people who were known as "*Tlacotin*". In ancient Mexico, indigenous males were sold to institutions as soldiers, where many of them were sold by their parents to work in agricultural fields, mines or to pay a debt. Indigenous women and young girls were sold as prostitutes, concubines, domestic servants, entertainers and many of them were also offered by their parents as a sacrifice to God (Von, 2007). It was not until 1519, when the *Conquistadors* invaded Mexico and the Spaniards went through the motions to enslave indigenous people to build the New Spain. Some historical documents describe that during the Spanish colonization, many African people were brought to Mexico as slaves for the construction of ports and mining activities. For example, the Government of Felipe-V brought 48,000 Africans, mainly from Guinea, who were forced to work in mining operations in San Luis Potosi (Quirós, 2013).

However, during the 20th Century human trafficking in Mexico has been closely related to prostitution and sex-work, moreover, it was controlled and operated by drug cartels (Astorga, 2000). At the later part of the century, trafficking in persons was primarily related to illegal migration into the United States. Thousands of Mexican young women were lured with false promises by *polleros* or "*Coyotes*" and trafficked into the U.S. for the purpose of sexual exploitation as well as maid servants (Ugarte, 2004). Currently, the U.S. Department of State estimates that as many as 20,000 young women and children are trafficked across the border from Mexico each year. Women and children who are transported to the United States from Mexico by traffickers face not only the risks inherent in being trafficked, but also the serious risks of the journey.

Each year, between 400 and 500 people are known to die while attempting to cross the border between Mexico and the United States (USDS, 2011). Young girls often unwittingly become trafficking victims when they are singled out by their "*coyotes*" during the journey of north. They are told they can travel at no cost, if they will agree to work later to pay-off their debts. These traffickers deceive and dupe the girls through false promises of jobs and other economic opportunities waiting for them in the United States. During their journeys, the girls are shown favouritism, and even given clothes, make-up, and gifts. Upon arriving at their destinations, however, they are informed that they owe a debt to their smugglers—and they will pay it off by working in the sex industry (Walters and Davis, 2011).

In the United States, these girls are often held in slavery-like conditions and forced into prostitution, domestic service, or forced labour. They are terrorized emotionally, forced to take drugs, moved frequently, locked up, raped, beaten, deprived of sleep, and starved. The smugglers knew from the start that exploitation would be the cost of the "travel now, pay later" deal (Smith, 2014; Walters and Davis, 2011). However, current studies affirm that over the last decade, international trafficking of women basically from Mexico into the United States has declined due to the complexity of obtaining a visa and strict patrolling at the international borders, resulting in a boom of internal trafficking in Mexico (COHA, 2009; Rusey, 2013; Wolfe, 2015). At present, Mexico ranks second in the world in terms of prostitution of under-age persons (Monroy, 2010). According to Azaola (Esteinou, 2011) the rapid increase in the number of children for commercial sexual exploitation is due to the following factors: (1) The deterioration of living conditions of poor families; (2) the promotion of child prostitution by close family members; (3) the use of sexual activities as a means of survival by street children who escape from an abusive home; (4) the recruitment of children as sex-workers by organized crime networks; and (5) the illegal transfer of children as sex-workers from developing countries to developed countries.

The above studies reveal how child prostitution has increased in the country, however, during the last few years, Mexico has undergone deep changes regarding trafficking of women (Azaola and Estes, 2003). The real extent of trafficking of women in Mexico is difficult to ascertain. There is little empirical data on trafficking of women in Mexico. To date, there are no official statistics on trafficking of women, but our previous research indicates that every year approximately 10,000 people are being trafficked within Mexico, particularly to the following six cities: Cancun, Acapulco, Mexico City, Tijuana, Ciudad Juarez and Monterrey, and approximately 5,000 are trafficked into the United States (Acharya and Bryson, 2014). This study also found that in Mexico 7 out of 10 trafficked women are being trafficked within the country and 3 out of 10 are taken abroad (Acharya, 2013). In addition, every day an estimated 400 women enter into prostitution (this figure includes trafficked and non-trafficked women) in Mexico City, out of which 80 per cent do so against their will (González, 2003).

In 2014, the National Citizen Observatory conducted a four-year analysis (January 2010 — July 2013) of human trafficking in Mexico including 31 States, the Federal District, and the Federal Government. The present study found persistently high levels of impunity for the crime, demonstrating how incomplete and contradictory official information contributes to bury the true scope of the problem. Over the time period, 16 states reported a total of 846 victims, while the rest failed to provide information. Jalisco had the highest number of victims, with 283, representing about a third of the total. This was followed by Baja California, with 136, and Puebla, with 122. The national Attorney General's Office (PGR) registered 347 victims during this time period, and the Ministerial Federal Police (MFP) registered 121 (ONCSJL, 2014).

Likewise, information regarding sex, age and nationality was provided for only a portion of the total victims reported by these States. Of these, around 87 per cent were women and approximately the same per cent were victims of sex trafficking, and nearly 90 per cent of victims were single, Mexican citizens and were under 18 years old (*Ibid.*). In the last few years, significant efforts have been made to understand the dynamics of Trafficking in Persons concern in the country. As discussed earlier, human trafficking in Mexico is basically related to sex trafficking and prostitution, however, the 2015 Trafficking in Persons Report indicates that Mexican women, children as well as men are also exploited in forced labour in agriculture, domestic service, food processing factories, construction, the informal economy, begging, and vending in both the United States and Mexico. Thus, this partial representation of human trafficking in Mexico in mass media as well as academia has created an obstacle for law enforcement, which we attempt to reflect in the following sections.

Media Representation of Human Trafficking in Mexico

It is important to note the complexity of media analysis, mainly in a tough issue like human trafficking. Doing research on human trafficking on the field for the media requires a critical perspective, for this, it is necessary to take into account two epistemological reflections. First Umberto Eco's stance on the role of mass media on societal change (Eco, 2004) and the second point pertains to Bourdieu's position on the media as a socially created role (Bourdieu and Kauf, 1997). According to Pierre Bourdieu (*Ibid.*), it is not important to have an ideological notion as the media is a product of the system, it is in charge of reproduction, therefore, we must always analyze the media taking into account its ability to control [society and/or masses]. Both reflections will guide us with a critical eye, because it is impossible not to have a transformative intention in this task of analyzing an area as sensitive as the human trafficking phenomenon.

In Mexico, as in other parts of the world, Information Technologies (IT) and mass communication play an important role in policy decisions, public opinion and in the most important topics in the social sphere. It is important to notice that in this country there are certain singularities in mass media, as there is an oligopoly on journalism and opinion at a national level, which is more clear and evident at local levels (Arreola, 2015). These oligopolistic practices are rooted on the historical partnership of dominant power groups with economic and political interests, to which the information that is communicated and even generated by the mass media has to be a reflection of the establishment on course (Huerta, Torres and Díaz, 2011). The way in which the Mexican system has been constructed to promote practices that benefit certain groups, is harmful and perverse towards social welfare and development of the country, mainly because these help replicate social practices in order to maintain a *status quo*, which directly affects the most fundamental human rights. The Mexican Government has ignored its responsibility and its role as a key promoter of social change, especially those actors who are key decision-makers at the political sphere (*Ibid.*).

Mexico is currently undergoing a Human Rights crisis because of the atmosphere of violence existing throughout the territory (Acharya, 2013; Uribe and González). Despite having legal recourse covering the entire cycle of trafficking, which are based on the prevention of the phenomenon through the prosecution of the offense up to the recovery and rehabilitation of victims, efforts made by the Mexican State have not been sufficient to stop this social malaise that affects thousands of people daily in the country. Thus, we see that human trafficking is a crime that violates the most fundamental human rights, carrying a variety of ailments at the time when the situation of trafficked individuals is analyzed and even the environment into which they are embedded and operate, which is full of all kinds of violence (Acharya, Gómez, Moctezuma, Morquecho *et al.*, 2011). This inhuman phenomenon is a crime that has a number of systematic academic elements, difficulting their introduction into the everyday vocabulary, even after there have been national and international efforts to socialize the complexity of its terminology (AN, 2008; CNDH, 2012; UNODC, 2007); this is when the media makes sense of the human trafficking issue.

As noted previously, the media is part of a corrupted system with naturalized practices of social actors, perpetuating ignorance about the trafficking phenomena among the general population. In most cases, the Mexican media interpreted human trafficking as a synonym of sexual exploitation. The important media including newspapers[4] and television showcased trafficking of women relevant to prostitution and sexual slavery. In Table 3.1, we have analyzed the basic terminology commonly used by national and local media in the country which makes the issue of trafficking in people incomprehensible.

As it shows, Type-I terminology reflects a misrepresentation of the most general epistemological notions of human trafficking, for example commonly calling it "Slavery of the 21st Century" or implies it is a synonym of sex trade; Type-II terminology evidences the lack of

Table 3.1: Terminology Used in the Media

Type I: Does not explain the phenomenon, confuses the types of trafficking	**Type II:** Misrepresentation of the phenomena
➢ Slavery of the 21st Century ➢ Sex-trade ➢ Illegal business ➢ Human trafficking network ➢ Slavery and exploitation of human beings	➢ White slave traffic ➢ Sexual exploitation ➢ Sexual slavery ➢ Forced sex-work ➢ Prostitution as a form of trafficking
Type III: Does not differentiate between types of trafficking and types of exploitation	**Type IV:** Does not reflect the variety and complexity of human trafficking forms
➢ Victims of trafficking, sexual or labour exploitation, slavery or capture by criminal groups ➢ Sexual and labour exploitation of people ➢ Bonded labour ➢ Servitude exploitation ➢ Exploitation by prostitution	➢ Sex Trafficking ➢ Victims of prostitution ➢ Pornography of minors ➢ Child trafficking ➢ Pornography

Source: Self-elaboration.

ethics on the historical process of the concept using obsolete terms such as white slave trade, or using modern misleading terms as sex slavery; Type-III terminology denotes axiological bias, confusing human trafficking and exploitation as the same or ignoring terms as forced labour, servitude and slavery; and finally Type-IV terminology points out the most specific epistemological notions, referring to issues that are far from human trafficking, such as prostitution or pornography, or understands human trafficking only as sexual exploitation, dimming the rest of the modalities, like servitude, forced begging and forced labour, among others (AN, 2008; CNDH, 2012; UNODC, 2007). Finally, from the media we can identify three key social stakeholders that explain the main issues on human trafficking occurring in Mexico. We clearly observe that none of the stakeholders speak about nor visualize this social problem in a single point of view, thus, this multi-imagination and misrepresentation have become an obstacle in the process of law enforcement and generating public policies. In Table 3.2, we have analyzed the discourses provided by each stakeholder representing the phenomena in the media.

Misrepresentation of Human Trafficking in Law Enforcement Process

From different discourses rendered by the Government of Mexico as well as the interpretation of different legislations, we can conceptualize that trafficking in persons as synonymous of sexual exploitation. For the

Table 3.2: Terminology Used in Media by Stakeholders

Stakeholders	*Content of Discurse*	*Typical Expressions*
Journalists	They use the wrong concepts, the term white slave trade is commonly used and focus their coverage on human trafficking for sex exploitation, and in many cases talk about sex work as trafficking itself.	• White slave trade • Pimping • Pimp • Vice houses • Prostitutes
Government Agencies	They talk about crime prevention and focus almost exclusively on the role of criminal organizations, hindering other actors involved. They often deny the existence of the phenomena on the territories in which they perform their duties.	• Protection of women and children • Criminal Organizations • Drug trafficking • White slave trade • It does not happen here
Non-Governmental Organizations	Accuse the unrest as a lack of support to the victims and the impunity of the Governmental Agencies. They have a clear understanding of the phenomena in a global and systematic manner.	• Sex trade • Forced labour • Human trafficking for sexual exploitation • Client and pimp

Source: Self-elaboration.

purpose of analysis, we have focused on the 2014 General Law to Prevent, Punish and Eradicate crimes on human trafficking and to protect and assist victims of these crimes. This law defines trafficking of persons in its Article 10 as: The action of capturing, trapping, transporting, transferring, holding, delivering, receiving and/or housing one or more persons for the purpose of exploitation. The same Article also defines "exploitation" as slavery, servitude, prostitution and other forms of sexual exploitation, labour exploitation, forced labour, forced begging, using minors for criminal activities, illegal adoption of minors, forced marriage, organ trafficking and illegal biomedical experimentation on humans. However, this definition and each type of exploitation and its punishment are explained in detail from Article 11 through Article 31 as shown in Table 3.3.

We can notice by Table 3.3 that, firstly, the definition of trafficking contained in Article 10 does not mention the "means" used in order to achieve the exploitation purposes, which reflects that, for this law, both trafficking and exploitation are almost synonymous. When we analyzed the explanation of "means", we found mainly the definitions of sexual exploitation, which is the most comprehensive and explained in Articles 13 to 20 and in Articles 26, 27, 28 and 29. As for the other forms of exploitation, Articles 22 and 24 only mention forced labour and forced

Table 3.3: Forms of Exploitation listed in the General Law of Human Trafficking

Article 11	Slavery is the dominance of one person over another. Under such dominance, free will over one's self and property does not exist.
Article 12	Servitude may take the form of: • Debt bondage, a condition reached due to the commitment of providing a service in order to pay a debt. • *Gleba*, which is the dominance over the people living on a determined geographical area, specifically the one used for agriculture.
Article 13	Exploiting someone through prostitution, pornography, public or private sexual exhibitions, sex tourism or any other paid sexual activity by means of: deception, moral or physical violence, abuse of power or vulnerability, harm or the threat of it, threat due to migratory status or threat of using any legal procedure.
Article 14	Benefit from the production of pornography in which the person was forced or deceived.
Article 15	Profit from the trade, distribution, exposure or circulation of pornographic material in which persons were exploited.
Article 16	Production of child pornography.
Article 17	Holding, acquiring or leasing child pornography.
Article 18	Moving people out or into Mexican territory in order to sexually exploit them.
Article 19	Offering labour opportunities different than sex-work, but with the intention of performing it later.
Article 20	Acquiring the services of someone under the conditions mentioned in Article 19.
Article 21	Labour exploitation takes place when someone illegally and unjustifiably benefits economically or in any other way through someone else's work. Such work degrades a person's dignity when it violates labour laws under unhealthy or dangerous conditions, disproportioned relation between the work performed and the payment received, or below minimum wage.
Article 22	Defines forced labour as obtained by use of force or harm or threat, whether physical or to their migratory status or threat of using any legal procedure.
Article 23	States forced labour or servitude does not happen when demanded in fulfillment of military service or any other civil obligation or a penalty.
Article 24	Forced begging occurs when a person asks for charity against their will by harming, forcing or threatening them, or by deceiving them.
Article 25	Use of minors to commit crimes in terms of the Federal Law Against Organized Crime.
Article 26	Receive or deliver a minor with the purpose of sexual exploitation or any other type of exploitation.
Article 27	Receive or deliver a minor by means of illegal adoption with the purpose of sexual exploitation or any other type of exploitation.
Article 28	Forcing someone to get married with the purpose of sexual exploitation or any type of exploitation.
Article 29	Sexual exploitation taking advantage of the marital or emotional relationship.
Article 30	Extracting, removing or obtaining an organ, tissue or cells from live human beings without the proper medical legal procedures in order to obtain an economic gain.
Article 31	Applying procedures, techniques or legally unapproved medication on a person or group of people.

Source: Self-elaboration.

begging, plus none of the other exploitations have been taken into consideration (CDHCU, 2014).

In spite of the above difference in concepts of trafficking in persons, the 2014 General Law to Prevent, Punish and Eradicate crimes on human trafficking explained different ways in which exploitation may occur and mentions some activities related to trafficking in persons that can be punished. For example, Articles 32 through 35 refer to leasing publicity spaces for deceitful advertising with the purpose of trafficking; own or manage press or electronic media that sells publicity spaces for deceitful advertising with the purpose of trafficking; leasing or owning properties to house or hold trafficking victims; and acquiring services from a person in a trafficking situation while being aware of the person's condition. Similarly, Article 36, states that revealing confidential information related to the crimes of trafficking is also a punishable activity. The other ambiguity of the law is that activities which are unrelated to exploitation or trafficking, even though they are closely related, will be investigated, processed and are punishable within the framework of trafficking law.

As we can realize, despite growing awareness of the much wider scope on human trafficking, most of the law remains focused on the issue of sexual exploitation, as it has been discussed earlier. In the 2014 General Law to Prevent, Punish and Eradicate crimes on human trafficking, 12 out of 20 forms of exploitation mentioned in Articles 11 to 31 corresponds to Trafficking in Persons related to sexual matters for example: forced prostitution, production, distribution and possession of child pornography, forced marriage with the purpose of sexual exploitation, among others. The rest of the activities mentioned are slavery, servitude, labour exploitation, forced labour, forced begging, child trafficking and illegal adoption, use of children for organized crime activities, forced marriage for servitude purposes, organ trafficking and illegal medical experimentation with humans (*Ibid.*). Nevertheless, most of those forms of exploitation listed is this law are not necessarily forms of trafficking or even exploitation by themselves. For this case Articles 14, 15, 16 and 17 understand as a form of exploitation just owning or obtaining a profit from the production or distribution of pornography in which victims of trafficking or children were used. That means that someone acquiring child pornography for self-consumption may be prosecuted in terms of the current anti-trafficking law. Also exploitation, according to Article 19, is not a form of trafficking as most of the behaviours and characteristics of trafficking are not present even though exploitation is present. As far

Table 3.4: Complementary Mexican Laws that Mention Human Trafficking

Law	Provision
Federal Code for Criminal Procedures	Article 194 section XVI defines trafficking in persons a severe crime.
Migration Law	According to Article 2, it is a form of organized crime.
Federal Law against Organized Crime	States on Article 2 section VI that trafficking in persons becomes organized crime when three or more people gather to commit the crime.
General Law on Women's Access to a Life Without Violence	Article 49 section XXIV demands each State in the Republic to develop and apply gender-based protocols to investigate crimes related to trafficking in persons committed against women.
General Law on Victims	Article 111 section II recognizes victims of trafficking in persons with obstacles to defend themselves and therefore are entitled to a special fund allotted to damages and recovery.
Administrative Law of the Attorney General's Office	Article 5 section XVII demands to prepare and apply gender-based protocols to investigate crimes related to trafficking in persons committed against women and minors.
Law on the Protection of Boys, Girls and Teenagers Rights	Article 31 demands observing adoption processes in order to prevent trafficking of minors. Article 47 section III states that federal and local governments should prevent, investigate and punish cases involving trafficking of minors. Article 103 section III forces parents or tutors to protect minors from trafficking.
Law on Refugees and Complementary Protection	Article 20 guarantees institutional assistance to those individuals in the process of being recognized as refugees. For this, trafficking in persons victims, among other cases, should receive special attention. Article 54 guarantees attention for a proper integration of refugees taking into account their context such as being a victim of trafficking.

Source: Self-elaboration.

as Article 20 is concerned, it is difficult to prove the awareness of the trafficking condition of the person hired; this behaviour does not fit as exploitation, even less so as trafficking.

Despite many researchers point out most of the victims of sexual exploitation are women, boys and girls (Acharya, 2015; Montiel, 2011), there is an increasing exposure in the media of trafficking for labour exploitation. Similarly, the Global Report of Trafficking in Persons (UNODC) indicates America as a region where the participation of trafficking for labour exploitation and trafficking for sexual exploitation share almost the same proportion with 47 per cent and 48 per cent respectively for victims detected between the years 2010 and 2012. However, here we must emphasize that the 2014 Mexican General Law to prevent, punish and eradicate crimes on human trafficking and to protect and assist victims of these crimes is not the only legal instrument that misrepresents human trafficking in the law enforcement process. There are other national legal recourses that have the same confusion and ambiguities, which we have listed in Table 3.4. However, most of these laws consider human trafficking as a "*crime*" and set aside the aspects of human rights violations, gender equality and the problem of migration.

The misrepresentation of human trafficking in legal tools has translated into the arbitrary application of law. In our analysis of the number of detainees held by Attorney General's Office as traffickers, we found that, in 2014, 70 people of Mexican citizenship allegedly conducted trafficking activities, out of which 58 were arrested under Article 13, which refers to exploitation through paid sexual activities; 5 were detained under Article 17, referring to acquiring or holding pornographic material in which trafficked persons were involved; 2 were accused under Article 10, transporting, transferring, holding, delivering, receiving and/or housing one or more persons for the purpose of exploitation; 1 was kept in obedience to Article 16, producing child pornography; and 4 were accused of other non-specified crimes contained on the anti-trafficking law. Nevertheless, most of these alleged traffickers (85.3%) focused on the sexual exploitation modality of the crime.

Here we can conclude that each legal document in Mexico addresses human trafficking mainly as a crime and is synonymous with sexual exploitation, and less as a phenomenon in which migration, gender and human rights are involved. This kind of misrepresentation and diverging definition leading the anti-trafficking policy is aimed more toward the prosecution process than toward protecting victims and preventing the phenomena, leaving the victims' rights unprotected and the root causes of the issue unattended, plus setting aside other forms of exploitation, such as labour exploitation taking place in agriculture and other dangerous or "dirty jobs" we discussed earlier, and therefore, in order to carry out a successful anti-trafficking policy the focus on the issue of trafficking in persons must change to a human rights-based approach to effectively protect the victim's rights and provide a better understanding of the gender, economic, cultural, social and migratory factors that trigger the phenomena.

Conclusion

By the end of the 20th Century and the early 21th Century, the human trafficking problem captured the sudden attention of mass media as well as governments worldwide. Both international and regional media distributed facts that women were being tricked into prostitution by organized crime. Research conducted by the media indicated trafficking victims are mainly young, uneducated, willing to move abroad and attracted by a flashy lifestyle, entertainment, clothes and the possibilities of their dream destination. Once they were trapped with promises, they were directly sold to pimps and pressured into prostitution through violence. The constant push by media at different levels created global waves of trafficking that rapidly became a political and social issue. At first, service providers and Non-Governmental Organizations (NGOs) simply provided assistance and help to individual victims, but later they began to develop comprehensive programmes and policies.

In the case of Mexico, human trafficking was brought into the spotlight by Government agencies and Non-governmental Organizations at the beginning of the 21st Century, when the 2001 Trafficking in Persons Report ranked Mexico as a source and transit country. According to the U.S. State Department, Mexican women, children and men were trafficked into the United States, Canada, and Japan for the purpose of sexual exploitation and forced labour, and Mexico is a transit country for persons from various countries, especially Central America and China. There is an increasing number of people from Brazil and Eastern Europe moving through Mexico, some of whom are trafficked Salvadorans and Guatemalans, especially children, trafficked into Mexico for prostitution, particularly at the Southern border. The report classified Mexico as a Tier 2 country, given that the government does not yet fully meet the minimum standards and there are no specific laws in place to prohibit the trafficking of persons, and this continued until 2003. However, since the 2002 Trafficking in Persons Report, the U.S. Department of State extensively recognized Mexico as a source, transit and destination country of women and children trafficked for the purpose of sexual exploitation.

In spite of the growing attention by Mexican media and Non-governmental Organizations, Mexico resisted until 2005 and that same year the Mexican Government ratified the Palermo Protocol. In 2007 it published the first anti-trafficking law, which was known as Law to Prevent and Punish Trafficking in Persons (*Ley para Prevenir y Sancionar la Trata de Personas)*. Later in 2012, the Mexican Government formulated a new anti-trafficking law, the General Law to Prevent, Punish and Eradicate crimes on human trafficking and to protect and assist victims of these crimes, reformed again in 2014. Nevertheless, during the last decade, the Mexican Government has made significant efforts to fight against human trafficking in the country, yet these efforts have not been observed. As far as our analysis, is concerned the central and nodal problem is misrepresentation of the human trafficking issue in the media and anti-trafficking law. Both media and Government agencies focus human trafficking on the perspective of sexual exploitation and involvement of organized crime, which overlooks other types of trafficking. As a consequence of the diverging point of view and definitions, the issue of trafficking seems to distance away from the realities of victimizations and moving closer to the sphere of political interest. However, in the present study we may conclude that the human trafficking problem in Mexico is a complex social problem and it is necessary to enable multidimensional focuses of attention to develop a comprehensive approach of political as well as *mediatic* stand, beneficial to victims and society as a whole.

Acknowledgement

This study was supported by the National Council of Science and Technology (CONACYT), Mexico, [CB-2013/223023].

Notes

1. Autonomous University of Nuevo Leon, Monterrey, Mexico; E-Mail: *arun.kumara@uanl.mx*
2. Autonomous University of Nuevo Leon, Monterrey, Mexico.
3. *Ibid.*
4. For example, on January 5, 2016 Mexican national newspaper *El Universal* published the article: Attorney General rescued 16 trafficking victims from Cancun. *http://www.eluniversal.com.mx/articulo/nacion/seguridad/2016/01/5/rescata-la-pgr-16-victimas-de-trata-en-cancun*

References

Acción por los Niños (AN). 2008. *Medios de Comunicación en Acción Contra la Trata de Personas: Manual para Periodistas*, Lima, Perú. Accessed on 14/12/2015. *http://www.accionporlosninos.org.pe/archivos/publicaciones/sm_23700_ManualPeriodistas.pdf*

Acharya, A.K.; Gómez, O., F.J., Moctezuma S., A.; Morquecho C., A.J.; Domínguez S., T.P.; Benítez, A., A.A.; Cervantes N., J.J.; Garza R., A.; and Quistiano V.,

M.V., 2011. *Perspectivas del Tráfico de Personas en México: Un análisis de las Entidades Federativas*. Monterrey, México, Universidad Autónoma de Nuevo León.

Acharya, Arun Kumar. 2013. Mujeres invisibles y victimización sexual en México. El caso de la trata de mujeres en Monterrey, *Estudios Sociales*, vol. XXI (42), Julio-diciembre, Hermosillo, México.

Acharya, Arun Kumar. 2015. *Trafficking of Women for Sexual Exploitation: A Study from Mexico*, Mexico, Pearson.

Acharya, Arun Kumar and Bryson C. Jennifer. 2014. "Trafficking of women and vulnerability to HIV/STI infection in urban Mexico", *Genus*, vol. 70 (2-3).

Anti-Slavery International (ASI). 2002. *Human Traffic, Human Rights: Redefining Victim Protection*, Anti-Slavery International, Thomas Clarkson House, The Stableyard, Broomgrove Road, London, SW9 9Tl, United Kingdom.

Arreola, F., 2015. Puede *@SanjuanaMtz quebrar a Proceso y @AristeguiOnline hace lo que se denuncia en su sitio*. SDPnoticias.com. Accessed on 28/12/2015. *http://www.sdpnoticias.com/nacional/2015/10/02/puede-sanjuanamtz-quebrar-a-proceso-y-aristeguionline-hace-lo-que-se-denuncia-en-su-sitio*

Astorga, Luis. 2000. "Traficantes de drogas, políticos y policías en el siglo XX mexicano". In Claudio Lomnitz (ed.), *Vicios públicos, virtudes privadas: La corrupción en México*, Mexico City: CIESAS.

Azaola, Elena and Estes, J. Richard (Eds.). 2003. *La Infancia como Mercancía Sexual: Mexico*, Canada y Estados Unidos, 1st Edition, Mexico: Siglo XXI.

Bourdieu, P., and Kauf, T., 1997. *Sobre la televisioìn*. Barcelona: Anagrama.

Burke, Mary C., 2013. *Human Trafficking: Interdisciplinary Perspectives*, New York: Routledge.

Busza, S., Castle J. and A. Diarra. 2004. "Trafficking and health", *British Medical Journal*, No. 328.

Cámara de Diputados del H. Congreso de la Unión (CDHCU). 2014. Ley General Para Prevenir, Sancionar y Erradicar los Delitos en Materia de Trata de Personas y Para la Protección y Asistencia a las Víctimas de estos Delitos, Última Reforma DOF 19-03-2014, Government of Mexico, 2014. Accessed on 10/12/2015. *http://www.diputados.gob.mx/LeyesBiblio/pdf/LGPSEDMTP.pdf.*

Council on Hemispheric Affairs (COHA). 2009. *Modern Day Slavery in Mexico and the United States*, Washington DC. Accessed on 21/12/2015. *http://www.coha.org/modern-day-slavery-in-mexico-and-the-united-states/.*

Comisión Nacional de los Derechos Humanos (CNDH). 2012. La trata de personas. CDMX, México. Accessed on 14/12/2015.*http://eleconomista.com.mx/sociedad/2015/09/11/cdmx-reconocida-combatir-trata-personas.http://www.cndh.org.mx/sites/all/doc/cartillas/8_Cartilla_Trata.pdf*

Eco, Umberto. 2004. *Universidad y mass media*, Cuadernos de Información y Comunicación, No. 9. Accessed on 25/12/2015. *http://www.uacm.kirj.redalyc.redalyc.org/articulo.oa?id=93500910.*

Esteinou, Rosario. 2011. "Selling bodies and Sexual exploitation: Prostitution in Mexico". In Rochelle L. Dalla, Lynda M. Baker, John Defrain and Celia Williamson (eds.) *Global Perspectives on prostitution and sex trafficking: Europe, Latin America, North America and Global*, USA: Lexington Books.

González, R., 2003. Violencia contra las mujeres deja un millón de víctimas anuales en

México, *CIMAC*, Mexico. Accessed on 16/12/2015.*www.cimacnoticias. com.mx/node/30338.*

Huda, S., 2006. "Sex trafficking in South Asia", *International Journal of Gynaecology and Obstetrics*, vol. 94.

Huertas Díaz, Omar; Torres Vásquez, Henry; Díaz Pérez, Nydia Cecilia. 2011. El leviatán de los mass media, el peligro de la otredad y el derecho penal: La construcción mediática del enemigo, *Revista de Derecho*, Barranquilla, Colombia: Universidad del Norte, No. 35, enero-junio.

International Labour Organization. 2012. *ILO global estimate of forced labour: results and methodology*, Special Action Programme to Combat Forced Labour (SAP-FL), Geneva.

International Labour Organization (ILO). 2005. *A global alliance against forced labour*, Global Report under the Follow-up to the ILO Declaration on Fundamental Principles and Rights at Work 2005, Report I(B), International Labour Conference, 93rd Session, Geneva.

McClain, N.M. and Garrity, S.E., 2011. "Sex Trafficking and the Exploitation of Adolescents". *Journal of Obstetrics, Gynaecologic, and Neonatal Nursing*, vol. 40(2).

Monroy, Paulina. 2010. México: pasividad ante explotación sexual infantil, *Contralínea*, México, CDMX. Accessed on 12-12-2015. *http://www.voltairenet.org/article 167246.html*

Office for Democratic Institutions and Human Rights (ODIHR). 2004. *National Referral Mechanisms: Joining Efforts to Protect the Rights of Trafficked Persons: A Practical Handbook*, Warsaw, Poland. Accessed on 14-12-2015. *http://www.osce.org/odihr/13967*

Observatorio Nacional Ciudadano de Seguridad, Justicia y Legalidad (ONCSJL). 2014. *Estadística sobre la eficiencia en el combate a la trata de personas en México: un ejercicio de acceso a la información 2010-2013*, Observatorio nacional ciudadano de seguridad, justicia y legalidad, México.

Quirós Vicente, Francisco Javier. 2013. Aspectos de la vida y sociedad novohispana del siglo XVIII, *Revista Académica de Investigación,* No. 13, August. Accessed on 14-12-2015. *http://www.eumed.net/rev/tlatemoani/13/novohispana.html*

Rusev, A., 2013. "Human trafficking, border security and related corruption in the EU", *Migration and security sector paper series*, Brussels: DCAF.

Skilbrei, May-Len and Tveit, Marianne. 2008. "Defining Trafficking through Empirical Work: Blurred Boundaries and their Consequences," *Gender, Technology and Development*, vol. 12(1).

Smith, Holly Austin. 2014.*Walking Prey: How America's Youth are Vulnerable to Sex Slavery*, 1st edition: Walking Prey, New York.

Ugarte, M.B., L. Zarate and M. Farley. 2004. "Prostitution and trafficking of women and children from Mexico to the United States". In, M. Farley (ed.) *Prostitution, Trafficking and Traumatic Stress*, USA: Haworth Press.

United Nations Office on Drugs and Crime (UNODC). 2004. *United Nations Convention Against Transnational Organized Crime and The Protocols Thereto*, United Nations Office on Drugs and Crime, Vienna. Accessed on 14-12-2015. *http://www.unodc.org/documents/treaties/UNTOC/Publications/TOC%20Convention/TOCebook-e.pdf*

United Nations Office on Drugs and Crime (UNODC). 2007. *Manual para la lucha contra la trata de personas*. Accessed on 14/12/2015. *http://www.unodc.org/pdf/Trafficking_toolkit_Spanish.pdf.*

United Nations Office on Drugs and Crime (UNODC). 2012. *Global Report on Trafficking in Persons 2012*, Research and Trend Analysis Branch Division for Policy Analysis and Public Affairs, United Nations Office on Drugs and Crime, PO Box 500, 1400 Vienna.

United States Department of State (USDS). 2011. *The Trafficking in Persons Report-2011*. Washington DC. Accessed on 11-12-2015. *http://www.state.gov/j/tip/rls/tiprpt/2011/.*

United States Department of State (USDS). 2015. *The Trafficking in Persons Report-2015*. U.S. Department of States, Washington DC. July. Accessed on 03/04/2015. *http://www.state.gov/g/tip/rls/tiprpt/2015/.*

Uribe Arzate, Enrique and González Chávez, María De Lourdes. 2007. La protección jurídica de las personas vulnerables, *Revista de Derecho,* No. 27, julio. Barranquilla, Colombia: Universidad del Norte.

Von Mentz, Brígida. 2007. "Slavery and unfree labour in ancient Mexico and the new Spain (especially in the 16th century)", *Studiahistorica, Historia Antigua*, No. 25, Universidad de Salamanca.

Walters, Jim and Davis, Patricia H., 2011. "Human Trafficking, Sex Tourism, and Child Exploitation on the Southern Border", *Journal of Applied Research on Children: Informing Policy for Children at Risk*, vol. 2(1).

Wolfe, Abigail K., 2015. "Human Trafficking and Commercial Sex Exploitation: Treatment Recommendations for an Invisible Population", *Doctoral Papers and Masters Projects. Paper 24*. Accessed on 03/12/2015. *http://digitalcommons.du.edu/cgi/viewcontent.cgi?article=1023&context=capstone_masters.*

Zimmerman, Cathy, Mazeda Hossain, Katherine Yun, Vasil Gajdadziev, Natalia Guzun, Msc, Maria Tchomarova, Rosa Angela Ciarrocchi, Anna Johansson, Anna Kefurtova, Stefania Scodanibbio, Maria Nenette Motus, Brenda Roche, Linda Morison, and Charlotte Watts. 2008. "The Health of Trafficked Women: A Survey of Women Entering Post-trafficking Services in Europe", *American Journal of Public Health*, vol. 98(1).

FOUR

RESOURCE-TRIBE-POWER COMPLEX AND EXCLUSION: A SCRUTINY

M.C. BEHERA

In contemporary academics and agenda of Government Organizations (GOs) and Non-Governmental Organizations (NGOs), the phenomenon of tribal exclusion occupies an important area of enquiry. It is because the phenomenon presents an alarming situation of contradictions in that the tribes get excluded with every development strategy aimed at their inclusion. Moreover, tribal exclusion in development process has become a critical concern in human rights violation and ethical trepidation. The academics, GOs and NGOs, therefore, study the phenomenon of exclusion both empirically and theoretically with focus on positive and normative perspectives. The present chapter, however, attempts to examine the cause of tribal exclusion drawing on the tribal worldview and its contemporary status in development process.

The chapter is organised into five sections. Section I advances an outline of the analytical frame, entitled *Resource—Tribe and Power Complex* to understand the issue of tribal exclusion, particularly in the process of state sponsored development programmes. Section II outlines a few cases of exploitation, inequality, deprivation and displacement those define contours of exclusion. In section III, reality gaps, i.e. examples of exclusionary inclusion have been presented drawing on author's field study and secondary sources. In section IV, the incidence of exclusion is explained in relation to unequal power structure in *resource-tribe-power* complex. In section V, we conclude the discussion.

Section I

Analytical Framework

The discourse on "tribal development" is not *tribe specific* in that it does not focus on development of individual tribes or tribe as a social category separately. It rather presents an integrationist model where tribal development forms an integral part of national development policies and programmes. The ideology of national development on the other hand, is invariably the nation's adaptation to ever shifting development paradigms in international development discourse, which began with intellectual idealism before 1960s, shifted to techno-bureaucratic viability of projects in 1960s and early 1970s and to participatory development in 1980s (Mohanty, 1991). From 1980s, the trend of shift is rapid and competing within the frame of privatisation, globalisation and liberalisation (Behera, 2006). Various strategies like sustainable development, human development, livelihood security, inclusive growth, development through culture and empowerment with focus on gender issue, environmental sustainability, climate change, and institutional decentralisation have been critical issues in international development discourse (Behera, *ibid.*; Chambers, 1993 & 2006). These strategies also have influenced the economic policies of the nation to which tribals are integrated. Needless to say, the concept of tribal development is a misnomer in that it is an integrated formulation within the aggregation of national development policy.

Traditionally, the tribals are self-reliant autonomous economic units (GOI, 2014:287). Later, these units have got integrated with gigantic economic system of national dimension. In the new system, they are not the decision-makers. The decisions on what to produce, how to produce, how much to produce and the mechanism of distribution, to which they are linked, are governed through principles formulated at a level different from the boundary of tribes. Their autonomy is largely defined within the frame of "eminent domain", "public interest", etc. in relation to development policies and priorities. Practically, the tribes find themselves shifted from their own complex to another which is altogether alien to them. Their own complex happens to be a holistic worldview (*see* Redfield, 1953 & 1962; Adhikary, 1984 & 1991 and Behera, 2008) within the framework of interconnectedness and integration of all aspects of life. This holistic worldview is presented by Vidyarthi (1963) with reference to the economic life of the Maler, a tribe in present Jharkhand that revolves round shifting cultivation within the frame of *nature-man-spirit complex*. In such a frame, a complete understanding of a particular aspect of life is possible in its relation to other aspects (Pertin, 2009). Vidyarthi (*ibid.*) presents the economic life as instituted in socio-political organisations and in faiths and beliefs of the Maler.

But in new worldview, the economic aspect of life is independent of religious outlook and social norms. Moreover, the ideological considerations of sharing, barter exchange, mutual cooperation, respect for nature and propitiation for its use do not form a part in the structure of the new complex. In it, the holistic worldview confronts a matrix of specialised aspects of life with a shift in power base from tribal autonomy. We designate this new situation as *resource-tribe-power complex* in contrast to *nature-man-spirit complex* to understand the emerging issue of *exclusion* in development process.

The terms which form the domain of the complex are conceptualised as under:

Nature *vs.* Resource: The *nature* component of *nature-man-spirit* framework is replaced with *resource* in view of its commoditisation and mobility beyond the tribal system. In tribe's worldview Nature is a free gift and the principle of exclusion[1] does not govern its use. A tribe considers nature as giving environment (Bird-David, 1990) or preserver and feeder (*thow-gew*) (Nimachow, 2011:193), but not a commodity to be sold. In the worldview, the nature has a supernatural (spirit) realm and its use requires propitiatory rituals for the presiding deities (Pertin, 2009). But use of nature as resources lacks not only the belief in nature-supernature connections, but the ideology of community ownership and sharing. Tribes encounter nature not as a "community of being" (Gadgil & Guha, 1992) in "universal kinship relations" (Barnard, 1978), but as a commodity detached from their worldview of *free gift* and *sharing*.

Man *vs.* Tribe: In our complex of *resource-tribe-power*, 'tribe' replaces 'man' that is apparently gender neutral[2], community specific and defines the community as an autonomous distinct micro unit. Naturally, tribes designate by names meaning 'man', though in a number of cases the nomenclature of a tribe is an outside import.[3]

In contrast to the connotation of 'man' in *nature-man-complex*, 'tribe' in *resource-tribe-power complex* is a socio-administrative category, ST, a common name applied to each and every group of the same kind. The focus of development is not on *tribe* as an autonomous micro group, not even on macro group consisting of a number of heterogeneous autonomous tribes, but rather on nation/public in which 'tribe' is a constituent. Arguably, 'man' (individual tribe) has become only a member in a larger group called tribe or Scheduled Tribe in India which further is a constituent of the nation like other population groups.

Spirit *vs.* Power: Tribes generally profess animism in different degrees in which each animate and non-animate object has a soul. The soul is the guardian/presiding spirit of the object. In tribal worldview, the spirit stands for power, both malevolent and benevolent. It punishes the wrong doers (Pertin, 2009). That is why during oath and ordeal the priests administer oath in the name of the Supreme power in order to identify the real culprit (Elwin, 1959: 211). Tribal people perform rituals to propitiate spirits responsible for disease, and other calamities. Even they worship spirits for good harvest, good health of human beings and domestic animals, safety and protection in forests, and in general, for general welfare of human kind and domestic animals (Kani, 1993; Basar, 2011 and Behera, 2015). Invariably, interaction of tribals with nature is governed by recognition to the power of spirits (also called supernatural beings, deities etc.). The fear of supernatural punishment for violation of norms maintains tribes' symbiotic relations with nature (Behera, 2008: 22, 24-15). The power embodied in spirits and recognition to its authority over human keeps the social order and relationship with nature in balance without any practice of exclusion.

The 'power' in resource-tribe-power complex has political and economic dimensions. In this complex government at different levels, business and corporate houses, bureaucracy-corporate house nexus, market etc. constitute power structure. Obviously, this structure differs from the power structure in traditional tribal community in that the former is not holistic and therefore, not instituted in other aspects of life. In this power structure, economic life is delineated with the use of *nature* as *resource* in the absence of social, cultural and religious aspects of life.

The complex, i.e. *resource-tribe-power* so formed is one of the domains within a bigger domain, operates mostly by itself without any connections with other domains such as ethics, sociality etc. Needless to say, tribal economic life has narrowed down to a specialised *resource-tribe-power complex* as compared to the holistic *nature-man-spirit complex*. Tribes encounter a power structure alien to them and a connection of resources to the national and international market demand (cf. Nongkynrih, 2012:38 for tribals' holistic aspiration *vis-à-vis* the political-economic aspiration).

In *nature-man-spirit complex* power is mediated by 'man' in between nature and spirit. But in *resource-tribe-power complex* power rests on the top vertex and percolates down the superstructure. Unlike 'man' as the mediating force between nature and spirit to ensure a holistic individual and community life, in *resource-tribe-power complex*, power is dominating with a view to achieve macro-economic growth in quantitative terms.

Section II

Contours of Exclusion

Contours of tribal exclusion are tricky and complex. The incidence of exclusion takes diverse forms such as inequality, exploitation, capability deprivation, class formation, displacement, loss of entitlement etc. and reflects in different conditions like marginalisation, poverty, backwardness, vulnerability and so on. Obviously, the question is why the concept of exclusion over other indicators and attributes to study adverse impact of development on tribes. Sen (2000) also draws our attention to recognise the versatility of the idea and its reach, i.e. *the language of exclusion* to avoid too much indiscriminate use of the term.

Admittedly, a contour of exclusion, whether, it is in the form of inequality, displacement or in any other form, is a multiplex interrelation of various forms and perspectives. The contour of displacement, for example, is a distinct form of exclusion, but it creates such other exclusionary conditions as indebtedness (Rath, 2010 and GOI, 2014:150-151), unemployment (GOI, 2014:128, 130) and migration (GOI, *ibid.*:284; ActionAid, 2005; Panda, 2006; Tripathy, 2010 and Jena, 2014), bonded labour [Rastogi, 2007; Mohanty, 2002 and Nazer (nd)] and human trafficking (Behera, 2013). Sen (1998 & 2000) calls it *relational roots of deprivation* following Adam Smith's *relational deprivation* frame of explaining impoverishment. What he has emphasised is interconnectedness of elements of exclusion. He comments, "Social exclusion can, thus, be constitutively a part of capability deprivation as well as instrumentally a cause of diverse capability failures".

The concept of exclusion is inclusive of all forms and perspectives which mark a difference in terms of indicators of development between

Table 4.1: Poverty among STs – Rural and Urban India (1983-84, 1993-94, 1999-2000, 2004-05 and 2009-10)

(in %)

Year	*ST*		*All-India*	
	Rural	*Urban*	*Rural*	*Urban*
1983-84	63.8	54.2	45.6	42.2
1993-94	52.2	42.4	37.1	33.7
1999-2000	45.9	34.8	27.1	23.7
2004-05 (Revised Est.)	61.9	35.0	41.8	25.7
2009-10	47.1	28.8	33.8	20.9

Source: Statistical Profile of Scheduled Tribes in India 2013, Ministry of Tribal Affairs, Statistics Division, Government of India, www.tribal.nic.in

tribals and other social groups. It presents tribals in a situation that does not belong to the one in which other social groups are characterised in terms of comparatively higher growth, better access to basic entitlements and opportunities. Apparently, the tribes and other social groups are found having been placed on unequal planes. In other words, the tribal group is categorically excluded from the plane on which other social groups find a place. In the situation of displacement, the people are directly excluded from their territory, resource base and many related aspects of life in the event of use of their customary resources in development projects. Arguably, exclusion not only indicates the conditions, nature and characteristics of the discrimination, but explains the process as such. In this regard de Haan (1997, cited in World Bank, 2011:3) also considers both outcomes and relations that constrain individuals from achieving these outcomes, and the outcome as an element of social exclusion.

Although contours of exclusion are many and diverse, a few representative ones are selected to drive the point of discussion home. Moreover, a detailed discussion on each and every contour is not the objective of present chapter and practically comparative and update data for tribals are not available for such purpose. However, whatever data are easily available in government records and micro studies of individual scholars and organisations are presented to draw attention to the scope and complexity of contours of tribal exclusion.

Poverty

Poverty is widespread in tribal areas. Data available are scanty and based on quantitative figures estimated on the basis of sample survey by NSSO, Government of India. Poverty in tribal area has both quantitative and qualitative dimensions. Quantification of tribal economic life is not so easy, as tribes have neither records nor the attitude for it. Obviously, sample data in quantitative terms would be often misleading. Nevertheless, a rough idea on tribal poverty is presented in Tables 4.1 and 4.2.

Statistics in Table 4.1 shows a declining trend of tribal poverty both in rural and urban areas. However, the same trend holds for the nation as whole. The striking point is that the rural urban gap of tribal poverty is 18.3 percentage point as compared to this gap (12.9% point) between all-India rural and urban population. In other words, rural STs are excluded from urban STs in terms of 'non-poor' category by 18.3 percentage point where it is 12.9 per cent at all-India level. The gap is evident between rural ST and national rural category (13.3% point) and between urban ST and national urban category (7.9% point). At any point of comparison, the ST category shows greater figures of exclusion than national average. Table 4.2 shows large percentage of ST population below poverty line and thus the greater extent of ST exclusion as compared to national average in some states. Tribes in different states suffer from different degrees of exclusion (Table 4.2). In Odisha it is highest for rural STs, while in Uttarakhand ST urban poor records the highest. At all-India level the rural urban gap is 14.0 per cent point. This indicates the extent of urban tribal poverty. Interestingly, the combined average of rural and urban poverty is not available for ST category and all social groups for a better comparison.

Table 4.2: Percentage of Poor STs in State More than National Average (2004-05) *(in%)*

State/India	*Rural*	*Urban*
Uttarakhand	Less than national average	64.4
Orissa	75.6	61.8
Karnataka	Less than national average	58.3
Uttar Pradesh	Less than national average	37.4
Andhra Pradesh	Less than national average	50.0
Madhya Pradesh	58.6	44.7
Maharashtra	56.6	40.4
Chhattisgarh	54.7	41.0
Jharkhand	54.2	45.1
Bihar	53.3	57.2
All India	**47.3**	**33.3**

Source: Same as Table 4.1.

It needs mention that equality between tribal and national averages does not mean that tribes are as better off as other groups in the country.

This is a statistical paradox. The gap between ST and all Social groups does not compare between ST and non-ST categories. In All Social Groups STs are included. So in case of no difference between the two, there is a gap. Low average of STs included in higher average of *other social groups* reduces the average of *all social groups*, making it less than the average of *other social groups* (All social groups present national average which is the average of the averages of STs and other social groups.). In other words, the level of exclusion in terms of gap in percentage point when compared with'other groups' is actually larger than it appears when compared with All Social Groups.

Table 4.3: Access to Bank Accounts and Durable Assets

Social groups	*Households possessing Bank Account and a few durable assets (in %),*									
	Bank account	*TV*	*Bi-cycle*	*Computer/Laptop*	*Mobile only*	*Both (land line & mobile)*	*Two wheeler*	*Four wheeler*	*TV, Computer / Telephone/ mobile phone & Scooter/ Car*	*Do'nt have any*
All Social Groups	58.7	47.2	44.8	6.3	53.2	6.0	21.0	4.7	4.6	17.8
ST	44.98	21.9	36.4	4.4	31.1	1.8	9.0	1.6	1.3	37.3

Source: Report no. 543 of NSS 66th round.

Table 4.3 shows that less ST households possess bank accounts. The same trend is noticed in terms of possession of durable assets like bi-cycle, computer etc. It is to be mentioned that bank account is a prerequisite to avail of some Government Schemes. So, possession of bank account does not show the credit position of the tribes as compared to other groups. Similarly, bicycles and computers are distributed to STs under various schemes. Obviously, possession figure does not indicate the *real purchasing power* of the tribe persons to understand how far they are outside of *below poverty line bracket*. Moreover, the migrant youths on return to villages also purchase some assets (GOI, 204:109) as a matter of demonstration effect. The asset inequality between STs and other groups is reported in Xaxa Committee Report (*ibid.*; 117-1180).

Education

Literacy level of tribal population is still below the national average.

Report No. 543 of NSS 66th Round, 2009-10, as shown in Table 4.4, records that ST literacy is 63.1 per cent against the national average of 72.8 per cent. Some micro studies also provide poor state of tribal education among tribals. Vacancies in jobs for ST category as seen in advertisements are a clear indication of low level of higher education. This means a few have access to higher education and obviously many are excluded in the process (Behera and Basar, 2009). The status of tribal education can be appreciated from Tables 4.4, 4.5, 4.6 and 4.7.

Table 4.4: Percentage Distribution of 'Not Literate' Persons of Age 15 Years and Above (*in %*)

Social group	*Rural*			*Urban*		
	Male	*Female*	*Total*	*Male*	*Female*	*Total*
ST	35.8	58.3	47.0	12.7	31.3	21.8
All Social Groups	26.0	49.8	37.8	10.4	23.6	16.7

Source: Same as Table 4.3.

Table 4.4 shows that non-literate ST category across rural-urban divide and male-female divide within the age group of 15 years and above is quite high as compared to national average. In fact this gap will appear more if compared with groups minus STs in All Social Groups. Conversely, the literacy level is low as shown in Tables 4.5 and 4.6 in all categories.

Table 4.5: Literacy Rate among Persons of Age 5 Years and Above for ST and All Social Groups (*in %*)

Social groups	*Rural*			*Urban*			*Rural + Urban*		
	Male	*Female*	*Total*	*Male*	*Female*	*Total*	*Male*	*Female*	*Total*
ST	70.1	52.6	61.5	88.0	72.0	80.4	71.7	54.4	63.1
All Social Groups	77.3	58.5	68.2	90.0	78.9	84.8	81.1	64.0	72.8

Source: Same as Table 4.3.

Census, 2011 (Table 4.6) records a gap of literacy average of 14.3 percentage point between ST and All Social Groups.This gap is 12.36 per cent point and 15.29 per cent point for corresponding male and female groups. Between ST male and ST female the gap of literacy stands at 19.18 per cent point. Evidently, the incidence of ST exclusion is more than national figures in all categories.

Table 4.6: Literacy Rate of All Social Groups and ST Population (2011)(*in %*)

Social groups	*Literacy*		
	Male	*Female*	*Total*
ST	68.53	49.35	58.96
All Social Groups	80.89	64.64	72.99

Source: Registrar General of India, Census 2011.

Working Papers, NCW, 1988-89 (quoted in Priyadarshini, 2015) provide a general idea on drop-out rates of ST children. The drop-out rate for tribals at the secondary level is as high as 87 per cent and for the girls it is almost 90 per cent. Consequently, there is a negligible per cent (0.06%) of tribal women in institutions of higher education. In fact, percentage of tribal population at different levels of education is also comparatively low. This is shown in Table 4.7 for persons of the age group of 15 years and above.

Table 4.7: Percentage Distribution of Persons of Age 15 Years and Above by Level of General Education (*in %*)

Level of Education	*ST*						*All social groups*					
	Rural			*Urban*			*Rural*			*Urban*		
	Male	*Female*	*Total*	*Male*	*Female*	*Total*	*Male*	*Female*	*Total*	*Male*	Female	*Total*
Up to Primary	26.4	21.7	24.2	17.6	16.7	17.1	25.3	22.0	23.7	15.9	17.2	16.4
Middle	18.3	10.3	14.3	19.3	15.3	17.3	20.5	13.5	17.0	17.5	15.3	16.4
Secondary	11.1	5.7	8.4	18.2	14.7	16.5	14.7	8.2	11.5	19.5	15.9	17.7
Hr. Secondary	5.7	2.7	4.2	14.3	11.1	12.8	8.0	4.2	6.2	13.9	12.1	13.0
Diploma/Certificate	0.6	0.3	0.4	2.6	1.0	1.8	1.0	0.4	0.7	2.9	1.3	2.1
Graduate & above	2.2	0.9	1.6	15.3	9.8	12.6	4.5	2.0	3.2	19.8	14.7	17.3

Source: Same as Table 4.3.

Health and Hygiene

Unfortunately, health institutions are few and far between tribal areas. The norms of establishing medical institutions do not favour the tribal demographic pattern. At present, the norms for Primary Health Centres (PHCs) is 1:20,000, i.e. one PHC for every 20,000 population and 1:3,000 for sub-centres in tribal areas are lower than the norms for other areas. But given the density of population many tribes would not have a PHC in a 100 km distance (Parida, 2016; Reddisekhara, Y., 2016; also *see* Pandey, 1996 and ICMR, 2003).

The Bulletin on Rural Health Statistics in India, 2005 provides comparative health indicators of SCs, STs and all group categories. The health indicators in terms of infant mortality, under 5-mortality and under-nutrition are the poorest for the STs as show in Table 4.8.

Table 4.8: Infant Mortality Rate of SCs, STs and All Social Groups (*in %*)

Categories	*Infant Mortality Rate*	*Under-5 Mortality Rate*	*Undernutrition*
SC	83.0	119.3	535
ST	84.2	126.6	559
ALL	70.0	94.9	470

Source: The Bulletin on Rural Health Statistics in India, 2005.

The data presented in *the Bulletin on Rural Health Statistics in India,* 2005 (Table 4.8) and *National Family Health Survey (NFHS)* 2005-06 (Table 4.9) show divergence with regard to infant and under-5 mortality rate. The gaps are 22.1 and 30.9 respectively. The reason of this gap could be sampling error. In a way this corroborates to the point that data on tribes are as vulnerable on reliability scale for comparison and interpretation as the conditions of tribes. Nevertheless, it is indicative of the trend of tribal vulnerability. Table 4.9 presents comparative health indicators which look discouraging for tribal health status.

Table 4.9: Comparative Health Indicators of STs (2005-06) (*in %*)

Health Indicators	*Scheduled Tribe*	*All-India*
Infant Mortality	62.1	57
Non-Natal Mortality	39.9	39
Post-Natal Mortality	22.3	18
Child Mortality	35.8	18.4
Under Five Mortality	95.7	74.3
ANC Check-up	70.5	77.1
Percentage Institutional Deliveries	17.7	38.7
Childhood Vaccination (Full Immunization)	31.3	43.5
% Households covered by a health scheme/insurance	2.6	31.9
Prevalence of any anemia (<12.0g/dl) in woman	68.5	55.3

Source: National Family Health Survey (NFHS), 2005-06.

The hygienic condition of tribes is reflected in terms of their access to basic amenities like latrine and bathing facilities, drinking water etc. the condition is also not encouraging like the health indicators. Table 4.10 presents accessing level of tribes. The figures shown will be more when compared with All Social Groups minus ST. The exclusion reflects in the absence of facilities. In comparison to 22.6 per cent of ST households having latrine facility within the premises 77.4 per cent is to be noted not having the facility within the premises. The same trend is noticed with regard to other facilities.

Table 4.10: Access to Basic Amenities relating to Hygiene

Social groups	*Facilities in %*							
	Good Houses	*Facilities within premises*		*Separate kitchen in side*	*Waste water outlet connected to (Closed drainage)*	*Main source of Drinking water in relation to premises*		
		Latrine	*Bathing*			*Within*	*Near*	*Away*
All Social Groups	53.1	46.9	42.0	61.3	18.1	46.6	35.8	17.6
ST	40.6	22.6	17.3	53.7	6.1	19.7	46.7	33.6

Source: Same as Table 4.9.

Land Alienation

The problem of land alienation is the most burning problem in tribal India. Whether they practise agriculture or depend on forests it is the land that stands as the only source of livelihood. Banerjee (2011:50) informs us that in Assam 90 per cent of tribal people depend on agriculture and about 70 per cent of tribal families have been practically rendered landless. The Annual Report of Ministry of Rural Development of the Government of India, 2004-2005 has registered 86,291 cases of land alienation involving 10,48,93 acres of land in undivided Bihar (including Jharkhand), which topped the list of tribal land alienation in India (Behera, 2013; also *see* Behera & Nath, 2004).

While referring to a sample survey conducted by the Department of Rural Development in 1988, Government of India, Rath (2010) informs us that about 30 to 55 per cent of tribal households had been affected by land alienation. He also reports that about 80 per cent of land was alienated to the non-tribals.

Hussain (2008:30) gives an estimate of acquisition of huge tracts of tribal land that is approximately 7015.60 acres by the Government of Assam for commissioning of Kopili Hydroelectric Project. The construction of capital complex in Guwahati of Assam due to shift of capital from Shillong in 1973 displaced and alienated 1,00,000 people of their land, nearly all of them tribal – majority of them being the Bodos. The land acquired for the purpose is estimated about 48,000 acres out of which more than 43,000 acres of land were part of Kamrup tribal belt (*ibid.*, 42-43).

Development Induced Displacement

Mega-development projects are the models of economic development recognised across the world. It may be hydro-power project like Sardar Sarovar in Gujarat and Hirakud Hydro-Power Dam Project constructed in Odisha during 1950s; industrial houses like Rourkela Steel Plant of Odisha or Bhilai Steel Plant in Chhattisgarh or BHEL in Andhra Pradesh; mining projects in Odisha as well as in other states which exploit ores like dolomite, iron, bauxite by both Private and Public Sector Companies. One will find these activities carried out in tribal areas as there are resources for such activities. Millions of tribal people have been displaced from their lands, their homes, their livelihoods, and their communities to make way for projects (*see* Behera & Nath, 2004).

Some figures of displacement are available for different projects. More specifically in Indian context the magnitude of displacement as calculated by Fernandes (2008) for the period 1951-2000 tunes to the extent of 21.3 millions while for academicians like Mahapatra (1999), the estimate accounts this to the tune of 25 millions. Another estimate puts it that some sixty million people have been displaced in the last seventy years. Fernandes (2008) maintains that in India, around 40 per cent of the estimated 60 million DPs/PAPs during 1951-2000 are tribals (*see* GOI, 2014:257).

In recent years Special Economic Zones (SEZs) and Protected Areas are also emerging as substantial people-displacing projects. In India, for protected areas alone, one estimate suggests that as many as 6,00,000 tribal people have been displaced. A study shows land acquisition by the Government of Andhra Pradesh to set up Special Economic Zones (SEZs) (Tripathy, 2014). Xaxa Committee (GOI, 2014) reports lack of basic civil amenities, low employment opportunities for tribal DPs/PAPs, deterioration of health (*ibid.*: 295), loss of status of women after replacement (*ibid.*:294), impoverishment (*ibid.*:296) and deterioration of general quality of life (*ibid.*: 289-290 and Padel & Das, 2010: 89-95; and 2008).

Tribal exclusion is both relative and absolute[4] along all the indicators like poverty, health, literacy, access to basic amenities and so on. The gap that exists between rural-urban and male-female divides within the group, and between STs and other social groups or all social groups measures relative exclusion. This trend holds true for level of poverty and access level to amenities. The absolute exclusion is marked by the deviation from 100 per cent achievement (Behera and Basar, 2010:38, fn.9).

Section III

Exclusionary Inclusion: Some Field Experiences

After Independence of the country, the government has been taking special care for the development of the tribals. Not only there are Constitutional safeguards and supportive institutional set up, but there are various schemes implemented to realise the objectives. Several of the schemes formulated during early plans are still active through five year plans along with new schemes. Development initiatives permeate through various five-year plans with the sole aim of protective discrimination and affirmative action for tribal development. Some of the strategies and schemes include Community Development Programme, Multipurpose Tribal Blocks, Tribal Development Block, Development Agencies, Primitive Tribal Groups, Integrated Tribal Development Projects, Modified Area Development Approach, Tribal Sub-Plan, Dispersed Tribal Development Programme, and Centrally Sponsored Schemes and many others etc. (Mohapatro, 2009:25-28 and Xaxa, 2012:25-26).

But various evaluation studies (*see* GOI, 2014) find that development objectives of the tribes have not been realised. Rather, they are found more deprived, marginalised and thus excluded in the process of development. Here, we present a few instances of schemes implemented to understand the nature and cause(s) of exclusion in the process of inclusion. The name of villages has not been mentioned for obvious reasons.

Case I: In 2010, the author was reported an event during the field study in a Paraja village of Lamptaput Block of Koraput district. The village is located about 10 kms away to the right from the road connecting Lamptaput Block and Machhakunda. The people of the village normally borrow money from the *kumtis* (traders) by auctioning tamarind trees during lean period. The *Kumtis* fix the rate which is about ten times less than the market price. One NGO intervened in 2008 and arranged the sale of tamarind to a whole seller in Vishakhapatnam. The villagers got good amount for tamarind. In 2008, the government electrified the village and people got free electricity. With electricity, more than 50 per cent of the families went to the *kumtis* to borrow money to purchase TV and radio in 2009. The *kumtis* got the opportunity of an unfair bargain and supplied them TVs and radios for which the tamarind trees were auctioned for three seasons. Before NGO intervention, whatever auction money they used to provide annually to a family would have procured one TV costing around Rs.7000. The condition of the villagers became worse and many migrated to Vijayawada, Rajmundry and Vishakhapatnam as wage labourers, and that to through these *kumtis*.

Case II: In 2002, the Government of India provided financial assistance to the Sulungs of Arunachal Pradesh for rehabilitation under Bonded Labour System (Abolition) Act, 1992. The money was distributed from the office of the Deputy Commissioner, Seppa. Sulungs from far away places like Bameng, Chiang Taju, Khenwa circles came with their family members to receive the money. Their former Nyishi masters arranged for their night halts and food. When they received the money, their Nyishi masters claimed the amount and in fact took away from them being food and lodging charges. Most of the Sulungs returned empty hand.

Case III: In 1986, the author recorded an event in a Galo village of West Siang district. Many families in the village availed of the Government scheme and converted the *jhum* fields to terrace fields in 1982. In 1984, they reconverted the terrace fields to *jhum* fields for they could not produce variety of crops they used to produce from *jhum* fields. A similar event is also recorded by Hussain (1993:55, 56-57; *cf.* 1984) in Yangse Valley of East Kameng district of Arunachal Pradesh.

Case IV: During field study in 1987 in Mishmi villages of the then Hayuliang sub-division of Lohit district of Arunachal Pradesh it was reported that the cattle and pigs supplied were eaten up as they started dying. The Mishmis do not take milk; they rather eat beef and pork. Elwin (1960:69-70) also mentions of unsuitability of exotic animals to the climate on high elevations and lack of knowledge of tribals to look after exotic animals properly.

Case V: During field study from 1983 to 1992 in Khampti villages in connection with Ph.D. assignment a number of events were reported which point to failure or misuse of schemes. There were also schemes which replaced the traditional technology. A few of them are as follows:

1. In many Khampti families the sewing machines supplied under IRDP scheme were found laying idle, though the ladies who were beneficiary under the scheme were given training in Block Offices. In one family, the machine is rented to a non-tribal tailor. It was reported

that tailoring unit was not practicable as it stood on the way of other necessary works like collecting fire wood and vegetables, fetching water, weaving clothes for family members, cooking, preparing local wine etc. Moreover, the villagers do not have enough clothes to stitch in a single tailoring unit that could run profitably in a village.

2. The Khamptis are traditionally famous for running hydro-powered rice mills and making paper and ink. Supply of diesel powered rice huller under employment assurance scheme has adversely affected the technology. In all the Khampti villages hydro-powered rice mills have simply vanished giving place to diesel powered rice huller. Due to availability of paper and ink in the market, except a few old persons, others had no knowledge of manufacturing paper and ink.

3. Under land reclamation scheme and introduction of plantation crops in 1980s, a Khampti chief converted the entire village common land to tea plantation. A case was filed in the court of the District Magistrate, Lohit District by the villagers, but the verdict went in favour of the Chief according to customary laws. As per custom, a family, with the permission of the Chief, occupies as much land as its members are capable of managing to meet their subsistence needs. The planter being the Chief justified his capacity to manage the land (of course with hired labourers) for his newly acquired consumerist needs. Due to shortage of common land and prospect of further extension of cultivable land many of the families migrated and established a new village.

Case VI: In 1987, the failure of low cost latrine scheme in Apatani villages of Arunachal Pradesh was reported during a field study. The Apatani houses are on raised platforms and to a corner below the platform they construct pigsty. Above the pigsty they construct the latrine, and the human excreta is used as food of the pigs. Due to low cost latrine, the pigs did not get enough food. Land being scarce, the Apatanis do not allow the pigs to stray because every piece of land is put under one or other type of uses. As a result the scheme was not successful.

Case VII: The construction of Andaman Trunk Road has been a bone of contention between activists and the government. Its adverse impact is well documented in the Report of Xaxa Committee (GOI, 2014:364-365). A London based organisation, "Survival", gives an account of the plights of the Jarwa people when they encountered development forces through the road (quoted in Behera, 2013).

It reports,

Outsiders are invading the reserve of the isolated Jarwa tribe in the

Andaman Islands, India...Despite a Supreme Court Order to Islands' Administration to close the highway which runs through the reserve; it remains open, bringing disease and dependency... The problem has become so acute that in some areas the once abundant wild pigs and fish are now scarce... The main highway which runs through the Jarwa reserve, known as the Andaman Trunk Road, is also bringing exploitation of the Jarwa. There are numerous reports of poachers and other outsiders sexually exploiting Jarwa women, and outsiders are introducing alcohol, tobacco, and alien food items on which the Jarwa are starting to depend. Those entering Jarwa land also bring outside diseases to which the Jarwa have no immunity.

Section IV

Resource-Tribe-Power Complex

The ideal state of *nature-man-spirit complex* does not appear in examples cited in section III. Development dynamics already indicate external linkages beyond the complex and thus the tribe. These linkages in Paraja village of Lamtaput, both traders and market, have turned the *nature* (tamarind and tamarind trees) to *resources*. The power equation being unequal, the Parajas are exploited and thus excluded from the fair bargain during transaction under market situation. A similar type of unequal power relation between Nyishis and Sulungs (Behera, 2004) has excluded the Sulungs from use of the assistance of rehabilitation. Sulungs are human resources for the Nyishis who wield authority over them. The complex is not tribe specific, rather, it is inter-tribal with Sulungs as resources, and Nyishis representing the power. Sulungs' worldview in their relation with Nyishis forms a type of resource-tribe (Sulung)-power complex.

Unequal power relations in the customary land tenure system of the Khamptis (*see* Behera, 1994) facilitated use of village common land as private resource, thereby excluding some families from its future use. The power dynamics along with people's perception of land in the customary frame was absent in development schemes of land reclamation. Moreover, the customary inequality could be transported to the modern process of development where the Chief operated within the resource-tribe (villagers)-power frame.

Within a short span of about 20 years from Chinese aggression in 1962, since when development of Arunachal Pradesh became a serious concern of National Government, the attitude of people was found responsive to new forces of development (*see*, Jha, 1985; Agarwal, 1885; Das, 1995 and Behera, 1994). It is therefore, not a surprise that the Galos and people in Yangse Valley converted *jhum* land to terrace fields in late 1970s and early 1980s. Nevertheless, the worldview of nature-man-spirit complex had its influence. In this worldview, ritualistic significance associated with *jhum* cultivation and some crops, multi-cropping practices, crop diversity and moreover, familiarity with the way of life which they found lacking in terrace cultivation made them to decide upon reconversion to *juhm* fields. The ideological perception of people in economic pursuits was not considered in the strategies of development interventions. A similar gap also exists in process when the Mishmis were supplied with cattle, Khampti beneficiaries with sewing machines and diesel powered rice hullers, the Apatanis with low-cost latrines and when Andaman Trunk Road is constructed in Jarwa territory. As a result schemes failed in objective realisation and people remained outside the desired benefit in all the cases.

In failures of schemes[5], unequal power equation is evident in the absence of people's participation in decision-making. The decision came from above the people whom development is meant for. Needless to say, the decision-makers held the power which people to be developed did not have. The exclusion is visible in the absence of people's participation in decision-making process and thus from realisation of the desired benefit.

There are studies which find tribal marginalisation in the process of their linkage to national development schemes.[6] Dréze and Gazdar (1977) and Maharatna (2000) clearly link the lower fertility and mortality rates to tribal integration with industrial and market societies that encroach upon traditional sustainable livelihood. Behera and Basar (2009) inform us that exclusion is inherent in selective and gradual process of implementation of schemes (also *see* Thorat and Newman, 2007; *cf.* Xaxa, 2012:27-28).

Though the studies had their distinct objectives and analytical perspectives, we can reason out the incidence of marginalisation, displacement etc. in the frame of unequal power relations. The planners, policy-makers, administrators etc. have their own perspectives, understanding and interest in view while they engage in tribal development. Land Act, Forest Acts etc. during colonial period had colonial interest in mind (*see* Bhukya, 2012). It is but natural of tribal exclusion from their resources to serve colonial interest. Criminal Tribal Act, 1871 can be viewed as a land mark of backward and forward forces of tribal exclusion. First, these people resorted to petty crimes for survival when they were rooted out of their traditional means of livelihoods consequent upon colonial policies (Radhakrishna, 2001). Second, the Act attached social stigma of criminality in the community and isolated it from its normal life and status. Regular reporting of the members of the designated criminal tribe to the police kept many of them away from securing gainful employment.

The hangover of these colonial policies has been looming large in the horizon of development endeavours after Independence. The Land Act (Fernandes, 2014) and Forest laws were operative even in the early years of first decade of present century (Mahapatra, 1993 & 1999a and Saldhana, 1993).

The power difference and exclusion is not unique to development interventions. It is institutionalised where there are unequal power relations between groups, for empirical data show that inequality in power relations has the potentiality of breeding practices for self-perpetuation; the practices often are visible flagships of "social good" carrying the invisible cargo of "immediate benefit", and all together operating as a process towards perpetuation of socially constructed and regulated dominance in power relations. Even under patriarchy, assuming all other power relations in the society constant, the women have various spheres of exclusion.[7] The society evolves mechanism to reinforce the power ideology and exclusion like the witchcraft among the Mundas (Kelkar & Devnathan, 1993). Moneylenders linked with tribal communities keep the tribes entrapped in perpetual debt by the mechanism of interest policies, thumb impression/signature in blank papers, advance of new loans to repay earlier loans or to meet social/religious obligations like marriage, curative rituals, payment of fines etc. or to meet full shortages. Sulungs' bonded relation with Nyishis has also such reinforcing mechanism (Behera, 2004).

A striking feature of exclusionary forces is that it gets carried over to a new system (*see* Behera & Basar, 2009:241; also *see* (Walton, 2007, cited in World Bank, 2011:2). The planter Chief of the Khampti village has successfully used his power to occupy community land for commercial motive whereas his power has the sanction under traditional norms of sharing and subsistence living. Dzuvichu (2012) informs us how the inequality of women in patriarchy in Naga tradition has been reinforced in state sponsored development programmes. A similar trend is reported by Sitlhou (2015) about Kuki women in the process of development within the frame of new power structure. The *moutana*, the practice of blood-money among the Bhills in Rajasthan as compensation to the victim family by the accused has been a serious law and order problem because of its extension to spheres in modern life. Doctors, drivers etc. are charged under this system when death occurs even at the time of discharging normal duties (Kataria, 2014). Conversely, development interventions have not been able to neutralise the exclusionary forces that existed in the tradition, for traditional power elites are found progressively included in the process of development (Misra, 1993 and Behera & Basar, 2010:38, fn.8 and 2009:240, fn.3).

Needless to say, in traditional tribal communities there were unequal power relations and incidences of exclusion, internal exclusion because of emerging power structure within *nature-man-spirit complex.*[8] This power is an intervening feature in between *nature* and *spirits*, rests on 'man' in the complex, redefines 'man's' mediating relation between nature and supernature and results in the practice of exclusion. The stronger is the intervening power the greater is the incidence of exclusion. In hunting-gathering community, the intervening power is minimal and rests on patriarchy. Consequently, ritualistic exclusion of women characterises patriarchal power structure of the community. A strong patriarchy often displays concentration of power in fewer hands or at different levels and therefore, more intense practice of exclusion in different fields like with hunting as mentioned earlier. Whether it is witch hunting, restriction of practices, or inheritance along male line, all these are mechanisms for reinforcing the phenomenon of female exclusion in a patriarchy (*see* Sitlhou, 2015 and Kelkar & Devnathan, 1993).

In chieftain type of societies, the power rests on the chief and in such societies the incidence of exclusion is more intense. In Nocte and Wancho communities of Arunachal Pradesh for example (*see* Dutta, 1978; Dutta 1990 and Srivastava, 1970) a section of people (Wangpan in case of the Wancho) do not have membership rights in the traditional village council. Even in gerontocracy of the Sherdukpens and Apatanis of Arunachal Pradesh, the exclusion practice is quite visible. In Sherdukpen community, members of the *Chao* clans do not have the right to head the village council, Jung and participate in decision-making (Sharma, 2013). The right rests on the members of *Thong* clans. Among the Apatanis the Buliang membership (both the member and the council are called

Buliang) is hereditary (Kani, 1993). Even in Monpa community the *tsorgen*, the head of the council, is elected from among those families who have *khraimi* (those who own taxable land) are eligible to the post of Tsogen Norbu (2008). 'Slaves' in tribal communities invariably constitute an excluded group (*see* Elwin, 1959).

We find that exclusionary process continues, often more intensely, even after the Government of India embarked upon planned process of development for general welfare and raising the standard of living of the marginalised groups like the tribals with policies of affirmative action and positive discrimination. Safely we can infer that the exclusionary forces are reinforcing in the frame of unequal power relations and have the potentiality of being carried over to new system. This is evident when the Government formed by 'elites' framed policies and implemented strategies of development for heterogeneous groups like tribals, SCs.

In the construction of tribe (ST), the power dimension is not homogeneous. Power heterogeneity exists when different tribes within the category have different levels of contact, pursue different occupations and display various levels integration in the development process. The first visible one is the PVTGs (Particularly Vulnerable Tribal Groups) within the ST category whose average development indicators is less than that of the ST as a whole, thereby making them economically more backward and vulnerable within the group. Statistics apart, field observations present their backwardness in strong terms.

Unequal relations persisted in spite of government's endeavour because backwardness existed in different degrees among various tribes before their integration with national development policies. A community with better technology, economy, etc. have the potentiality of exerting power over the one with less of them. Empirical data suggest that agriculturist communities have developed an unequal power relation with neighbouring hunting gathering societies[9] (Behera, 2004 and Woodburn, 1988). As the communities have different levels of development, competition among them does not ensure a level play ground and a fair chance of equal share. This is another dimension of unequal power relations as two unequal partners compete for at least equal share. It does not come as a surprise when Behera and Basar (2009:236-241) report us that traditional elites of Arunachal Pradesh have proportionately a major share in the development process than the common people. In the process of development, elites have been created during early years who endeavour to continue by creating opportunities.

This justifies intra-tribe inequality, for the tribes were not homogenous before their integration in development process. They pursued a wide range of occupations, ranging between hunting-gathering and white collar jobs (Vidyarthi and Rai, 1985) and displayed different levels of cultural contact[10] (Elwin, 1944). Obviously, the aristocratic Raj Gonds, Khamptis and others, at the higher level of contact, responded better to development forces and therefore portray better indicators in the field of literacy, health and market connections than nomadic tribes like Birhors or hunting-gathering tribes like Sulungs who have the least level of contact. Contact with Christianity has positive impact on tribal literacy; it is evident from statistics of higher literacy of tribal states like Mizoram (94.4%), Nagaland (86.5%) and Meghalaya (86.1%) in Northeast India where majority of tribes profess Christianity. Even within ST groups, caste-communities in Sipiti and Juansari-Bawar areas have been listed which have better social dynamics of acceptance than PTGs. The dynamic difference justifies Mina tribes' major share in white collar jobs than Bhils. Except field observations, we do not have comparative indicators to present various degrees of exclusion even within the ST category.

The inequality and further marginalisation of these groups have been criticised in terms of Western model of development ideology and structural strategy of centralised plans, top-down approach, macro-perspective and sectoral coverage. What is inherent in structural strategy is unequal power relation. Those who are involved in development process are 'others' to those whom development is meant for. The 'others' form a system of decision-makers for the development those outside the system. Even the representatives of tribes in the system represent the system than the tribal worldview of life and development. No doubt, the people call these representatives as cultural outsiders, the *dikhu*, those who belong to the culture beyond the tribal communities (Mahapatra, 1980 and Alam, 1993). The unequal power relations coupled with vested interests reinforces the exclusionary process.

The concern for tribal development has a base imbued to contemporary ideology of human rights, democracy, empowerment, equality and so on. Undoubtedly, it is positively a right consciousness towards achieving what humanity deserves and abolishing what narrow human mind created for various divisions. But the problem begins here. The efforts to raise the level of living of tribals are made keeping the western standard of living as ideal. Unfortunately, during colonial period, their resources got linked to Western ideology of development and the tension of relations began from there. Notwithstanding this, efforts are, however, directed to secure a standard of living for the tribals following the ideals of Western principles of development—market, money, maximisation, mass production, high level of consumption and so on. This contradicts the symbiotic relations between the tribes and the resource base (nature) in the process of securing material means of existence. Of course, tribal view of development at present is neither the traditional level of subsistence living, nor the high level of a consumer economy, the complexity of which is yet to be understood. They want a shift from traditional development paradigm, but within the conservation paradigm of their culture. The 'others' also emphasise on conservation of tribal culture *vis-à-vis* development (*see* UNDP, 2004)[11] , for the role of culture in general is recognized through a majority of the Sustainable Development Goals (SDGs), including those focusing on quality education, sustainable cities, the environment, economic growth, sustainable consumption and production patterns, peaceful and inclusive societies, gender equality and food security. But ironically, the development and conservation stand in opposite camps and the tribes are reduced to the status of cultural refugees, the *dikhu.*[12]

In the development model that we have adopted tribal resources are exploited to maintain regional, national and international consumption level. The trade off between the level of development and the resources they sacrifice in no way testify the others' welfare motive or efforts to correct the wrongs. The tribes bear the cost of a level of development, which otherwise do not mean much to them given their status of deprivation and marginalisation, but the cost not only makes their present vulnerable but denies their access to resources in future. This is reflected in displacement, land alienation and other contours we have outlined in Section III of this chapter.

In resource-tribe-power complex, both resource and power are external to tribal worldview; obviously each of them has separate connotation and function. In the power structure the 'tribe' stands in the periphery or outside. Its representatives conform to the ideological requirement inherent in power structure than to tribal needs. The participation in decision-making or giving consent is divided along political party affiliations along with the traditional power base in villages. There are also manipulation and stage management by outside forces like administration through a group of vested interest from within the community (GOI, 2014: 350-351; Misra & Sivaiah, 2009:193; also *see*

Padel and Das, 2010) to show that decentralisation strategy works in order. In this context, Basar (2011) with reference to villagers' participation in joint forest management comments that decentralisation is a strategic innovation to reinforce forces of centralisation.

Of course, there is a reversal in structure with focus on decentralisation, peoples' participation etc. There are three Acts namely—Land Acquisition Law of 2013, Forest Rights Act, 2006[13] and PESA, 1996 that provides for tribal participation and seeking their consent. In these Acts power relations have not been considered. In the absence of data on their functioning the extent of tribal exclusion cannot be ascertained. But given the nature of power differences along party lines, inequality in development indicators indicating unlevel ground for competition, incidence of exclusion cannot be avoided. This can be safely argued with example of *moutana,* reinforced by integrating customs with modern system, which has created law and order problem in tribal areas of Rajasthan and Gujarat despite modern Panchayats and laws. Moreover, forest relations and decentralised governance at Panchayat level are not all that constitute the tribal worldview and tribal way of life.

In this context mention may be made that regulations could not prevent tribal land alienation, for tribal land is a resource and linked to national interest through the national power structure. There are examples of land allotment to refugees and MNCs in tribal areas by state machinery.[14] The Jhum Land Regulations of 1947-48 recognises the customary rights of tribals of Arunachal Pradesh on land (Elwin, 1959:65f). Nevertheless, their lands in Tezu and Bomdila areas have been transferred to Tibetan refugees, in Chowkham and Diyun areas to Chakma refugees. Allotment of tribal land of Nyiamgiri to Vedanta or to other MNCs in other projects stands witness to the overriding power beyond tribal customary practices.

In resource-tribe-power complex which governs the tribal life, especially their development, exclusion is embedded.

Section V

Conclusion

Tribals had their self-reliant economy before they encountered external forces. Even in self-reliant pursuits within nature-man-spirit complex power inequality existed beginning with patriarchy and extending across chieftaincy and other socio-political institutions like gerontocracy, social divisions etc. So, the complex did not ensure inclusiveness in all spheres of life, for patriarchy practised ritualistic and other types of exclusion for women. In other words, exploitation, inequality and exclusion are inherent characteristics in unequal power structure. The existence of unequal power structure in itself builds on exclusion of one group. As a matter of fact, sections without or with less power apparently form the group which remains outside of the power wielding group. With power differences, it is but natural that the priorities, perspectives, opportunities, interests, working plan etc., also differ. Field experiences we have presented in Section III and tribal land alienation in the process of their welfare within decentralised frame we have discussed in Section IV substantiate to the proposition that interests, working plan etc. differ between power groups.

In contemporary development discourse unequal power relations are quite obvious at least in terms of effective participation in policy formulation, in market transactions, resource perception etc. between the tribes and 'others'. The relations between the two are produced and reproduced to serve interests of the 'others'. The 'others' ironically ride the horse of maximisation principle of production and consumption in contrast to subsistence living of the tribals. The former includes policy-makers, administrators, planners, corporate houses, international relations, market, non-tribal traders, and above all governments having a role to play in tribal development. Obviously, development concerns place tribes and others in two power blocks. The interface, however, does not have a level playing ground; it is rather intertwined with sets of unequal access to resources, different levels of consumption and production ideology and unequal opportunities for participation and expressions of capabilities. Always the relations carry overt and covert interests, meanings and values of the 'others' into which the 'tribals' are included. The result is a growing hiatus between objectives and achievement in tribal development resulting in tribal exclusion.

We began with the assumption that nature-man-spirit complex provides ideal situation for inclusion. But we found that inequality of power relations even within it creates exclusion. Arguably, in unequal power relations in a process, exclusion is an inherent characteristic. We can safely infer that tribal inclusion in development process will only be attainable with autonomy of tribals in the decision-making process within the frame of unequal power relations.

Notes

1. Access to Nature/community resources by one member does not exclude the other members of the community from its use. Every member of the tribe has access to use Nature to satisfy material needs within the prescriptions of the cultural norms.
2. The designation of a tribe like Puroik, Birhor or Nyishi etc. which means 'man' is gender neutral; it denotes both male and female. In some tribes, the designation of the tribe itself may not denote 'man'(human), but the vocabulary system has the term that denotes 'people'. Nyi in Galo means human. The Galos use *yame* for boys and *nyijir* for girls. But the terms of address to male and female of different positions and relations after marriage are based on classificatory distinctions and from the terms the sex of the addressee is known. Personal communication with Dr. Jumyir Basar, Associate Professor, AITS, Rajiv Gandhi University, on 15th June, 2016.
3. *See* Showren, 2009 for the designation of Daphla to the community who call themselves Nyishi. Similarly, Abor (Nyori,1993) is an outside designation for the Adis and Aka (Nimachow, 2011) for the Aka community.
4. Xaxa (2012:3) presents two forms of exclusion on the basis of accessibility and deprivation. Sen (2000) also presents two forms of exclusion, namely active and passive.
5. *See* Nongkynrih (2012:41-42) for adverse impact of broom grass scheme.
6. Integration with market economy made tribes "consumers from producers" (Nongkynrih, 2012:46) and from a state of autonomy to perpetual dependent (Haimendorf, 1898:51-78).
7. Exclusion has different dimensions and exists in areas of participation in rituals, decision-making and all types of economic activities, inheritance, ownership, alliance sphere, and so on. Denial of opportunities, freedom of participation etc., are in fact practices of exclusion. It reflects unequal treatment to members in the group, even within prescribed norms. Exclusion results in deprivation, inequality, entitlement rights and marginalisation in social process. Conversely, deprivation, marginalisation etc. are indicators of the incidence of social exclusion.
8. *See* Gupta (2012) for class formation within Mog tribe of Tripura.
9. Between two neighbouring tribes, the smarter and industrious one may own the resources of the other and thereby making them poorer and poorer. The land of the Dangi Bhils in Dang district of Gujarat has shifted to the smart and industrious Konkanas over the years. The Dangis, on the other hand have become poorer and poorer and migrate to different places and work as wage-labour for livelihoods (Patel, 2014:102).
10. Elwin (1944) attributed the causes of tribal plights to their contact with outside culture.
11. In September 2015, the United Nations General Assembly adopted the "2030 Agenda for Sustainable Development" with 17 ambitious universal goals; and UNESCO's Culture Conventions hold key to their implementation. UNESCO believes culture as both an enabler and a driver of the economic, social and environmental dimensions of sustainable development.
12. The *dikhu* is a cultural refugee; s/he is considered to be an outsider to his/her own

culture though s/he is a member of it. S/he is not a member of any other culture either, for his/her identity lies in his/her membership of the community s/he belongs to. Earlier, the Santhals considered any outsider a *dikhu*, especially, moneylenders, traders etc. belonging to the exploiting class.

13. Joshi (2014) highlights the complexities while implementing FRA in Gujarat and analyses it in the background of Adivasis struggle over forest land. Particularly, he focuses on the irregularities in the process of implementation of FRA by forest department, sometimes deliberately, which trigger off protests and agitations by the tribal communities.
14. Tribal ownership of land is governed by their customs. But do tribals own land when land deeds are required to prove ownership? See Bhukya (2012:67-70) for the conflict over land between tribes and government along with outsiders.

References

Action Aid. 2005. "From Hunger to Suffering ... a Journey: Migrant Workers in the Brick Kilns – Interventions report". Hyderabad: Action Aid.

Adhikary, A.K., 1984. *Society and Worldview of the Birhor: a nomadic hunting and gathering community of Orissa*. Calcutta: Anthropological Survey of India.

——1991. "The Tribal Worldview: Changing Perspectives", in B.N. Saraswati (ed.), *Tribal Thought and Culture*, New Delhi: Concept Publishing Co.(p) Ltd. pp. 105-20.

Agarwal, A.K., 1985. *Northeast India—An Economic Perspective*. Allahabad: Chugh Publications.

Alam, Javeed, 1993. "Fragmented Culture and Strangulated Existence: Jharkhand's Culture Encounter with the Modern". In Mrinal Miri (ed.), *Continuity and Change in Tribal Society*, Shimla: IIAS, pp. 11-22.

Banerjee, Nirmalya, 2011. "Tribal Land Alienation and Ethnic Conflict: Efficacy of Laws and Policies in BTAD Area". *Refugee Watch*, Issue No. 37, June 2011.

Barnard, A., 1978. "Universal systems of kin categorization". *African Studies,* Vol. 37, pp. 69-81.

Basar, Jumyir. 2011. "A Study of Indigenous Knowledge System in Development Policies and Programmes with Special reference to Resource Management by the Galo of Arunachal Pradesh". Unpublished Ph.D. thesis submitted to Rajiv Gandhi University, Itanagar.

Behera, D.K. and Nibedita Nath. 2004. "Impact of Mega Dam Project on the Land Sources of the Project Affected Indigenous People of Kalahandi District, Orissa". *Man and Life*. 30(1-2). pp. 1-18.

Behera, M.C. and Jumyir Basar. 2010. "Formal Education in Arunachal Pradesh: issues of exclusion". In M.C. Behera and Jumyir Basar (eds.), *Globalisation and the Marginalised: Issues and Concerns for Development*, (co-edited), New Delhi: Commonwealth Publishers, pp. 21-50.

——2009. "Implementation of Development Schemes and Exclusion: A Study with reference to growth of education in Arunachal Pradesh". *The Oriental Anthropologist*, Vol. 9, No. 2 (July-December, 2009), pp. 233-253.

Behera, M.C., 1994. *Planning and Socio-Economic Development of the Tribals*. New Delhi: Commonwealth Publishers.

——2004. "Slavery or Institutionalising Efforts at Perpetuating the Source of Labour?: The case of the Nyishi-Sulung Relationship", *Man and Life*, Vol. 30, No. (1-2), January-June, 2004, pp. 27- 40.

——2008. "Understanding Forager Worldview and Changing Ideology of Human-Nature Relationship (A Study with reference to Sulung, Nyishi and Khampti Tribes of Arunachal Pradesh in North-East India)". In Panchanan Mohanty, Ramesh C. Malik and Eswarappa Kasi (eds.), *Ethnographic Discourse of the Other: Conceptual and Methodological Issues*, New Castle, UK: Cambridge Scholars Publishing, pp. 8-38.

—— (ed.). 2006. *Globalising Rural Development: Competing Paradigms and Emerging Realities*, New Delhi: Sage Publications.

—— 2013. "Tribal Development in India: Reality Contours of Possibilities". *5th Prof. Ajit Kumar Mitra Memorial Lecture* delivered on April 28, 2013, Koraput: COATS.

—— 2015. "Nyokum Yullow and Religious Outlook of the Nyishi: A note on familiarity and Emic-Etic Rationality". In *The Researchers', Special Issue* — Volume I, Issue II, December-2015.

Bhukya, Bhangya. 2012. "The Eternal Colonial Legacy: *Adivasis* and Land Assertion in Andhra Agency". In Dev Nathan and V. Xaxa (eds.), *Social Exclusion and Adverse Inclusion— Development and Deprivation of Adivasis in India*, New Delhi: Oxford University Press, pp. 63-78.

Bird-David, N., 1990. "The Giving Environment: Another Perspective on the Economic System of Gatherer- Hunters". *Current Anthropology*, Vol. 31, No. 2. pp. 189-96.

Chambers, Robert, 1983. *Rural Development, Putting the Last First*, Longman Scientific & Technical, England.

——*Challenging the Professions, Frontiers for Rural Development*. London: Intermediate Technology Publications.1988 reprint.

—— 2006. "The State and Rural Development: Ideologies and an Agenda for the 1990s". In M.C. Behera (ed.), *Globalising Rural Development: Competiting Paradigms and Emerging Realities,* New Delhi: Sage Publications, pp. 59-77.

Das, Gurudas, 1995. *Tribes of Arunachal Pradesh in Transition.* New Delhi: Vikas Publishing House.

de Haan, A., 1997. "Poverty and Social Exclusion: A Comparison of Debates." *PRUS Working Paper 2*, Poverty Research Unit, University of Sussex, Brighton, United Kingdom.

Dréze, J. and H. Gazdar, 1997. "Uttar Pradesh: The Burden of Inertia". In J. Dréze and A. Sen (eds.) 1997. *Indian Development: Selected Regional Perspectives*, New Delhi: Oxford University Press.

Dutta, P.C., 1978. *The Noctes.* Shillong: Directorate of Research, Government of Arunachal Pradesh, Itanagar.

——1990. *The Wanchos*, Directorate of Research, Government of Arunachal Pradesh, Itanagar.

Dzuvichu, Rosemary, 2012. "Development and Women: The Discourse in Nagaland". In Dev Nathan and V. Xaxa (eds.), *op. cit.*, pp. 81-93.

Elwin, V., 1944. *The Aboriginals*. Bombay: Oxford University Press. First published in 1943.

——1959. *The Philosophy for NEFA*, Government of Arunachal Pradesh, Shillong (presently at Itanagar), Arunachal Pradesh.

——1960. *Report of the Committee on Special Multipurpose Tribal Blocks*. New Delhi: Ministry of Home Affairs, Government of India.

Fernandes, W., 2008. "Sixty years of development-induced displacement in India: Scale, impacts, and the search for alternatives". H.M. Mathur (ed.). 2008. *India Social Development Report 2008* (pp. 89-102). New Delhi: Council for Social Development, Oxford University Press.

——2014. "Tribal Customary and Formal Law Interface in North-east India: Implications for Land Relations". In M.C. Behera and Jumyir Basar (eds.), *Resources, Tribes and Development*, Jaipur: Rawat Publications, pp. 159-172.

Gadgil, M. & Guha, R., 1992: *This Fissured Land: An Ecological History of India*, OUP, Delhi.

GOI, 2014. *Report of the High Level Committee on Socio-Economic, Health and Educational Status of Tribal Communities of India*. New Delhi: Ministry of Tribal Affairs, Government of India.

Gupta, Malabika Das. 2012. "Class Formation among the Tribals: A Case Study of the Mogs of Tripura". In Dev Nathan and V. Xaxa (eds.), *op. cit.*, pp. 94-110.

Haimendorf, C.V.F., 1989. *Tribes of India: The Struggle for Survival*. New Delhi: Oxford University Press.

Hussain, Zahid, 1984. "Eco-System and Human Response." In L.S. Gassa (ed.) *Garo Hills—Land and the People*. Guwahati: Omsons Publications, pp. 52-64.

——1993. "Constraints in Development of settled Agriculture in the Mountain Eco System in North-East India". In K. Alam (ed.) 1993. *Agricultural Development in North-East India: Constrains and Prospects*. New Delhi: Deep & Deep Publications, pp. 52-58.

Hussain, Monirul, 2008. *Interrogating Development—State, Displacement and Popular Resistance in North-East India*. New Delhi: Sage Publications.

ICMR, 2003. "Health Status of Primitive Tribes of Orissa". *ICMR Bulletin*, Vol. 33, No. 10, October, 2003.

Jena, Sanjeeb Kumar, 2014. "Multidimensional Enormities of Migration: A Case Study on Migratory Tribal Labour of Koraput District of Odisha". In M.C. Behera and R.C. Parida (eds.), *Investing in Globalisation—Policy, Participation and Performance in Odisha*, New Delhi: Commonwealth Publications, pp. 45-75.

Jha, S.D., 1985. *The Wealth of Arunachal Pradesh*. New Delhi: Mittal Publications.

Joshi, Satyakam, 2014. "State, Forest Policy and Tribals: Some Ground Realities of Implementation of the Forest Rights Acts (2006) in Gujarat". In M.C. Behera and Jumyir Basar (eds.), *Resources, Tribes and Development*, Jaipur: Rawat Publications, pp. 191-215.

Kani, Takhe, 1993. *The Advancing Apatanis of Arunachal Pradesh*. Ziro: Takhe Omang.

Kataria, S.K. (ed.) 2014. *Moutana, the Blood-Money Custom in Tribals*, Jaipur: National Publishing House.

Kelkar, Govind and Devnathan, 1993. "Women's Law Rights and Witches". In Mrinal Miri (ed.), *Continuity and Change in Tribal Society*, Shimla: IIAS, pp. 109-118.

Mahapatra, L.K., 1999a. "Tribal rights to land and the state in Orissa". In D.K. Behera and G. Pfeffer (eds.). 1999. *Contemporary Society: Tribal Studies* (pp. 135-151). New Delhi: Concept Publishing Company (Pvt.) Ltd.

Mahapatra, L.K., 1999. *Resettlement, Impoverishment and Reconstruction in India: Development for Deprived.* New Delhi: Vikas Publishing House.

Mahapatra, Sitakanta, 1980. "The Insider Diku: Boundary Rules and Marginalised Man in Santhal Society". In P.C. Mahapatra and D. Panda (eds.), *Tribal Problems of Today and Tomorrow*, Bhubaneswar: Sabari Cultural Society, pp. 2-3.

Mahapatra, L.K., 1993. "Customary Rights in Law and Forest and the State". In M. Miri (ed.), 1993, *op. cit.,* pp. 84-96.

Maharatna, A., 2000. "Fertility, Mortality and Gender Bias among Tribal Population: An Indian Perspective." *Social Science and Medicine,* 50 (10): 1333–51.

Misra, K.K., 1993: *Tribal Elites and Social Transformation*, Inter-India Publications, New Delhi.

Misra, K.K. and N.Venkata Sivaiah, 2009. "Minor Forest Produce and the Problem of its Ownership by the Gram Sabha in the Scheduled Areas of Andhra Pradesh". In *The Oriental Anthropologist*, vol. 9. no. 2, (July-December, 2009), pp. 179-196.

Mohanty, A., 1991. "Poverty Alleviation Strategy—An Overview", in B. Mishra (ed.), *Poverty, Unemployment and Rural Development*, Ashish Publishing House, New Delhi.

Mohanty, R.P., 2002. "Profile of Bonded Labour System in India with Special Reference to a Primitive Tribal Community of Orissa". In R.N. Pati & Jagannath Dash (eds.), 2002. *Tribal and Indigenous People of India—Problems and Prospects*, New Delhi: APH Publishing Corporation, pp. 129-152.

Mohapatro, P.C., 2009. "Problems of Tribal Development in Orissa". In Pyarimohan Mohapatra (ed.), *Sustainable Development in Bonda Hills*, Koraput: COATS, pp. 19-38.

Nathan, Dev and Virginius Xaxa, 2012. "Introduction and Overview". In Dev Nathan and V. Xaxa (eds.), *op. cit.*, pp. 1-15.

Nazer, M. (nd). *A Study of Land Alienation and Indebtedness among Tribals in Tamil Nadu*. New Delhi: Government of India (Planning Commission), http://www. Planning commission.nic.in/reports/sereport/ser/stdy_land.pdf), retrieved on 8/4/ 2013.

Nimachow, Gibji, 2011. *The Akas: Land and People*. New Delhi: Commonwealth Publishers.

Nongkynrih, A.K., 2012. "Development, Environment, and Broom Grass: A Sociological Perspective." In Dev Nathan and V. Xaxa (eds.), *op. cit.*, pp. 36-51.

Norbu, Tsewang, 2008. *The Monpas of Tawang—Arunachal Pradesh.* Itanagar: Director of Research, Government of Arunachal Pradesh.

Nyori, T., 1993. *History and Culture of the Adis*. New Delhi: Omson Publications.

Padel, Felix and S. Das. 2008. "Cultural Genocide: The Real Impact of Development—Induced Displacement". In Hari Mohan Mathur (ed.) 2008. *India: Social Development Report 2008* (*Development and Displacement*). New Delhi: Oxford University Press/Council for Social Development,103-115.

Padel, Felix and Samarendra Das. 2010. "Resettlement Realities: The Gulf between Policy and Practice". In M.C. Behera & Jumyir Basar (eds.), *Interventions and Tribal Development—Challenges before Tribes in India in the Era of Globalisation*, New Delhi: Serials, pp. 61-100.

Panda, A., 2006. A Peport on Migration. Western Odisha Rural Livelihoods Project. Mimeo.

Pandey, G.D., 1996. "Highlights of Tribal Health Research Under Indian Council of Medical Research". *ICMR Bulletin*, 26(3 & 4): 21:28.

Patel, Arunbhai B., 2014. "Custom of revenge among Tribals in Poshina Strip Area of Khedbrahma Taluka: 'A Chadetaru' System". In S.K. Kataria (ed.) *op. cit.*, pp. 100-106.

Parida, P.K., 2016. "Tribal Health Problems in Odisha: An Overview". In M.C. Behera (ed.), *Interventions, Familiarity and Continuity—Dynamics in Tribal Communities*, New Delhi: Commonwealth Publishers, pp. 223-240.

Pertin, Otem, 2009. *Rethinking Tribal Institutions*. New Delhi: Commonwealth Publishers.

Priyadarshini, Priyanka, 2015. "Tribal Development: Perspectives, Programmes and Critique." In *Asian Mirror—International Journal of Research,* Volume II, Issue V, November, 2015, pp. 34-37.

Radhakrishna, Meena, 2001. *Dishonoured by History—Criminal Tribes and British Colonial Policy*. Hyderabad: Orient Longman.

Rastogi, Archi, 2007. "Uttarakhand tribal community bound to bonded labour". *Down to Earth,* March 31, 2007. Retrived from http://www.downtoearth.org.in/node/5758 on 11/4/2013.

Rath, Jagannath, 2010. "Poverty and Trends of Exploitation among the Tribals: A Case Study of Kandhs in Koraput District of Orissa". Unpublished Ph.D. Thesis of Berhampur University, Koraput: COATS.

Redfield, R., 1953. *The Primitive World and its Transformation,* Cornell University Press, Ithaca.

Redfield, R., 1962. "The Primitive Worldview". In M.P. Redfield, (ed.), *Human Nature and Study of Society: The papers of Robert Redfield,* The University of Chicago Press, Chicago, pp. 269-280.

Reddisekhara, Y., 2016. "Medical Communication and Utilization of Public Health Services among Konda Reddy of Andhra Pradesh, India". In M.C. Behera (ed.), 2016, *op. cit.,* pp. 251-270.

Saldhana, I.M., 1993. "Customary Rights and Colonial Regulations: Thana Forests in the Nineteenth Century". In M. Miri (ed.) 1993, *op. cit.,* pp. 70-83.

Sen, Amartya, 1998, "Social Exclusion: A Critical Assessment of the Concept and Its Relevance." Paper prepared for the Asian Development Bank, Manila.

Sen, Amartya, 2000. "Social Exclusion: Concept, Application, and Scrutiny". *Social Development Papers No. 1*. Manila: Office of Environment and Social Development, Asian Development Bank.

Sharma, Anita, 2013. *The Sherthukpens of Arunachal Pradesh*. New Delhi: INTACH & Aryan Books International.

Showren, Tana, 2009. *The Nyishi of Arunachal Pradesh—An Ethnohistorical Study*. Delhi: Regency Publications.

Sitlhou, Hoineilhing, 2015. "Patriarchal Bargains and Paradoxical Emancipation: Issues in the Politics of Land Rights of Kuki Women". *Indian Journal of Gender Studies*, 22(1) 92–115, DOI: 10.1177/0971521514556949, Sage Publications. Downloaded from ijg.sagepub.com by guest on June 6, 2016.

Srivastava, L.R.N., 1970: *Among the Wanchos of Arunachal Pradesh*, Directorate of Information and Public Relations, Arunachal Pradesh, Shillong.

Thorat, Sukadeo and Katherine, S. Newman, 2007. "Caste and Economic Discrimination: Causes, Consequences and Remedies". In *Labour Market Discrimination and Urban Sector, Research Series, Social Exclusion, 1(1)*, New Delhi/New Jersey: Indian Institute of Dalit Studies/ Princeton University, pp. 1-7.

Tripathy, S.N., 2014. "Globalization, Deprivation and the Predicament of Displaced Tribes in India". In M.C. Behera and Jumyir Basar (eds.), 2014. *op. cit.*, pp. 140-157.

——— 2010. "Distress Migration in Tribal Orissa: A Study in KBK Districts". In M.C. Behera and Jumyir Basar (eds.), 2010, *op. cit.*, New Delhi: Commonwealth, pp. 51-69.

UNDP, 2004. *Human Development Report 2004—Cultural Liberty in Today's Diverse World.* New York: The United Nations Development Programme.

Vidyarthi, L.P., 1963. *The Maler: A Study in Nature-Man-Spirit Complex of a Hill Tribe.* Calcutta: Bookland.

—— and B.K. Rai, 1985. *The Tribal Culture of India.* New Delhi: Concept Publishing Company (p) Ltd.

Walton, M., 2007. "Culture Matters for Poverty, but Not Because of a Culture of Poverty: Notes on Analytics and Policy." Unpublished paper, New Delhi / Cambridge, MA: Centre for Policy Research/John F. Kennedy School of Government, Harvard University.

Woodburn, James, 1988. "African hunter-gatherer social organization: Is it best understood as a product of encapsulation?". In Tim Ingold, David Riches and James Woodburn (eds.), 1988, *Hunters and Gatherers I: History, Evolution and Social Change*, Oxford: Berg.

World Bank, 2011. *Poverty and Social Exclusion in India.* Washington, DC.: World Bank.

Xaxa, Virginius, 2012. "Tribes and Development: Retrospect and Prospect". In Dev Nathan and V. Xaxa (eds.), *op. cit.*, pp. 23-35.

FIVE

IN SEARCH OF EDUCATION'S PROMISE

Indian Tribal Children Leaving Home for the Hope of a Better Future

CHRISTINE FINNAN

I owe my connection to the Indian anthropological community and to the indigenous tribal children of Odisha to Dr. Deepak Kumar Behera. He not only provided me with deep insights into the situation of tribal people, but he also introduced me to a number of communities and schools in Odisha. Specifically, he introduced me to the Kalinga Institute for Social Sciences (KISS), which served as the research site for this chapter. During an initial visit in 2011, Dr. Behera and I were introduced to a sea of 16,000 KISS students who joined together in greeting and prayer for us. I was amazed by the sight of so many children and by the bold vision of KISS's founder Dr. Achyuta Samanta. Dr. Behera's reaction was more measured. He raised concerns that KISS could exacerbate the decline of tribal languages and leave children with only a superficial knowledge of their tribal cultures. But, he also expressed appreciation for KISS's commitment to tribal children and acknowledged the draw KISS has for tribal families. As Dr. Behera describes in the introduction to *Contemporary Society: Tribal Studies* (2015) tribal children will remain vulnerable and marginalized without high quality educational opportunities so he understands why Dr. Samanta focuses on education as a way to move tribal people out of poverty.

To many anthropologists, KISS is the anathema of what should be done to address tribal people's marginalization and vulnerability. KISS takes children out of their communities to live in an institutional setting in which the language and culture resembles mainstream India rather than any of the 62 different tribal groups represented at KISS. Concerns that children will lose their traditional tribal languages and cultures are real and compelling, but I posit in this chapter that these concerns should be examined in light of a more expansive definition of culture, a definition that highlights tribal parents' cultural conceptualizations of the *future*. Building on the growing recognition in anthropology and sociology that conceptualizations of the future are critical aspects of culture (Appadurai, 2013; Miyazaki, 2004; Vaisey, 2009), I maintain that parents' and students' experience of KISS serves as an example of the "variety of ways in which human beings absorb newness into frames that they always carry with them before the fact" (Appadurai, 2013: 285). KISS has grown rapidly and is attractive to tribal parents because it taps into parents' and children's cultural conception of the future; it presents itself as a hopeful institution, and it gives children the "capacity to aspire" (Appadurai, 2013) to be change agents for their communities.

I had the opportunity to spend six months at KISS in 2014-2015 conducting research aimed at better understanding why families send their children to KISS, what students gain and lose by attending KISS, and the beliefs, values, and assumptions underlying the KISS school culture.[1] With the help of three Indian research partners, we conducted over 160 interviews with students, former students, teachers, administrators, staff members, parents, and visitors; we observed in multiple sites across campus and visited several tribal villages. In addition, I reviewed documents, internet resources, and videos. The following discussion reflects my analysis of these data, with an emphasis on how KISS provides a platform for tribal families' hopes and aspirations for the future. Before delving into the KISS data, I provide a review of the literature on the link between schooling, hope, and aspirations.

Universal Education: Real or False Hope?

Schools' promise of hope for a better future is very attractive to parents and children. As Katherine Anderson-Levitt (2005) graphically describes in "The Schoolyard Gate", children in much of the global south are eager to enroll in school; they clamber to get inside the schoolyard gate while their northern peers dream of escape from confines of school. Considerable research on the sacrifices families and children make to attend school supports this observation. Children travel long distances; parents pay fees they cannot afford, and children delay involvement in the workforce because they hope that schooling will lead to a better future (Bolton, 2015; Froerer, 2012; Frye, 2012; Jeffries, Jeffries & Jeffries, 2004; Vavrus, 2007). The belief in education's promise has become nearly universal.

Unfortunately, across the world, education's promise for most poor children has been unfulfilled. Research points to disconnections between official governmental nods to the importance of universal education and their willingness to provide necessary funding and human and capital resources for adequate schools for the poor. Some wonder if governments pledge support for universal education only to "look modern" or to receive funding from international agencies (Anderson-Levitt, 2003; Bolten, 2015; Cregan & Cuthbert, 2014; Frye, 2012; Steiner-Khamsi, 2004). Others suggest that providing poor quality schools serves as a means of maintaining status hierarchies and further subjugating the poor (e.g., Apple, 2015; Bourdieu & Passeron, 1990; Frierer, 1970; Kumar, 2015). Around the world, the poor face the reality that education is needed for occupational and social advancement, but that the schools their children attend are insufficient.

Despite poor quality schools, children remain hopeful about education's promise, and they desire to be identified as students. The label "student" describes not only a current status—someone who goes to school—but also future aspirations. These aspirations are tied to local, national, and international assumptions that education leads to better employment and bright futures (Cregan & Cuthbert, 2014; Frye, 2012). It also carries connotations of superior social standing and behaviours that are often associated with the attainment of adulthood (e.g., increased knowledge, self-restraint, and social skills) (Bolten, 2015; Clemensen, 2015; Frye, 2012; Jeffrey, Jeffrey & Jeffrey, 2004). For example, Margaret Frye (2012) found that in Malawi, female secondary students made the seemingly irrational decision to continue in school and delay marriage, despite dismal job prospects, because they absorbed the national narrative of a bright future through education. Nana Clemensen found that even young children position themselves as educated because of "the powerful symbolic value of schooling and its representations, reaching well beyond the tangible realm of school" (2015: 245). As the preceding section illustrates, too often these promises are false and are primarily the product of national campaigns to promote poorly conceptualized and underfunded school systems or reforms (Drahos, 2004).

Schools can also provide a venue for students to develop what Arjun Appadurai (2013) describes as the "capacity to aspire." He suggests that, "aspirations about the good life, about health and happiness, exist in all societies" (p. 187), that they are a natural part of cultures. But, he adds that the capacity to aspire is not evenly distributed in any society, with the relatively rich and powerful being more apt to fully develop this capacity. He continues:

> The capacity to aspire is thus a navigational capacity. The more privileged in any society simply have used the map of its norms to explore the future more frequently and realistically, and to share this knowledge with one another more routinely than their poorer and weaker neighbours (p. 188).

One thing schools can do to move children out of poverty is help students develop this navigational capacity, the ability to "read the map" toward attainable aspirational futures. India, like most countries, upholds education as a primary vehicle for poverty eradication. It provides compulsory primary education, and nearly all Indian children are enrolled in primary schools across India (UNICEF, 2015). However, as in most societies, the promise of poverty eradication through education is curtailed by the poor quality of schools serving children living in poverty (ASER, 2015; Kingdon, 2007; Kumar, 2015; Sedwal, 2011). Despite their limitations, schools remain hopeful institutions. Parents continue to believe that their children will have brighter futures if they are educated; students aspire to be "educated people", and schools have the potential to bring poor students' "capacity to aspire" to the same level as more affluent students.

KISS as a Hopeful Institution

I never thought of schools as hopeful institutions until I conducted research at KISS. I knew that schools prepare students for the future, but I did not see the significance of hope in this process. Drawn to KISS with questions about why parents send their children away to a residential school, about what students gain and lose by attending KISS, and about what beliefs, values, and assumptions underlie its school culture, I realized that hope was central to each of these questions. Parents send their children to KISS in hopes of giving them a better future; students have the opportunity to develop the capacity to aspire (a form of hope) while at KISS, and KISS promotes itself as a hopeful institution. Before exploring the connection between hope and schooling further, I will provide some basic information about KISS.

KISS is a residential school providing free education, room and board, medical care, vocational, athletic and artistic training to 25,000[2] indigenous children from 62 different tribal groups. Located in Bhubaneswar, the capital of the state of Odisha, it is funded primarily by profits from its sister institution, the Kalinga Institute of Industrial Technology (KIIT), a well-respected for-profit university; both institutions were founded by Dr. Achyuta Samanta. KISS receives no governmental funding or other support because Dr. Samanta uses the profits from KIIT to support KISS. Students as young as six enter KISS in grade one and can continue their studies through post-graduate education either at KISS or by qualifying to attend KIIT as part of a guaranteed 5 per cent reservation for KISS graduates. Students live at KISS ten months a year, going home to their villages for only two months during the summer. KISS has been in existence for 26 years, and word of its goals and programmes has spread across Odisha's tribal belt. Parents' eagerness to send their children to KISS is reflected in the 50,000 applications KISS receives annually for about 2,000 openings.

While all schools have a school culture that binds the school community together (Finnan & Swanson, 2000), KISS's school culture is more explicit, public, and pervasive than that of most schools. Some aspects of KISS's school culture are prominently displayed on its website, in promotional materials, and across campus; others become evident after spending time at KISS. Some aspects of its school culture are reflections of beliefs and values emanating from the wider society, such as the value of education and the inadequacy of Government schools. Other aspects of KISS's school culture are specific to KISS, such as its promotion of itself as a place where hopes are nurtured and achieved and its commitment to preparing students to be change agents and give back to society.

KISS's Commitment to Education as the Route to Poverty Eradication

On November 12, 2014, I attended a Class 9 English class. The teacher asked the 24 girls and 30 boys to open their books to page 105 to begin a lesson on The First Step. She asked the students if they knew what "first step" means. When they did not respond, she said that Dr. Achyuta Samanta took the first step to empower tribal children through education. She opened a discussion about the importance of education. One student said that a country, state, and community cannot develop without education. She then asked why some children are not able to be educated.

Male student 1: Parents are not aware about education and due to poverty, they are not able to educate.

Male student 2: If girls are not educated, then they live in darkness and are not able to know about education, health, sanitation, which is useful for their future.

Field notes
November 12, 2014

As this vignette illustrates, KISS was established on the belief that education is the route out of poverty, and this belief permeates its school culture. Dr. Samanta, who grew up in poverty, attributes most of his success to his education; KISS attracts a staff that shares this belief, and KISS parents and children sacrifice their time together because of their belief in a better future through education. KISS's belief in the transformative power of education is omnipresent on campus, on its website, and in popular press reports. The KISS homepage features a rotating set of photos and captions that express core beliefs, especially its commitment to Educate, Enable, and Empower. Dr. Samanta's statement, "Poverty creates illiteracy, and literacy eradicates poverty", appears on signs on the KISS campus and in articles about KISS. The belief in education's transformative power features prominently in articles about KISS that appear in the popular press. The following are several examples from news stories about KISS:

- "Illiteracy restricts employability. Empowered by education, tribes can make a quantum jump in life, become role models and catalyst of change in the community." Textbox in article about KISS appearing in *Uday India* (September 1, 2012).
- "Education is weapon against poverty" Headline in article about KISS appearing in *The Sunday Tribune*. Chandigarh (September 23, 2012).
- "Dr. Samanta with KISS children: unwavering education

empowerment belief" caption under photo of Dr. Samanta and children in an article appearing in *Education World* (April 2012).

Interviews with KISS students, teachers, staff, and parents reveal their unquestioning adoption of this belief. They point to examples of successful students and to the limited options available if they did not have the opportunity to study at KISS. For example, a KISS pass-out (graduate) who is currently enrolled at KIIT said that if he had not attended KISS, he would be similar to his friends:

> Most of my friends are labourers and some friends are migrant labourers working in other states of the country under difficult conditions. If I had not come to KISS, I might as well be like my friends; I would still be continuing as a labourer, too.

A KISS administrator said that they advise students to:

> ... just try to stick to your study and whatever difficulties you are facing... you may not get all the things at one time, so slowly, slowly things are happening. But do not think that will be a hindrance for you in life; be educated. After that, you will see your own path... Education, good behaviour, peaceful coexistence, how to speak. ...Education is the top priority. Be educated by any means. Education will empower you. Our slogan is "educate, enable, empower" you must have seen it?

KISS as a "Beacon of Hope"

The titles of the following articles illustrate the centrality of hope to the KISS story:

- "Merchant of Hope", *India Empire* (June, 2012) by Anjay Sinha.
- "Beacon of Hope", *Uday India* (March 20, 2010) by Vaishalit Tanwar.
- "Kiss of Hope", *Discover India* (October, 2009) by Satyendra Patnaik.
- "Achyuta Samanta: A Light of Hope Flickering Beyond the Dark Tunnel" *Uday India* (April 11, 2009) by Bibhuti Pati.

These articles focus on the promise of hope for a better future by emphasizing Dr. Samanta's rise from poverty and KISS's role in giving hope to its students. KISS also emphasizes hope in promotional videos that contrast hopelessness at home and hope at KISS. These videos begin with scenes of beautiful countryside in the hilly tribal lands and of proud people living their traditional lives,[3] but the scenes quickly shift to present images of environmental destruction and pan across faces expressing hopelessness and despair. The voice-overs tell how tribal people are unable to live their traditional lives given environmental degradation through encroachment of lumber, mining, and hydroelectric schemes and fear of Naxalite uprisings.

This sense of hopelessness for tribal people's traditional lifestyle was reiterated in interviews with students and parents. Most students described their villages fondly, but they believe that their futures would have been constrained if they stayed there. Many older KISS students and those attending KIIT said that their friends are living lives much like their parents' lives; they are married and working as laborers. When asked about their futures, KISS students describe high aspirations for continued study and professional work, primarily as doctors, nurses, engineers, and teachers. As one KISS student currently studying at KIIT said when asked what he would have done if he did not attend KISS, "All friends of my village are married and working as labourers at minimum price in the village. If I had not come to KISS, I would be a labourer in my village." Instead, he is studying for a Diploma in Electronics and Telecommunications, and he hopes to obtain a Bachelor of Technology from KIIT and work as an engineer. Teachers also cite poor conditions and hopelessness in villages to explain why parents send their children to KISS. For example, one teacher said:

> All parents want the betterment of their children. Parents know that they have no sufficient resource for the betterment of the children. Now, they get an option at KISS for betterment so they send their children to KISS. In this school they get all type of facilities like free food, education and all type of training for skill development of the children, which is better than other schools.

Free education from Class 1 until the student leaves KISS/KIIT is critical to the hope and optimism that surrounds KISS. Nearly all parents said that one reason they chose to send their children to KISS is because it is free. Although attending Government primary and secondary school is technically free, parents often cannot afford to pay for fees and provide the supplies necessary for attendance. For example, one parent, when asked why he is sending his child to KISS said, "As it is a good school and all type of services provided to tribal children is free of cost which are better than our home, so I had decided to send my children to KISS… It is not possible for me to provide service and education like KISS. So he might attend village school now."

Becoming Change Agents and Giving Back to Society

> Each of the students passing out from KISS is becoming a Change Agent for the future. Empowerment through education and sustainable livelihood are no longer confined to only phrases, rather it has been proved that all these have been possible because of KISS.
>
> A Social Revolution
> *Hindustani Times*
> February 2013

At KISS, students are encouraged during assemblies, in academic classes, and during mentoring sessions to be change agents and give back to society. They also see the practice of giving back in Dr. Samanta's[4] life, in sacrifices of KISS staff, and in role models of older students. The commitment to being change agents has also shaped students' career aspirations, with many students saying that they want to become doctors, nurses, and teachers in the future. Some students are not waiting until they finish at KISS to give back to their communities. They are taking the initiative to make changes in their villages when they visit. The following student comments are examples:

- Every year that I go back, I coach the students to study. I have about five or six children who come and study under me. I have been doing this for the last three or four years. I have been continuing to do this, and the children have also passed out from 10th.
- I am able to teach the tribes, the school children and drop-outs, at my village while I go there in vacation. I have counselled their

parents. Thus, it has generated a kind of community fellow feelings within me.

- While I was doing a science project on hardening of soil, climate change, I went to my village and made people aware of this and told them to switch over to organic fertilizer instead of using chemicals. We discussed on the issue of soil erosion too. I used to give tuitions to the children at village who needed it the most.

Many of the female students teach lessons they learn about health and hygiene, especially women's health, to the women and girls in their villages. According to a KISS administrator, the village women and girls will listen and trust one of their own, while they will ignore someone from outside. The KISS students, meanwhile, gain confidence about the value of what they are learning and their ability to make a difference when they help their communities during their summer breaks.

Students and their families also describe long-term goals to help their communities. Several students and former students offered ideas such as the following:

- I cannot do as much as Dr. Samanta has done for KISS. But one thing I can assure, that I can help the students at the KISS school that are running in the district level in terms of financial support after I get a job and earn money.
- I love my community, and I love my village. First of all, I shall go back to my village after finishing my study here and doing specialization in medicine and open up a hospital there. Then, after I will see if I can pursue any other higher studies or not.

Parents assume that, through education, their children will give back to society. Below are several responses to the question, "How can KISS students make a positive effect on society?"

- If my daughter is highly qualified after passing out from KISS, she can make the rest of us understand new things and will do good for the community.
- An educated person will make positive change to society. If my son becomes educated and gets a good job, then other members of our society are inspired and send their children to school.
- He can help change the society. He can help the village in overcoming the problems we face in day-to-day life, like water

crisis, unemployment etc. If he becomes an engineer, he will be an asset for the society.

Dr. Samanta is committed to KISS students becoming change agents in their communities. In fact, his plans for future expansion hinge on KISS students carrying the KISS culture to the satellite centers he envisions for the future.[5] As he says:

> You will see how I have planned. These KISS students will be change agents to run the rest of KISS in their own districts in Odisha. That is my hidden agenda… It's easy to say "they will be change agents", but how will they be change agents? After getting graduation we should provide the avenues. No policy maker provides the avenues, only speaking, "Make them change agent". If we start the 30 branches in 30 districts, we will make them change agents. They will run the show as teachers, managers, and supervisors. They will really act as change agents in their community. They imbibe everything here.

According to a KISS administrator, even if KISS students do not work in the KISS satellite centres, they can serve their communities as teachers and nurses in government facilities, "All the teachers we create will have a job. The more nurses we create, [they] will have a job. The Government of India has a lot of jobs reserved[6] for them, but they never get those posts because they are not qualified. They will be qualified so they will get the jobs."

DISCUSSION AND CONCLUSION

As I described in the introduction, Dr. Behera introduced me to KISS, and he shared the ambivalence I have heard from other visitors about educating tribal children in an institution of KISS's size and scope. It is true that KISS removes children from their tribal cultures, and that KISS students face the prospect of limited linguistic and cultural fluency when they return to their villages.[7] KISS students live most of their lives within the confines of a large institution, learning its expectation for appropriate behaviour and aspirations, and they interact primarily with KISS students and staff. I use the term ambivalence because, although people have questions and concerns, they also recognize why families send their children to KISS – for the hope of a better future through education.

The data presented above illustrate how KISS builds on these hopes, how it unquestioningly accepts the global assumption that education is the best route out of poverty, how it projects itself as a hopeful institution, and how it builds students' capacity to aspire to be change agents and give back to society. KISS exists because Dr. Samanta experienced the transformative power of education, and he wants other poor children to have the same opportunity to succeed. He also realizes what the academic literature supports, that universal schooling may be key to poverty eradication, but its impact is limited by serious problems in education delivery to the poor and by entrenched issues of poverty (e.g., lack of food, adequate housing and clean water, environmental degradation, corruption). KISS exists because the Government schools serving tribal communities are so inadequate and because it also provides immediate relief for families unable to provide sufficient food, clean water, and medical services for their children.

Does KISS provide a better quality education than village schools? Based on student enrollment and achievement numbers provided by KISS, it is difficult to draw firm conclusions[8], but indications are that it does. For example, where student and teacher absenteeism is a serious problem in village schools, KISS classes are always offered, and children are not allowed to skip class. Where learning levels in Indian rural schools are low (ASER, 2015), large numbers of KISS students pass mandatory state tests.[9] In addition to academic classes, KISS also provides vocational training and athletic and artistic opportunities unavailable in village schools. These opportunities provide alternative livelihood options for students who struggle academically, and they may keep students in school longer than if they were studying in their villages.

KISS students also frequently hear success stories of fellow KISSians and words of encouragement from highly esteemed visitors. KISS students have real and accessible models for their aspirations; for example, several KISS athletes qualified to join the Indian 2016 Olympic team; girls' and boys' rugby teams won international competitions in London and Manchester; fellow KISSians travelled to the United States for summer English language programmes, and five per cent of KISS graduates qualify each year to continue their studies in fields such as engineering and medicine at KIIT.[10] These role models are visible evidence that tribal children can have the navigational capacity to make aspirations real

(Appadurai, 2013). Couple these success stories with the exhortations of Dr. Samanta, KISS personnel, and many national and foreign visitors that they are special and can make a difference for their communities, and with their isolation from peers and adults who have dropped out of school and struggle to make a living, KISS students' capacity to aspire grows.

The centrality of hope in KISS's school culture presents a future in which tribal children are no longer vulnerable and marginalized. A focus on the future aligns with a reframing of the concept of culture alluded to earlier. This orientation, grounded in the theories of George Herbert Mead (1959) and William James [1981 (1890)], emphasizes the temporal nature of culture. Yes, we live in the present, but our culture also shapes our understanding of what went before, the traditions, histories, stories, and "this is what we have always done" aspect of culture. More importantly, culture also frames our anticipation of what will be, our hopes, wants, plans, and expectations. To Steven Vaisey (2009), culture combines a focus on the past, in which it *justifies* present actions by tying them to how things have been done, and a focus on the future, in which culture *motivates* actions by positing how things can be done. Arjun Appadurai (2013) warns that anthropologists have emphasized the past, to the point that, "the future remains a stranger to most anthropological models of culture" (p. 180). He argues that when the future is seen as a "cultural fact", culture is no longer an impediment to development and change, but serves to define "collective horizons" and "collective aspirations" (p. 180).

KISS certainly celebrates the past through oft-told origin stories, in particular Dr. Samanta's rise from poverty to be a prosperous and prominent philanthropist and the rise of KIIT and KISS from nothing to world-renowned institutions. It also encourages students to retain their tribal languages and cultures, to talk with their elders when they are home, and to be proud of their tribal heritage. But, the culture that surrounds KISS is primarily that of motivation and aspiration; it is looking forward. KISS students learn that they are in the process of becoming someone; they are building the capacity to hope.

Notes

1. Funding for this study came from a Fulbright—Nehru Academic and Professional Excellence Award (Research), a College of Charleston Faculty Development Grant,

research funds from the Department of Teacher Education and Department of Sociology and Anthropology, and by a one-year sabbatical granted by the College of Charleston. I also received considerable support from the faculty and staff of KISS and KIIT. Sasmita Sahoo, Sasmita Mohanty, Sujay Pati, and Sugyan Mishra assisted with data collection and formative analysis.

2. The school population in 2015-16 was 25,000; it was 22,500 in 2014-15 when data were collected.
3. See https://www.youtube.com/watch?v=ZfkWjJ_iaL4 and http://www.kiss.ac.in/video/all.html
4. Dr. Samanta's story is told repeatedly. He grew up in poverty following his father's death, but through hard work, education, and the kindness of others, he became a highly successful man by founding the for-profit Kalinga Institute of Industrial Technology (KIIT). Rather than enjoy the material benefits of wealth, he lives very simply and channels profits from KIIT into supporting KISS.
5. KISS is planning to develop satellite campuses in 30 districts in Odisha. The satellite campuses will provide the same services as the main Bhubaneswar campus in students' local communities. The satellite campuses will serve younger children so that they do not have to travel so far from home. The main campus will eventually serve primarily students seeking more advanced education.
6. The Indian Constitution sets aside a portion of government jobs to people of the Scheduled Castes and Scheduled Tribes.
7. We asked parents and students if students had trouble fitting in when they come home and very few mentioned any issues with language fluency. Some parents said that their children missed the "luxury" of life at KISS.
8. Because of KISS's rapid growth its systems for tracking students over time are limited. For example, I was unable to obtain clean data on drop out rates and employment rates for graduates.
9. In Odisha students are required to pass a state exam to complete Standards 10 and 12. In 2015, all of the 12th standard students who took the exam passed, and in 2016, 95 per cent of the 1,300 10th standard students who took the exam passed it. I have not been able to confirm that all eligible students took the exams.
10. One student was selected to join the Indian archery team. In 2011 the under-13 boys' rugby team won the International Rugby Tournament in Manchester, UK, and in 2014 the under-13 girls' rugby team won the same tournament in London.

References

Anderson-Levitt, Kathryn. 2005. "The Schoolyard Gate: Schooling and Childhood in Global Perspective." *Journal of Social History,* 38: 987-1006.

Apple, Michael. 2015. "Reframing the Question of Whether Education Can Change Society." *Education Theory*, 65 (3): 299-315.

Appadurai, Arjun. 2013. *The Future as Cultural Fact: Essays on the Global Condition.* London: Verso.

ASER (2015) Annual Status of Education Report (Rural) 2014. *http://*

img.asercentre.org/docs/Publications/ASER%20Reports/ASER%202014/fullaser2014mainreport_1.pdf

Behera, Deepak Kumar. 2015. "Introduction". In *Contemporary Society: Tribal Students.* (ed.) D.K. Behera. New Delhi: Longman.

Bolten, Catherine, E., 2015. "A Great Scholar is an Overeducated Person. Education and Practices of Uncertainty in Sierra Leone." *Journal of Anthropological Research* 71:23-47.

Bourdieu, Pierre, and Jean-Claude Passeron. 1990. *Reproduction in Education, Society and Culture.* Second Edition. London: Sage Publications.

Clemensen, Nana. (2015). "Staging an Educated Self: linguistic displays of schooling among rural Zambian children", *Anthropology and Education Quarterly*, 46 (3): 244-259.

Cregan, Kate, and Denise Cuthbert. 2014. *Global Childhoods: Issues and Debates.* London: Sage Publications.

Drahos, Peter. 2004. "Trading in Public Hope." In *Hope, Power, and Governance*, (ed.) V. Braithwaite. *The Annals of the American Academy of Political and Social Science*, 592: 18-38.

Finnan, Christine, and Julie D. Swanson. 2000. *Accelerating the Learning of All Students: Cultivating Culture Change in Schools, Classrooms, and Individuals.* Boulder, CO: Westview Press.

Friere, Paulo. 1970. *Pedagogy of the Oppressed.* Translated by Myra Bergman Ramos. New York: Herder and Herder.

Froerer, Peggy. 2012. "Learning, Livelihoods, and Social Mobility: Valuing Girls' Education in Central India: Valuing Girls' Education in India." *Anthropology and Education Quarterly,* 43(4): 344-357.

Frye, Margaret. 2012. "Bright Futures in Malawi's New Dawn: Educational Aspirations as Assertions of Identity." *American Journal of Sociology,* 117 (6): 1565-1624.

Jeffrey, Craig, Patricia Jeffery, and Roger Jeffery. 2004. " 'A Useless Thing!' or 'Nectar of the Gods?' The Cultural Production of Education and Young Men's Struggles for Respect in Liberalizing North India." *Annals of the Association of American Geographers,* 94 (4): 961-981.

James, William. 1981 [1980]. *The Principles of Psychology*. Cambridge, MA.

Kingdon, Gita Ghandi. 2007. "The Progress of School Education in India", *Oxford Review of Economic Policy, 2,*168-195.

KISS home page. Accessed May 12, 2015.http://www.kiss.ac.in/media/index.html

Kumar, Krishna. 2015. *A Pedagogue's Romance: Reflections on Schooling*. New Delhi: Oxford University Press, India.

Mead, George Herbert. 1959. *The Philosophy of the Present.* Arthur E. Murphy, (ed.) La, Salle, Ill.: Open Court.

Ministry of Tribal Affairs. 2013. *Statistical Profile of Scheduled Tribes in India. 2013.* New Delhi: Government of India. Accessed May 15, 2015. http://tribal.nic.in/WriteReadData/userfiles/file/Statistics/StatisticalProfileofSTs2013.pdf

Miyazaki, Hirokazu. 2004. *The Method of Hope: Anthropology, Philosophy, and Fijian Knowledge.* Stanford: Stanford University Press.

Pati, Bibhuti. 2009. "Achuta Samanta: A Light of Hope Flickering Beyond the Dark Tunnel." *Uday India.* 16, no. 14.

Patnaik, Satyendra. 2009. "KISS of Hope." *Discover India.* October: 20-21.

Sinha, Anjay. 2012. "Merchant of Hope." *India Empire.* June.

Sedwal, Mona and Sangeeta Kamet. "Education and Social Equity in Elementary Education." In *Who goes to School? Exploring Exclusion in Indian Education*, edited by R. Govinda, 87-122. New Delhi: Oxford University Press, 2011.

Steiner-Khamsi, Gita. "Globalization in Education: Real or Imagined?" In *The Global Politics of Educational Borrowing and Lending,* edited by G. Steiner-Khamsi. New York: Teachers College Press, 2004.

Tanwar, Vaishalit. 2010. "Beacon of Hope." *Uday India.* March 20.

UNICEF. 2015. India. Statistics. Accessed June 3, 2015. *http://www.unicef.org/infobycountry/india_statistics.html*

Vaisey, Stephen. 2009. "Motivation and Justification: A Duel-Process Model of Culture in Action." *American Journal of Sociology,* 114: 1675-1715.

Vauras, Frances. 2007. *Desire and Decline: Schooling Amid Crisis in Tanzania*. New York: Peter Lang.

SIX

HINDUTVA AND THE QUEST FOR PURITY

How Popular Hinduism is Marginalized

HARALD TAMBS-LYCHE

Introduction

Literature about *Hindutva* and 'Hindu fundamentalism' in general has stressed its conflictual stance against other religions, notably Islam and Christianity. This important issue has tended to mask—at least to foreign observers—the increasingly salient conflict lines within Hinduism itself. The diversity of the Hindu tradition is vast, and though Brahmin influence ('sanskritization'—Srinivas, 1952, 1962, 1967) has worked for centuries to produce a degree of integration among cosmopolitan, national and local elites, an opposition persists between their views and the numerous popular variants of the religion. It has often been stressed that there is no organized Hindu 'church', comparable to what exists in Christianity, and that this absence explains, at least partly, the enormous diversity that is so characteristic of Hinduism. The argument of this chapter, however, is that the pressure for integration from above has increased enormously in recent years, and that this increase is closely related to the politics of *Hindutva* as well as to changes due to economic growth.

It may well be argued that this pressure from above is not new: I have elsewhere noted (1991) how the combination of urban middle-class dominance and Congress rule produced similar effects in Saurashtra some forty years ago. Central to my argument, then, was the link between urban middle-class culture and the traditional, 'non-violent', values of the merchant castes. This, I hold, is still a crucial point: as I have noted elsewhere (2011, 2016) Brahmin influence has tended, since the late nineteenth century at least, to integrate with a broader bourgeoisie, where elements of Brahminism merge with Merchant caste values. Thus, the rise of *Hindutva* must be seen as closely connected to the expansion of the bourgeoisie, and, recently, of liberalist capitalism (Desai, 2011).

Within Hinduism, this corresponds largely to a growth in Vaishnava influence. Vaishnavism, like Jainism, and in a distant past Buddhism, has historically had a main base in the merchant castes. With modernization, Vaishnavism came to be identified with a large part of the rising bourgeoisie, while Shaktism—the worship of the Goddess, often including animal sacrifice, became relegated to the category of "popular religion". As an informant from the Shaivite minority of a Brahmin caste in South Kanara affirmed: "Vegetarianism is not there in the Vedas. It all came from the Vaishnavas". Vegetarianism has, indeed, become one of the main ways in which Hinduism has "modernized" or reformed itself, as a comparison of its present spread with the information of the "tribes and castes" volumes of the early twentieth century will show. This means that animal sacrifice has become emblematic of the "barbarian" or "medieval" practices that should be reformed. This is why I choose the abolition of animal sacrifice as a main theme in the present chapter.

Hindutva may be conceived as a "political" ideology, but its religious component stems, as I argue, from a particular mix of Hindu values selected from these principal constituents of the bourgeoisie. Thus seen, *Hindutva* represents a drive to purify as well as to unify Hinduism around middle-class values. With the tremendous growth in size and influence of the middle class in recent years, the pressure to integrate popular Hinduism with its dominant values has increased tremendously.

Deepak Behera has, for many years, focused on marginalized groups. These have often been *Adivasis*. My point in this chapter is to show that popular Hinduism, too, is being pushed to the margins in contemporary India, and that the forces involved are basically the same as those that threaten other marginal cultures.

This chapter is organized around two case studies. Sheikh's article (2008) on the conflictual changes in the cult of the Goddess Bahuchara, in Gujarat, will be used to outline some of the issues, as presented by the author. The second example comes from the work Marine Carrin and I have done together in South Kanara. Karnataka. There, the main temple of the Mogaveera fishermen, at Bennekudru, has been the object of a long struggle between those who want—and who finally seem to have succeeded in—purifying the cult, and those who, in the first decade of the 21st century, wanted to return to the 'old ways'.

Bahuchara Temple, North Gujarat

Bahuchara's temple, situated on the boundary between the North Gujarat and Saurashtra regions, is traditionally regarded as one of the three *Shakta Pithas* in this part of India. While well known in Gujarat, however, the temple rarely attracted pilgrims from outside Gujarat and Rajasthan (Sheikh, 2010: 84). Though the Gaekwads of Baroda, in whose territory the temple was situated, took some interest in it (Manajirao Gaekwad was healed by the Goddess in the 1770s), the devotees of Bahucharaji "were seen as culturally and politically subversive", as Sheikh puts it (2010: 85). As a Shaktist temple, and a place of animal sacrifice, it was increasingly seen as 'primitive' and 'unorthodox' in a Gujarat which, from the mid-nineteenth century, saw the impressive growth of the strictly vegetarian Swaminarayana movement. This movement, indeed, was a major vector in the development towards the present Vaishnavite, "non-violent", and vegetarian culture that dominates the middle class in Gujarat today, and saw popular Shaktism as its main adversary (Tambs-Lyche, 1995, 1997, 2001, 2004). But even within the Shaktist fold, Bahuchara and her temple was in a special position. It was well known for the *hijadas* (eunuchs) that served the sanctuary. These cross-gender attendants were shocking, not just because they were rumoured to recruit some of their members by forced castration, but also because of their ribald or obscene performances, as exemplified by their role in Rabari marriages (Westphal-Hellbosch and Westphal, 1974). Indeed, it was said that Bahuchara had the power of turning men into women or *vice versa*, and as if this was not enough, the *kamalias*, temple servants in this Hindu temple, were Muslims, and dressed in female attire (Shah, 2010: 85).

The bulk of Bahuchara's devotees belonged to the Koli caste, classified as a "criminal caste" by the British. Farmers from the periphery, the Kolis were "armed peasants" and formed an important part of the armed forces of many rulers in Gujarat. Some of these rulers, and the Koli peasants in general, were apt to supplement their income by raids on villages of the more settled areas—a practice which may be classed under 'politics' in pre-British days, but which the British labelled as 'criminal'. As the most numerous of all Gujarat castes, Kolis were the archetype of the people merchants, other members of the growing bourgeoisie, and lawful peasants in the more settled areas saw as 'barbarian', 'wild', and 'uncivilized' (Tambs-Lyche, 2002a, 2002b). Finally, the temple received substantial earnings from pilgrims and devotees, which "successive administrations sought to regulate and safeguard" (Sheikh, 2010: 85). All this, of course, reflected on the notoriety of the Bahuchara temple, and these stereotypes—of Kolis as well as of this particular goddess—were still current in Gujarat in the seventies when I started my fieldwork there.

Yet Bahucharaji was recognized as a powerful goddess, in spite of as well as because of whatever the urban elite found undesirable. She would "grant favours, especially of male children, and cure diseases...The goddess was also the protector of *hijadas* and representative of their sacral authority. Her appeal, though restricted to Gujarat and southern Rajasthan, reached far beyond her core non-Brahminical local base" (Sheikh, 2010: 85-86).

The origin of the Goddess is contested. Local Kolis claim she was a Koli. Charans claim most of the goddesses of Gujarat to be deified women from their own caste, who are seen even in life as prospective *satis*—in the sense of particularly pure or holy women—with a female power (*shakti*) surpassing that of other mortals (Tambs-Lyche, 1997), leading many Charanis to live as venerated saints (Basu, 2004). In 1935, the Charan author G.S. Mahiya wrote a book setting out the more specific claim that Bahuchara was a Charani of the Detha clan, born in Ujala village, Marvad, who lived around 1309 C.E. (Mahiya, 1935; Sheikh, 2010: 88-90). Brahmins, however, tend to look at Bahuchara as a *puranic* goddess, originally called Balatripurasundari. This claim was made by R.J. Desai in a book published in 1937, explicitly as a refutation of Mahiya's thesis (Desai, 1937; Sheikh, 2010: 89-90). In his *History of Bahucharaji (Shri Bahucharajino Itihas)* of 1919, B.G. Bookseller prefers to attach the goddess to the Krishna cycle, claiming she was the child that Yashoda gave away in exchange for Krishna. But he in his turn claims that the first shrine to Bahuchara was built by Rabari and Bharwad pastoralists (Bookseller, 1919: 13; Sheikh, 2010: 91).

With regard to these conflicting claims, we should note the differential positioning of their perpetrators. Kolis are a community politically and culturally marginalized by the intrusion of more formally organized states into their territories. In the area around Bahuchara's temple, this process had begun early: any state formation tends to be wary of an armed and independent-minded peasantry led by their own chiefs inside or just beyond their frontiers. When Baroda took possession of the territory in 1721 (Sheikh, 2010: 87) they came into lasting conflict with the local Rajput and Koli chiefs, who often managed to wrest their lands from the Gaekwad's control. It was probably to strengthen this control that the Gaekwads assigned three revenue villages to the temple (*ibid.*) and it is again typical of increased state control during the colonial period that these villages were resumed by Baroda state in 1933 (Sheikh, 2010: 90). By then Kolis had long been classed as a criminal caste. And when land reforms were introduced after independence, it was the Patidar farmers, long associated with areas under state control, rather than the Kolis who benefited from them (Sud, 2007). Traditionally, Kolis were goddess worshippers and Shaktists, and animal sacrifice was an integral part of their religion, around Bahuchara but also elsewhere in Gujarat.

Rabaris and Bharwads are pastoralist castes. While the Bharwads are mainly herding sheep and goats, the Rabaris are the traditional breeders and herders of camels. The latter, especially, are often nomadic and tend to live outside the village society of agriculturalists. They stand, therefore, somewhat apart from the caste order, though they were regarded as the highest of the pastoralist castes and certainly saw themselves as superior to the peasants. Rabaris were sometimes allied to the ruling houses, however, with the special task of guarding the frontiers. As nomads of the wilderness they were not easy to govern or control.

Charans were, in the traditional set-up, part of the elite, as bards and genealogists to the Rajputs, including the ruling families. But like their patrons, they were Shaktists and devotees of the Goddess. Some still practiced their older occupation as buffalo herders, and were "brothers of the blanket"—*daghlabhai*—of the pastoralist castes. Part of the caste may thus be regarded as marginal to the caste order and the power set-up. But it was the Charans who produced and perpetuated the myths of the Rajput aristocrats, and we may see them as the guardians, and the sacred figures, of the martial, Shaktist tradition of the ruling houses in Western India. As such, they were intimately connected with the princely states, and when these disappeared, the Charans were greatly weakened in power and influence. This paved the way for a relatively unbridled advance of the Bhakti ideology of the bourgeoisie.

Brahmins play an ambiguous part in the scenario I am sketching here. Traditionally, they served in both Shaktist and Bhaktist temples. In general, Brahmins in priestly service tended to share the religious ideology of their patrons. But the majority of Brahmins were not priests. In Gujarat, many—such as the Shrimalis—were chiefly merchants, and tended to share much of the ideology of other merchant castes. From at least the 18th century onwards and especially during the British period, more and more Brahmins were absorbed into the growing bourgeoisie. Among the Brahmin castes, then, Shaktists have been gradually losing out to Bhaktists throughout the modern period, until we may now safely include the vast majority of Brahmins among the *bhakti*-oriented middle class. The most often recounted miracle of Bahucharaji is variously placed in the time of the Delhi Sultanate or the Mughals. Desai placed the miracle in the earlier period:

> "Sultan Alauddin II, known as *khuni* (bloody) conquered Patan (the capital of Gujarat) and began to destroy Hindu shrines. After destroying Rudramala in Sidhpur, he went towards Bahuchara. There were many fowls (*kukada*) there—they are the vehicles of Bahuchara—and the Muslims ate them. One escaped. At night, (the escaped) rooster began to call "*kukade kuu Bahuchari*" at which all the fowls in the stomachs of the soldiers came alive, tore their bellies and came out" (Desai, 1937: 21; cited and translated by Sheikh, 2010:92).

The story of the miracle may indeed be ascribed to the time of the Sultanate, for it was cited by Shridhara in 1508 and by Vikram Samvat in 1565. By then, it had become proverbial (Sheikh, 2010: 93). It is clear, then, that Bahuchara's cult and temple was well established by that time. The *Bombay Gazetteer* claims it was built in 1152 C.E., and both the temple and its adjoining village are mentioned in an inscription of 1280 C.E. (Sheikh, 2010: 86).

Yet criticism of the temple and its cult also began early. A Jain writer, Gunavijaya, in 1621 describes a complaint made in the fourteenth century by the merchant Kochar, to the Mughal governor about the practice of blood sacrifice, said to be practiced by the Bhils, at the temple. The text claims that such sacrifices were stopped, by order of the Sultan. Kochar was named governor of fourteen villages around the temple, and even had the fish in the temple pond protected. As Sheikh underlines, the story shows how the Gujarat sultans employed Jains to pacify turbulent groups such as the Bhils, showing "the unease of elites with practices at the temple and attempts to regulate them" (2010: 92).

But if animal sacrifice had been banned at Bahuchara in the fourteenth century, it was certainly resumed later: like most goddess shrines in Gujarat, the temple continued to be associated with animal sacrifice until the practice was prohibited by the Gujarat state in 1972. Throughout this period, Shaktism was opposed and criticized by the supporters of Bhakti-inspired Vaishnavism (Tambs-Lyche, 1997). With modernization from the British period onwards, its merchant base expanded into a broader bourgeoisie or 'middle class', taking in a large part of the Brahmins, and, in Gujarat, the Patidars (Tambs-Lyche, 2011b). In Gujarat, the castes in this group are known as the *savarna* (Sud, 2007, Yagnik and Sud, 2004). The pressure on *shakti* religion, which as we have seen has been present since the late middle ages, has increased proportionally to the strength of the middle class.

This sets the stage for the present situation. In 2007, the BJP Government began a major assault on this 'unorthodox' sanctuary to assure its place within the *bhakti*-oriented middle-class religion that is the base for *Hindutva*. That year, Chief Minister Narendra Modi laid the foundation stone for a new temple (Sheikh, 2010: 87). By 2009, the old temple was being pulled down, and a new marble structure was built in its place (2010: 97, n.5). The Madhya Sthan, the auxiliary temple where animals used to be sacrificed, was tended by the *hijadas*. They were then staging a sit-down outside the temple to save it from the demolishing workers (2010: 97, n.6). There was then an ongoing court case concerning the rights of the *hijadas* and the *kamalias* in the temple and its cult.

The new temple is now fully active. The rites of the temple no longer include animal sacrifice, but the community of *hijadas* still controlled the Madhya Sthan in 2012 and conferred blessings on their disciples.[1] Indeed, says Wikipedia, Bahuchara is now considered the "patroness of the *hijada* community in India".[2] I have found no recent source mentioning the *kamalias*, however: on the face of it, it seems unlikely that the Modi government would have left a Muslim community in charge of ritual at an important Hindu temple, which the state had taken the initiative to rebuild. With animal sacrifice banned, the *kamalias* removed, and the *hijadas* confined to their own particular building, the purification of Bahuchara's temple has come a long way. The implication of the BJP Government in rebuilding the temple points to the class interest behind these changes, as behind the trend to make popular Hinduism conform to middle-class norms.

Bahucharaji is a rather special figure among the Shaktist goddesses of Gujarat, but all have become vegetarian by state decree. Shakti Mata, the guardian goddess of the Jhala Rajputs, is herself somewhat special, since she first appeared in the cremation grounds, stressing the Tantric associations of this enigmatic deity. Here she met the future founder of the Jhala dynasty, married him, and begot the next generation of Jhala rulers (Mayne, 1920). But when I visited the temple of Shakti Mata in Dharangadhra in the early 1990s, I found myself listening to Bhajans, as soft and peaceful as those sung for Krishna, in honour of the goddess composed by a local devotee. And between 1974 and 1987—I do not have the precise date—the traditional Brahmin priests of Khodiyar's temple near Bhavnagar had been sacked. They had terminated animal sacrifice in accordance with the law, but they were of the old guard of local priests, who did not claim any Sanskrit learning. It was found improper, I was told, that this, the most important goddess temple in Saurashtra, should be tended by "uneducated and almost illiterate" priests, so they were replaced with properly educated ones. What became of the old priestly community, I do not know.

Benakudru Mahasathi Temple, South Kanara

The Benakudru temple is situated on an island in the estuary complex of the two Sita rivers near Barakuru in Kundapur District, South Kanara. It is regarded as the chief temple of the Mogavira fishermen's community, and its members come from all along the South Kanara coast for the main temple festival in December. The Goddess, here, was known as Mahasati, the great sati: she also presides over an older temple farther south, at Kodi west of Brahmavara. Mahasati (or Masti) was sometimes said to be a form of Mariamman or of Kali, but as Mahasati she is a local figure: in North Kanara we find a large number of Mahasatis, but they are usually represented only by a memorial stone. Only the Mahasati of the Mogaviras has risen to the status of a goddess. The priests were Mogaviras: no Brahmins officiate at Benakudru, even today. The temple committee, too, has only Mogavira members.

The Benakudru temple was the seat of a line of *gurus*—with *guru*-ship transferred patrilineally — who advised or directed the religious affairs of the Mogavira community from the eighteenth century to 1966 (Uchila, 2013: 145). These *gurus*, like their counterparts in other low-caste communities, certainly had a 'sanskritizing' influence. They were also instrumental in improving the status of the fishermen. In their time, animal sacrifice was not terminated, but it was moved to a distinct site outside the temple. The first *guru* established himself at Kodi, but at a date which cannot be determined exactly, the seat of the *guru* as well as, more generally, the religious centre of the community was moved to Benakudru. The move should probably be placed in the late eighteenth century, since the last *guru* took office in 1905 and there were at least four *gurus* at Benakudru before him (Uchila, 2013: 145).

The last *guru* died without offspring in 1966, and it was decided not to seek a new *guru* in a related line, but to terminate the succession (Uchila, *op. cit.*). This did not mean that the institution disappeared completely, for the last *guru* is seen as surveying and protecting the community from the other world. The *gurus* are still venerated, and I shall return to that point.

In December 1996, when we first visited the temple, the goddess was still called Mahasati, though it was also stated that she was the same as Mariamman, and, less insistently, identical with Kali. Thus, while her specific identity was merging with that of better-known South Indian or all-Indian goddesses, she retained her fierce character. As in the times of the *guru*, fowl were sacrificed for the goddess' oracular sessions, but outside the temple, out of view of the public and the officiating priests. Cockfights also remained an integral part of the Goddess' annual festival in January, but they, too, were held at a distance from the temple, just outside the walls of the temple enclosure. Thus, the sacrificial traditions of the temple were maintained, but in a discrete manner. In short, the accent then was on 'purifying' the temple and 'Brahmanize' the ritual.

Still, there were several *bhuta* sanctuaries attached to the temple. The *bhutas* are found everywhere in South Kanara, and may be said to be the deities of the Tulu-speaking part of the population. They are also called *daivas*, which the protestant missionaries translated as 'Devils'. More accurately, they are demi-gods, occupying a place between the Hindu gods and the humans. Like *satis*, the *bhutas* are seen as having lived on earth: some are clearly deified humans, like the twins Koti and Chennaya, warrior heroes of the Billava community. There are *rajandaivas*, linked to the old chiefdoms, as well as *bhutas* particular to a specific caste (Carrin and Tambs-Lyche, 2003). The latter include Bobbariya, who is the guardian *bhuta* of the Mogavira community, and who particularly protects the men at sea. Other *bhutas* seem to be a kind of double of the Hindu deities. This is the case with Malesariya, who in the Benakudru temple stands as a double for Mahasati: unlike the latter, she receives animal sacrifice directly in front of her sanctuary, inside the temple grounds. The *bhutas* at Benakudru also included Koliaramman, a female *bhuta* said to have been installed there by (Koli) fishermen from Maharashtra. We were told, at that time, that this deity really had nothing to do with the temple, and should be taken away.

In December 2003, when we returned to Benakudru, the new chairman of the temple committee had decided on a radical change of policy. It was argued that the Mahasati's powers had diminished since the past, and that this was due to mistakes committed by the earlier committees. This year, we observed Kali coming to the temple, danced by a Pambada medium. She was dressed as a young girl—probably because, as Mahasati, she died young—and she did not have the protruding tongue so prominent elsewhere in Kali's iconography, or in the appearance of most of the fierce female *bhutas*. Kali effectively danced the story—the term *paddana* used for the epics of the *bhutas* was employed—but in contrast to the dance of the *bhutas*, she stopped the dance at various times to ask questions of the audience, or to respond to their questions. Her talk was not in the majestic tone of the oracles of Mariamman, which we had observed in several temples of that goddess: nor did she speak in an authoritarian and threatening tone like most *bhutas*. Instead, Kali behaved like an insolent, mocking girl. The highlights of the play—for we had the impression of a theatrical performance—were clearly the dialogues with the Mogaveera priest—here, the head of the temple committee—and with the audience. Through her remarks, Kali in fact made a discourse on the present state of local society. At the end of the dance, fifty cocks were sacrificed before the dancer, in the temple grounds. Asked, she said she was satisfied. There was also, as part of the festival, animal sacrifice to Koliaramman, the Maharashtrian *bhuta*.

There was an interesting incident when one of the fifty cocks to be sacrificed to Kali, escaped. Priest, attendants, and members of the audience all ran to catch the fowl, causing a break in the ritual sequence. What was striking was that nobody seemed to fear the potential fury of the deity with regard to what, in a Brahmanical context, might have been seen as a ritual fault or at least a bad omen. People laughed. They seemed to regard this episode simply as fun. Unlike earlier practices, then, animal sacrifice, this year, was at the centre of proceedings. There was also quite a big cockfight. At that time, animal sacrifice had not yet been banned in Karnataka, but cockfighting was prohibited. Asked about this, the chairman of the temple committee said nobody would interfere, since this cockfight was part of a religious ritual, and not a commercial affair.[3]

The whole atmosphere was light-hearted, and nobody we met criticized the turn the ritual had taken. There was no apparent trace of the earlier attempts to purify the temple or to explain away the non-Brahminical sequences. Of course, it may well be that the partisans of the earlier temple committee were staying away from the ritual this time. It would indeed have been interesting to know more about the political leanings of these very different committees, but, unfortunately, we have no information on this. What was clear, however, was that this "return to tradition" was an affirmation of Mogaveera independence from the religious and cultural pressure of the higher castes.

When we returned to the temple again in 2016, all this had changed again. We were told that animal sacrifice was no longer performed—though later, it was admitted that Malesariya still received such sacrifice. Mahasati did not. She was no longer said to be Mariamman or Kali; she had now become Durga Parameshwari. Durga does not appear in oracular performances, though Malesariya still does. In 2003, this *bhuta* had served as a double of Kali/Mahasati, and Kali had danced and accepted her animal sacrifice in front of the sanctuary of Malisaraya. Now, it was clear, the *bhuta* was seen as quite separate from Durga, and the latter had no part in such sacrifice. Animal sacrifice, then, had been separated from the main cult: indeed, it had been marginalized.

The temple itself has been renovated, a project which had in fact been started by the committee which was in power in 2003. Among the *bhutas* at the temple, Koliaramman has disappeared. As to the cockfight, the committee members present just said it is forbidden by law. The house of the *gurus*, still there in 2003, has been pulled down, but in its place a monumental memorial hall for the *gurus* has been built —quite close to the ground where we had witnessed the great cock sacrifice then. To put it briefly, the present temple committee had accomplished the goals of the policy as stated in 1995/96, and no mention was made of the 2003 interruption. The Benakudru temple had been purified and its main ritual would now be quite acceptable to a high-caste, middle-class audience, though Brahmins still have no part in the ritual, and the temple remains under the exclusive control of the Mogaviras.

The point I want to make, here, is that developments at Benakudru have followed the same general trajectory as at Bahuchara: a radical change in ritual practices so as to conform to Middle-class standards.

But while the Bahuchara temple has effectively been taken over by new groups—a middle-class take-over in fact—the reforms at Benakudru have all been done by the Mogaviras themselves. Clearly, however, as the 2003 interruption shows, this has not happened without important internal conflict in the caste.

Why should the Mogaviras, who control the temple, reform their practices to conform to middle-class standards? To explain this, we must look at the socio-economic changes within the caste. Ever since at least the seventies, fishing has contracted as an occupation for two reasons: first, mechanization and other technical improvements mean that fewer men catch more fish. Secondly, over-fishing has lead to reduction in catches. More and more Mogaviras have, through education, effectively entered the middle class. Even in 2003, we were told that the Mogaviras had become sensibly richer than their neighbours on the coast, the Billava toddy-tappers, even if the latter, too have risen considerably on the socio-economic scale. Thus, with many of the Mogaviras adopting a middle-class lifestyle, it is no wonder that middle-class values should influence their religious practices. But how, then, can we explain the sudden turn 'backwards' around 2003? I can only suggest here that this fisherman caste is in a particular position, compared to other castes. Unlike the agricultural castes, they traditionally lived—as many still do—in separate villages, with no other caste present. Traditionally, they were largely self-governing: they adjudicated their conflicts through their own Panchayats, sometimes referred to as the *katte* system—and since these conflicts took place in their own villages, nobody interfered. Economically, they sold their fish but otherwise remained free of interference. Thus, unlike the Kolis around Bahuchara, they largely orchestrated their own 'sanskritization', as also their own reactions to it. This is not to deny the importance of state interference; cockfights had long been illegal, and in 2015 animal sacrifice has also been banned in Karnataka.

In 2016, we also re-visited another important Mogaveera sanctuary, the Mariamman temple at Urva in Mangalore. During earlier visits to the temple festival, cocks were sacrificed in a narrow line outside the temple, clearly as a part of the festival though invisible from the temple itself. Now, we were told, the practice had been officially terminated. But, said one of the temple attendants, in case of illness such sacrifice is still the better remedy. People want to do it. Government should not interfere in religious practices, he said.

Tamil Nadu Politics of Animal Sacrifice

It may not have been incidental that animal sacrifice had been reestablished at Benakudru in December 2003. On the 28th of August that year, the Chief Minister of Tamil Nadu, Jayalalitha, had decreed the enforcement of a 1950 Act banning animal sacrifice, an Act which had largely remained a dead letter since (Good, 2015: 10). A few months later, the decree as well as the 1950 Act was repealed, in face of considerable opposition especially in the Southern parts of the state, as well as from several opposition parties. Good feels this U-turn was made in view of the forthcoming election, which, in fact, was carried by the opposition. These events were quite widely published and discussed, and may well have given a spurt to those among the Mogaviras who were in favour of the tradition of animal sacrifice.

The events also underlined the political dimension of the ban on animal sacrifice. In Saurashtra, I had noticed this in the 1980s (Tambs-Lyche, 1991) where, in fact, the political constellations were quite different: it was the Congress Party which had, in 1972, banned animal sacrifice, and the quite perceptible grumbling against the law was most noticeable among castes which were then on the way to becoming OBCs – Bharwads, Kolis and others. This made them side with the opposition against the Congress, and, later, with the BJP. Later, however, it has become quite clear in Gujarat that the BJP, like the Congress earlier, was the spokesman, in this as in other matters, of the urbanized middle class. This is eminently clear from the reconstruction of the Bahuchara temple described above.

In Tamil Nadu, Jayalalitha's decision to ban animal sacrifice was seen as a move to reinforce her alliance with the BJP, and it was opposed by the DMK, which tended towards the Congress. The most fervent adversaries of the ban, however, came from the Communist parties. The General Secretary of the CPI-M stressed that animal sacrifice was "part and parcel of the lives of *Dalits* and other backward classes and the order would offend them". Karunanidhi, the DMK leader, argued from a regionalist stand that the order was "an attempt at destroying Tamil culture" (Good, 2015: 11).

It seems clear, then, that the reaction to the ban followed two lines of argument: the ban strengthened the consciousness of animal sacrifice as 'culture' and 'tradition' for those who opposed the ban, while at the same time, the controversy strengthened the opposition between an urban, middle-class elite eager to purify and reform Hinduism, and a number of generally rural, lower-class groups who wanted to assert their religious independence from elite, and Brahmin influence. The feeling that the government should respect religious tradition seems indeed to be strong.

Conclusion

Animal sacrifice was central in Vedic times, while opposition to such sacrifice can be traced at least to the time of the Buddha and of Mahavira, the founder of Jainism. Many of the current traditions of such sacrifice can be traced to the early medieval period, and the buffalo sacrifice became the royal ritual *par excellence* in the high middle ages. As I have stressed for Saurashtra (1997), the opposition between the Shaktist religion of the castes that formed the core of the political system and the non-violence of the merchant castes runs like a red thread through the history of that region. But the coming of the modern state, from at least the sixteenth century onwards, produced a situation where the merchant castes—gradually growing into a bourgeoisie—gained more and more influence. This had to do with the growing sovereignty of the rulers over their vassals, the creation of a mercenary, royal army, and the increasing financial dependence of the rulers on the merchant castes. The trend continued and was strengthened in the colonial period, when the rulers could no longer function as warlords. It paved the way for the pre-independence period, where the bourgeoisie, providing the main base for the independence movement, forced the rulers into a dead end, where they became the allies of the losing British.

The demise of the rulers deprived the supporters of animal sacrifice of its elite support. As Fuller puts it, the bourgeoisie was engaged in a "rediscovery of Hindu cultural and religious values associated with the nationalist movement" and they came increasingly to view Hinduism as 'corroded from within by a host of indefensible, barbaric medieval customs' (2004: 100), which included the 'superstitious' practice of 'blood sacrifice' (2004: 101). The class base of this reformed Hinduism is clearly evident, and no less so with the spectacular expansion of the middle class in recent years.

All this inevitably leads to the marginalization of animal sacrifice, along with a number of other practices current in popular Hinduism. In 1950, when the state of Tamil Nadu banned animal sacrifice, elite domination of Indian politics was largely taken for granted. Thus, in the debate preceding the 1950 Act, D.S. Ramachandra Rao "contented that human beings are cruel by nature, but it was the task of the more enlightened and civilized … to educate the general population in higher ethics" (Pandian, 2005: 2316; cited by Good, 2015: 9). This paternalist attitude to folk culture was quite typical of the Congress period, and continues under the present government.

Since the 1980s, however, such elite domination cannot be taken for granted—as Jayalalitha discovered to her cost in 2003. The OBC movements now tend to challenge the 'liberal' bourgeoisie everywhere, to the point where they have taken over the rule in some of the States (Jaffrelot, 2005). In this situation, socio-religious reform in India is "almost always a double-edged sword, which tends to reinforce superior values precisely as it seeks to undermine superiority itself" (Fuller, 2004: 103).

Still, the long historical trend, which has tended to marginalize popular Hinduism and animal sacrifice as its most controversial component, is continuing, and under the present government the pressure from *Hindutva* to create a standardized, middle-class Hinduism is increasing. At the same time, the widening base of Indian democracy, with increased participation by the OBC and even the *Dalits,* means that the urban middle-class can no longer have everything their own way. The road to *Hindutva* cannot be by elite pressure alone, and it is evident that enormous efforts are made to 'reform' the lower castes. In Bahuchara Mata's temple, elite pressure succeeded only against considerable resistance from the lower castes. Among the Mogaviras, the restoration of animal sacrifice in 2003 shows that the reform met considerable resistance, yet today, the reform seems—on the face of it – to have won the day. But there is grumbling: hidden resistance, in Scott's sense (1985), is certainly continuing. Whatever the outcome, the struggle within Hinduism—with animal sacrifice as one of the foci of conflict—is certainly one of the main conflict lines in India today. The marginalization of popular Hinduism is advancing at the moment, but the outcome of the struggle is not yet clear.

Notes

1. This is clear from the following videos on internet: Sheila Simkin: "Blessed by a Eunuch in Bahucharaji Temple, Gujarat", http:/www.Travels with Sheila.com, dated 14-6-2011; Vidyuanathan Ramaswami: Pavaiya: the sexless devotees of goddess

Bahucharaji (no date), accessed 16-6-2016; "Transgender Story", Sathiyam TV Special, www. Sathiyam TV, dated 19-10-2012, accessed 16-4-2016.

2. Wikipedia.org, article 'Bahuchara Mata' accessed 16-1-2016.
3. In a recent article, Michael Dusche (2016) reports an incident concerning the cockfight at a large *bhuta* festival in Tulu-speaking North Kerala. Here, the police descended and took about 25 participants in the cockfight to jail. Soon after, one of the policemen involved died, while another lost his leg in an accident. Finally, the police returned to the place and staged a ritual of reparation, praying the *bhuta* to excuse their mistake.

Bibliography

Basu, Helene. 2004. *Von Barden und Königen: Ethnologische Studien zur Gättin und zum Gedächtnis in Kacch (Indien).* Frankfurt am Main: Peter Lang.

Bookseller, B.G., 1919. *Shri Bahucharajino Itihas.* (The History of Shri Bahucharaji). Mahesana-Bahucharaji: Published by the Author.

Carrin, M. and H. Tambs-Lyche. 2003. "You don't joke with these fellows. Power and Ritual in South Kanara, India*." Social Anthropology*, no. 1, 2003: 23-42.

Desai, R., 2011. "Gujarat's Hindutva of Capitalist Development", *South Asia*, XXXIV, 3: 354-381.

Desai, R.J., 1937. *Bahucharaji mata-nu prakatya ane sahitya-man teno ullekh.* (The appearance of Bahuchara Mata and literary notices of her). Ahmedabad: Published by the Author.

Good, A., 2015. "Animal Sacrifice and the Law in Tamil Nadu, South India". Paper presented at the 5th Asia and Pacific Congress, Paris, September 2015.

Fuller, C.J., 2004. *The Camphor flame: Popular Hinduism and Society in India* (revised and expanded edition), Princeton and London: Princeton University Press.

Jaffrelot, C., 2005. *Inde: la démocratie par la caste*. Paris: Fayard.

Mahiya, G.S.S., 1935. *Charanadevi Shri Bahucharaji (Chunval Pithadhishvari)*. (The Charan Goddess Bahucharaji, Goddess of the Chunval Shrine). Bombay: Shri Charan Jnyati Hitvardhak Sabha.

Mayne, H.,1921. *History of the Dharangadhra State*. Calcutta: Thacker, Spink & Co.

Pandian, M.S.S., 2005. "Dilemmas of Public Realm; Secularism and Religious Violence in Contemporary India", *Economic and Political Weekly,* 40, 22-23: 2313-20.

Ramaswami, Vidyanathan: Pavaiya: the sexless devotees of goddess Bahucharaji (no date), *www.youtube.com/watch? V=udlRm5_Vo-U; accessed 16-4-2016;*

Scott, J.C., 1985, *Weapons of the Weak: Everyday forms of Peasant Resistance*. New York: Yale University Press.

Simkin, Sheila: "Blessed by a Eunuch in Bahucharaji Temple, Gujarat", *http:/ www.Travels* with *Sheila.com,* dated 14-6-2011, accessed 16-4-2016.

Sheikh, Samira, 2008, "The Lives of Bahuchara Mata", in E. Simpson and A. Kapadia (eds.): *The Idea of Gujarat: History, Ethnography and Text*, pp. 84-99. Delhi: Orient Blackswan.

Srinivas, M.N., 1952, *Religion and Society among the Coorgs*. Oxford: Oxford University Press.

—— 1962, *Caste in Modern India and Other Essays*. Bombay: Asia Publishing House.

—— 1967, *Social Change in Modern India*. Berkeley: University of California Press.

Sud, Nikita, 2007. "From Land to the Tiller to Land Liberalization: The Political Economy of Gujarat's Shifiting Land Policy", *Modern Asian Studies*, 41, 3: 603-38.

Tambs-Lyche, H., 1982. "The Merchantization of Saurashtra." *Journal of Social Science* (Dhaka), No. 16: 39-50.

Tambs-Lyche, H., 1994 "The Concept of Maya in the Vacanamrtam of Swami Narayana", A.W. Entwhistle and F. Mallison (eds.) *Studies in South Asian Devotional Literature*. Delhi: Manohar Publishers, pp. 192-209.

Tambs-Lyche, H; 2001. "Swami Narayan: Une hagigraphie récente au Gujarat" *in* F. Mallison (ed.), *Constructions hagiographiques dans le monde indien*. Paris: Champion: 257-281.

Tambs-Lyche, H., 2002. "Koli, Rajput, Kanbi, Patidar: revendications identitaires au Gujarat hier et aujourd'hui" *in* M. Carrin and C. Jaffrelot (eds.), *Tribus et basses castes: Résistance et autonomie dans la société indienne, Purusartha 23,* Paris, EHESS: 265-297.

Tambs-Lyche, H., 2002. "Townsmen, Tenants and Tribes: War, Wildness and Wilderness in the Traditional Politics of Western India". *In* R. Behera et G. Pfeffer (eds). *Contemporary Society— Tribal Studies*, Vol. 5, Delhi: Concept Publishing Company (P) Ltd., pp. 208-29.

Tambs-Lyche, H., 2004. *The Good Country. Individual, Situation and Society in Saurashtra.* Delhi: Manohar Publishers.

Tambs-Lyche, H., 2011. *Business Brahmins. The Gauda Saraswat Brahmins of South Kanara.* Delhi: Manohar Publishers.

Tambs-Lyche, H., 2011. "The Quest for Purity in Gujarat Religion: A Bird's Eye View", *South Asia,* special issue "Religion in the Making of a Region", XXXIV, 3: 333-353.

Tambs-Lyche, H., 2017. *Transaction and Hierarchy: Elements for a Theory of Caste.* Delhi: Manohar Publishers.

"Transgender Story", Sathiyam TV Special, www. Sathiyam TV, dated 19/10/2012, accessed 16/4/2016.

Uchila, S.K., 2013. *A Study of Mogaveera Community*. Mumbai: Dakshina Kannada Mogaveera Mahajana Sangha (Uchila), and Mogaveera Mahajana Seva Sangha (Mumbai).

Westphal-Hellbosch, S. and H. Westphal. 1974. *Hinduistische Viehzüchter im nord-westlichen Indien, vol. 1: Die Rabari.* Berlin: Duncker und Humboldt.

Wikipedia.org, article "Bahuchara Mata" accessed 16/1/2016.

Yagnik, A. and N. Sud. 2004. "*Hindutva* and Beyond: The Political Topography of Gujarat." Paper presented at the Conference on State Politics in India in the 1990s, LSE Crisis States Programme, London School of Economics *(http://www.crisisstates.com/download/india/yagnik&sud.pdf,* accessed January 2011).

SEVEN

PARADOX OF DEVELOPMENT AND ANTI-POLITICS IN MALKANGIRI DISTRICT IN ODISHA, INDIA[1]

JENS SEEBERG AND RIKKE AARHUS

Development and the Creation of the Cut-off Area

This chapter describes healthcare—one of the key services of the modern state and a measure of its level of development—in the shadow of a large dam, another material symbol of development, in Odisha, India. Odisha has one of the largest concentrations of tribal population accounting for approximately 22 per cent of the state's population. If Odisha is one of the poorest states, the southernmost district of Malkangiri is one the poorest districts in India, and within Malkangiri district, Kudumulugumma block must be one of the poorest blocks in the entire country. This is so not only because of lack of economic development in a general sense; it is so because of one specific development project, which dates back to 1962, and following which point in time there has been no development possible in the so-called Cut-off Area. This was probably not the intention or even included in the discussions, when Nehru and Khrushchev agreed on a hydroelectric power plant as part of India's Third Five-Year Plan. What they did agree was, with Soviet engineering expertise, to construct the Balimela dam across the Machkund river in Malkangiri to meet the increasing power needs of the neighbouring state of Andhra Pradesh. The project involved the flooding of a large area along the river banks that was inhabited by Scheduled Tribes. Those living on the western bank were moved to the resettlement villages that were subsequently constructed and given acronym names: RSC-1, RSC-2 etc., standing for Resettlement Colony. These are still village names 50 years later. The households that complied with this resettlement plan were paid INR 500 per individual. However, not all agreed to the plan. Those living along the eastern river had their land there, and their ancestors and identity were buried in those hilly fields. They refused to comply and withdrew to the strip of land adjacent to the mountains that separate the district from Andhra Pradesh, soon to realize that a lake took shape that was too time-consuming and expensive to cross for any daily needs. They came to inhabit the "Cut-off Area", as it was appropriately named, and area where no compensation could be paid, nor could the electricity that soon would travel in the wires above them reach down to the ground level where they lived—a fate that they, unknowingly, shared with their former neighbours in the numbered Resettlement Colonies.

In 2004, when the authors first visited the Cut-Off area, an estimated 37,000 people were living there.[2] The launch—a small square barge that was dangerously overloaded with people and goods to get value for money, four Rupees per person—took four hours from departure at Chitrakonda to reach the clay bank that was identified as harbour on the Cut-off shore. After a short stop it returned back. It was not possible for people from the Cut-off area to reach the hospital in Chitrakonda and return the same day. In fact, due to the opening hours of the hospital and the early, albeit somewhat unpredictable departure time of the launch, they would have to spend 48 hours of travelling and two overnight stays, in addition to the hours of walking between their village and the clay bank harbour, to manage to be seen by a doctor, if, that is, they were not unlucky that he had gone out for some personal business. It was little wonder that there was only one registered tuberculosis (TB) patient in the Cut-off Area, named Anand. It was more like a small miracle. However, when we found him, Anand was left with an empty medicine box. He had finished the medicine in less than the prescribed two months and had done so without the existence of relevant support mechanisms for supervised treatment. Anand had no medication for the four months continuation phase, and he had fallen down from a Salop tree when he was tapping palm beer and hurt his leg too badly to be able to make the necessary journey to the hospital in Chitrakonda, across the water, had he wanted to.

In the Shadow of the Balimela Dam

This visit was the point of departure for development of four studies to assess the situation in seven villages on both sides of the water, and one of these studies was undertaken by RA under the supervision of JS, who was also in charge of an interdisciplinary research project in the district. RA's study, described in the following, focused primarily on the Paraja tribe, which was one of the largest original inhabitants, indigenous groups in the area. We use the term '*Adivasi*' as it is used in the area. In the context of a society dominated by high-caste Hindus, in Malkangiri District both people classified as "Scheduled Tribes" and as *Dalit* (Scheduled Castes) identify themselves as, and are called, *Adivasi.* Only few *Adivasi* people lived in Chitrakonda, as most of the town's inhabitants were non-local people. *Adivasi* villages were scattered around Chitrakonda in a radius of one to 30 km. Most of these were resettlement villages established after the construction of the Balimela dam.

Public transportation was only available to a few of the villages. Most of the villagers would walk, travel by boat or go by bicycle to Chitrakonda, which was the centre for trade, medical treatment and education in the area. A hospital was established in Chitrakonda at the time of the construction of the hydropower project. However, the hospital was not the only place where *Adivasi* people would seek treatment. In fact, most consulted other providers, if provider is broadly understood as anybody who would provide care for the sick against some form of payment. In many *Adivasi* villages, there were traditional healers (locally known as *disari*, *gurumai* and *alekh*), who were often consulted in case of health problems. At the time of fieldwork, in 2005, there were three privately-owned medical stores in Chitrakonda.They were frequented by *Adivasi* people as they could get both medical advice and medicines there, although the chemists had little or no formal training. *Anganwadi* workers covered all villages, either living in the village or in a neighbouring village. Most *Anganwadi* workers were illiterate, which, according to their supervisor, was an obstacle for fulfilling their duties. Some providers practised biomedicine with only a little or no biomedical knowledge. They were known as doctors among villagers and as 'quacks' among government providers. In Chitrakonda, three registered medical practitioners (RMPs) had clinics at the time. Government-employed multipurpose healthworkers (MPHWs), most of them female, also covered the area. Ideally, they should live in the villages they worked in but in practice most lived in Chitrakonda and travelled by bicycle and/or boat to the villages.

Tuberculosis in and Around Chitrakonda

Thus, villagers had a broad spectrum of providers to seek treatment from, and many made use of more than one provider. In what follows, we shall focus in particular on tuberculosis (TB), since this disease is the target of the Government Programme known as the Revised National Tuberculosis Control Programme (RNTCP). While we noted that Anand was only partially treated for TB in the Cut-off Area, the only formally recognized centre for TB treatment in the area was the hospital in Chitrakonda. Contrary to WHO and Government standards, TB medicines were also sold at medical stores, prescribed by RMPs, and some traditional healers also claimed to be able to cure TB. In the following, 'provider' will be used to refer to government-employed health personnel only, as they are officially recognized providers of TB treatment. RNTCP, based on the DOTS strategy, was introduced in the district of Malkangiri in 2001. Before this, TB patients were mainly referred to a private Christian missionary hospital in Lamtaput in neighbouring Koraput district. Many villagers still linked TB with Lamtaput. At the hospital in Chitrakonda, the lab technician was trained under the RNTCP. Multipurpose Health Workers (MPHWs) were trained and worked as DOT providers, responsible for overseeing to oversee that patients took their medicines every second day during the initial two-months treatment phase. In some cases, the MPHW had informally trained an *Anganwadi* worker or a local villager as a DOT provider, when a positive case was identified in the village ("spot training"). Among providers, it was generally believed that there were many undiagnosed TB patients in villages. Often, providers blamed the patients for this: villagers were thought to consult traditional healers instead of Government doctors and "not to care about health". Providers would also mention problems with those patients actually coming to the hospital: they often failed to deliver the three required sputum tests; they did not adhere to the treatment regimen; and they did not have any confidence in the hospital doctors until their condition deteriorated. So, according to providers, if TB treatment was not successful, villagers/patients were responsible for this. A few providers, however, were sensitive to the difficulties faced by patients in getting treatment in Government hospital, such as lack of transportation, unsuitable opening hours and the frequent absence of health care staff. Common negative stereotypes among providers, who in their private lives condemned tobacco and alcohol for religious reasons, were that all *Adivasi* people smoked and drank excessively. Many providers linked drinking and smoking to TB, either as a cause, an aggravating factor, or a reason for the patient not being able to follow the treatment. Providers also talked about villagers' unhygienic houses and living conditions and bad food habits and pointed to a relationship between these conditions and the diseases they suffered from, thereby effectively blaming *Adivasi* people for their impoverished and vulnerable life conditions. Bur the front-line health workers also worked under frustrating circumstances.

MPHWs who, in most cases, acted as DOT providers, faced heavy workloads combined with the absence of any recognition for their efforts. Going to the villages was physically strenuous, and some MPHWs feared going there due to personal experiences of, or rumours about, drunken people, people demanding money or medicines, or fights. When reaching a village MPHWs might not find the patients there, and villagers did not wish to present their health problems. Almost all villagers in the study villages had heard of TB and could cite an example of someone who (apparently) had died from TB, although they could not always describe the symptoms of the disease. Those who knew of TB feared it as it was considered fatal. Few villagers were aware that TB medicines were supposedly available at the hospital in Chitrakonda free of cost as they were accompanied by prescriptions of other drugs, including unnecessary cough syrups and vitamins. In combination with transportation costs, this practice undermined the claim that the treatment was free.

A commonly mentioned symptom associated with TB was cough. Cough was often treated with different medicines bought from medical stores and/or from traditional healers. Some villagers often believed that alcohol and tobacco could cause TB, but most did not know the bacterial cause of the disease. For most villagers, the Government hospital was often the last resort. They were of the opinion that medicines at the hospital were of inferior quality compared to medicines from medical stores and RMPs. In addition, their preference for injections was rarely fulfilled at the hospital. Villagers experienced ending up paying for 'free' services at the hospital. Compared to the examination and behaviour of RMPs, villagers found examination procedures less thorough and the behaviour of providers more offensive at the hospital. Many villagers expressed insecurity about going to the hospital and interacting with providers. They also often experienced that the hospital was either closed or providers were not available when they went there. Traditional healers were often consulted, either in combination with another provider or as the sole treatment provider.

Local healers enjoyed great respect in the villages and took part in many spheres of village life and were highly trusted in health matters. MPHWs came to the *Adivasi* villages about twice a month. Villagers felt less insecure interacting with MPHWs than with hospital providers. However, villagers complained that the MPHW came irregularly, that he/she came in the middle of the day when many were working in the fields, that the MPHWs were not able to treat any other condition apart from malaria, and that some of them demanded money in exchange for the government-supplied medicines they brought. The authors did not come across any MPHW who sold government-supplied medicines. But some MPHWs told how they sometimes sold medicines they had bought in medical stores, e.g. injections, a practice that was observed by RA.

Interaction between Patients and Providers

Choosing a suitable provider in case of illness was a difficult task for villagers. Quality and availability of medicines, payment, opening hours, trust as well as previous experiences affected their choice. Personality and behaviour of the provider also played a major role. Experiences from contexts other than health also influenced the decision. Conflicts from everyday life in the village and experiences with a provider outside the medical sphere affected whether a certain provider, whether government or private was consulted in case of helath problems. In Chitrakonda, provider-patient interaction was largely influenced by the fact that patient and provider did not belong to the same ethnic group (Barth, 1969). Unequal social status and power equations influenced interactions and their outcome. Ethnic identities worked to identify as a specific *Adivasi* community *vis-à-vis* other groups (*ibid.*:13). Both in Chitrakonda and in the villages surrounding it, people made a clear distinction between *Adivasi* people and "Odia people". *Adivasi* people were people who belonged to "Scheduled Tribes" as well as low-caste people who lived in villages. Odia people (literally meaning people from Odisha) were here understood as those who lived in Chitrakonda, including both non-tribal people from Odisha and other states, notably the bordering state of Andhra Pradesh. According to this classificatory scheme, the majority of providers working in the area were Odia while the patients in the study were *Adivasi* people.

Adivasi people were considered among the lowest in the social hierarchy and were expected to behave in a highly respectful manner towards Odia people. Clothes, habits, adornments, language and appearance served as social markers that allowed *Adivasi* and Odia people to categorize each other. Differences between Odia and *Adivasi* people were especially stressed by Odia people and served to distinguish 'us' from 'them', often involving disrespect and symbolic violence. *Adivasi* people tried to diminish the differences to get accepted by Odia people, to appear to be similar to them and therefore increase their opportunities and status. This was seen when men from villages came to Chitrakonda dressed in trousers and shirts in contrast to the waist cloth and shirt they wore in their village setting. The characteristics (drinking alcohol, smoking etc.) attributed to *Adivasi* people affected the way a provider treated a patient. Providers often looked down upon patients and justified their behaviour by referring to these stereotypes. Communication between providers and patients is one example of how a person's ethnic identity shapes the way one is perceived by others (*ibid.*:15). Often diagnosis and recommended action were not explained to patients, since it was considered to be a waste of time due to their perceived ignorance and carelessness. *Adivasi* people, on the other hand, would never ask for a diagnosis themselves due to their inferior status.

Instead, AR often observed villagers discussing what the patient was suffering from after a consultation, and she was sometimes asked about the diagnosis. A set of taken-for-granted rules governed the interactions restricting what could be said and done (*ibid.*: 16). Examples of such rules were: the provider was always right; the patient should only speak when asked to; the patient should not make any demands; and the provider did not have to behave politely and make the patient feel at ease. One of the consequences of these implicit but effective rules was that patients did not always report all symptoms or any previous treatments to the provider. Family history of TB and other important information was thus not available during clinical decision-making. Whether the rules of interaction could be changed or challenged depended upon the different 'capitals' the patient could bring to bear on the situation.

Capitals are resources which can be economic, social and cultural and have asymbolic value (Bourdieu, 1986). Odia providers were generally more powerful in the interactions as they controlled more capital than *Adivasi* patients, in addition to the hierarchy between patient and healer. They had more social capital due to their higher social status; they were literate and economically better off. Even literate *Adivasi* people were not able to benefit from this capital as they were presumed to be ignorant and primitive due to their ethnic origin. However, being literate often gave them confidence to ask questions, and they felt less insecure dealing with providers than their illiterate kinsmen. The inequality between patient and provider was further enhanced by the fact that not all *Adivasi* people spoke Odia (the official language of Odisha), and many did not speak it fluently. The providers, who spoke Odia, had the power to decide in which language the interaction should take place. This meant that patients sometimes had insurmountable communication difficulties in expressing themselves and in understanding what was said. Only literate *Adivasi* people asked questions if they did not understand the providers.

Several MPHWs explained how difficult it had been for them to understand the villagers when they first came to the area, but that with time they had learned key words in local languages. However, as the area was not considered attractive to be posted in, there was a relatively high turnover of MPHWs, and patients therefore frequently encountered new MPHWs who had yet to acquire even the most basic local language skills. Language problems were also observed at the hospital, although these were largely denied by hospital staff. Such problems were seen, for instance, when a patient was told to have a sputum test. When the patient did not understand what to do and remained seated, the doctor would tell the patient to leave the room without further explanation. As a consequence, it happened regularly that patients did not get the prescribed test done, because they had not understood what to do and where to go.

Social Distance

From the above, it is clear that many non-medical factors influence treatment of diseases in Chitrakonda. As the providers complained, there were problems with patients not coming to the hospital, not reporting symptoms to MPHWs when they went to their villages, or not showing interest in treatment. However, this was not on account of the patients' perceived ignorance and carelessness about health as the providers claimed, but due to a pragmatic way of handling their misfortunes (Whyte, 1997). *Adivasis* did not have much confidence in government providers or medicines. They had bad experiences of absentee providers and of rude and disrespectful behaviour towards them. These experiences influenced villagers' preference for non-governmental providers. To be seen as an equal (and equally) human being and not being branded negatively on the basis of ethnic background was important for them. Hence, the practice of providers to treat them as ignorant, abusers and incapable of understanding messages constituted a significant access barrier, exacerbating the social distance in everyday life between Odia and *Adivasi* communities. Even if physical distance constituted another important access barrier, the villagers seemed to find it easier to overcome this than the social distance.

However, unable or unwilling to directly and openly question this social hierarchy, both Odia providers and *Adivasi* villagers said physical distance was the biggest obstacle to accessing treatment at the hospital. Social distance was less obvious for those who were part of the social hierarchy and had grown up embedded in its framework, and rather than articulate the issue openly *Adivasi* villagers would demonstrate their resentment against this treatment through their preference for traditional healers. Furthermore, despite the alleged barrier of distance, villagers—at least those residing on the Chitrakonda side of the Balimela Dam—regularly made use of medical stores and RMPs and went to the weekly market in Chitrakonda. To most people in the Cut-off Area, this was not an option, and they generally did not appear on the mental horizon of formal or informal healthcare providers in the town.

Dam-Health Dynamics

Development as a discursive trope and a material articulation works at many levels in the above scenario. Development is demonstrated by the hydroelectric prestige project of the sixties which was essential for the production of electricity for urban and industry consumption but not for village development in the area where it seriously disturbed the infrastructure of the original inhabitants. And development is demonstrated in the government-funded healthcare system that is set-up to replace traditional forms of treatment with biomedicine. Lack of original connectedness and the negative impact of one development project (the dam) on another key development area (the health system) complement Ferguson's argument in "the Anti-Politics Machine". He uses this term to capture the usually unintended effects of the workings of the development industry in Lesotho in the context of development projects that often fail to meet their stated objectives (Ferguson, 1994). Ferguson, while pointing to the uniqueness of the circumstances of Lesotho as a nation state surrounded by South Africa, and discussing the rationale of development projects that systematically "fail" according to their own stated objectives of poverty reduction and increase in agricultural production, defines two sets of "side effects" of development projects: growth of state administration and bureaucratization in geographical (and administrative) areas that were not well accessed/accessible for the State machinery earlier, and at the same token, delinking this process from the political consciousness.

Poverty, and its reduction, is defined as a 'technical' problem, not a political one. Along with this depoliticising—or because of it—development projects can carry out highly sensitive activities under the disguise of 'development', such as expanding state power to control populations—or control populations more effectively—than was the case before 'development' took place, says Ferguson (*ibid.*). Ferguson wonders to what extent these mechanisms are indeed unique to Lesotho or whether they represent general and generalizable dynamics that—to varying degrees—are part of the workings of the development industry globally. He notes that "development" projects all-over the world tend to be formed by a shared, context-independent "development" expertise as one reason why the Lesotho experience would be part of a very general phenomenon; another standardizing effect comes from the tendency to standardize programmes into "packages" of standard available "inputs" (*ibid.*: 258).

In the case of Malkangiri, perhaps as a within-state parallel to Lesotho, the district may be seen as being surrounded by more powerful centres of government that decides on the use of the district's natural resources for external benefit and to the detriment of the people living in the district, while placing this decision exclusively in the realm of the national and state politics, disregarding and actively ignoring the politics of *Adivasi* rights—a concept that was even weaker at the time of the construction of the dam than today.

Both hydro-power infrastructure and health system are developmental milestones from the perspective of the state, but their systemic de-linking is an act of "anti-politics". The two—the dam and health—are, of course, dynamically entangled, but ignoring this makes it possible to also ignore their paradoxical and conflicting developmental effects. Damming the river and creating the lake changed the ecology in favour of certain species and not others, hence improving breeding conditions for the Anopheles mosquito, the vector of the parasite causing malaria, and its construction was followed by an increase in the incidence of the dangerous *P. falciparum* malaria. This epidemic change, it should be noted, co-occurred with the effective cutting off of a large area and a substantial population from meaningful access to services normally associated with the development of the "modern state", such as education and health care (Prince, 2013).

A syndemic is an epidemic of co-morbidities and social conditions that mutually reinforce each other (Singer, 2009). The increase in malaria came to interact syndemically with a host of other conditions that were common in the area on both sides of the dam, involving anaemia, splenomegaly and fever (all potentially linked to malaria) as well as upper respiratory tract infection, musculo-skeletal diseases, goitre, eye diseases such as cataract, dental problems, skin diseases and ear diseases, as well as widespread undernourishment of children (Sahu, Satapathy, Sahani, Bhattacharya & Seeberg, 2005), all of which had to be managed without treatment, or with a precarious combination of traditional, herbal and/or randomly accessible biomedicines distributed through informal channels. A systematic comparison of health status of villagers on both side of the Balimela Dam showed a statistically significant difference with higher prevalence of splenomegaly in the Cut-off Area compared to villagers closer to Chitrakonda, but otherwise villagers on both side of the dam suffered from the predominantly treatable conditions mentioned above to similarly high degrees, pointing to the astounding efficacy of normalized social distance as a barrier to health care. We propose that the workings of what Ferguson called the anti-politics machine have played an important role in keeping 'development' represented by the dam and 'development' represented by state funded health care in separate domains. Both are seen by the state as 'technical' rather than 'political' matters, something that itself, of course, represents a politics of ignoring *Adivasi* society.

As far as the disruption of *Adivasi* society by the dam is concerned, it may be defined as collateral damage by the state, and the 'choice' of tens of thousands of *Adivasi* inhabitants to stay at ancestral land in the Cut-off Area seems to have been interpreted by state representatives as a justification for the state to withdraw from all responsibilities in the area. The above analysis shows, however, that even if this withdrawal of state responsibility were somehow to be remedied, the performance of social distance would continue to outweigh the importance of physical distance as a barrier to access to health care. Importantly, social distance is intrinsically political and irreducible to a "technical issue". Hence, we argue that the systematic domination of *Adivasi* communities by the dominant society as exemplified in the present study can be directly measured in the extremely high incidence of unaddressed yet medically treatable diseases—a syndemic relationship that Farmer has defined as an expression of structural violence (Farmer, 2001, 2005).

Notes

1. Parts of this chapter constitute an edited version of a text previously published by Aarhus (2005).
2. The authors wish to express their gratitude to Dr. Nilakanth Panigrahi, who organised and participated in this visit.

References

Aarhus, R. (2005). Overcoming social distance: Interactions between tribal TB patients and non-tribal providers. In R. Addlakha and J. Seeberg (Eds.), *Accessing TB Services in a Tribal District: The Malkangiri Project, Orissa* (pp. 59-70). New Delhi: DANTB.

Barth, F. (Ed.) (1969). *Ethnic groups and boundaries. The social organisation of culture difference.* Bergen, Oslo, London: Universitetsforlaget.

Bourdieu, P. (1986). The forms of capital. In J.G. Richardson (Ed.), *Handbook of Theory and Practice for the Sociology of Education* (pp. 241-258). New York: Greenwood.

Farmer, P. (2001). *Infections and Inequalities: The Modern Plagues. Updated Edition with a New Preface.* Berkeley: University of California Press.

Farmer, P. (2005). *Pathologies of Power: Health, Human Rights, and the New War on the Poor (with a new preface by the author).* Berkeley: University of California Press.

Ferguson, J. (1994). *The Anti-Politics Machine. "Development," Depoliticization and Bureaucratic Power in Lesotho.* Minneapolis: University of Minnesota Press.

Prince, R.J. (2013). Situating Health and the Public in Africa. Historical and Anthropological Perspectives. In R.J. Prince and R. Marsland (Eds.), *Making and Unmaking Public Health in Africa: Ethnographic and Historical Perspectives* (pp. 1-54). Athens: Ohio University Press.

Sahu, T., Satapathy, D.M., Sahani, N.C., Bhattacharya, A., and Seeberg, J. (2005). Health status of tribal population in an unreached area of Malkangiri district. In R. Addlakha and J. Seeberg (Eds.), *Accessing TB Services in a Tribal District: The Malkangiri Project, Orissa.* New Delhi: DANTB.

Singer, M. (2009). *Introduction to Syndemics: A Critical Systems Approach to Public and Community Health,* San Francisco: John Wiley & Sons.

Whyte, S.R. (1997). *Questioning Misfortune: The Pragmatics of Uncertainty in Eastern Uganda* (Vol. 4), Cambridge: Cambridge University Press.

EIGHT

ITINERANT AND SUBALTERN MUSICIANS OF WESTERN ODISHA[1]

LIDIA GUZY

Itinerant subaltern Priest-Musicians

Sarmangalia

The *Sarmangalia* is an itinerant non-Brahmin priest of the goddess Mangala. He wanders from village to village, accompanied by his wife and children. The *Sarmangalia* carries the goddess Mangala with him in a portable wooden altar, devoting the utmost care to her.[2] The *Sarmangalia* and his family usually have no fixed abode but camp outside the villages by the roadside, sheltered by provisional plastic tents.

The worshipping chant of the *Sarmangalia* can be heard from far away[3] :

"*Dukho nee*
Take the pain.
Sukho dee
Give the happiness.
Suke suke rohu
Let the happiness remain.
Apoti nahi
I have no wish.
Bipoti nahi
I do not know any danger."

"*Ma Mangala likes the sound*", the *Sarmangalia* explains while playing the *Sarmangalia dhol* drum. This is a small wooden drum made from lizard leather on the left and from goat's leather on the right side. The *Sarmangalia* plays the drum with a stick in his left hand, while his right hand scratches the skin. The deep, monotone sounds he produces are conceived to evoke and represent the goddess Mangala. As he plays the *Sarmangalia dhol* drum and sings the songs of the goddess, the *Sarmangalia* begs for food for himself and his family as well as for food offerings for the goddess. In the morning and evening the *Sarmangalia* conducts his ritual worship (*puja*) by food offerings to the goddess and by playing his drum. He mixes the sacrificial food (*bhog*) and distributes it among the villagers.

The *Sarmangalia* purifies the village he visits with some flattened rice mixed with cow dung. It is believed that the *Sarmangalia*, who is also called *deheri* which means local healer, cures the physical or psychological ailments of those who give him donations. The sound of the *Sarmangalia dhol* drum is assumed to appease and satisfy the goddess Mangala and to represent at the same time her voice and religious advice. It is believed that the drum's sound chases away bad dreams (*barna sapna*), protects against witchcraft (*tondei*)—especially when played at crossroads—and shields against bad spirits (*bhut-pret*). Both the *Sarmangalia*'s *puja* and the sound of his drum are thought to prevent or heal illnesses such as small pox (*mata*), chicken pox (*bosonto*), fever (*jhoro*) and all kinds of skin diseases (*khosa kujri*) or mental stress. Besides these healing procedures, the *Sarmangalia* priest also sells self-made talismans (*dongria*) which are supposed to contain *Aryuvedic* medicine. (*see* Photographs 1, 2 and 3).

The activity of the *Sarmangalia* represents the link between ritual migrant music and healing. His performance is a performance of cure, or a "performance of healing" as outlined by Laderman and Roseman (1996: 1-16). The deep resonating sound of the *Sarmangalia* drum and the transportable altar of the goddess create an atmosphere of unfamiliarity, of temporality and thus of ritual effectiveness. The temporary character of his stay in a village, the ephemeral place of devotion which is established with the portable altar, the movement inherent in the *Sarmangalia*'s performance as well as the liminal, nomadic group he forms together with his wandering family all contribute to a continuum of strangeness around him which is effective on his ritual clients.

Photograph 1: *Sarmangalia* priest with his *Sarmangalia* drum, on the way to Padampur, 2006, L.G.

Photograph 2: Portable altar of goddess Sarmangala, on the way to Padampur, 2006, L.G.

Bhairavi

Another local category of wandering priest-musicians are the *bhairavi*, also called *Mali konti* or talisman-makers. They fashion talismans from the *tulsi* tree and play the *kanjoni,* a tambourine made from lizard leather.[4] The *bhairavi* also teach theatre (*nato kirtan siksan*) and carry out ear invocations (*kana mantra*). They whisper secret spiritual advice into the ear of their barren or otherwise physically ill patients (*dukhi sukhi kosti*) who ascribe healing power to their whispering. They offer their services to everybody except the marginalised Gonsia and Ganda, considered as

Photograph 3: Sarmangalia worshipping goddess Sarmangala through the sound of *sarmangala* drum, on the way to Padampur, 2006, L.G.

"untouchable" (*achhut*). Even so the *bhairavi* are of a low and contested social status themselves, they still act within the socially constructed categories of "untouchability", maintaining what superiority they are able to secure in relation to other social groups.

Generally, *bhairavi* are regarded as healers for general purposes, such as skin diseases, stomach pains, mental frustration and the prevention against any kind of evil external influences. For healing and preventive purposes, the *bhairavi* make talismanic threads which they sell while roaming from village to village. Similar to the *Sarmangalia* families, the *bhairavi* priest-musicians move between the month *moxir* and *choit* (from December to April) with their wife and children. During the rainy season, the *bharavi* families stop their wandering and stay at a temporary home. As in the case of the *Sarmangalia*, their nomadic lifestyle is imagined to be essential for the effectiveness of their healing powers. The migrant-musician thus heals while passingby.

While the male *bhairavi*'s specialisation is mainly to play *kanjoni* music in performing their ritual activities, the *bharavi* women are specialised in tattooing. They tattoo the women of the village communities they visit, but their trade is restricted to executing designs and patterns determined by these communities. For men, tattoos (*juti)* are not regarded as necessary: "*Education (bidha) is enough for men*", people tell. For women however, tattoos are held to be effective after death, as a last covering of the carcass. In their tattoos, according to local beliefs, the forefathers (*pitru*) live on. As one legend tells, the god of death, *Jom*, will ask each woman: "*Do you have your tattoos*?" If she has not, *Jom* will chase her away from the world where the deceased and the ancestors live. He will shout: "*Go away! Your body is impure/not covered* (*pinda suddha nahi*)!" If she is expelled from the kingdom of *Jom,* the dead women could become a homeless ghosts (*pret*), and thus dangerous for the living. Tattoos are considered to convey an impression of injury and aesthetic mutilation, having an inverse effect in terms of spiritual security. Tattoos are seen as signs of a woman already wounded, marked by her blood. This symbolic "impurity" and aesthetic imperfection gives her a spiritual guarantee not to die a bad death that could turn her into a *pret* and not into an ancestor (*pitru*), which is the aspired state of good death.[5] The male *bharavi*'s music and the female *bhairavi*'s tattooing seem to fulfil complementary roles: through the aesthetically distancing character of migrant ritual music and of tattooing the female bodies, male and female clients are protected from all kind of ailments in their lifetime as well as after death (*see* Photographs 4 and 5).

Photograph 4: Bhairavi with his *kanjoni*, on the way to Padampur 2005, L.G.

Jawara geet musicians: Another example for the traditional connection between music and the task of healing illness is the *jawara* music (*geet*), played to chase away *Mata*, the goddess of the small pox and chicken pox (*guni sendri*), as well as to cure all kind of *raga* (illnesses

Photograph 5: *Kanjoni* Instrument, with tatooing ingrediences, 2005, L.G.

of the skin). *Jawara geet* musicians belong to the caste of the *Ghansya*, a Harijan category which is considered even lower than the Ganda. Their traditional occupation is the skinning of dead animals for the manufacturing of drum-skins. *Jawara geet* is performed by a singer or a group of singers, accompanying themselves by the playing of *mandal* drums. *Jawara geet* may be performed as a cure for acute illness or in the context of a preventive ritual.

In case a villager acutely suffers from one of the diseases named above, a singer of *jawara* music (*jawar gayak*) or a group of singers and players might be called, in order to sing nine nights and nine days in his village. As an invitation to perform in a village, the *jawar* singer is given a lemon (*lembu*); he then has to donate the lemon as an offering to the goddess *Mata* and her manifestation Durga. The cutting of a lemon is considered auspicious. "*When goddess Mata sees the lemon, she will be happy* (devi Shanti heba)", explains a villager. According to a local legend, the lemon symbolises the head of the demon Moisasur who, in the shape of a buffalo, was beheaded by the beautiful goddess Durga.

As a general prevention against *mata* and *raga* diseases, *jawara* music is traditionally played on the ninth night (*noworatri*) of the month *choit* (April) and during *noworatri*, the ninth night of the month *dusshara* (October). During *dusshara* the goddess Durga is venerated synonymously as *Mata*. The *jawara* singersare acting as ritual assistants (*sevako*) to the local healer named *gunya* or *baiga* who, with the help of the *jawara* music, puts himself into a state of trance. He becomes *boil*—entranced by the goddesses—and in this state is supposed to be able to heal and protect from illness. The *baiga* acquires his healing and protective power while being venerated as the goddess *Mata* and at the same time venerating the goddess himself.

Today, *jawara geet* is only rarely practised in Bora Sambar. Only some famous *jawara* singers and players still perform their music. As skin diseases could in recent years be significantly reduced by means of state or NGO sponsored health campaigns, *jawara* performances are no longer demanded by the village populations of the region. Another reason for its decline is that *jawara* players try to escape their low social status connected to their traditional profession and musical activity.

In many villages of Nuapara district however, local altars known as *mata gudi* are found. Dedicated to the goddess *Mata*, they indicate the memory of the tradition of *jawara geet*. And still, in front of almost every house in the region, dry lemons can be found hanging on the veranda. These apotrophaic symbols remain, even when the music has perished.

Gopijantra

Another category of itinerant priest-musicians are the *gopijantra*, literally the "musical machine" (*jantra)* played by the friend "*gopi*" of Radha. Radha is worshipped as the beloved girlfriend of the god Krishna who, in Hindu mythology, is the incarnation of the god Vishnu.[6] *Gopijantra* thus denotes both, the one-stringed instrument made out of a melon (*lou*) and a string as well as the itinerant priest-performer. Sometimes, the *gopijantra* is also called *ekatara*, literally the one-stringed musical instrument.

For the *gopijantra* performer, the instrument itself is the altar of the goddess Sarasvati, the Hindu goddess of wisdom and learning. By lighting an incense stick (*duppo katti*) the *gopijantra* daily worships his instrument. Playing the instrument means an act of worship (*puja*) directed towards the goddess.

A *gopijantra* features as the itinerant singer of the mythical local narrative (*katani*) of Gowind Chandra, a famous folk tale of Orissa, which meanwhile has been written down in the Gowind Chandra book (*bohi*). The *gopijantra* walks daily around 3 to 5 kilometres while begging, singing and playing. In the evening he returns to his home. Locals consider his activity as a religious devotion and an act of asceticism.

Daily, the *gopijantra* sings the well-known rhythmic chant of Gowind Chandra:

Gowind Chandra Katani[7]

"The father of Gowind Chandra is Manik Chandra.
The mother of Gowind Chandra is the goddess Mukta.
Before Gowind Chandra was born,
Jom, the God of death decided that Gowind Chandra will live only 19 years.
In his 19th year he shall die, Jom said.
Only his mother knew this.

....

Anxious, she has forbidden her son to leave his home.

....

The only way for Gowind Chandra to be saved (mukti), was to leave the house—not as a son, but as a wandering ascetic (baba). Only as a baba he could mislead the god of death.

....

In order to meditate Gowind Chandra left mother and father.

...

Photograph 6: A *Gopijantra* singer playing his *gopijantra* lute, met on the roads to Padampur, 2004, L.G.

The meaning of the story—as the *gopijantra* explains—is that one crucial way to salvation (*mukti*) lies in the devotional practice of singing religious stories while begging. Here, the local concept of worldly renunciation and religious devotion amalgamates with the trans-regional Hindu value of asceticism[8] and the Indian Hindu mysticism of the *bhakti* tradition.[9] While begging and singing, the *gopijantra* accepts food or

Photograph 7: *Dopara* drum player, on the way to Raipur, 2008.

money donations (*vikhya*) from donors who in this way hope to attain good *karma*—performing good deeds to accumulate a "spiritual capital" for the next life. The Hindu worldview's central category of *karma* is, in short, a religious theory of action, which postulates that all the deeds of an individual have an effect on his or her next existences. Consequently, all situations and occurrences of the present life can be traced back to moral achievements or failures in a previous existence. Donations—"gifts" in terms of their socio-anthropological value—are meant to realize their value in an economy of soteriological reciprocity which aims at a final spiritual release. While the performance of the *gopijantra* is in its narrative and conceptual content embedded in the trans-regional Hindu mythology and its ideological context, the idea of goddess worship through the specific sound of a particular musical instrument and especially the identification of instrument and sound with the voice and utterances of a goddess seems to be an element specific to the Bora Sambar region.

Cherchela

The *cherchela* is a begging musician who plays a big round and thin membranophone, the *dopara*, which reminds of an oversized tambourine. The *dopara* is made from the wood of the *khorol* tree (*khorol kat*) and is strung with goat's skin (*cheli chamara*). This big and thin instrument is played with a *timsi*, a small bamboo stick for the left hand and a stick (*kondha*) from the wood of the local *sisu* tree (*sisu kath*) for the right hand. Due to this handling of the instrument, which resembles that of the *dhol* and the *nissan* drums of the *ganda baja* orchestra, the *dopara* membranophone is considered—especially by Ganda musicians—as the ancient instrumental origin of the *ganda baja* orchestra. Musically, the *dopara* drum might substitute the *dhol*. The *cherchela* musicians explain that *dopara* music is played especially for the worship of goddesses such as Sarasvati, Samley, Lakshmi and for gods such as Ganesh and Vishwakarma (*see* Photograph 7).

"*Cherchera par is the rhythm of begging (vikhya magiba)*", the listeners of the *dopara* music tell. While playing the rhythm of begging, the *dopara* performer goes from door to door in order to collect voluntary donations. Giving donations (*vikhya deba*) to wandering and begging musicians in form of food or money is considered a religious merit (*karma*). The value of donations (*vikhya deba*) to the *cherchera* follows the same logic of an ascetic and devotional tradition already encountered in the case of the *gopijantra*.

Porushram

With the *porushram* we come across the case of a specifically local tradition of the oral transmission of a pan-Indian epic. The subaltern *porushram* musician is a local devotional musician and singer who has taken a special religious initiation in order to lead his life together with his wife as a *porushram*—a wandering beggar-musician (*porushram dikhya*), devoted to the worship of the pan-Indian god Rama and to the recital of the narrations of the *Ramayana*. Together with the *Mahabharata*[10], the *Ramayana* belongs to the great lyrical epics of Indian cultural history. It tells the saga of the divine hero Rama, his beautiful wife Sita and the dangerous king Ravana. Its author is the saintly poet Valmiki[11] , the origins of the text are considered however to trace back to the period around 4th century BCE. The *Ramayana* epic is very popular in lay Hinduism and its contents are publicly declaimed or musically presented in sung narrations, the so called *kata*. *Porushram* is originally the name of a mythical figure, the creator of the god Rama, whose symbol is an axe. Retelling the stories of the *Ramayana*, the *porushram* roams the streets with an axe on his shoulder and utters the name of god the Rama. "*The porushram is always on the street (bate bate jiba)*", the people tell. Often the *porushram* is blind, making a living by wandering from door to door together with his wife, singing the story of Rama and begging for alms.

The *porushram* goes about his trade only in the morning hours. According to the prescriptions of his religious devotion, he is supposed to return after getting one meal a day. But besides this internal religious explanation, a practical reason might be that in the rural context with its poor infrastructure it is necessarily to reach home before sunset. As going by foot requires time to reach one's destiny, the return home requires the greater part of the day.

Photograph 8: *Porushram*, Chichinta village, 2007, L.G.

Devgunya: *Music and Exorcism*

Another subaltern priest-musician is the *devgunya*, literally the exorcist of gods (*dev*= god, *gunya*=exorcist), who chases away malevolent forces. *Devgunya* designates at the same time (a) the *Devgunya*, a local subaltern community; (b) a ritually specialised non-Brahmin priest; and (c) a lyre-like chordophone, also termed *veena*, played only by the *Devgunya* community. The non-Brahmin priest-musician called *devgunya* specialises in the worship of the goddess Lakshmi—the goddess of wealth and rice. One could understand *devgunya* as "the exorcist priest of the goddess Lakshmi" as it is believed that with the music of his lyre-like string instrument *devgunya* bad spirits (*bhuta*) are chased away. The chordophone *devgunya* is considered holy by the *Devgunya* community, representing the goddess Lakshmi as well as the goddess Mangala, the clan goddess (*ishta devi*) of the *Devgunya* community. The sound—*sur*—of the instrument is believed to invoke both goddesses.

Photograph 9: *Devgunya*, at Bisipalli village, played by Anand Benya, 2009, L.G.

The *devgunya* chordophone is a bar zither of about 1.20 metre in length, consisting of a bamboo bar, in the middle of which a resonance body fashioned from a melon gourd is fixed. It is strung with one string made out of cow's gut sinew and decorated with seven moulded knobs topped by seven mussel shells. On the left side of the bar a bronze casting and on the right side a wooden handle is attached. The musician presses the string with his left hand and plucks it with the right hand in order to create the sound.

The microcosmic morphology of the instrument corresponds to the divine macrocosm of the *Devgunya* community: The seven little knobs topped by mussel shells represent the seven notes and the seven sister-goddesses. The *bara bhai bentkar*, the twelve mythical brothers of the Binjhal community, are said to reside in the bronze casting. The cow's gut sinew used as string stands for "untouchability", but also for the strength of the instrument. No god can touch the instrument because of this untouchable string. This also explains why the very sound of the untouchable string is believed to drive away malevolent elements. The sounds of the *devgunya* zither and the recitation of the *devgunya* priest-musician expel bad dreams, bad spirits (*bhuta*) and bad thoughts. The local term for the exorcising power of the music of the *devgunya* is *baja dwara. Mantra dwara* denotes the power of the spoken word that, during the playing of the *devgunya* instrument, assumes the same exorcising power. When summoned, the *devgunya* goes to his mentally and physically suffering clients, where he plays and sings in order to chase away the malevolent elements haunting them. This musical exorcism is called *devta nacha*, the dance of the gods, which is also the name of a song sung on this occasion accompanied by the *devgunya* chordophone:

Devta nacha geet
Played with the devgunya chordophone[12]

Chai chai chai olo
Look my dear Chaichai [pet name of the goddess Lakshmi]
Saas Pindiche banaa lugaa
The mother in law wore decorated linen clothes.
Toor kaahin kimaa
Why you are wise?
Hatara sukhuaa-Jhuri
The sign is the salty dry fish [a metaphor connected to death]
Uppar bandhar Chooli kilo
The snail is at the surface of the pond [the snail may be seen as a metaphor for life, the pond as an image connected to the fertility of women and to goddess worship]
Amar devi naat karuche
Our goddess is dancing.
Chum Chhum Chhumre guri [an onomatopoetic phrase alluding to the tinkling sound of women's foot chains]
Amar devi nat karuche
Our goddess is dancing.
Bohi Pindiche gailo
The daughter in law wore a [simple] hand loomed *saree*
Mor kahi ki mana?
Why should I also wear it?
Baari Baaina
The aubergine of the garden [metaphorical allusion to wealth and prosperity]
Tali Bandhar Gholi
and the snail of the pond
Sarge ude dhuli
which also influenced the heaven's atmosphere
Payejhal bajila

Photograph 10: *Sarangi* player Jalandar Benya of the Devgunya community, at Bisipalli village, 2004, L.G.

[all] sounded in her feet.
Mor mane bhabile
This is what I thought.

The metaphoric language of the *devgunya* constructs a symbolic link between the microcosm of vegetables and animals and the macrocosm of the gods, which is expressed in the image of the divine dance and the sound of the dancing feet of the goddess Lakshmi. Lakshmi is symbolised and worshipped in India through the image of her feet, painted by women with rice paste on the threshold of their houses. The symbol of the goddess' feet alludes to wealth, prosperity and happiness, which are thus invited to come into the particular house. The sound of the goddess' feet relates on the one hand to a common acoustic metaphor of femininity and sensuality commonly expressed through the soft tinkling sounds of foot anklets accompanying the steps of women's feet. On the other hand, it is associated with the worship of the goddess through the sound of music which in this case again is conceived as both, the manifestation of the goddess herself and the medium of her worship.

The *devgunya* instrument is played particularly in the yearly ritual services for the goddess Lakshmi (*Lakshmi puja*). During her worship in the month of *maxir* (November/December), the exorcising power of the goddess is believed to be especially effective in protecting and preventing from all kind of misfortune and evil. In the course of this worship, the local epic Lakshmi *purana* is sung. The singing of the Lakshmi *purana* is intended to support the power of the music by the power of recitations and words (*mantra dwara*). The *devgunya* cither is considered by the Devgunya community as their sacred instrument which may never be sold. Their secular instrument, used for begging, is the *sarangi* (*see* Photograph 10).

Only men of the Devgunya community are entitled to play music. Devgunya women create small portable altars of the goddess Lakshmi—Lakshmi *murti*—made out of rice seeds, which are sold during the time of the ritual services of the goddess. The members of the Devgunya caste consider themselves to be the descendants of Narad, the mythical saint (*rishi*) and musician of the *Vedas* who, with his musical instrument, the chordophone *tampura*, is believed to have transmitted worship practices through his theory of sound. Narad's theory of sound is generally connected to the evolution of north Indian ("classical") *raga* music. It expounds that the universe and the cosmos were created by the sound (*nada*), the word (*shabda, vak*) and the rhythm of Shiva's drum (Daniélou 2004: 148).[13]

In establishing a connection with the mythological context of the pan-Indian Hindu narratives and Vedic texts, the subaltern *devgunya* musicians thus ascribe a special cultural dignity to their ancestry, intended to counter their factual social marginalisation.

Conclusion: Music, Movement, Migration and the Role of Social Margins

In the Bora Sambar region, music, movement, migration and social marginality coincide. Music moves. It moves with musicians themselves living on social margins. Music moves from village to village along the routes of the itinerant non-Brahmin priests and musicians, and it moves by means of its sound vibrations. Its transgressing character is physical in the wandering movements of its performers and the rhythmic, sometimes dancing movements of their performance. But it is also metaphysical as it represents the sonic presence of the Divine. Regarding the wandering priest musicians or nomadic artists who offer their "musical services" to the villages of the Bora Sambar region, their mobility and marginality is held to be a crucial reason for their ritual efficacy.[14]

The diverse subaltern non-Brahmin priest-musicians and itinerant musicians of the Bora Sambar region keep a storehouse of cultural and musical wealth. Through their various musical traditions, they preserve a unique cultural consciousness and a local system of ideas and values about divinity, death and healing.

Ritual sound can establish an aesthetic distance, which becomes effective in the healing and exorcising powers ascribed to many of the discussed musical practices. The sound—*sur*—itself is associated with motion and linked to spiritual liberation (*mukti*). The effect of aesthetic distancing is metaphorically intensified by the migrant, wandering status of most of the musical performers. The attitude of begging, involved in particular traditions of migrant music, hints to connections between local concepts of religious musical performances and trans-regional religious traditions, such as the hegemonic Hindu value of asceticism.

All of the diverse musical traditions of the subaltern itinerant musicians of the Bora Sambar region are connected by social marginality and often to ambivalent and dangerous rituals and situations of life—a social and ritual condition which classifies the non-Brahmin priest-musicians as "impure", as of a precarious and ambivalent social status. I would suggest that the symbolic identification of precarious and ambivalent ritual music with its performers, hints to a convergence between the medium music and its message: the transitional, migrant or passing character of music represents both: (1) the ritual transition and the ritual transformation of spiritual impurity; and (2) the ritual passing and banishing of ailment. These transformations always imply a precarious being in-between the worlds. The liminality of the ritual music seems, in consequence, to stigmatise its performers socially.

Furthermore, the sounds of the specific instruments of priests-musicians of the Bora Sambar region are on the one hand acoustic metaphors and a sonic language expressing indigenous theories of sound and the sacred. On the other hand, the importance of sound in the region demonstrates the interplay between trans-regional Hindu narratives and local concepts, indicating significant effects of hegemonic Hindu value-ideas in the region. Itinerant subaltern musicians on the social margins of Western Odisha represents, cherish and harbour a unique intangible cultural heritage of the Eastern Indian region.

Notes

1. This article represents a part of my monograph Lidia Guzy, 2013, Marginalized Music. *Music, Religion and Politics from the Bora Sambar Region of Western Odisha*. Lit Verlag: Basel/Berlin.
2. Some *Sarmangalia* prient-musicians also carry the goddess Thakurani with them.
3. Documented by the author on a road to Padampur, 20 December, 2006.
4. The instrument of the *bhairavi* bears a remarkable similarity to that of the wandering Mahima Dharma ascetics of Orissa (Guzy, 2002).
5. For a further discussion of the categories of bad or good death *see* Alex/Heald, 2008.
6. According to the mythology of the Hindu epic *Mahabharata* and to its local narrative counterparts, Vishnu is believed to have been raised in a cowherd's family, vigorously playing the flute and often engaging in romantic episodes with cowgirls or other girlfriends (*gopi*).
7. Documented by the author on November, 15, 2004, on the roads to Padampur.
8. According to Louis Dumont's fundamental analysis, an Indian ascetic is an "individual outside the world" (*individu hors le monde*), who has left the world of castes, as opposed to the "individual in the world" – i.e., in the caste system. Ascetics, in the eyes of the faithful, have already reached in this earthly life the highest stage of religious release from the cycle of rebirths – *moksha*. (Dumont, 1986: 324-350); on the diversity of modern ascetic traditions in South Asia, *see* Ishwaran (1999).
9. The *bhakti* movement played a crucial role in the historical period of the Indian Middle Ages (around the 12th century C.E.). The concept of *bhakti* emphasizes an intimate relationship to a personal god. In contrast to the "proper conduct" (*karma marga*) of Brahmanism and the "proper knowledge" (*jnana marga*) of Indian philosophy, the *bhakti* movement introduced the "devotional love of god" (*bhakti marga*) as the way to salvation. Its religious aim was to direct one's concentrated feeling towards a god while attaining indifference to worldly concerns; on the broad phenomenon of the *bhakti*-tradition in India, *see* Biardeau (1994).
10. The *Mahabharata* is a heroic poem that was collected between 400 B.C. and 400 A.D. and consists of more than 1,00,000 *śloka* (double verses). It contains myths, legends, parables and fables of an ethical, teaching character. The most famous section of the *Mahabharata* is the *Bhagavad-Gita,* "The song of the magnificent". The *Mahabharata* epic contributed greatly to the widespread popularity of the god Vishnu in South Asia (Glasenapp, 1986: 66-93).
11. For the retold Valmiki's version by Krishna Dharma *see* Valmiki, 1998.
12. Recorded by the author on October 18, 2003, at Bisipalli village, played by Anand Benya, transcriptions and translation by Surendra Kumar Sahu.
13. The ancient Indian Vedic literature bears witness to the existence of very early indigenous theories on music and sound. Collections of religious hymns (*saman*) similar to the oldest *Rig Veda* hymns can be found in the *Samaveda*, the textbooks of the *udagatri* priests for *Soma* sacrifices (Nijenhuis, 1974: 1). Fragments of *Rig Veda* (*Samaveda*) which are of unsure date (around 1750-500 B.C.E. according to Michaels (1998: 67) or much older – about 4000 B.C.E. according to Klostermaier (1994: 477-82)) expound through their hymns the spiritual and ritual characteristic

of sound as *vak,* the sacred word, speech or language (Doniger O'Flaherty, 1981: 61) which is equated with a goddess, especially with the goddess Sarasvati. Mystical texts of the *Upanishads* (secret teachings and Vedic tracts dealing with philosophical issues) of the late phase of the Vedic religion (1000—500 B.C.E.) show that the voice itself is considered holy. The most important holy verse (*mantra*) is the syllable "*Om*", considered as the expression of the creative process of the universe, originating from *shabda-brahma* (the ultimate in form of a sound). For later periods, "(t)*he most outstanding examples are the linguistic theories of the grammarian Bhartrihari (5th century C.E.) and of the Kashmir Shaiva philosopher, left-handed tantrist and poet Abhinavagupta (11th centrury C.E.) or the Nada Brahman of the musicologists who claim the world is sound*" (Wilke, 2008: 31).

14. Christine Guillebaud (2008) describes analogous phenomena for the region of Kerala, where itinerant musicians offer their services to families of high status in order to treat malevolent influences and to protect from misfortune. In Kerala and in Orissa, the mobility of these musicians is seen as a crucial reason for their ritual efficacy.

References

Alex, Gabriele/Suzette Heald (ed.) 2008. *Good Deaths, Bad Deaths: Cultural Perspectives on Death and Dying*, Special issue of Curare, Vol. 31, 1.

Biardeau, Madleine. 1994. *Études de Mythologie Hindou II. Bhakti et Avatara.* Pondichéry: Publication de l'École Française d'Extrême-Orient.

Dumont, Louis. 1986 (1966). *Homo Hierarchicus. Le Système des Castes et ses Implications.* Paris: Tel Gallimard.

Guillebaud, Christine. 2008. *Le Chant des Serpents. Musiciens Itinérants du Kérala.* Paris: CNRS Publications.

Guzy, Lidia. 2002. Baba-s und Alekh-s – Askese und Ekstase einer Religion im Werden. Vergleichende Untersuchungen der asketischen Tradition Mahima Dharma in Orissa/östliches Indien. Berlin: Weissensee Verlag.

Guzy, Lidia. 2013. *Marginalized Music. Music, Religion and Politics from the Bora Sambar Region of Western Odisha.* Lit Verlag: Basel/Berlin.

Ishwaran, Karigoudar (ed.) 1999. Ascetic Culture: Renunciation and Worldly Engagement. In *JAAS – Journal of Asian and African Studies,* Vol. XXXIV, (1).

Klostermaier, Klaus K., 1994. *A Survey of Hinduism.* Albany\ New York: Suny Press.

Laderman, Carol / Marina Roseman (eds.) 1996. *The Performance of Healing.* London: Routledge Publications.

Michaels, Axel. 1998. *Der Hinduismus. Geschichte und Gegenwart*, München: C.H. Beck.

O'Flaherty, Wendy Doniger (ed.) 1981. *The Rig Veda. An Anthology: one Hundred and Eight Hymns.* Selected, translated and annotated by Wendy Doniger O'Flaherty. Harmondsworth: Middlesex, England, New York.

Wilke, Annette / Axel Michaels / Cornelia Vogelsanger (eds.) 1994. *Wild Goddesses in India and Nepal.* Proceedings of an International Symposium. Bern and Zürich: Bern: Lang (Studia Religiosa Helvetica 2).

Wilke, Annette 2008. Sound and Sense. Sonic Perception in Hindu India. In Lidia Guzy (ed.), *Religion and Music.* Berlin: Weissensee Verlag: 15-60.

NINE

CHILDHOOD IN CULTURE:
Navigating Between India and Brazil

LUCIA RABELLO DE CASTRO AND MARCELA RABELLO DE C. CENTELHAS

Introduction

Academic life in the present globalized world has been gradually modelled after hegemonic economic principles of efficiency, productivity and competitiveness. These have insidiously slipped into the social practices, discourses and teleologies that have so far oriented the search for knowledge, the love for discussion and exchange of ideas and the relevance of transmission, altering altogether the meaning and fate of what academy in our present world is for. Jacoby (1987) cautions us that present academic life is more akin to credentials, titles and celebrating one's self-reputation than interested in securing the freedom of thinking. It seems that we are heading for an academic life whose insignia of distinction lie on the competence for celebrity and egocentric entrepreneurship incommensurably distant from the cherished ideals of solidarity, critical thinking and political engagement.

The present volume of felicitation for Professor Deepak Kumar Behera opens-up for us a precious opportunity to celebrate an intellectual and an academic life that has remained faithful to his ideals. As Hannah Arendt has noted, courage is a public quality (2002), which today very few are willing to cultivate as it may put in risk one's public esteem. We praise Professor Behera for his unremitting courage as he stands as an inspiration for all of us who feel sometimes impotent before the imperatives of this new era. Those who have had the privilege of belonging to the circle of Professor Behera's colleagues have had a chance to share and learn from his serene standpoint against such a prevailing academic reality of competitiveness. His zest to share with colleagues what he has been able to obtain for himself was remarkable: his knowledge, know-how, projects, ideas and whatever useful information. He practised what he professed, and generosity with colleagues was his mark. He could maintain along his life a compassionate and acute outlook on disagreements and disputes, providing a third party standpoint of oxygenation and support so that none could find him/herself put aside on account of his/her beliefs. The faith in others and in their good judgement makes him, not only a distinguished colleague, but one who is able to integrate wisdom and professional knowledge.

In the contribution to this volume, we undertake a dialogue with Professor Behera's work on children and tribal people. His extensive research on these two social groups has produced a unique understanding of the social issues that affect these groups today, specially in face of the new legislation that is purported to safeguard their rights and demands. Notwithstanding advances formally coded in legal dispositions, the question that needs to be asked remains: to what extent people's lives in these groups have been improved? If not, what accounts for the resistances to change the *status quo*? We have brought forth the notions of culture, vulnerability and marginalization as key theoretical concepts in Professor Behera's work to discuss these questions. These notions make up a three-fold analytical stance from where to highlight present challenges concerning the plight of these social groups.

In order to enhance the discussion in view of a trans-national frame of analysis, we have navigated between Professor Behera's contribution and Brazilian scholarship on children and tribal people. As India and Brazil stand as two emergent countries in the international capitalist order, part of the BRIC' countries, they share multiple similarities in terms of the present social, economic and political conditions. The purpose here is to establish a potent dialogue on common problems and dilemmas that are interposed in these two countries' search for social equality and development.

CULTURE AND THE EDUCATIONAL INSTITUTIONALIZATION OF TRIBAL CHILDREN: NAVIGATING BETWEEN INDIA AND BRAZIL

It seems quite evident that within the scope of present anthropological scholarship revisiting the concept of culture should consist of an important task. In the extensive contribution of Professor Deepak Kumar Behera, it is possible to identify such a concern as a leading aspect of his ethnographical work and research projects, specially those related to tribal and indigenous peoples in contemporary India. In different moments (Behera, 2003; Behera and Pfeffer, 2009) he has addressed the significant and structural difference between the culture of tribal[1] peoples and that of urban westernized societies, emergent in interethnic contexts such as those of state intervention and tribal educational institutionalization.

The effort to converge the concern with the concept of culture and the study of tribal peoples can be taken for granted to some extent, in that the contact with these peoples, as these stand for a "radical alterity" in relationship to the anthropologist or to the national society, would imply a process of objectification of the latter's culture and values (Wagner, 2009). However, it is important to consider that today culture consists of a fundamental notion to describe differences and act thereupon in an ever increasing globalized world; in this sense we can affirm that such a notion does not belong mainly or solely to academicians, but also to tribal and indigenous people themselves. It is possible then to raise the issue about the demand of an ampler discussion in the human and social sciences about its meanings and the political and social consequences of its uses (Carneiro da Cunha, 2009).

In the history of the anthropological sciences the concept of culture emerges tinged with a certain ambiguity expressing both a totalizing phenomenon, once everyone belongs to a culture, and a particularizing one, as all cultures all unique and distinct. Irrespective of the genealogical dimension of the concept, we argue that over and above its different meanings the idea of culture introduces a social relationship, one that is constituted in the encounter—absolutely asymmetrical—between West and East, or still, between "primitive" and "modern" peoples. Insofar as a relative conception of culture has introduced the equivalence among different cosmologies and ways of living, it is noteworthy that invariably the notion of culture is likely to produce limits, geographies and alterities that introduce a division between "us" and "them". This should not lead to a total rejection of such an important concept, but brings forward the urgency to analyse its implications in anthropological research, mostly in ethnographic work.

If the notion of culture is embedded in a colonial heritage as it was coined in this asymmetrical encounter between the West and indigenous peoples, producing thus a hierarchical separation between them, nonetheless it is possible to say that its contemporary use has been recognized and appropriated by a great number of indigenous peoples as a way to affirm their autonomy in search of their rights. This tribal and indigenous process of updating the concept of culture is present in distinct contemporary interethnic relationships, encompassing recent endeavours to rescue and affirm the value of tribal and indigenous cultures and languages, to deal with tribal and indigenous demands for territory and to legitimate indigenous and tribal representativeness in political disputes. In this context of "reinvention of culture", to borrow an expression from Roy Wagner (1981), a process that calls our attention, on account of its importance in public debate and as a good point to illustrate our argument, concerns the educational institutionalization of indigenous peoples and tribal communities.

The relationship of indigenous peoples with the Brazilian state—or with the "whites", as the non-indigenous are usually called in Brazilian ethnology—has been qualified by disrespect and violence towards their ways of living, as part and parcel of a more comprehensive colonizing enterprise in other parts of the globe as well. In Brazil it is esteemed that before the arrival of the Portuguese colonizers in the 15th century there were between 3.5 to 6.0 million indigenous peoples (Denevan, 1992)[2] scattered in the whole national territory. Today, indigenous groups count a little over than eight hundred thousand people. During the 20th century, specially in the 1970s, when the future of the indigenous peoples became a topic in the public debate of the country, the disappearance of these populations was even cogitated as an irremediable fact. Nevertheless, in the last thirty years, demographic data have in fact shown a steady increase in the number of these peoples[3] who, though they represent only 0.4 per cent of the whole Brazilian population, possess a great cultural diversity spread in two hundred and forty six different peoples, and one hundred and eighty different languages.

It is also possible to affirm, without incurring in an exacerbated optimism, that indigenous peoples have so far not only *not* disappeared, but also have succeeded in organizing themselves in different social movements that have had a strong influence on the elaboration of the Brazilian Constitutional Law of 1988. By this Constitution, called by some as "Citizen Constitution", indigenous peoples in Brazil have succeeded in obtaining both the legal recognition of their original territories, as well as the right to a differentiated education that is attentive to their ways of living and social organization. According to the official documents that establish the "Directives for a National Policy of Indigenous Education" (MEC, 1994), indigenous schools should be planned in view of the particularities of each people or community, devising methods and pedagogical materials different from those of conventional schooling so that it is possible to teach and develop mother indigenous languages. These principles express thus a novel perspective on the relationship between the state and the indigenous peoples that is not based, at least formally, in the attempt to assimilate and incorporate the indigenous peoples into the national society, but to recognize them as a cultural alterity and seek to respect their social organization, languages, customs, beliefs and traditions.

Despite its promising rhetoric, there is still a great distance between legal dispositions and the concrete reality of indigenous peoples in Brazil. In order to have a more realistic dimension of the schooling situation of the indigenous peoples, it is necessary to analyse the extensive ethnographic work dedicated to this topic that allows us to establish an interesting comparison between the Brazilian and the Indian contexts. In general, the overall issue—that very much relates to the concern with the concept of culture that we mentioned earlier—consists of interrogating about whether the school as a social space meant to support the cultural transmission processes of Western societies can be changed to serve the process of cultural transmission of indigenous cultures.

Cohn's (2004) analysis of an experience of schooled learning in a Xikrin village, indigenous people in the North of Brazil, questions whether and how it would be possible to accommodate "an indigenous education" with "an indigenous school education". The Xikrin understand, differently from the "whites", that learning is something that takes place in every moment of life and that it involves the teaching of a specific repertoire of behaviours associated with each learning situation. Respect (*pia'am*) consists of a central aspect of the adult-child teaching for Xikrin people, since it entails the necessary silence and humility before those who teach, the elders. The question then is how to incorporate such an important aspect of a schooling educational project insofar as the latter demands that indigenous children actively participate in learning (for instance, responding and making questions, something which is in conflict with the notion of respect—*pia'am*). In this sense, there are challenges to be faced in the project of an indigenous school education.

The insightful contribution of Professor Behera (2003) on the process of educational institutionalization of tribal children in Orissa, India, poses this challenge in still more concrete terms alongside his detailed and acute ethnography of the daily life in *Ashram* schools. His main argument points to the fact that this institutionalized educational process positions children between two cultures, the tribal and the modern westernized one, as the school does not seem receptive to native experience and values. Differently from the tribal context where learning takes place through the transmission of familial traditions and alongside the daily activities of social and material reproduction, the process of educational institutionalization is confined within a specific institution separated from the village and the family and directed at the disciplinarization of child bodies and the time of childhood.

Although situated quite far away from Orissa, the ethnographic work of Benites (2013) on the indigenous school education of the people Ava Kaiowá, inhabitants in the Centre of Brazil, also points to this tension between education in the community and education at school. The social and territorial organization of the Kaiowá people is based on extended families which are kin groups relatively autonomous linked by relationships of affinity, mostly consanguinity. These groups possess a unique history and tradition that is considered a valuable heritage to be transmitted to the younger ones, in order to perpetuate the indigenous way of good living (*teko vy'a*). Children's education is centred on the figure of the grandmother, taking place at different social spaces, but mainly through domestic work, play, and ritual situations (sacred and profane). It is noteworthy that, similar to those tribal contexts studied by Behera (2003), the processes of learning, socialization and value transmission of these indigenous children are not exclusive to a single institution but cut across all daily activities.

As we have remarked before, despite institutionally legal dispositions in Brazil to assure a differentiated education to indigenous peoples, ethnographic work (Benites, 2012) has shown how in the real context of village schools indigenous education remains controlled by Christian missionary organizations in which a civilizing and assimilationist perspective prevails. The loss of control over the educational process by the family and the imposition of values and educational syllabus completely decontextualized from their own are frequent complaints of the Kaiowá people in relation to these schools. This distance between family and school is also remarked by Behera (2003), who indicates the need for a reorganization of the division of labour in tribal communities as children have to attend school and be absent from their homes.

Behera (2003) not only draws attention to the fact that as tribal children have to leave for school they have to separate themselves from their family and their native territory, but also to the problematic meaning of the future that this educational institutionalization process allows them to construct. Behera emphatically affirms that from children's point of view (and sometimes also parents') school teaching in *Ashram* schools does not allow them to draw plans for the future. As he describes, school curricula are meant and serve the purposes, demands and values of urban modern societies, and not to what is valued in local communities. Chemistry, physics, geometry and geography are taught instead of hunting, agriculture, ethnomedicine and fishing. Furthermore, the process of learning is seriously jeopardised as teachers do not speak the native languages of their pupils frequently imposing their own language which children do not understand.

Such an intergenerational relationship between students and teachers is thus problematized by Behera's ethnographic work (2003). The teachers in *Ashram* schools come from a non-tribal context; they not only do not speak their students' native languages, but also demonstrate a negative judgement towards their customs and traditions. As teaching is often a secondary activity for these adults, their dedication to the task becomes fragile weakening interpersonal relationships with children. In an engaged and committed attitude towards children's well-being, Behera notes that abuses are sometimes committed by adults in these schools, such as attributing to students their own (teachers') domestic labour, deviating school material and applying too severe punishments for students' trifle errors.

As he analyses the institutional arrangement of these schools based on an extremely rigid routine, bad conditions of hygiene, housing and eating, an excessive workload undertaken by students, and above all, an evident incompatibility of the school ethos with the values held by the tribal peoples, Behera (2003) criticizes the colonial and authoritarian dimension in the process of educational institutionalization of tribal children: ".... why should tribal children today be exposed to an educational system that was devised one hundred years ago in Victorian colonial times and is thoroughly authoritarian?" (Behera, 2003:191). After students have passed through their educational years, which is supposed to offer them perspectives and possibilities of social mobility, these youth return definitely to their communities as they cannot find well paid urban employment. Above all, they are subjectively divided, or as Behera puts it, they are positioned "in between two cultures, the civitas and the tribal".

Despite the fact that indigenous school education can be criticized to contain a colonial dimension, both Cohn (2004) and Benites (2012) suggest that there may exist an indigenous interest in these new spaces of learning, the schools, in the Brazilian context. This interest, apparently paradoxical, reveals that though indigenous peoples may have quite distinct values and modes of living from the urban middle classes, they consider that the mediation and contact with the world of the "whites" is necessary for their own survival and for the reproduction of their peoples and cultures. To be able to use certain codes and languages, specially written language (for the Kaiowá people, the "language of the paper") propitiated by school learning, is regarded as a possibility to negotiate with a world characterized by the logic of laws, propriety and contract. These populations which have been historically marginalized from public decision processes, see in school learning the possibility that their children can inhabit these two worlds, the indigenous/tribal and the civitas, in view of safeguarding their recently obtained position of rights holders.

The issue at stake here, which is directly related to the discussion of the concept of culture as suggested earlier, is whether such a mediation can be possible. As schools are generally organized as an institution modelled after the Westernized modern project as far as transmission and socialization are concerned, how is it possible to conceive it as a locus of transmission of cultures that do not necessarily organize their knowledge and traditions in a corpus to be transmitted by a specific institution? This question, raised here with the intention to provoke discussion, leads us to our initial concern: the idea of culture forwards similarities and differences once it maps out differences between distinct social groups. These relationships thus produced find expression in the case of the educational institutionalization of tribal and indigenous peoples. For indigenous/tribal peoples, the demand of schooling brings about an impasse of two quite incompatible world visions, one related to their own indigenous/tribal education and the indigenous/tribal school education. To adhere to the latter can mean the distancing, and even the rejection, of their original cultural values and also the appropriation of a system of thought and values that is alien to their own origin.

As insightfully notes Behera (2003), to be between two cultures leads to social and subjective sensitive issues, even in face of the fact that the relationship between "modern" and "primitive" groups today is less asymmetrical than used to be a few decades ago. Indigenous and tribal peoples have struggled bravely and resisted to "disappear" or, to "become whites". Considering that the educational institutionalization of indigenous and tribal peoples may hinge on aseemingly insoluble problem today, it seems at least necessary to recognize the singularity of the processes whereby these tribal peoples learn and teach to make the case for what can be named as an indigenous/tribal pedagogy.

THE VULNERABILITY AND THE MARGINALIZATION OF CHILDREN: NAVIGATING BETWEEN INDIA AND BRAZIL

The issue of the vulnerability and the marginalization of the child is at once associated with the acknowledgement of the legal status of children as 'minors' before the law. As such, children are considered to be not yet full human beings capable of independent choice and decision-making. Their vulnerability stands for their not fully developed cognitive and moral capacities, which seems to legitimate social and cultural practices of protection and regulated participation in social life (Kulynych, 2001). The reality thus created by legal dispositions is mainly subsidised by a gamut of psychological theories which, along the 20th century, have produced a theory of the human subject as a developing being, born under-socialized and immature, whose lifelong trajectory will lead him or her to maturity and psychological completion. 'Developmentalism', as a widely diffused scientific paradigm, has contributed to ground the repertoire of juridical and cultural representations and practices about children's lesser capacities and restricted involvement as co-partners in the construction of the social world (James & Prout, 1990).

The taken-for-granted truth of children's vulnerability confers an essentialized nature to children, one which inescapably positions children as inferiors as regards to their elders on whom they must depend, trust and be subordinated to. However, a more critical outlook on children's vulnerability should interrogate about its conditions of possibility, that is, how is it that children are vulnerable? Or, what are the historical, cultural and political conditions which are responsible to produce children's vulnerability? Therefore, the issue of vulnerability as a moral and psychological condition of the human (child) subject should entail a more analytical perspective conducive to a less simplistic understanding of its process (= when and how one becomes vulnerable), its cultural and political underpinnings (=what are the conditions which produce vulnerability) and its mode of subjectivization (=who are those that become significantly vulnerable).

We take Deepak Behera's rich scholarship on children's vulnerability and marginalization as an insightful approach to tackle this issue in view of deconstructing the regime of truth that has been consolidated about children and childhood. Furthermore, we take this opportunity to establish a dialogue between Behera's contributions and Brazilian scholars concerning the issue of vulnerability and marginalization of children.

Children's vulnerability and marginalization have been two important themes in Behera's scholarly contributions in the area of child studies. His analytical perspective is deeply entrenched in his view of children as agents and co-partners in the social construction of the world we live in (Behera & Trawick, 2001). This may sound today as quite a well-established idea espoused by child researchers all-over the world emulated by the ideals set by international conventions on the rights of the child (Cohen, 1996). Accordingly, the acknowledgement of the equal worth of the child *vis-à-vis* her adult counterpart represents a paradigmatic shift in the way modern societies have come to consider children and their social presence. However, as pointed out by Behera and Pramanik (2012), "this treaty can at the most be regarded as a provisional result" (p. 80). Rather than considering the sufficiency of legal dispositions, the authors underline their instrumental value in terms of bringing about new social practices and altering customs and traditions. After all, it is the latter which proves crucial in determining children's position and well-being. Significantly, thus, stands the authors' observation that legal frameworks can have small impact on the practices they are meant to regulate and change, and in this case, the status of equal worth legally prescribed to children mostly represents an abstract norm rather than an enforced reality. If representations about children's moral and legal positions seem resilient to top-down definitions of their worth, dignity and competence, one should examine how other concurrent definitions are produced in daily social interactions between children and their elders. Through the ethnographer's labour of bringing out the tensions, contradictions and conflicts in the daily lives of children, it may be possible to extricate the views that inform how relationships between adults and children are constructed and which values and normative ideas they tend to affirm.

Children's social lives in schools have been a significant dimension of Behera's vast ethnographical work. If children have been granted new entitlements by recent legal dispositions, it is in schools, better than anywhere else, that one should look for the advances in conferring children their due worth: "There is no place, more suitable than school to show this respect", note Behera & Rashmi (2012:81). As a norm-bound institution, modelled by ideals, schools should incorporate new challenges resulting from the recent normative changes in children's legal status, so as to give them a place of genuine respect in disputes, conflicts, disciplinary measures, the examination system as well as in the participation of the school in general. Nevertheless, the authors' conclusions point that schools tend to reproduce certain deep-engrained beliefs that corroborate a highly hierarchical and authoritarian child-adult relationship based on the sole authority and power of the latter.

The plight of school children is that of being entrapped by a totalitarian system of oppression corroborated by both parents and school staff who are in unison in producing "over-burdened children" (Behera & Pramanik, 2012; Behera & Pramanik, 2001). It is this central concept in Behera & Coll.'s work that characterizes the process of producing vulnerability in children, not as an essentialized attribute of their supposed nature, but as the result of diverse social and cultural practices in which children are positioned. Two encompassing practices account for the production of "over-burdened children" in modern childhood in India: the overall competitiveness that qualifies adults' expectations and demands from children, and presides over the organization of all school activities; and, the unfair structure of power relationships that dominate child-adult relationships in the school and the family contexts.

Diverse ethnographic studies conducted by Behera and Collaborators have highlighted the pervasiveness of competition as a cherished value held by parents who want to make their children "achievers and performers" (2012:87), despite whatever emotional and existential costs this might engender. For children, complying with parental demands and expectations seems a must in face of other imminent negative consequences, such as disappointing them and losing their own self-esteem. On the other hand, teachers and school staff act in accordance with parents' wishes, "... Principals of the schools today have become like film producers. They give what the audience wants", affirm the authors (2012:86). Rote learning, a huge academic overload and a child unfriendly atmosphere altogether are used to instil in children the idea that the only possible alternative left is compliance with the elders' expectations even if this might mean giving up their own personal projects and dreams and experiencing school learning as a pointless and irrelevant activity. The ideological legitimation for such an endeavour is made under the plea of "the best interests of the students". Although negotiation, resistance and non-compliance do occur, children are left with little scope for altering this oppressive context in view of yet another element that concurs to consolidate the social imaginary that there is no way out: discipline and physical and psychological punishment.

Behera and Pramanik state that "...Traditionally in our society, children are viewed as the property of their parents" (2012:89) which already positions children as dependent on authority figures, seen as knowledgeable and omnipotent individuals. Physical punishment, as well as humiliation, stands as an acceptable way to persuade children to acquiesce to adults' demands, at home or at school. As noted by the authors, "it was observed that some teachers punish the students on a regular basis. It appears as if giving punishment has become their habits" (2012:87). The authorised and legitimated position of adults to act as the sole arbiter over a child's behaviours structures the position from where children can act and respond in their social relationships with adults. The taken-for-granted truth of adults' omnipotence entails the impotence of children, their *vulnerability,* as an effect of a mutual understanding of the lesser position of the child and her limited possibilities of action. Thus, the projected surplus of power and knowledge on the adult's figure simultaneously implies the imagined frailty of the children's, an already given décalage that fixes the latter in a condition of impairment and vulnerability. Children's resentment, fear and psychological breakdown seem to be other side effects of such a structuring of child-adult relationships, also to be found in other social relationships of oppression and domination (Scott, 1990).

"Over-burdened children" understood as an iconic expression of a complex process of producing acquiescent, fearful and vulnerable children interrogate the legitimacy of the sovereign rule of adults over them. Acting on behalf of children and in their best interests can lead, as Behera *et al.* have shown, to claim what is not defensible: the silencing of subjects and their moral and psychological degradation. Furthermore, it is argued that what seems important—children's zest and enthusiasm for learning—

is lost along the educational process meant to foster only ambition, competitiveness and a non-compassionate self. One can wonder how these cognitive and moral choices can serve a democratic society much in need of human capabilities such as solidarity, cooperation and compassion (Young, 2002).

Besides the ills inflicted to children and the creation of dubious conditions for self-realization, Behera & Pramanik remark on the cultural inadequacy of the present educational system in India. They ask: "Why Indian students have to be exposed to an educational system invented over a hundred years ago, in colonial India, that is wholly authoritarian?" (2001:172). We would add, why is it that southern colonized countries seem so reluctant to re-invent their present and futures? In a way, the sovereign position of Europe and North America in dictating what development or education consist of seems to be reproduced alongside intergenerational lines, adults dictating what children should do in the name of their best interests. The authors argue then for a more culturally sensitive way of reinventing the intergenerational tie, instead of maintaining the one originated in colonial India characterised by its harshness and authoritarianism. We quote the authors at length: "It is necessary to invent pedagogical methods not based on competition as the main motivational factor which leads to self-realization… […] if a child is raised in a non-competitive context, she has more chance to attain success even in a competitive world. The fact of not being the first does not break her down emotionally. Thus, she can be more successful. If she is more successful, she can do it at her own pace, with a healthy understanding of others. She is not devoured by anxieties of comparison with others and competition…. The understanding and the acceptance of one's own and others' talents is something that is worth cultivating. Cooperation with others contributes to harmony within oneself and in relationships with others" (2001:173). Thus, this cautionary observation points to the fallacy embedded in the prevalent ideal of competitiveness which from very early takes hold of children's lives. For Behera, educational practices informed by such a perspective can only bring about worn-out and overburdened children incapable of loving learning and self-defeated, very much like the plight of modern adults under unattainable demands described by Ehrenberg (2010).

In what follows we try to establish a dialogue between Behera's seminal concept of children's vulnerability, understood as the production of a structure of practices and norms, that seem to go unquestioned under the legitimacy of the ideology of the best interests of the child, a naturalised power structure between adults and children, and an oblivious adhesion to an ethos of competitiveness in social relations.

Brazilian scholarship echoes Behera's views on children's overburden (Castro, 2014) understood as a process constituted in social relationships between children and adults. However, the context of production of vulnerability is mainly located within structural social inequalities which positions children, specially those of the lower classes, in the least favourable place to negotiate a better off deal for themselves. Vulnerability, or as it is often referred to in Brazilian literature (Janczura, 2012), concerns "social vulnerability" part and parcel of the social issues and contradictions originated under the capitalist mode of production which tend to deepen social differences and legitimate them under the guise of inherent natural differences among individuals and social groups. Studies of social vulnerability focus on the social violence inflicted on some groups of children that, despite their legal rights concerning basic education, health and provision, are left to their own (ill) fate to respond to social demands and aspirations of self-realization.

The promulgation of the Statute of Children and Adolescents in Brazil in 1990 (Brazil, 1990), following a period of intense public debates, contributed to a reconfiguration of discourses and issues concerning poor and abandoned children (Castro & Kosminsky, 2010), whose fate was often criminalized and institutionalized. The main thrust of the Statute consisted in promoting a significant detour from an elitist image of 'the child', based on the habitus of the upper classes, to encompass under the categorization of children and adolescents all of those under the age of 18. Thus, a reordering of the social imaginary was forwarded firmly established on clear-cut State and society's obligations towards children under this new legislature. Despite many advances in this respect, as cautioned earlier by Behera & Pramanik (2012), laws do not change social practices only by decree. If criminalization and institutionalization of poor children came to be under scrutiny, or yet, outlawed procedures, universal rights to education, health, provision and leisure have not become so far cherished values and unquestioned prerogatives for all children, irrespective of their social class, gender and ethnic origin.

The new legislature made special provision for those children who, on account of their social and ethnic condition, suffer more adversities and disadvantages. Risky social conditions have comprehended a gamut of situations: from abandoned children to school drop-outs, from ill-fed or undernourished children to drug-addicted adolescents, all of them demanding from the state specific public policies and welfare programmes. Therefore, two main tenets emerge out of the recent configuration of social issues concerning poor children in Brazil: they are expressed in the notions of social risk and children's pro-activism (CNPD, 1998). The former assumes implicitly that children in these situations may fare less successfully if not granted with special provision from the state (ironically enough, the state claims to grant special provision when it has not been able to grant children with their basic universal rights). The latter regards children as necessarily motivated and driven to change their situation in the direction of a more universal norm of childhood based on middle class habitus and ideals. Once these expectations concerning these children fail, the understanding of what constitutes social risk approximates that of a social problem. From being looked after in a special way these children can be looked as potential social problems whose remedial treatment is often institutionalization and criminalization (Teles, 2008). Therefore, the notion of social vulnerability produced in the context of the new legal arrangements of the 1990s in Brazil faces challenges concerning these novel forms of marginalizing children even if the present context seems more aware of their plight offering them more legal provision and protection.

Brazilian scholarship on the social vulnerability of children articulates the notions of social risk and public policies in order to access and evaluate how conditions of poverty and social disadvantage *disable* children from their own aspirations of self-realization and social dignity. It is important to note that such a scholarship has often highlighted the multiple and severe shortcomings of recent public policies which have been implemented to counter the effects of social risk in childhood (Paiva *et al.*, 2013). As such, social vulnerability has remained a perverse effect of structural adversities that, though understood in light of determining social conditions rather than of inherent deficiencies of individuals, have jeopardised the plight of many Brazilian children to this day.

Final Considerations

The closing of the present contribution on the notions of culture, vulnerability and marginalization for a volume that celebrates and honours the life and academic trajectory of Professor Deepak Kumar Behera could not but refer, even if briefly, the relevant implications between anthropological research and academic engagement. As we noted earlier, in an academic world regulated by the imperatives of social competitiveness, individualism and efficiency, the distinct commitment of Professor Behera to his values and beliefs is of paramount importance, as it makes it possible to sensitize society with respect to the wider political implications of issues, such as tribal children's education and children's overburden in schools.

Professor Behera's dedication to the study of childhood and tribal peoples has brought to light not only significant empirical and analytical contributions to the humanities, but also has stimulated and widened public debate on the participation of children and tribal peoples in the decision-processes of public life. His work has made it possible, as many are already aware of, the reclassification of tribal communities from "Primitive Tribal Groups" to "Particularly Vulnerable Tribal Groups", altering the pejorative colonial connotation of the former. This fact, adding up to many others of his extensive and engaged career as a social scientist and researcher, expresses what Asad (1973) affirms about social research as an enterprise committed to knowing about the world *and,* most importantly, being affected by it.

It is in the bosom of our relationship with the world that social research takes place, positioning thus ethnography and field-work as privileged places from which to establish a more proximate contact between the researcher and his or her object, and a research frame that goes beyond the structural and formal categories of knowledge. In this chapter, we have discussed how legal dispositions, such as the Directives for a National Policy of Indigenous Education in Brazil (Brazil, 1994), and the Brazilian Statute of Child and Adolescent (Brazil, 1990), despite the significant social advances they forwarded, have so far neither conduced to a more effective participation of children in their intergenerational contexts, nor a greater respect for tribal cultures in the process of educational institutionalization.

Both the discussions brought forth by Professor Behera, as well as those proposed by Brazilian researchers, have succeeded in revealing the challenges to conciliate a "tribal/indigenous education" with a "tribal/indigenous school education". The separation of the family, the asymmetrical relationship with teachers, the extenuating routine of study and work and the disrespect for the mother language of the students are a few, out of many aspects, which point to the difficulties for indigenous and tribal peoples to make use of an institution whose origin is alien to their worldview and traditions. What ethnographic work is able to demonstrate is that to effectively evaluate the present situation of tribal education, be in India or in Brazil, empirical studies are necessary to investigate how social relationships are constructed in these social spaces under the impact (or not) of those legal dispositions and state policies.

Likewise, as we examine the notions of vulnerability and marginalization in childhood in interlocution with Professor Behera's contribution, we are led to affirm that they are the product of political, social and historical conditions, and not a natural attribute of children's subjective constitution. Vulnerability and marginalization are produced by, and interact with, other aspects, such as social inequalities. In the same way that tribal education as prescribed by legal dispositions is far from achieving its cherished educational ideals of diversity and equality, children's rights have not inspired different social and educational practices, neither have they changed the adult centric perspective of incapacity and submission attributed to children.

As the researcher critically evaluates his or her methodological and theoretical advantage point to analyse social issues, such as children's and tribal peoples' participation in public life, the social and political dimensions of scientific work are brought to light. If social research is directed at knowing about the world and being affected by it, the ideal of scientific neutrality must be problematized once (political) engagement becomes a constitutive part of the process of knowledge production. We understand engagement here not as an empathic and dedicated attitude of the researcher towards her or his object of study, but, more radically, as a repertoire of multiple responsibilities, affects and moralities that are implied in this devoted commitment.

This commitment, far from distancing the researcher to secure objectivity in his or her work, consists, in fact, in making it possible to gain a more insightful perspective of the wider and more complex net of relationships of one's object of study. This does not seem to be possible in the absence of a committed stance towards what we study, or of a more acute sensitivity to see beyond canonical procedures or established formulations. The radicalism of methodology as a political issue brings us to Gramsci (2000) for whom the research process also consists of a movement of self-constitution and inventory. Professor Behera's sensitive and committed ethnographic work is tinged with this radicalism once we apprehend in his contribution that the subject and the object of inquiry are never absolutely separated.

Notes

1. Throughout this chapter, we will make a distinction between the terms "tribal" and "indigenous" people, as the former is mainly associated with how these social groups are referred to in India and in Professor Behera's work, whereas the latter, in Brazilian anthropological scholarship.
2. These data are based on an estimation made by researchers grounded on archaeological findings and historiographical accounts of Portuguese travellers of the 16th century. They are not deemed exact precision and on that account are object of dispute among anthropologists and researchers of indigenous issues.
3. The census of 1991, 2000 and 2010 have estimated respectively 292,131, 734,127 and 817,963 indigenous peoples living in urban and rural areas in Brazil. Without any doubt, the abrupt increase between 1991 and 2000 does not only represent a population increase, but also concerns an increase in the number of people declaring themselves as indigenous. For a lengthier discussion on the topic, *see* Oliveira, 1999.

References

Arendt, H. (2002). *O que é a política? Org. Ursula Ludz.* (3rd ed). Rio de Janeiro: Bertrand.

Asad, Talal. 1973. Introduction. In T. Asad (ed.), *Anthropology and the Colonial Encounter.* New York: Humanities, 9-19.

Behera, D.K. and Trawick, M. (2001). Children and Childhood in Metropolitan Cultures: An Introduction. *International Journal of Anthropology,* 16 (2-3), 57-64.

Behera, D.K. and Pramanik, R. (2001). A sobrecarga das crianças escolares: reflexes a partir de uma pequena cidade da India. Em L.R. de Castro (ed.), *Crianças e jovens na construção da cultura.* Rio de Janeiro: Nau/Faperj, 153-178.

Behera, D.K. (2003). In Between Two Cultures: The Porcess of Educational Institutionalization of Tribal Children in Orissa, India. In K. Malone (ed.), *Child Space: An Anthropological Exploration of Young People's Use of Space.* New Delhi: Concept Publishing Company (p) Ltd)., 178-192.

Behera, D.K. and Pfeffer, G. (2009). An Introduction in Behera, D.K. and Pfeffer, G. (eds.), *Contemporary Society: Tribal Studies. Vol.8, Structure and Exchange in Tribal India and Beyond.* New Delhi: Concept Publishing Company (P) Ltd., ix-xvi.

Behera, D.K. and Pramanik, R. (2012). School Children Negotiating Space and Time in Eastern India. *The Oriental Anthropologist,* 12 (1), 79-95.

Benites, T. (2012). *A escola na ótica dos Ava Kaiowá.* Rio de Janeiro: ContraCapa.

Brazil/1990. *Estatuto da Criança e do Adolescente.* Brasilia: Conselho Nacional dos Direitos da Criança e do Adolescente.

Brazil/1994. *Diretrizes Para a Política Nacional de Educação Indígena.* Brasília: Ministério da Educação.

Carneiro da Cunha, M. (2009). *Cultura com aspas e outros ensaios.* São Paulo: CosacNaify.

Castro, L.R. (2014). Challenges to Children's Autonomy in a Braziiian State School. *The Oriental Anthropologist,* 14(2), 237-250.

Castro, L.R. and Kosminsky, E. (2010). Childhood and its Regimes of Visibility: An Analysis of the Contribution of the Social Sciences. *Current Sociology,* XX (X), 1-26.

CNPD, 1998. *Jovens acontecendo nas trilhas das políticas públicas.* Brasília: CNPD.
Cohen, C. (1996). Children's Rights: The Changing International Legal Paradigm. In D.K. Behera and G. Pfeffer (eds.), *Childhood and Complex Order.* Delhi: Manak Publications. 113-131.

Cohn, C. (2004). Os processos próprios de ensino e aprendizagem e a escola indígena. *Cadernos de Educação Escolar Indígena—3o grau indígena,* (3)1, 94-111.

Denevan, W. (1992). Native American populations in 1492: recent research and revised hemispheric estimate in: Willian Denevan (ed.), *The Native Population of the Americas in 1492.* Madison: The University of Madison Press, xvii-xxx.

Ehrenberg, A. (2010). *O culto da performance.* São Paulo: Ideias e Letras.

Gramsci, A. (2000). *Cadernos de cárcere v.2.* São Paulo: Civilização Brasileira.

Jacoby, R. (1987). *The Last Intellectuals.* New York: Basic Books.

James, A. and Prout, A. (1990). *Constructing and Reconstructing Childhood: Contemporary Issues in the Sociological Study of Childhood.* London: The Falmer Press.

Janczura, R. (2012). Risco ou vulnerabilidade social? *Textos e Contextos,* 11(2), 301-308.

Kulynych, J. (2001). No Playing in the Public Sphere: Democratic Theory and the Exclusion of Children. *Social Theory and Practice,* 27, 231-264.

Oliveira, J.P. (org.). (1999). *A viagem de volta: etnicidade, política e reelaboração cultural no nordeste indígena.* Rio de Janeiro: ContraCapa.

Paiva, I., Bezerra, M., Silva, G., Nascimento, P. (2012). *Infância e juventude em contextos de vulnerabilidade e resistência.* São Paulo: Zagodoni.

Scott, J. (1990). *Domination and the Arts of Resistance.* New Haven: Yale University Press.

Teles, N. (2008) (ed.). *Um olhar sobre o jovem no Brasil.* Brasilia: Editora do Ministério da Saúde.

Wagner, R. (1981). *The Invention of Culture.* Chicago: University of Chicago Press.

Young, M. (2002). *Inclusion and Democracy.* Oxford: Oxford University Press.

TEN

INDIGENOUS KNOWLEDGE AND EMPOWERMENT AMONG *ADIVASIS* IN JHARKHAND

MARINE CARRIN

I propose to unravel the weave of *Adivasi* knowledge in Jharkhand (Central India) to show how they revolve around three dimensions, the emergence of an historical consciousness, the feeling of a shared identity related to language, and to culture and ecological diversity.

Adivasi societies in Central India have often developed a policy of resisting global, capital, savage and corrupt industrial exploitation.The Indian State legitimises its current policies for structural adjustment and liberalisation by promising economic growth for all; but this programme seem necessarily to entail for the rural poor the need for a different model of welfare. For activists and development agencies, sustainability has become inseparable from social equity. This ideology has resulted since two decades in activists trying to mobilize tribal groups for sustainable development (Baviskar, 1997). But *Adivasi* assertion has taken a different direction towards a kind of minority identity politics. I shall explore claims about the tribal relationship to nature by showing that these claims do not only concern tribal economy, but aim at redefining the role of Adivasis themselves in rethinking their world. For instance, they maintain "sacred groves" as religious emblems of indigenous knowledge. But, *Adivasi identities have been shaped by history. It would be wrong to streotype Adivas merely as forest people, though the sylvan surroundings in which they live have fostered creativity art and knowledge.These talents are reflected in Mundari songs, arts and crafts, in their work and thought as well as in different aspects of their life.* Besides, it is not by chance that current concern over biodiversity in a globalizing world has in many ways put hope in tribal practices which are regarded as sustainable. Yet, biodiversity also comes with the promise of a different lifestyle contrasting with the homogenized consumerism which dominates today's capitalist economy.

Indigenous knowledge has often been discussed mainly as folk-medicine and folklore: this perception is generally devoid of subjectivity, since tribals are perceived as subalterns and thus muted. I am trying to articulate *Adivasi* answers to exploitation and deprivation as indigenous knowledge taking into account *Adivasi* sense of history as well as their efforts for organizing their survival and representation. In privileging indigenous knowledge as a departure point, I argue that *Adivasi* societies are able to produce strategies of resistance, not simply in terms of protest, but also in forging new ideas.

Indigenous Knowledge as Resistance

During the colonial period, Mundari discourses have internalized the categories of domination in producing counter-hegemonic discourse, and as Guha (1983) has brilliantly shown, Santal rebels in 1855 also appropriated the symbols of the colonizers.

When we read G. Prakash' seminal essay "Science between the Lines" we understand that the study of the Indian archive involves the analysis of colonialism in culture, as "modernity eclipsed little knowledge and empowered an elite that enunciated the discourse of science" (1996:58). But has indigenous knowledge really been eclipsed? If not, what is an indigenous theory? Indigenous knowledge as local knowledge tries to aggregate and unify experience into a whole that can be perceived, shared and transmitted as *Adivasi* sensitivity.

On the basis of reinvention of Adivasi *pasts, I shall show through littérature and diverse forms of commemorations, how indigenous tribal groups in Jharkhand and Orissa have succeeded in staging various politics to adress the State while articulating their claims as cultural and political rights. For example, in Jharkhand, mass mobilization during hunting has become a way to adress political and economic claims on the Forest Departement and the Police. In these cases, the confident use of 'culture' reminds us of Sahlins'* (1999) *concept of culturalism which links cultural identity to the reformulation of rights. But, while Adivasi societies try to assert their identities by claiming access to collective rights and resources, the modern liberal State, which is premised on individual rights, fails to find adequate responses to group claims.*"

Sarna Religion in Jharkhand

The State of Jharkhand, founded in 2000 as a 'tribal' state, with the Munda, Santal, Ho and Oraon as the largest tribal populations, has a Hindu majority, due to immigration from the plains. Muslim, Christian, Sikh came since the mediaeval period with the result of alienating the tribal lands and making a new landlord and moneylenders class emerge. The forms of social organization are varied depending on the size and scale of the population: small bands of food gatherers can be contrasted to larger tribes of settled agriculturists such as the Munda and the Ho, which have produced chiefdoms and kingdoms. Even on the same scale of political organization under chiefs, more or less included in the participation of modern village councils, we find many kinds of variations: matrilineal or patrilineal kinship organization, rules of residence, succession and inheritance as well as variations concerning the position of women, the transmission of knowledge and skills between the age groups and the various types of religious specialists.

Today, most *Adivasis* in Jharkhand do not agree with the view they were backward Hindus in the past, as stated by sociologist Ghurye (1943) and reiterated by Bose (1967) who explained the Hindu model of tribal absorption resulting in tribal communities becoming underprivileged and marginalized communities. If this picture was observed during the post-Independance period until the 1960s, it has changed radically in the 1970s. under the influence of tribal movements which found a political resonance in the Jharkhand Party. Since the 1970s, most *Adivasis* groups tried to assert their identities though some of them chose to become Christians. Yet we observed a return to paradigms of religious indigeneity, such as a special attachment of tribal groups to the land, clan organization, double priesthood, old kingdoms and ancestors cults. It was no more question to imitate the religious practices of the Hindus, a trend known as sanskritization (M.N. Srinivas, 1967), but to find a religious identity common to the *Adivasis* under the banner of the Jharkhand Party.

The identity crisis has led the tribals, often called animist by others, to use the word Sarna for their religion. Sarna, the sacred grove, is a piece of virgin forest left untouched when the village was founded. Felling its trees is taboo. In this reinvented religion, the supreme being is seen as self-created, omniscient, and the source of life. He is often called Dhorom, or Dharmo. Other important concepts are *buru* and *bonga.* The two are often joined, *bonga* being a gloss of *buru*. *Buru* is a hill, where sacrifice is often performed: *Buru bonga* denotes one of the village spirits. *Maran Buru,* the chief deity worshipped by the Santals, means "Big Mountain". *Sin* (tree) *Bonga* is one of the main deities worshipped in the Sarna. Village rituals represent the cosmic order, as well as the agricultural cycle and its associated taboos. The Flower festival, *Baha bonga* for the Santal, *Sarhul* for the Munda, the Oraon and the Kharia, celebrates the blooming of the *mohua* flowers and the ripening of the first fruits, associated with fertility and the ancestors. *Baha* focuses on the possession of three young men, who go to the forest to pluck the flowers, associated with *Maran Buru,* Jaher Era (the guardian of the sacred grove), and their five sons. When the youngsters return to the Jaher with the flowers, they bring a necklace and a bow and arrow, emblems of the Jaher deities. The village priest questions them as oracles, and they predict the crops. The priest presents the flowers, representing fecundity, to the married village women. The flowers provoke possession, as does the alcohol made from them. During Baha, the priest dedicates sacrificial animals to the Sarna bongas, and offers rice-beer libations to the possessed youngsters, then to the older men and women. The men cook the sacrificial meat, shared by all.

Women are excluded from sacrifice and possession. In most Mundari groups, they are banned from ploughing, but they transplant paddi and "marry" the seedlings. Thus women, like ancestors, participate in the renewal of the lineage. While ancestors fix the breath associated with bone symbolizing the lineage, the women fix the soul of the paddy. Here, fecundity and transplantation merge symbolically, mediated by flower and uterus (*Baha*) (Carrin, 1986). Sohrae is the Santal cattle festival where cows are worshipped. Here, the Santal express ideas of ritual space, as the assistant priest sacrifices some of his blood to *bonga* dwelling at boundaries. Among the Santal, the Munda and the Ho this sacrifice marks the frontier between the village and the forest. The three festivals of Baha or Sarhul, and Sohrae and condense the essential religious preoccupations of the Mundari groups. They underline the passage from shifting cultivation with hunting and gathering, to settled agriculture with cattle. Mundari groups also worship Hinduized deities such as the Karam tree, associated with purity and asceticism, as well as different kinds of village boundaries.

The *Adivasi* as an Intellectual

In a previous work (Carrin, 2017) I have explored how *Adivasi* intellectuals emerged and how they have contributed to the making of indigenous knowledge. I shall briefly evoke how the colonial transformations affected the discourse of the tribal leaders who claimed a history and culture for their own group.

Santal oral knowledge is producing its own devices, such as rhetoric and analogical reasoning, to sustain indigenous theories of knowledge which, of course, have been influenced by the ideology of writing. The Scandinavian missionaries, who arrived in 1867, taught roman script to their Santal collaborators, who travelled about the villages and collected stories, dictated to them by a vast number of informants (Carrin and Tambs-Lyche, 2008). Here, we have examples of Santal writing since the eighteen-nineties, which offer a testimony of the social and cultural changes. We see, here, how indigeneity was constructed by the *Adivasi* themselves around different figures, such as rebels, prophets and *gurus* which emerged in the second part of the nineteenth century.

Later, the *Adivasi* elites allied themselves to missions to use legal channels in their resistance to exploitation (Carrin, 2009). The process of class formation and the development of *Adivasi* elites, which started at the beginning of the twentieth century, accelerated from about the time of First World War. In the thirties, Ragunath Murmu, a Santal teacher, reacting against the idea of writing Santali in different Indian scripts, invented a new alphabet, the signs which were motivated by ideo grammatical elements, but arranged alphabetically. Murmu argued that his script was phonetically more coherent and expressed *Adivasi* sensitivity rooted in daily experience thus defining a new kind of knowledge. Each symbol had a meaning and the symbols correspond to the pronounced sounds. They evoke "the sign language of branches" which is used during a hunt. The new script was then used to print the first newspapers, which were read by Santals living in other States.

The introduction of writing had the effect of pointing native thinkers in new directions of effort and creativity. In Jharkhand as well as in Orissa, the invention of Murmu's script in the thirties, and its implementation in the fifties, has allowed young generations to develop a new feeling of identity which has since developed in a large network of cultural associations operating in several states. But Murmu also started a religious movement, calling youth to teach the script and to perform in village theatre. Later, other young authors wrote dramas where they developed social themes. To some extent, the same schema developed among the Kharia, under the leadership of Pyara Master, and among the Ho under the inspiration of Lako Bodra. The Oraon, also having their own script have not achieved the same diffusion of the script, while the invention of a script among the Sora was more a religious affair since the new script did not develop in a literature. Still, indigenous script represent a kind of code which defines indigenous knowledge, sensitivity and religiosity.

This kind of knowledge is conveyed among the Santals through discursive strategies aiming at representing Santal identity. The same argument could be applied to the Ho and the Kharias, who, parallel to the Santal, had prophets and *gurus* reinventing their identity. The case of the Mundas is slightly different since they were not dispossessed of their lands and participated in state formation when the king (*raja*) of Chotanagpur was himself a Munda. These *gurus* were also social reformers and they often established schools and cooperatives but, above all, their religious influence contributed to make *Adivasis* feel pride in their new knowledge. The introduction of writing probably allowed another texture of knowledge which emerged from the colonial encounter, the narrative (Carrin, 2015a). But writing, which circulated in a restricted way, did not obstruct oral expression. Comparing the Santal theory of language and their theory of history, I will assert that these bodies of knowledge have been systematized since the colonial period, or at least that the missionaries who have introduced writing among the Santals, have also tried to influence the process of learning (Carrin and Tambs-Lyche, 2008).Then prophets and *gurus* propose a new knowledge seen as *Adivasi* sensitivity, which could be shared by all, inducing new balance of power in *Adivasi* societies formerly dominated by chiefs and priests.

Indigenous Knowledge and Resistance

Among Mundari groups, indigenous knowledge cannot be reduced to a collection of folk-tales and religious texts, since social actors produce their own ways of reasoning. It is a situated knowledge in the sense of Lave and Wenger (1991), which results from a distinct system of transmission where different social actors (such as ancestors, grand parents, chiefs, priests and other figures of authority) mediate language devices, mythic and ritual elements as well as a body of rules governing exchanges between kin, contracts, privileges and inheritance. Though formerly, indigenous knowledge was not equally shared, today, it is appropriated by youth who call indigenous knowledge "ancestors' knowledge" to differentiate it from school (or government) knowledge (*sarkar bidia*). In remote villages, children are appreciative of indigenous knowledge stressing the protective role of the village priest, while other youth, living closer to cities like Jamshedpur, are praising a new kind of knowledge, informed by the history of labour and claims for *Adivasi* rights (Carrin, 2016).[1]

Later on with the formation of the Jharkhand Party by Jaipal Singh, an Oxford educated Munda, in 1950, these differences became less important, though the Jharkhand Party as a symbolic and cultural matrix was able to encode new meanings and became capable of rallying different forms of protest. The political discourse which was developed by the Jharkhand Party involved a difficult compromise between the idea that indigenous people had rights over the land and that they also represented indigenous knowledge and wisdom. These ideas have contributed to create the political space of Jharkhand where *Adivasi* populations have been emotionally invested in asserting their identity.

Reinforcement of Traditional Authority

The Santal, as opposed to the "western individual", seem not to put forward an ideology of "rationality".They rather say that their behaviour is always guided by the voice of the ancestors, or the "custom" (*colon).* But thin should not lead us to underestimate the rationality of Santal thought. I have tried to identify situations where men and women were trying to evaluate their work and their decision-making processes. In other words, the Santals use practical reason in a perfectly rational manner in their daily routine, or even when they undertake some new task. But, for different reasons, their rational strategies may fail when they feel that the conditions of social justice and equity are not fulfilled. When discussing what kind of lessons to take from failures, the villagers feel they could achieve a certain control of technical knowledge but that social knowledge was more problematic.

While men discuss the difficulty of innovating in agriculture and cattle breeding, since they have to compete with the *outer* world, women succeed in being efficient in the *inner* world, the town market, where they mainly compete with other *Adivasi* communities. To succeed in having one's rights recognized is also very strenuous, since you have to go to some office and sign papers—but sometimes the papers which would identify your ownership over a piece of land have disappeared. You have to know your rights, but this is useful only if officers want to grant you your rights. This kind of statement refers to the corruption that villagers experience in daily life (Stuart Corbridge; S. Jewitt and S. Kumar, 2004: 17-54). Due to corruption, they say, social knowledge does not work properly. Then, "we cannot learn from this experience (*priyog*)". This is why ancestors' knowledge is the true knowledge, which implies to know what will happen after death. What is important is the capacity of vision (*nelnel*) which enables some priests to foretell the future (Carrin, 2018). Santal adults think that educated people lose this power of vision whenever they live in town and distance themselves from Nature.

Political Strategies

To-day, the Munda, the Santal and the Ho are promoting their traditional structures of Authority to avoid direct confrontation with the State administration, perceived as oppressive and corrupted. They launch grass-roots initiatives, trying to conciliate the traditional forms of self-government with political participation. These initiatives represent answers to the stigma *Adivasi* societies have internalized, since they seem to trust more their own leaders than non-*Adivasi* government representatives.

This search for a relative autonomy, through a revival of traditional leadership, does not exclude people from addressing government as in other parts of India. Jharkhand, then, offers a labyrinth of ideologies built on laws, religious movements and political forces such as the MCC (Maoist Communist Comity) which have even succeeded in pervading the market economy. In this context A. Shah (2007) defines Jharkhand State as a market of protection since protection is becoming a commodity which is controlled by the MCC, the Marxist Coordination Comity (MCC) and the People's War Group (PWG). The Hindu high castes, through the RSS, have equally become very active in the region, as well as on the Orissa border (Angana Chatterji, 2009).

The possibility for resistance exists, but has to follow some legal channels, which is not always possible since corruption prevails. In the last twenty years, with the emergence of tribal self-rule, assertions of right have found a new meaning. This has led to the reformulation of *gram sabha* which means a village assembly, which shall consist of all the adult members of a village including women, and implies an attempt to harmonize electoral rolls, seats, reservation of posts, keeping in mind that *Adivasis* have often been outraged and oppressed.

Let us note however, that the Recognition of Forest Rights of 2006 acknowledges some of the everyday violence that forest laws impose on *Adivasi* existence. The provisions of the Act take into account the different contexts in which forest dwellers live in the country as well as their relationship to the forest. The forest Act has allowed activists to move from development delivery to empowerment, and from planning to conscious participation. But in some states, the *Adivasi* village assemblies are being subverted by officials in order to favour the marketing of forest produce (such as bamboo or eucalyptus) with the backing of State Government, and against the interests of the *Adivasis*. Mining has been at the centre of the development debate since officials and middle class interest groups assert that the surest way to development is to intensify mining. *Adivasi* labour in mines has a long history, but the situation of the workers has greatly deteriorated both in terms of stability of employment and conditions of safety.

Reinventing Indigenous Knowledge

It is the shared feeling of loss which allows the present generations to imagine themselves as similar to the ancestors, a metaphor which does not imply that they control a finite corpus of knowledge: rather, this corpus, layered with indigenous theories, admits fragmentation and is reactivated from time to time by prophets who aim at redefining ruptures in order to re-enchant the world. Santal, Munda and Ho traditional structures of authority have been partly reinvented through the influence of religious movements—such as the *Sarna Dhorom*.

To-day, the "Return to the Sacred Grove" is known under different names in the different communities, but the phenomenon is always linked to séances of public possession where religious brotherhoods celebrate their own rituals. Even so, this quest expresses the pan-tribal dimension of the Jharkhand movement, whose leaders organize "conferences" to imagine the hard core of a common tribal religion. They have redefined the meaning of the sacred grove, the emblem of the ancestors, symbolized by a grove of *sal*[2] trees, sheltering the stones that represent the tribal deities. Intertribal commissions of village priests have decreed the equivalence of certain religious festivals, as celebrated by different Mundari groups. The village chiefs have revived the village political system, insisting on the importance of the council of intertribal hunts, which traditionally allowed everyone, irrespective of ethnic origin, to appeal to the "judgement of the burnt forest". More recently, the construction of custom, such as cults inspired by ecological movements, have become part of the subtle process of reinvention of tradition.

Performing Indigeneity

The Logo Buru festival, held in the first week of November, has both a cultural and a political meaning, since it includes dancing and singing as well as narrating the old myths. But simultaneously, the presence of the tribal leaders, including the then Chief Minister of Jharkhand, Sibu Soren, seems to convey that, "we are coming to thank the *Buru bongas* (mountain deities) for all we have achieved". We can look at the Logo Buru festival as the raising of the banner of indigeneity, while participants want both to renew with the ancestors and to invent themselves as a new kind of citizens.

The notion of performance, embedded here in a ritual context, means that 'performativity', as a mode of bodily or vocal action, is demarcated from quotidian interaction and defined by communicative intent (Hughes-Freeland, 1998; Schieffelin, 1998). For most Santals, the pilgrimage works to revive the sense of belonging to a sacred landscape, seen as a "pristine place", untouched by development, and this is particularly important for those who work in mines or in the steel plants of Jamshedpur, Rourkela or Bokaro. For the Santals who come from other states, the performance gives them the opportunity to share the revival of a tradition which is strong in Jharkhand, since it is linked to the politics of the State. Without describing the whole pilgrimage, I shall present one of its main sequences which epitomizes what we could call the Santal version of *Adivasi* consciousness of history.

Pilgrims walk towards Logo Buru cave which is located on the top of the hill. They should arrive at the top of the hill before the night, as—many informants stressed—it is important to watch the sunset on the cave of Logo Buru. This cave stands for the mythic Harata cave, where the Santal ancestors are said to have stayed seven years.

The night is spent in singing and dancing, while people cook the food they have brought. Young Santals play the flute and violin, and some young men decorate their heads with peacock feathers, as they do for the traditional hunt. The next morning, the Chief Minister, followed by other officials, enter the cave one by one. They peep through a hole which allows them to contemplate Cae Champa, the old Santal Kingdom. Some participants say that the image is rather like a wrecked ship at sea, while others see only a dark hole. The leaders are followed by the ordinary people (Carrin, 2015b).

The pilgrimage enables laymen, politicians, and writers to share the contemplation of a mythical kingdom, whose paradoxical existence nobody can localize on a map or fix in time. It allows mutual recognition of a common culture, but also invites the participants to share the luring experience of the loss of Cae Campa. Since the past cannot be seen, it is an enigma, unless its mirror effect is imagined through the evocative device of the cave. Some pilgrims who peep into the cave say "they have not been able to perceive the truth" while others state that "they have understood better the meaning of the loss." All, however, enjoy the place. While this is going on, the activists of the indigenous Santal script, ol'chiki, do a *puja* of burning incense sticks before the image of Ragunath Murmu, the inventor of the script and to other *Adivasi* heroes.

Nobody knows for sure when this pilgrimage started, but these last years, Santal writers and intellectuals have been very active in the organization of the performance. I always had the feeling that it was important to consider the pilgrimage as an old practice, though I am sure it did not exist when I started my fieldwork in the seventies. Answering my question with a sibylline smile, Digambara Hasdak, a Santal linguist, commented: "In Logo Buru, we try to forget the present time to come closer to our ancestors.Take Logo Buru as the image of the past encapsulated in a pristine place". Obviously the pilgrimage, like many pieces of Santal literature, worked in the minds of some informants as a means to experience truth, revealed by the contemplation of the cave.

Conclusion

Indigenous knowledge is defined as a bundle of emotions (*rasa*) influenced by the seasons and the memories of places—even if it does not exclude "some thinking". Experiencing the loss is a way to revive the image of the ancestors who were wandering from place to place in a landscape not yet destroyed by mining or forest exploitation. During the pilgrimage to Logo Buru Santal and other *Adivasis* enjoy singing, thus sharing emotions. Singing together allows them to forget awareness of differences among them. The pilgrimage to Logo Buru is organized by writers who often are retired employees who have been working in Jamshedpur. These writers have generally struggled against Companies and they often advise younger people about their right, but they also teach the youth how to look at life for selecting the small events which can make a good plot. This does not mean that differences of knowledge and awareness do not exist among them. I will not stress the gap between the Santal elite and illiterate villagers, since I want to underline the growing influence of writers in village life, as when village youth perform in the dramatic pieces the writers have wrought. Are Santal writers succeeding in forging cultural models for younger generations? Is Santal literature able to reflect a comprehensive image of *Adivasi* society for non-literate villagers who often get somebody to read to them the Santal newspaper in the village? How well is indigenous art, such as wall-painting or songs, able to convey *Adivasi* sensitivity along with literature? This last point is important since it means that non-literate adults can communicate through ritual, or art, with writers and educated youth. And finally, to what extent is Santal literacy—which has only recently emerged at the interface of the oral and written worlds—able to produce a sensitivity which can be shared and appreciated by *Adivasis* and non-*Adivasis*? Finally, to what extent can art and literature build new forms of agency and citizenship among *Adivasis*, by forging a new type of consciousness, pervaded by egalitarian ethos and a new imaginary capable of formulating paradigms of self-governance, and of asserting *Adivasi* rights?

Moving along rights does not allow local communities to really address the State, in issues like mining or water. Political participation still has a long way to go before it can reflect democratic principles. Though *Adivasi* assertion through art and literature has been positively acknowledged by different states, the access to vital resources such as forest, mines and water remains problematic since the State of Jharkhand— but also West Bengal or Chhattisgarh—are perceived as backing the business interests

I conclude that Mundari societies are able to formulate their cultural claims, but that the State and the different group interest are not always ready to accept *Adivasi* empowerment. Following the example of Ragunath Murmu and other inventors of script, Santal, Munda or Oraon writers have struggled to inform powerful constructions of social and political identity using mythic images such as Logo Buru. We may wonder whether these writers will succeed in promoting *Adivasi* literature in the Indian public sphere, and to what extent Santal or Munda indigenous theories will be able to sustain the process of a changing knowledge? I hold, however, that indigenous theories of knowledge are not useless repertoires, but that they contribute to revitalize language and ethnicity to forge a sense of belonging which, opposing *memocide*, takes care of memory work. It is this capacity for reflexivity which allow *Adivasi* communities to imagine answers to their endangered identity.

Notes

1. For an analysis of how Santal youth view traditional knowledge, See Carrin M. (2016) "The Making of Santal Youth of Jharkhand", In M. Carrin, H. Tambs-Lyche, D. Blanc (eds.): *Transfer of Knowledge and Children Agency: Reconstructing the Paradigms of Socialization: A Cross-cultural Perspective,* Delhi: Primus, pp. 127-149.
2. *Shorea Robusta*, L.

References

Banerjee, Prathama (1999) "Historic Acts? Santal Rebellion and the Temporality of Practice", *Studies in History*, 15: 209-246.

Banerjee Prathama (2002) "Re-Presenting Pasts: Santals in Nineteenth Century Bengal", in Partha Chatterjee and Anjan Ghosh editors, *History and the Present,* pp. 242-273.

Baviskar, A. (1995) *In the Belly of the R. Tribal Conflicts over Development in the Narmada Valley,* Delhi: Oxford University Press.

Bose, N.K. (1967) *Culture and Society in India,* Bombay: Asia Publishing Company.

Carrin-Bouez, M. (1986) *La fleur et l'os: symbolisme et ritual chez les Santal,* Paris: EHESS.

Carrin, M. (1997) *Enfants de la Déesse, Dévotion et pretrise feminine au Bengale*. Paris: Éditions du CNRS et maison des Sciences de l'Homme.

Carrin, M., (2002) Le Retour au bosquet sacré. Réinvention d'une culture *Adivasi*. In M. Carrin et C. Jaffrelot (eds.): Résistance et autonomie dans la société indienne, *Purusartha,* 23: 233-264.

Carrin, M. (2009) "The World of Tribes, Revolutionary Movements and Ethnic Withdrawal", C. Jaffrelot (ed.) *Contemporary India,* London: Penguin, pp. 543-568.

Carrin, M. (2012) "Hinduism and Tribal Religions in India," in: K.A. Jacobsen *et al.,* eds., *Brill's Encyclopaedia of Hinduism,* vol. IV, Leiden, pp. 588-602.

Carrin, M. (2013) "Jharkhand, Alternative Citizenship in an Adivasi State", Peter Berger and Frand Heideman (eds.) *The Anthropology of Modern India,* London: Routledge Publications, pp. 185-198.

Carrin, M. (2014) "The Santal as an Intellectual", in M. Carrin, G. Toffin and P. Kanungo, *The Politics of Ethnicity in India, Nepal and China,* Delhi: Primus Books, pp. 77-100.

Carrin, M. (2015a). *Le parler de dieux: le discourse ritual Santal entre l'oral et l'écrit (Inde),* Nanterre, Société d'Ethnologie.

Carrin, M. (2015b) "Performing Indigeneity on a Sacred Hill, Logo Buru" in: Ciocca & S. Das Gupta, *Out of Hidden India: Adivasi Hisories, Stories, Visual Arts and Performance, Anglistica AION,* Vol. 19, No. 1: 37-50.

Carrin M. (2016) "Transmission of Knowledge and the Making of Santal Youth," M. Carrin, H. Tambs-Lyche, D. Blanc (eds.): *Transfer of Knowledge and Children Agency: Reconstructing the Paradigms of Socialization,* Delhi: Primus, pp. 127-149.

Carrin, M. (2018) *Children of the Goddess, Devotion and Female Priesthood in Bengal.* (Translated from the French by Harald Tambs-Lyche), Delhi: Primus Books.

Carrin, M. and Tambs-Lyche, H. (2008) *A Peripheral Encounter: Santals and Missionaries, 1867-1900,* Delhi: Manohar Publishers.

Chatterji, Angana, P. (2009) *Violent Gods Hindu Nationalism in India's Present, Narratives from Orissa,* Gurgaon: Three Essays.

Corbridge, S., S. Jewitt and S. Kumar (2004) *Jarkhand: Environment, Development, Ethnicity.* Delhi: Oxford University Press.

Damodaran, Vinita (2005) "Indigenous Forest Rights, discourses and Resistance in Chotanagpur, 1860-2002", in G. Cederlof and K. Sivaramakrishnan (eds.) *Ecological Nationalisms: Nature, Livelihoods, and Identities in South Asia,* Delhi: Permanent Black: 115-150.

Elwin, V. (1954) *Tribal Myths of Orissa,* Bombay/New York: Oxford University Press.

Ghurye, G.S. (1959) *The Scheduled Tribes,* Bombay: Popular Prakashan.

Ghua, Ranjit (1983) *Elementary Aspects of Peasant Insurgency in Colonial India,* Delhi: Oxford University Press.

Hugues-Freeland, F. (1998) (ed.) *Ritual Performance, Media,* London: Routledge Kegan Paul.

Lave, J. and E. Wenger (1991) *Situated Learning. Legitimate Peripheral Participation,* Cambridge: Cambridge University Press.

Prakash, Gyan (1996) *Science between the Lines,* Oxford: Oxford University Press.

Sahlins, M. (1999) "Two Three Things that I Know about Culture", *Journal of the Royal Anthropological Institute,* 59(3): 399-421.

Schieffelin, E.L. (1998) "Problematizing performance", F. Hugues-Freeland (ed.) *Ritual Performance, Media,* London: Routledge Kegan Paul, pp. 195-207.

Shah, A. (2007) "Keeping the State Away: Democracy, Politics, and the State in India's Jharkhand", Govind Kelkar and Dev Nathan. *Journal of the Royal Anthropological Institute,* 13 (1) March: 128-45.

Shah, A. (2010) *In the Shadows of the State: Indigenous Politics, Environmentalism, and Insurgency in Jharkhand, India*. Durham: Duke University Press.

Srinivas, M.N. (1967) *Social Change in Modern India,* Berkeley: University of California Press.

Sundar, N. (2009) (ed.) *Legal Grounds: Natural Resources, Identity, and the Law in Jharkhand*. New Delhi: Oxford University Press.

Xaxa, Virginius (1999) "Transformation of Tribes in India: Terms of Discourse", *Economic & Political Weekly*, Vol. 34, No. 24 (June 12-18, 1999), pp. 1519-1524.

Xaxa, Virginius (2005) "Politics of Language, Religion and Identity: Tribes in India", *Economic & Political Weekly*, Vol. 40, No. 13 (March 26-April 1): 1363-1370.

ELEVEN

COUNTERING THE IMPOVERISHMENT RISK THROUGH EFFECTIVE AND REALISTIC PLANNING OF R&R ACTIVITIES

A Case from Central India

M. CHAUHAN AND S.C. PANDEY

Introduction

In recent decades a new development paradigm including poverty reduction, environmental protection, social justice, and human rights has been articulated where development is seen as both bringing benefits and imposing costs (Robinson, 2004). However, among its greatest costs has been the displacement of millions of vulnerable people. India has one of the highest rates of development-induced involuntary displacement in the world. The development process undertaken during post-independent India has resulted in impoverishment of millions of people. Development projects, such as dams, mines, wildlife sanctuaries and industries have already displaced about 21.30 million people from 1951 to 1990 in the country (Fernandes, 1994). His latest update estimates that large dams, huge industrial and mining projects, communication networks and power projects have uprooted as high as 60 million of people in India. This is tragical, because in one side the number of displaced people has increased, and is going to increase further during years to come and on the other side a large majority have not been properly rehabilitated yet (Fernandes, 1994). This is because rehabilitation of the

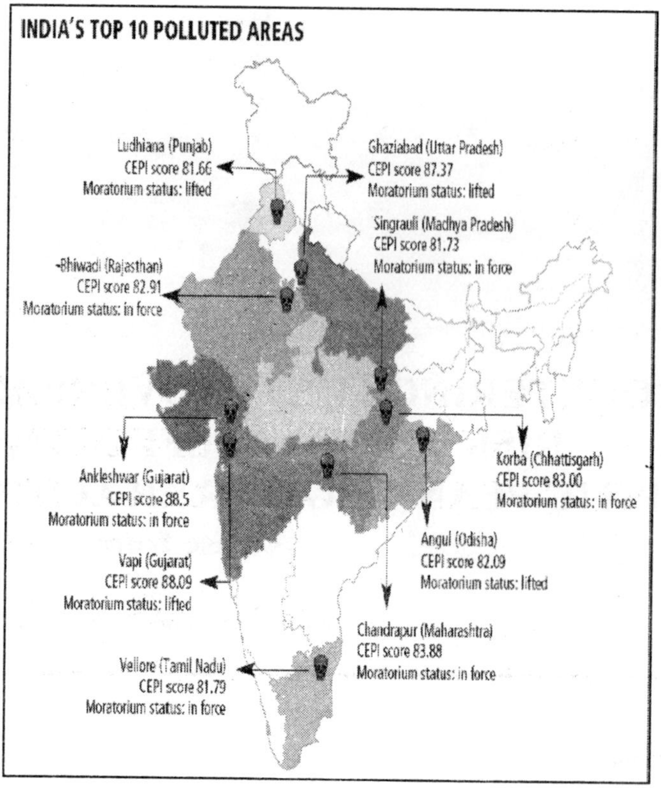

Map 1: India's Top 10 Polluted Areas

Source: http://www.downtoearth.org.in/content/gentle-critical-pollution

affected persons is not an easy task. According to (Sharma & Singh, 2009):

> Non-Governmental Organisations (NGOs) did not come forward to rehabilitate and resettle the displaced because they had reservations against such "anti-people" projects. They were more into advocacy and agitations against mega projects appropriating people's sustainable sources of livelihood.

The Singrauli Region

The Singrauli region of Madhya Pradesh (MP) and Uttar Pradesh (UP) is a nerve centre for thermal power of India. In terms of electric power and coal, the region is fast emerging as an energy hub of India. The region has been demarcated an area of over 3,000 sq. km. spread across the borders of UP (Sonebhadra district) and MP (Sidhi and Singrauli districts) for thermal power production and continues to be considered as South Asia's biggest industrial area (Greenpeace, 2011). Government of Madhya Pradesh claims that the total installed capacity of all power plants at Singrauli is around 10 per cent of total installed capacity of India.

The region has seen the systematic appropriation of prime agricultural land. Initially, it was for a dam and reservoir and later on for coal mines, coal-fired power plants, coal slurry disposal areas, railroad lines and other infrastructure, and eucalyptus plantations (Clark, Fox, & Treakle, 2003). The social and demographic profile of the area has undergone a significant transformation with the massive industrial changes due to the landscape. There has been more urbanization, depleting natural resources and more requirement of industrialized workforce.

Today, the region of Singrauli is poised at the centre of a debate in which the emphasis on double figure economic growth and political arguments for large-scale energy generation remain alarmingly disconnected from the voices of discontent on the ground. Inaugurating the Rihand Dam in 1964, Pt. Jawaharlal Nehru had promised that the Singrauli would become the "Switzerland of India". After his promise of about five decades, Shri Shivraj Singh Chauhan, the Chief Minister of Madhya Pradesh wants to develop Singrauli into another Singapore. In both the cases large tracts of agricultural lands, common lands and forest continue to be overtaken for extensive industrial expansion and displacement of communities.The end-losers of such a state of affairs will be the Project Affected Persons (PAPs) unless and until they will be resettled and rehabilitated properly.

Aim and Objectives of the Study

The study aimed at assessing the effectiveness of the resettlement and rehabilitation measures that were undertaken by NTPC Ltd. (Indian Power Company) in the project area of Vindhyachal Super Thermal Power Station (VSTPS) to mitigate the expected impoverishment risks due to development-induced displacement projects by the affected population. Following were the specific objectives of the study:

1. To assess the resettlement measures undertaken by the VSTPS.
2. To study the impact of community development activities on the socio-economic and cultural conditions of the communities.

3. To assess the changes in the quality of life among the village communities through project interventions.
4. To identify requirement of modification in the existing activities in order to take care of the changing needs of the people.

Methodology

As per the record of NTPC, a total of 20 villages have been displaced either partially or completely due to set up of VSTPS (Stage-I & Stage-II). Out of these 20 villages researchers were able to identify people displaced from around 18 villages due to the set up of VSTPS. The PAPs from these 18 villages have been found residing in the 26 villages in the vicinity of around 14 km from the existing plant site. Out of these 26 villages, researchers have taken up 11 villages (R&R Colony - 4 sectors on purposive sampling and other 7 villages on random sampling) for the study.

An in-depth study of all related literature including understanding of the interventions made by NTPC was done. The information was collected from primary as well as secondary sources. Data from primary source were collected through semi-structured interview/questionnaires/focused group discussions with community or community representatives. Feedbacks have been taken from the people for whom Community Development activities have been carried out. Feedback of at least 8 respondents in each category has been taken. A total of 603 respondents were covered under the study to see the standard of living of the people covered under various Community Development initiatives of the VSTPS.

Methodology for Computation of Standard of Living Index

The National Family Health Survey-II, a nation-wide survey at the district level, conducted in 26 states of the country jointly, East-West Centre, USA, USAID, UNICEF, Population Research Bureau, Washington DC, initiated by Ministry of Health and Family Welfare and coordinated by International Institute for Population Sciences, Mumbai, has developed an index to measure the Standard of Living in the household. This Index (Standard of Living Index – SOLI) will be adopted to measure the standard of living in the present study. (*http://www.nfhsindia.org/anfhs2.html*)

Table 11.1: Villages Affected by Stage-I

Sl. No.	*Village*	*Private Land (in acre)*	*Govt. Land (in acre)*	*Submerged (in acre)*	*Total*	*PAFs**
1.	Jainagar	590.93	86.58	—	677.51	286
2.	Keoti	119.99	02.41	—	122.40	107
3.	Parjasari	273.61	15.00	—	288.61	033
4.	Sarswahial	090.38	10.78	—	101.16	050
5.	Chanduli	620.55	44.07	—	664.62	496
6.	Pipraraja	173.36	21.56	—	194.92	044
7.	Telgawan	069.20	17.45	—	086.65	097
8.	Matwai	335.10	40.52	—	375.62	500
9.	Jaitpur	425.08	58.35	—	483.43	481
10.	Pipralal	183.38	10.55	—	193.93	023
11.	Nawadih	59.97	00.44	56.94	117.35	020
12.	Rampur	04.20	—	—	004.02	006
13.	Atraila	86.06	15.14	08.68	109.88	043
14.	Shapur	443.80	349.91	557.64	1351.35	118
	Total					**2304**

*Project Affected Families

Source: NTPC-VSTPS, 2010.

Table 11.2: Villages Affected by Stage-II

Sl. No.	*Village*	*Private Land (in acre)*	*Govt. Land (in acre)*	*Submerged (in acre)*	*Total*	*PAPs**	*HSO***
1.	Judi	133.41	05.24	18.22	156.87	230	176
2.	Uska	143.15	19.50	89.70	252.35	190	010
3.	Amratali	142.76	04.47	117.72	264.95	120	108
4.	Churchuria	193.83	06.05	290.67	490.55	175	090
	Total	**613.15**	**35.26**	516.31	**1164.72**	**715**	**384**

*Project Affected Person, ** Losing only house

Source: NTPC-VSTPS, 2010.

Area of the Study

Vindhyachal Super Thermal Power Project (VSTPP) was planned as 2240 MW Power project in two stages (Stage-I 6×210 MW) + Stage-II 2×500 MW) during 1981-82 and the foundation stone for this project was laid by late Smt. Indira Gandhi, the then Prime Minister of India on 12th November, 1982. For the project total 6,178 acres of area was identified. Out of which 3,189 acres of land was acquired for the plant and township and balance 2,989 acres of land was acquired for the Ash Dykes meant for disposal of the ash generated from utilisation of coal. A total of 20 villages were affected out of which 14 villages were affected during setting up of Stage-I and the remaining 6 villages for construction and expansion of Ash Dykes (*see* Tables 11.1 and 11.2). The land for plant area spread over 10 villages was acquired earlier and Stage I (6×210 MW) of this project was completed in February 1991 when all these units were commissioned.

Box 1: Revised RAP (Rehabilitation Action Plan) 1999 Provisions

1. Land losers to get Rs. 70,000 per acre for purchase of land, the registration charges, development charges @ Rs. 10,000 per acre after purchase of land. The land entitlement or equal to acquired land subject to a minimum of 2 acres and maximum of 5 acres.
2. Losing only house would get Rs. 70000 as lump sum rehabilitation grant.
3. Land losers who are employed elsewhere in Government. or in PSUs would be benefited by ex-gratia amount depending on the quantity of land acquired subject to maximum of 5. acres at reduced amounts, w.r.t (a) above.
4. Those losing their house or house and land would get a developed plot of 60x40 sq. ft. size in Resettlement Colony (RC) and Rs. 20,000 towards house disturbance and house construction assistance. Those who don't opt for plot in RC will be entitled to get Rs. 15,000/- as cash in lieu of plot.

Source: NTPC Ltd.[1]

Observation and Findings

1. Resettlement and Rehabilitation Measures

1.1. Land acquisition and their consequences on agriculture

Study depicts that before acquisition 484 PAPs had land but after acquisition landholding reduced to 414 PAPs. The average landholding per family has decreased from 7.88 acres to 0.256 acres among the PAPs, who still retain some pieces of land or purchased land at other places. About 83 per cent PAPs admitted that their land was acquired in the year 1986; about 7 per cent said that in the year 1983 and the remaining stated that the land was acquired after 1987. In addition there were other acquisitions; it includes the acquisition of the trees in the land, well and tube-wells.

Box 2: Agriculture Production and Productivity

Before the land acquisition, the PAPs had a total of 1655.81 acres of agricultural land but at present their land holding is only 183.77 acres. The decrease in landholding has led to the decrease in production from 7909 quintal (before the land acquisition) to 847 quintal (at the time of survey). Although the market value of the products increases day by day, the gross income from cultivation before the land acquisition was Rs. 24,96,142 and after the acquisition it decreased to Rs. 4,90,300.

About 39 per cent PAPs, who were previously involved in cultivation of *Kharif* crops, have decreased and remained less than 4 per cent. As on date the level of agricultural involvement in *Rabi* crops is almost negligible.

The reason for the decrease in percentage of cropping pattern is the loss of land and also the change in the occupational pattern and food habits.

1.2. Land acquisition and their consequences on livestock

In pre-acquisition, the total livestock possessed by villagers was 5056, which came down to 1367 during the post-acquisition. The average livestock per PAP decreased from 10 to 3 whereas the range has increased from 130 to 46. This is because some of the PAPs have started dairy practices. About 81 per cent of them accepted that their income from livestock was reduced, but about 19 per cent disagreed with it. About 95 per cent PAPs accepted that they were not able to maintain the number of livestock any further; about 5 per cent said the reduction in livestock was due to the reduction in the grazing ground and increase in diseases.

1.3. Land acquisition and their consequences on nature of employment

Before the land acquisition, the percentage of the PAPs involved in agriculture and labour was about 70 and 12 respectively; around 5 per cent were involved in service, including government and private services. Besides, 11 per cent of the PAPs were non-workers and about one per cent each was engaged in self-employed and dairy activities respectively. In post-acquisition period many PAPs became landless and their earning pattern also changed. The main occupations became daily wage labour, agricultural and non-agricultural, self-employment, services etc. As on date only 19 per cent PAPs are involved in agriculture. However, majority of them, i.e. about 60 per cent are engaged in labour work and the service sector.

1.4 Land acquisition and their consequences on income and expenditure

Although many PAPs have lost their land and have changed their mode of livelihood from agricultural sector to non-agricultural sector, the average annual income per PAPs has increased by almost Rs. 36,369. It was observed that the sum of annual income of all the respondents was in increasing trend. Before the land acquisition, the income and expenditure of the PAPs were Rs. 1,72,29,050 and Rs. 1,20,61,151 respectively. After the land acquisition, the income and expenditure has increased to Rs. 4,14,13,150 and Rs. 3,13,92,000 respectively. However, this increase is not only due to the impact of NTPC Ltd. intervention, but also due to the impact of inflation.

1.5 Land acquisition and their consequences on firewood and fodder

Before acquisition, about 13 per cent PAPs were collecting fodder from their own land, 32 per cent from the forest, 29 per cent from the village pastureland and less than half per cent from the market. After the land acquisition, only one and half per cent PAPs collect firewood and fodder from their own land, about 7 per cent from the forest, slightly more than one per cent from the village pastureland and more than 64 per cent from the market. As on date some of them have purchased stove or gas, *chulha*, heater etc.

Box 3: Firewood and Fodder

Before the land acquisition, the PAPs of these villages collected the sum of 3512 quintals of firewood annually, as the family size grew the need for more fuel result in more fire wood which comes to 99,257 quintals an additional annual expenditure of Rs. 1,702.45 on firewood for its purchase from the market. About 17 per cent PAPs were not affected in collecting firewood by the land acquisition, while about 83 per cent were affected by it.

1.6 Payment of Compensation and utilization pattern

About 99 per cent PAPs have received the rehabilitation amount and only 5 PAPs stated that they did not receive it. The PAPs have utilized the amount for more than one purpose. About 36.5 per cent of them have utilized the compensation money for construction of new house, 17 per cent utilized it to meet their day-to-day needs and about 14.5 per cent PAPs utilized it for purchase of land and its development purpose. Around 1.8 per cent of PAPs have spent their compensation amount in the wedding of their young ones or self, and around 6.1 per cent saved the compensation amount to meet their future needs.

Box 4: Compensation paid for tree, well and tube-wells

An amount of Rs. 1500 per fruit bearing tree, having a girth of three feet or less and Rs. 3000 for trees having a girth of more than three feet have been distributed along with the rehabilitation amount. There are about 233 PAPs whose open wells have been acquired along with the land and an additional amount of Rs. 15,000 per well has been given to them. Those PAPs whose tube-wells have been acquired are given an additional amount of Rs. 31,000 per tube-well.

1.7 NTPC intervention and benefits for PAPs

About 14.3 per cent PAPs said that the project is beneficial in the future. However, about 75.6 per cent PAPs said that the project is not beneficial for them at present or in the near future. The PAPs says till date only few development works has been done by VSTPS and so after 20 years no more changes will be expected in the future. There is a decrease in *kuchcha* houses and an increase in the number of mixed and *pucca* houses. Electricity was prevalent in most of the houses of the PAPs before the land acquisition, which has increased slightly after the acquisition. Regarding the main fuel for cooking, the use of LPG has increased among the PAPs with subsequent decrease in the use of charcoal and kerosene. Finally, regarding consumer durable there is a marginal increase of these assets in each household.

1.8. NTPC intervention in livelihood restoration

None of the PAPs which were interviewed have received training on the special course in ITI (Industrial Training Institute), 25 PAPs are running small shops and out of them 18 are satisfied with their present occupation. About 40 unskilled PAPs are working in NTPC Ltd. and out of them 32 are satisfied. Only 3 are skilled worker and they all are satisfied. 15 PAPs are working on contract, out of which 14 are satisfied.

1.9. NTPC intervention and consequences on social structure

The prevalence of child marriage has decreased to a certain extent after the project intervention. The *pardah* system and the female mortality rate are decreasing, while the dowry system is increasing. The women's role in decision-making in household matters is decreasing, the education scenario for girls have increased. Regarding occupations, due to land loss, the migration rate has increased. About 2 per cent PAPs say that their social status has been affected because of their landlessness, but the rest do not feel so. Around two per cent PAPs say that their family was disintegrated after the land acquisition. About 3 per cent PAPs accept that conflict and corruption has increased. According to them intra-community/caste level conflicts have increased. However, remaining 97 per cent disagree with this view.

2. Community Development Activities

2.1. Demography of sample villages

Table 11.3 depicts that more than 75 per cent families belong to Scheduled Caste and Other Backward Classes.

Table 11.3: Category-wise Family Detail

Villages	*No. of Families*						
	*ST**	*SC***	*OBC****	*General*	*Total*	*BPL#1*	*APL#2*
Navjeevan Vihar Sector-I	10	50	100	125	285	20	265
Navjeevan Vihar Sector-II	25	60	150	20	255	80	175
Navjeevan Vihar Sector- III	10	200	150	40	400	350	50
Navjeevan Vihar Sector-IV	30	60	120	30	240	200	40
Harrei West	10	40	2	105	157	70	87
Harrei East	10	40	11	60	121	50	71
Gahilgarh East	2	100	150	40	292	10	279
Gahilgarh West	2	15	330	30	377	15	362
Juwari	50	120	150	80	400	100	300
Banauli	5	300	500	2	807	350	457
Telgawan	10	60	40	10	120	60	60
Total 11 Villages	**164**	**1045**	**1703**	**542**	**3454**	**1305**	**2149**

* Scheduled Tribe, ** Scheduled Caste, *** Other Backward Class, #1 Below Poverty Line, #2 Above Poverty Line.

Source: Field Survey, 2010.

It was observed that more than 35 per cent project affected families are living Below Poverty Line. Due to limited options of earning sources in the locality more than 80 per cent families of Navjeevan Vihar Sector-III and Navjeevan Vihar Sector-IV fall under BPL category. The family members of these villages are mostly dependent on labour work. According to villagers, the amounts received enabled the people to replace only up to 30 per cent of their lost assets. Although lands were acquired all at once, evictions were carried out at different points of time. Thus, for instance, the first round of evictions was for the power projects, townships and its associated infrastructure. In this round, the people involved were categorised subsequently as Stage-I in the NTPC's Resettlement and Rehabilitation Policy. The second round of evictions was for the construction of permanent ash dykes and this took place in the late 90s. The compensation amount, disbursed many years prior to the evictions, got spent by the people much before they had to move.

2.2. Health and Sanitation

In last couple of years VSTPS is organizing health awareness camps in the area. However, the comparative health status indicators for the year 2005 and 2008 states that there are marginal improvements in the project affected areas (Table 11.4). During the survey work it was observed that people are least bothered about their health. There is lack of health seeking behaviour among the communities.

Table 11.4: Village-wise Health Status Indicators (I) for Year 2005 and 2008

Villages	Health Status Indicators									
	IMC* (No.)		MMC** (No.)		U5MC*** (No.)		Birth Case (No.)		Death Case (No.)	
	2005	2008	2005	2008	2005	2008	2005	2008	2005	2008
N. V. Sector-I	7	6	5	4	9	8	5	6	3	3
N. V. Sector-II	6	4	5	4	8	7	6	7	3.6	3
N. V. Sector-III	8	7	6	5	10	9	5	5	4	3
N. V. Sector-IV	6	7	4	3	8	8	10	8	5	4
Harrei West	5	4	3	2	7	5	6	7	5	6
Harrei East	4	3	2	1	6	5	6	8	3	5
Gahilgarh (E)	5	3	3	2	6	6	5	6	7	5
Gahilgarh (W)	4	3	2	2	5	4	6	6	6	4
Juwari	8	7	5	5	9	9	7	8	5	4
Banauli	5	4	3	3	7	6	6	8	5	5
Telgawan	4	3	3	2	5	4	5	5	3	2

*Infant Mortality Cases, ** Maternal Mortality Cases, *** Under 5 Mortality Cases

Source: Field Survey, 2010.

Table 11.5 reveals that there are marginal improvements in the cases of measles and tuberculosis, however number of malaria cases have increased more than 12 per cent. Except Telgawan, Juwari, Harrei (W) and N.V. Sector-IV, all other villages, the number of malaria cases have increased drastically.

It was observed that out of 11 villages, only one village have health related infrastructure. However, the PHC at Navjeevan Vihar Sector-I is also not operational and the existing structure is in deteriorated condition.

The resettled colony, i.e. Navjeevan Vihar Sectors-I, II, III and IV

Table 11.5: Village-wise Health Status Indicators (II) for Year 2005 and 2008

Villages	Health Status Indicators					
	No. of Measles cases		No. of TB* cases		No. of Malaria cases	
	2005	2008	2005	2008	2005	2008
N. V. Sector-I	10	11	5	8	125	149
N. V. Sector-II	14	16	6	0	86	126
N. V. Sector-III	12	13	6	5	115	135
N. V. Sector-IV	16	12	5	7	133	130
Harrei West	5	4	1	1	43	32
Harrei East	8	2	2	1	52	61
Gahilgarh (E)	14	12	3	3	106	145
Gahilgarh (W)	8	5	2	3	96	115
Juwari	10	12	4	3	87	76
Banauli	10	8	6	7	112	121
Telgawan	5	4	2	0	74	65
Total 11 villages	**112**	**99**	**42**	**38**	**1029**	**1155**

* Tuberculosis

Source: Field Survey, 2010.

have the basic sanitation facilities (*Sulabh Souchalayas* and Community Toilets). However, these structures are in deteriorated condition. In addition, there is absence of regular and sufficient water supply in these structures. Remaining 7 villages do not have the basic sanitation facilities. People of these villages go in open fields for latrines and toilet purposes.

2.3. Education

VSTPS is providing scholarships for SC/ST poor students who are studying in Government schools. In some of the villages such as Gahilgarh (W), Banauli and Telgawan, VSTPS is running Adult Education programme. This programme is for the people who missed the regular education system due some unavoidable reasons. In last couple of years, the literacy rate among female of 15-24 years age group has increased more than 5 per cent (Table 11.6).

Table 11.6: Overall Literacy Rate Among 15-24 Years Age Group

Villages	*Overall literacy rate (15-24 years age group) in %*					
	Male		*Female*		*Total*	
	2005	*2008*	*2005*	*2008*	*2005*	*2008*
Navjeevan Vihar Sector-I	70.00	74.00	55.00	60.00	62.50	67.00
Navjeevan Vihar Sector-II	56.00	60.00	48.00	55.00	52.00	57.50
Navjeevan Vihar Sector-III	48.00	50.00	40.00	42.00	44.00	46.00
Navjeevan Vihar Sector-IV	44.00	52.00	41.00	42.00	42.50	47.00
Harrei West	70.00	76.00	58.00	64.00	64.00	70.00
Harrei East	70.00	74.00	58.00	62.00	64.00	68.00
Gahilgarh East	58.00	60.00	40.00	50.00	49.00	55.00
Gahilgarh West	58.00	62.00	43.00	52.00	50.50	57.00
Juwari	54.00	58.00	40.00	44.00	47.00	51.00
Banauli	52.00	56.00	44.00	48.00	48.00	52.00
Telgawan	60.00	66.00	48.00	50.00	54.00	58.00
Total 11 Villages	**58.18**	**62.55**	**46.82**	**51.73**	**52.50**	**57.14**

Source: Field Survey, 2010.

2.4. Recreation and Socio-Cultural Practices

VSTPS is organising various recreational and socio-cultural activities like annual sports functions, celebration of festivals etc. in the area. About 54 per cent responded that the activities were good, whereas 39 per cent and 7 per cent responded that the activities were average and poor respectively. They also responded that there are changes in socio-cultural practices among the communities due to project interventions in the area. People are finding less space to play and have fun, games like *gulli danda, bhaura danda*, and other local games are lost. Festivals like *Diwali* and *Holi* are celebrated in less space as there is change in the housing pattern.

2.5. Vocational Training, Agriculture and Livestock

None of the PAPs which were interviewed have received training on the special course in ITI, 25 PAPs are running small shops and 18 are satisfied. About 40 unskilled PAPs are working in NTPC Ltd. and out of them 32 are satisfied. Only 3 are skilled worker and they all are satisfied. 15 PAPs are working on contract, out of which 14 are satisfied. In R&R Colony, there is no cultivable land whereas in other villages people do farming. However, most of the cases only those people are farming who have irrigation facilities of their own. In Juwari, the farmers are making less usage of their land as most of the farmers have their houses in the R&R Colony. In Telgawan, the farmers whose land is nearer to the canal are also taking 2nd crops. In R&R colony, the mortality rate of livestock is very low. One of the reasons could be because people keep less in number, which provides spaces for better care provisions. However, in other villages, the livestock annual mortality rate varies from 3-7 per cent. These areas have fodder insufficiency and most of the cases cattle eat plastic bags which leads to death.

3. Broad View of Overall Assessment of Community Development Initiatives

Table 11.7: Overall Assessment of Community Development Initiatives

Ratings	*Broad Areas and determination of the respondent*						
	Education	*Health*	*VT**	*Disability*	*Sports*	*Agriculture*	*Livestock*
Excellent	0 (0%)	0 (0%)	0 (0%)	0 (0%)	0 (0%)	0 (0%)	0 (0%)
Very Good	0 (0%)	0 (0%)	4 (2.5%)	0 (0%)	0 (0%)	0 (0%)	0 (0%)
Good	33 (38.75%)	0 (0%)	13 (13.75%)	6 (5%)	46 (53.75%)	0 (0%)	0 (0%)
Average	39 (45%)	33 (36.25%)	34 (40%)	38 (43.75%)	34 (38.75%)	44 (50%)	52 (60%)
Poor	16 (16.25%)	55 (63.75%)	37 (43.75%)	48 (51.25%)	8 (7.5%)	44 (50%)	36 (40%)
N =	**88 (100%)**	**88 (100%)**	**88 (100%)**	**92 (100%)**	**88 (100%)**	**88 (100%)**	**88 (100%)**

* Vocational Training

Source: Field Survey, 2010.

Table 11.8: Details of Infrastructural Facilities and Amenities of PAPs Before and After Land Acquisition

Infrastructural facilities	*Pre-acquisition No. of PAPs*	*Post-acquisition No. of PAPs*	*NET CHANGE in Per cent Points*
Pucca	.3	2.4	+2.1
Kaccha	98.4	4.7	–93.7
Mixed	1.2	92.8	+91.6
Toilet facility			
Own pit toilet	.5	1.2	+0.7
No facility	99.5	98.8	–0.7
Source of lighting			
Electricity	—	99.0	+99.0
Kerosene	100.0	.9	–99.1
Gas or oil	—	.2	+0.2
Main fuel of cooking			
Liquefied natural gas	—	2.3	+2.3
Coal	—	1.6	+1.6
Wood	100.0	84.8	–15.2
Other fuel	—	11.4	+11.4
Source of drinking water			
Tap	.2	.2	–
Hand pump	11.4	.7	–10.7
Well in residence/yard/plot	88.1	80.9	–7.2
Public well	.3	18.2	+17.9
Separate room for cooking			
Yes	100.0	100.0	—
No	—	—	
Ownership of house			
Yes	100.0	100.0	—
No			
Ownership of agricultural land		.2	
4 for 5 acres or more	17.0		–16.8
3 for 2.0-4.9 acres	3.0	.9	–
2 for less than 2 acres or - acreage not known	79.0	99.0	–78.1
0 for no agricultural land	1.0		+98.0
Ownership of irrigated land			
Household owns at least - some irrigated land	94.6	.5	–94.1
No irrigated land	5.4	99.5	+94.1
Ownership of livestock			
Own livestock	90.9	5.1	–85.8
Not own livestock	9.1	94.9	+85.8
Durable goods ownership			
Car or tractor	—	.9	+0.9
Moped/scooter/motorcycle	3.3	90.0	+86.7
Telephone	.5	.3	–0.2
Colour television	—	4.2	+4.2
Bicycle	92.7	2.4	–90.3
Electric fan	—	.9	+0.9
Radio	.4	.9	+0.5
Bullock cart	.9	...	–0.9
Black and white television	2.3	.2	–2.1
Other	—	.2	+0.2

**Source:* Field Survey 2010.

Table 11.9: SOLI (Standard of Living Index)

Categories of Standard of Living Index	*Before acquisition (B)*		*After acquisition (A)*		*Net change in percentage points (A-B)*
	Frequency	*Per cent*	*Frequency*	*Per cent*	
Low	139	23.1	34	5.6	–17.5
Medium	464	76.9	569	94.4	+17.5
Total	**603**	**100.0**	**603**	**100.0**	

**Source:* Field Survey, 2010.

4. Change in Quality of Life

Taking into consideration all the above indicators, as proxy to the living standard of the PAPs an index known as "Standard of Living Index" (SOLI), has been formulated (*see* Table 11.8).

Table 11.9 depicts the results of the index before and after the land acquisition, the result shows that there is a decrease of 17.5 per cent points in the PAPs, regarding the low standard of living and subsequent increase in the middle and high standard of living. Agricultural land, irrigated land and livestock influence the present index. Thus, although the PAPS might have more income level, saving or asset, the index is more influenced by the previous indicators.

Recommendation

1. Although it is more than 20 years, NTPC should continue to take up community development work in the nearby villages and in those villages which are affected by the project. Special care has to be given in the R&R Colony where all the development activities taken up by the station. VSTPS need to revisit their community development activities as per the requirement of the communities. This need arises because after a sustained effort of more than 20 years, still the area has more than 35 per cent families who are living Below Poverty Line. In some of the cases, it is more than 80 per cent.

2. At present most of the community development initiatives seem to be the event specific. However, it should be the combination of both result as well as process oriented. There is a need to prepare a comprehensive community development project/programme for all the neighbouring villages in the field of education, health, safe drinking water, sanitation, livelihood promotion, agriculture development and special

attention for children, youth, women and disabled. The project\programme should be for a period of 6 to 8 years and to be executed properly in order to minimize the impoverishment risks due to displacement. The comprehensive community development project\programme should be designed in such a way that its activities should be the combinations of both, curative as well preventive in nature.

3. Financial support for women and men (educated and uneducated) who want to start business, may be provided in the form of loans through banks. Three types of revolving funds for (i) Women, (ii) Youth and (iii) Farmers need to be introduced in the area. VSTPS should capacitate and empower the community by their own staff or with the support of good NGOs, so that community can manage these funds effectively on sustainable manner. In addition, VSTPS should promote to have a Village Development Fund in each village in order to maintain and repair the existing infrastructures when and where required.These activities may lead towards ownership of community towards community resources.

4. There is need to remove the dependency syndrome among the community as the people feel that all their problems have to be solved by NTPC Ltd. It can be done through a systematic withdrawal plan. Need of the community should be prioritised and should be addressed in phases. The withdrawal strategy document should have combinations of both, activity as well as programme withdrawals.

5. Villages, where people have lost all the surrounding land and where people are suffering of pollution due to ash ponds and smoke etc., should be acquired by NTPC and the people may be relocated to colonies of rehabilitation or elsewhere. However, this should be done on mutual agreement of both the parties.

6. Adequate budget should be allocated for community development programmes. It should not be a fixed percentage of profit earned by the company on a particular year.

Note

1. Resettlement and Rehabilitation Policy, 1989 undertaken by the Government of Odisha (Angul-Talcher Belt).

References

Agrawal, D. (1998). "Preventing Impoverishment from Displacement: The NTPC Experience." In: *Development Projects and Impoverishment Risks, Resettling*

Project: Affected People in India. H. Mohan Mathur and D. Marsden (eds.), New Delhi: Oxford University Press.

Beck, T., and Ghosh, G.M. (2000). "Common Property Rights and the Poor", *Economic & Political Weekly*, 35 (3): 147-53.

CEA. (2004). *Coal requirements in Thermal Power Plants.* CEA.

Clark, D., Fox, J., and Treakle, K. (Eds.), (2003). *Demanding Accountability: Civil Society Claims and the World Bank Inspection Panel*, Rowman & Littlefield.

CPCB & IIT, Delhi (2010), *Comprehensive Environmental Assessment of Industrial Clusters*, New Delhi.

Das, M.K., Awasthi, A.K., Pandey, R., Dwivedi, A., and Kaul, M. "Mapping of Forest Types and Land Use/Land Cover of Singrauli Coal Field Area Using Satellite Remote Sensing Techniques". *Journal of Tropical Forestry*, January-June 2007, Vol. 23 (I&II).

Dewan, R., 2008. "Development Projects and Displaced Women". In Mathur, H.M., (ed.) *India Social Development Report 2008: Development and Displacement.* Delhi: Oxford University Press/Council for Social Development.

Envirotech East Pvt. Ltd. (2008). *EIA Report for Vindhya Nagar NTPC Singrauli.* Kolkata.

Fernandes, W. (1994). *Development— induced Displacement in the Tribal Areas of Eastern India*- Indian Social Institute, New Delhi.

Fernandes, W. (Ed.). (2007): "Singur and the Displacement Scenario". *EPW*, 20 January.

Government of Madhya Pradesh (2011). Destination Singrauli: The brochure illustrates various projects that are taking shape in Singrauli, January 2011.

Greenpeace India Society (2011) "Singrauli: The Coal Curse" a fact finding report on the impact of coal mining on the people and environment of Singrauli, Bengaluru.

Labour and the Union Budget (2008). *Assessment of Displacement and NTPC Rehabilitation and Relocation Policy, Labour File*, Vol. 6, Nos. 2 and 3. pp. 32-36.

Pandey, G.K., "Management of Thermal Power Plants in India", Paper presented at BAQ 2006, at Yogykarta, Indonesia, Advisor, Ministry of Environment and Forest (Government of India), S.K. Tyagi, Scientist, & B. Sengupta, Member Secretary, Central Pollution Control Board, New Delhi (India).

Robinson, W.C. (2004). *Risks and Rights: The Causes, Consequences, and Challenges of Development—Induced Displacement.* Washington, DC: Brookings Institution—SAIS Project on Internal Displacement.

Sharma, R.N., and Singh, S.R. (2009). "Displacement in Singrauli Region: Entitlements and Rehabilitation". *Economic & Political Weekly,* XLIV (51).

TWELVE

FOREST, LIFE AND LIVELIHOOD

For Tribal Development, The Promise must be Delivered

RANJU HASINI SAHOO

> When a tribe was asked by Elwin (1958) what does he think of heaven and hell he described heaven as "Miles and Miles of Forest without Forest Guard" and hell as "Miles and Miles of Forest without any *Mahua* trees".

This simple world-view of a tribe of Central India speaks volumes about the symbiotic relation between tribes and forest, the top up approach to conserve and protect the forest as well as development strategies for tribal communities of India. Nevertheless, this simple world-view of the tribe provides enough materials not only to the anthropologists, but also to the rest of the social scientists, administrators, policy-makers and planners to think about the forest management *vis-à-vis* tribal development.

Through review of literature, the researcher endeavours to analyse the history of forest management in Central India, tribal unrest in Chhattisgarh and Orissa which has thrown some light on this simple yet a complicated tribal notion about hell and heaven.

A Brief Glimpse on History of Forest Management

From the historical perspective, the relation between tribal and forest is very well explained in the research work of Rangarajan (1996). Thus, he explained ownership of more than one-fifth of the land area of British India by the Forest Department made it not only the largest land manager in the sub-continent, but one of the largest forestry enterprises in the world.

Guha (1983) argues that the practices of colonial forestry were largely an outgrowth of the revenue and strategic needs of empire. The colonial period is seen as an ecological watershed because it disrupted the relationship of forest-based communities with the land. Customary restraints on the use of trees had earlier ensured deforestation. Gadgil (1985) sees the period up to AD 1800 as a time of 'equilibrium' between people and nature. Guha (1989) again argues that the genesis of colonial forestry lay in a drive to obtain timber for shipping in Malabar in 1806. But it was the need to ensure a creation of the Forest Department in 1864.

Rangarajan (1996) has very vividly explained that the first Superintendent of forests, John McLelland, blamed Sweden agriculture of the Karens for the destruction of teak. The German forester, Dietrich Brandis, became Superintendent in 1856. Major Seaton began encouraging tribals to grow teak saplings in their rice fields. Once tribal Sweden cultivators moved on to fresh plots, the trees became Government property. Brandis enforced strict regulations to control shifting agriculture and curb fines. Both strategies, encouraging inter-cropping and fire control, aimed to increase teak regeneration.

The common elements of early British forestry in India were already evident by this time in several provinces. The local inhabitants were either totally excluded, or else incorporated into a regime of control. Either way the wider British interests in timber and revenue were paramount.

Forest rules became more stringent after the formation of the Central province in 1861. The rise in demand for timber for public works led to increased conflict between the government and villages. Rural land users soon faced fresh problems because of the new strictures against cutting young trees. Forsyth (1889) admitted that the administration had concentrated on railway timber, but had ignored man demand for wood for construction. Everyone of teak forest had been closed off and only inferior sorts of wood permitted for rural use.

The early initiation for preventing fires and excluding cattle from government forests laid the ground for a wider regime of control under the Forest Act of 1878. Foresters had often equated conservation with the strict exclusion of private tree users from forests. There were no private user rights in reserved forests, which covered over one-fifth of the land area. By 1881 forest officers had a chance to implement their schemes for strict exclusion in these lands.

The extension of Government Control over forests after the Forest Act of 1878 also worked tribal land rights. The inclusion of land in reserved forests was not merely intended to protect timber, but reflected a deep-seated belief that there was no one fit to become proprietor of these extensive tracts.

Joshi (1990) has explained that after the rebellion on 1910, which is popularly known as 'Bhumkal' in Bastar, the Forest administration was directly taken over by the British Diwan and his staff. Hereafter, case was taken to prevent or to at least minimize the gross abuse of forest rules by the subordinate staff of the forest administration; for it was well-known that what the tribesmen grudged most was not the forest rules, but the men who implemented them. The Government's aim was to ensure increased revenue from local forests without creating resentment of people living in the forests.

Anderson and Huber (1988) while evaluating a project of World Bank and GOI which was implemented in 1975 sought to industrialize a backward region and to deal with the problem of national balance of payment explained, "In Bastar the measures taken to a report on the rebellion to the Foreign Department Secretary, the government was informed of the main grievances of the tribals: the inclusion of village land in reserves of forest, with a subsequent forced removal of villagers and the burning down of their dwellings; and, in general, the high-handed treatment and unjust exactions on the part of Forest Officials. The report admitted that these and numerous other grievances were largely genuine. In the judgement of the very experienced anthropologist, C. von Furer-Haimendorf, thus arose a conflict between the traditional tribal ownership and the state's claim to the entire forest wealth.

It is important to see the situation in Bastar comparatively; other tribal areas of India have experienced more profound upheavals, including confrontations with military forces. The sense of relative opportunity in Bastar for new forest tribe government relations was borne out by many experienced observers. Some options seemed to remain open; not everything was closed with sabers drawn. The dean of foreign observers of the tribal situation in India, C. von Furer-Haimendorf, sensed this during a jeep journey through Bastar in the late 1970. He visited Gond villages and weekly markets, travelled to the remote Abujh Mar Hills, and spoke to tribals and officials. The good situation there, he said, could be credited to efforts of enlightened and liberal civil administration to control the exploitative relations of tribal and non-tribal people in Bastar. Thus, the tribal people lead a life in accordance with their own traditions and inclinations. This optimism contrasted strongly with the foreboding he felt about the pine project, as we shall see.

Beyond the causes listed above and the responses made by the corporation, the tribal study concluded that the overall tribal reasoning followed a more profound logic. "Forests are so interwoven with the tribal life that it is beyond the imagination of a tribal to survive without forests, because of the ecological setting of a tribal village, socio-religious equilibrium, and economic dependence. The tribal's psychological as well as economic dependence on forests is paramount and is reflected in all walks of their life." Now, that the forests are curtailed, the tribals are apprehensive and suspicious. The tribal owns land and has a right over forests. The moment this relationship is converted into money which he cannot handle, he is at the mercy of a system which he does not know. Perception of the pine project was based on the tribals understanding of tribal and non-tribal relations in Bastar. The corporation did not come to buy or steal their land.

At the 1978 Conference of Ministers of Tribal Welfare and Forestry, Prime Minister Indira Gandhi stressed together need to restore ecological balance in India by giving to the tribals a right over trees and a right to their use in specific assigned areas. The concept of *nistari* embraces the rights she desired, yet in Bastar as elsewhere these rights have been curtailed or otherwise limited. In a reserved forest, such rights extend only to satisfaction of personal/household needs and preclude the felling of timber, but in a protected forest, these strictures are relaxed. Without fences and other boundaries, tribal have *de facto* expectations of using forest for their needs.

Citing the 1973 Annual Report, Commission for Scheduled Castes and Scheduled Tribes Jones (1978) points out that the net revenue from exploitation of tribal forests in the Central Tribal Belt, including Bastar (assuming that tribal forests comprise 50 per cent of Total), was Rs. 243 million in 1969-1970. In the same year, the special tribal programme expenditure was only Rs. 109 million, that is, tribal expenditures were only 44.8 per cent of revenues from tribal forests. The benefits of such an arrangement are clear. Observers say this ratio of revenue to expenditure was similar throughout the period of the Bastar project.

Taking cue from John's (1978) Anderson and Huber (1988) again endeavoured to substantiate the cause of failure of tribal development.

Thus, the main reasons are—firstly, the laws and special tribal programmes have failed because of the power of the non-tribal landlords, money-lenders and traders who control the tribal economies and local panchayats (councils). These groups in alliance with non-tribal government servants—development and revenue officers, administrators and magistrates—have been able to circumvent the laws and regulations and to divert development funds intended for tribals to their own use. Second, the development programmes have failed because they have often been transferred without modification from the culturally and environmentally different plains areas and because their implementation has been left to poorly trained and culturally prejudiced non-tribal officers. Third, the programmes have failed because they have not involved tribals in their own development. The use of the term "uplift" demonstrates the government's philosophy of development. Development is something done to tribals by non-tribals, not a process in which the tribals are actively involved and control. Fourth, the funds allocated for tribal development have been totally inadequate for the immense task of providing the necessary infrastructure and inputs. It seems that funds spent by the Government of India in tribal areas are considerably less than the value of the minerals and timber extracted from these areas.

From the Report of Glasfurd (1862), Sunder (1999) explains how the forest of Bastar was exploited for construction purpose of nearby states. Thus, she explains as early as 1862, Glasfurd was bemoaning the devastation of the teak forests of Bheji and Sukma under the unchecked felling of contractors and state creditors, who supplied the timber market at Rajamundhri by floating logs on the Godavari. Glasfurd estimated that in the three *zamindaris* of Bhapalpatnam, Kotapilly and Bheji, in 1861 alone 30,000 logs had been cut and exported to Rajamundhri to feed the demand from the Madras railway and the District Engineer's Department, upper Godavari works.

Again from the Record Room data of Jagdalpur Collectorate, Sundar (1997) cites examples of the indigenous concept of village boundaries and sites for cultivation being 'given' to their inhabitants by the earth. People go back annually over long distances to worship gods that were left behind when villages were deported from reserved areas. In 1914, in eighteen villages of Konta Tehsil out of 126 tenants who had deserted, 72 had returned and resettled. Yet others wished to come back and reoccupy villages in the Golapalli reserved forest from which they were turned out. The ranger's advice to them to select some other village was met with "half consenting, half decrying". He reported his conversations with the people to the Diwan. "They always said that they cannot go to any other village than those in which their ancestors had lived for centuries together. They seem to be much prejudiced as they think that they would sustain a great loss of life and property if they occupied any other village than those belong to their forefathers".

Citing the correspondence of Rook (1906) to Panda Bajineth Diwan, she explained how the later favoured the local rights when he wrote—

> "In a landlocked state like Bastar, villagers cannot do much damage to reserves so long as there is no outside demand for forest produce. Even want on felling except for *dhya* cannot amount for much.... The questions of rights of user are a very delicate one and every endeavour must be made by the Forest Settlement Officer to satisfy the people for to have them at enmity with the Forest Department augurs ill for the well-being of the reserves".

Grigson (1938) refuted the two point's criticism that shifting cultivation causes the passing of much fine forest and foretells desiccation and erosion. Others condemns *penda* is a lazy method of cultivation.

The shifting forest cultivation is criticized from two points of view. The forestry enthusiast laments the passing of much fine forests, and foretells desiccation and erosion. Others condemn *penda* as a lazy method of civilization the former forgets that in most of this area the forests have been too remote and inaccessible ever to be exploited, and that, even though some fine timber has been sacrificed, much that has gone was hopelessly over-mature. Vast areas of forest have been reserved by the State, and it has not been possible to work half of these reserves. The Maria does not range through his forests clearing patches for cultivation at random. He has more or less definite rotations and the clearings after two or three years cultivation may get twelve or fourteen years rest, at the end of which they have a dense forest growth.

It is a superficial criticism that condemns *penda* cultivation as lazy. The clearing of the land, especially if it be covered with heavy timber, is most arduous.

Shifting Cultivation

Elwin in *The Baiga*, wrote about the shifting cultivation of Baiga tribe that needs the attention of Scientific research. Elwin wrote about the practice of shifting cultivation around the world. Thus he wrote:

> "What is known to the Baiga as *bewar* is practiced throughout the tropical and sub-tropical regions of the world. It is the common method of cultivation in the forests of south America, in many parts of Africa and Mauritius, in Melanesia and the Atlantic Island, in Assam, in Ceylon, and in the remoter forest area of South and Central India. It is known as sartage on the French and Belgian Ardunnes as 'forming' in West Africa as *kohola* in the south-east Solomon Islands as *cheta* by the *vedda*. In *India*, the *dahi* and *koman* cultivation of the Bhuiya or Orissa the *penda* of the Baster Maria, the *jhum* of the Assam hill tribes, the *podu* of the *khond* of the Baster joy pore, the *beora* of the Pahari Korwa of *jashpur*, the *taungya* of the Burma hill tribes, are all, with some variations akin to the *bewar* of the Baiga".

Shifting Cultivation in the Legend of Baiga Tribe

The Baiga were established in the practice of *bewar* by Bhagavan himself who, when he called all the tribes of the world together to make a king, at first chose the Baiga. But Nanga Baiga begged that the Gond, his brother, might be king in the place. Bhagavan was pleased at this request, and, as a mark of his favour took Nanga Baiga by the hand and placed him on his throne by his side. He granted hid prayer to make the Gond kind, but he gave the Baiga an even greater blessings.

All the kingdoms of the world, "he said, may fall to pieces, but he who is made of earth and is Bhumiaraja, lord of the earth, shall never forsake it." You will make your living from the earth. You will dig roots and eat them. You will cut wood and carry it on your shoulders. Your wife will pack leaves and shell them. You must not tear the breasts of your Mother the Earth with the plough like the Gond and Hindu. You will cut down trees and burn them and sow your seed in the ashses. But you will never become rich, for if you did you would forsake the earth, and then there would be no one to guard it and sow seed in the ashes of burnt trees; and when he had taught him everything he called him to receive gifts of seed.

This legend is told, and believed, throughout the length and breadth of the Baiga country, Mandala and Niwas, in Rewa and Dindori, in Baihar, in Bilaspur, in Pandaria. In the old days it was the foundation of the conamic and social of the tribe. Every Baiga who has yielded to the plough knows himself to the standing on *papi-dharti*, on sinful earth, or as we first touched the plough, says Mahatu, "a man died in every home and Hothu of Talaipani confessed to me that he had at one time used a plough". "But my children have always been weak and sickly on account of it. If even one Baiga in a village touches the plough, we are all affected." This is a perfectly genuine religious belief, which the most vigorous propaganda has left unshaken. Dhan Singh of Pandpur once told me that if some magician were to come to him and ask him to choose the three things that he most wanted and that he Baiga most wanted in the world, he would say, "frist give us back our jungle". Then let us have free *kandabari* (root-plantations). And third, let us hunt freely once more. We do not want riches, only these three things" (Elwin, 2007).

The researcher while in an evaluation work in 2015-16 from the discussion with Sabitri Patra associated with Devote Trust, an NGO which works for the development of Kutia Kandh in Odisha came to know the following relevant information.

Forest and Shifting Cultivation

Kutia Kandh solely depend on forest and cultivation. They do not have capability to work outside and eke out a living. They have calculated that approximately 80 varieties of food and everything they get from forest like fruits and roots and medicinal plants in various seasons. Hence, they do not have anything to bye from market except cloth and salt. Even they get light from the fire of *Sisham* tree and in the night their house is lighted by burning this particular wood and take their food in the night and discuss the issues of the house and village.

Method of Cultivation: Where to Start How to Start through Traditional Knowledge System

Every village has their own boundary and own hills. For example a village have eight hills, then they decide which hill is to be cultivated in which year.

They take the help of Dishari to decide if it is good or bad by testing rice before him. If the rice is broken than it is not good.Then the deity of the particular hill is also asked through Dishari what she wants like egg, rice water etc. They have that option. If the deity is agreed than they start the cultivation and the time and day is decided and every body participate in the cultivation. It is a community affair. After the day is decided then everbody participate.They have their technique of cutting the tree that regenerates the tree once again.Then they burn the trees and bush.

Rich Bio-diversity

They use the local variety of seeds which is 26 varieties of seeds to sow and within that 26 varieties they have 45 sub-varieties of seeds, thus the shifting cultivation is rich in bio-diversity. Life and culture is deeply associated with shifting cultivation: While cutting, eating and collection of crops they have their song, dance, drama and worship. They have their ritual to the trees and deities. They never eat the harvested crop before offering the same to the deities during the associated festivals.

Rosencranz and Lele (2008) have rightly opined that the Supreme Court has played an important role in increasing awareness about the sorry state of forest governance in the country. But it cannot constitutionally or practically manage India's forest. It should invoke the Constitutional Duty of the State (Under Section 48A) to prepare comprehensive legislation for a more decentralized, locally sensitive and sustainable use oriented forest governance system.

Tribal Unrest

Citing the tribal unrest of Koyas of Malkangiri in 1879, 1880, Kandhas of Phulbani in 1850, Saoras in 1890 and 1940 Das (1972) explained how the tribal resisted the alien ruler who overlooked their own traditions and felt needs. Bhuiyans and Juangs of Keonjhar were equally vociferous against the native chiefs. These uprising were suppressed by the force.

Again he explained the tribal upheavals in parts of Andhra Pradesh bordering on Orissa have shown that tribals who have openly broken the law, understood very little of individual ownership *versus* public ownership, private enterprises *versus* socialism, they understood only one point, that is, that most of their land have been under the possession of non-tribals before a few years. Prospects of shifting cultivation were curbed by forest regulations. Economic life has not improved.

The Forest Policy Regulation (1952) drastically cut down the rights of the tribals in the forests. Forest was taken as national wealth and was to run on a commercial line. But the policy regulation overlooked the very existence of those groups of people who have been living for centuries in the forest.

Bhowmick (1981) in his research work *Forestry, Tribe and The Forest Policy in India* explained and analysed and compared between Forest Policy of 1894 and National Forest Policy of 1952.

Thus, the tribals who formerly regarded themselves as lords of the forests were through a deliberate process of law, turned into subjects and brought under the control of the Forest Department. The traditional rights of the tribals were no longer recognized as rights. In 1894 they became "rights and privileges" and in 1952 they became "rights and concessions" now they are regarded as concessions.

Shukla (1992) explained how discontent against forest contractor results into Koi Revolution, 1859. The people of Bastar were discontented by the new forest regulations under which the teak forest of Bastar was contracted with the timber merchants of Hyderabad. The unpopularity of the timber merchant Haridas Bhagwandas of Hyderabad as a forest contractor was contributory cause of 1859 revolution.

Until 1850, the greater part of Southern Bastar was a country rich in teak forest, poor in communications, and of little economic or political importance. A feudal system prevailed then among Kois, who while recognizing the sovereignty of the Rajah of Bastar, lived to all practical purpose under the Jurisdiction of their tribal heads then known as *Zamindars*. The tribal villages of Bastar fell into the hands of Hyderabad traders and were being exploited. There teak forests were being denuded by the timber merchants for the British railways.

The Kois had no illusions to the seriousness of the situation. They knew that the triumph would be short-lived and that the destruction of their villages could only be a matter of days. But Pam Bhoi (Zamindar of Bhopalpatnam), Ram Shay (Zamindar of Kutru), Jugga Raju and Jumma Raju (Zamindars of Bhiji), Nagul Dora (Zamindar of Photkel), and Kunyu Dora met together and joined hands. They decided that henceforth not a single teak tree would be allowed to cut by the timber merchants and jointly they lodged a campaign against the timber merchants. Thousands of Koi allowed them in resisting the oppressive merchants. "They were continually carrying fire and swords in the dense teak forest and burnt the timber-shops and cut the heads of the sawmen" (Glasfurd, 1862). It was not like the "Chipko Movement" of the North India. It was like the one human head cut off in lieu of one teak tree. The Hyderabad Nizam had to withdraw his agents from Bastar and Glasfurd (1862) had to cancel forest-deed with the Nizam.

Cultural Diversity, Cultural Identity and Environment

Before concentrating on issue of development it would be very apt to present here the very well explained viewpoints of Vatsyayan (2003) regarding various interfaces of culture and cultural diversity with the domains of all that we understand by the term natural environment and issues of cultural identity.

Thus, she explained many definitions have been given of cultural diversity and cultural identity. Perhaps without repeating all these one may say that culture is that which remains when all else is lost. It is the ultimate test of value, individual and collective.

As well recognized today, there are parts of the world, especially the non-industrialized world, which despite all the degradation, are great reservoirs of bio-diversity. This is evident in the rich forests of South America, Africa and parts of India. Equally important are the landscapes at higher altitudes, comprising glaciers, mountains and sources of great river systems. Equally important are the oceans and vast expanses of the seas which intermingle. Besides, there are the extensive deserts, be it of Africa or Asia, Sahara, Gobi or Thar. This earth, our planet, at its primary level comprises the natural landscapes with its distinctive mix of aquatic life, flora and fauna. While the oceans, land masses and mountain, landscape and forests are diverse, together they form an interconnected, highly interdependent, integrated eco-system. It is on this primal, primeval landscape that human habitation came to be Agriculture and agricultural patterns, and all that we understand by the term sedentary lifestyles evolved later. Diversity of cropping patterns and bio-diversity of seeds and harvests and concurrency were the natural consequences. Now, this diversity is the natural pattern. Both the natural as also human landscape is indigenous. It is in these parts (both the primal as well as the secondary as agriculture) that a sizeable population of the world in all continents lives. We designate them as indigenous people, tribals, nomads or pastoralists, or village communities of small cohesive societies. The natural environment, the flora, fauna, and the climate are the first determinants of cultural diversity. Societal structures, and value systems and worldviews, evolve in time, giving each group a distinctive identity. The cultural identity is sustained even if there is displacement in physical space and time. There are countless examples of this from all parts of the world, the Hopis, Zunis, Maoris and thousand others.

Bio-diversity and Cultural Diversity

Vatsyayan (2003) very lucidly explains that the culture of these tribal groups is as diversified as is the natural landscapes. Bio-diversity is as basic as cultural diversity. If in the natural sphere multiple seeding patterns and bio-diversity are essential for the maintenance of ecological balances, between oceans and the mountains and glaciers, the river systems and the oceans, so also is the necessity to nurture and sustain the cultural diversity of these groups of the population of the world. UNESCO has correctly identified the fund of traditional knowledge of these people in respect of flora-fauna-herbs-plants, water sources identification and conservation and methods and technologies of food gathering and food production. Besides, they are creators of exquisite craftsmanship, with local material, bamboo, coconut fibre, jute, banana, cotton, wool and much else. The very first necessity in any action plan is not only to recognize the distinctiveness of each of these groups but to accord them priority and dignity as givers in a post-modern 21st century developmental process. The so-called developed world and the developed sections of society within the developing countries must acknowledge their seminal contributions in the making of world civilizations. This is a debt to be paid to them after long centuries of neglect and even exploitation of the natural environment and them as custodians of the natural environment in the wake of a misplaced and today universally recognized counter-productive subscription to a single uni-linear and uniform progressive paradigm of development.

Today after the experience of a failure to maintain ecological balances, and harmony between and amongst people, international organizations and national governments have to radically modify their policies and programmes. They, the landscape and the people cannot be confined to reservations in place or as a patronizing attitude of protection as museum pieces. They and their knowledge and skills have to be accorded equal priority and acknowledgement in terms of cultural rights, human rights, empowerment, as that given to the height attainment in modern science and technology. The worldview of most of the indigenous people ranging from Australia to Asia to Africa or Latin America was characterized by the one common and unifying principle of considering all life-plant, animal and human—as one interconnected system. Also, there was and continues to be a notion of the 'sacred' as distinct from institutionalized religion or faith. There is thus a common uniting principle, almost perennial and a diversity, of cultural patterns. It is necessary to evolve multiple strategies in order to ensure that these groups are sustained, if the rhetoric of sustainable development is to become reality. Many regulative systems of the state will need to be radically modified. Future action plans at local, national and international levels have to address themselves to the question of evolving multiple structures of administration. For example, the societal structures varied from headman to a group of elders, but in essence it was all that we understand as local self-government and participatory processes of control, rather than an objective set of rules dissociated from life's immediate experience and reality. There are innumerable instances of what we may term as the indigenous methods of self-governance in the vastly diversified groups across the globe. These are or have been replaced by monolithic structures. Naturally, there is disruption, or even eruption. A corrective has to be found. A beginning can only be made by reorienting the attitudes, policies and programmes of development agencies. The traditional wisdom we wish to harness should be a part and parcel of an entire total holistic lifestyle and not a constituent apart (Vatsyayan, 2003).

On the Concept of Development

On the concept of development Ratha (1981) has explained the 5th Schedule aimed at safeguarding the interests of the tribes in land, to give them protection against exploitation, to protect their way of life and to develop the scheduled areas and Scheduled Tribes.

The concern for tribal development, therefore, appears to be oriented towards bridging the gap between tribal and non-tribal so that the latter can become partners in the new productive processes and developmental programmes. This obviously means that the income level of the tribals must increase. Their economic development must be the first concern; without economic development the rest cannot follow.

According to Schneider (1975), Development is a multidimensional process to progressively improve the social, cultural, economic and human conditions of the people all vital sectors necessary for a balanced growth of the society. Due emphasis should be paid to establish a meaningful link between the local and national level of development and of the world at large.

Development should also mean a tangible effort to bring effective freedom to this important segment of society in order to unify the people for the greater task of nation building.

Elwin (1963) also emphasized that the problem of tribal development, then bails down to not one of carving out an exclusive destiny for tribal society. Here is a section of humanity simple, tough and hardy, convinced of the sureness of its own way of life. Their existence was depended during the centuries of their forest and mountain existence, upon the principles of challenge and response. Rigours of climate have not driven them away from their homelands nor obliged them to abandon their way of life. But then they do not suffer from the obstinacy of adherence to the beliefs. They open a frank and willing to manage when faith and reason convince them change is necessary.

Singh (1987) has explained the importance of the role of social anthropologists who were probably the first among the social scientists to describe man in his environment and habitat and to highlight their interdependence. In recent years in spite of the warnings by anthropologists this relationship has come under severe stress with the sharp deterioration of soil, pollution of air and water, and reckless destruction of forest, which has led to the recurrent cycles of drought and flood. Mining has ravaged land, and together with new projects displaced indigenous communities. Their rehabilitation in their environment poses a problem.

In a corollary to Singh's (1987) lamentation Navlakha (2008) has also apprehended the similar situation when he explained the situation in district Dantewada in Chhattisgarh, which figures in the PM's speech has a rural literacy level of 21 per cent; 1,161 out of 1,200 villages have no medical facility of any kind. The People's Union for Civil Liberties (Chhattisgarh), in a publication dated March, 2004, report, after investigation, on the occurrence of deaths due to hunger and malnutrition in Hirpal and Gidam block of the district. An all-India fact-finding report had noted that while the people of Dantewada are extremely poor, their land is extremely rich, both in terms of minerals and forests. When the State Government talks of "development", it appears to have in mind the development of these resources for private profit as against the development of its people. The State Government has signed deals worth Rs. 13,000 crore with industrial corporations and is determined to push them through. It is this process which is being heralded as ushering in development. But what do you do if the people who own or till these lands do not want his development. Well, the simple way of dealing with them is to brush aside their opposition. We may arrive at a concession if we look into the suggestion of Agrawal (2008) whose concept of development is linked to indigenous institutions. Thus, having faith upon the management capacity of the indigenous institutions for its natural resources he emphasized on an alternative approach to development. He expressed that "Indigenous institutions provide alternative approaches to development, which are holistic. A case in point is the Maori tribe of New Zealand, which has a holistic perspective on well-being." According to them "employment, economic development, learning, food production, health, natural environment, wisdom of ancestors, culture and vibrant social institutions are all interdependent and interrelated". They do not recognize "sectoral demarcations between social, cultural and economic areas" (Durie, 1998 in Loomis, 1999). In Maori customary lore, people are integrally related to nature rather than dominant over it (Loomis, 1999). This is true for many indigenous communities and institutions world over.

Constitutional Provisions

Singh (1994) has highlighted the Constitutional provisions meant for the protection from social and economic exploitation and injustice as well as for providing positive steps to the Scheduled Tribes for their socio-economic development. For the welfare of these people, the Constituent Assembly adopted Article 46 of the Constitution, which reads as follows:

> "The state shall promote with special care the educational and economic interests of the weaker section of the people, and, in particular, of the Scheduled Castes and the Scheduled Tribes, and shall protect them from social injustice and all forms of exploitation."

Article 244, 244 (A) and Fifth Schedule provide Constitutional provisions for the Administration of the scheduled areas and tribal areas. It referred to the administration and control of scheduled areas and Scheduled Tribes. For example, apart from conferring special powers to Governors of States, it had been laid down that regulations may be promulgated in the scheduled areas to prohibit or restrict transfer of lands from members of Scheduled Tribes, to regulate allotment of land to them and to regulate moneylending business.

Scheduled Area Regulation, 1969

The Act of 1969, deals more effectively with the problems of land alienation. It empowers the Deputy Commissioner to restore wrongfully alienated tribal land, without any bar of limitation. This regulation is applicable in the entire scheduled area.

Prior to the Constitution, the term "Scheduled Tribes" was not in vogue, but the tribes were variously termed as aboriginals, *Adivasis*, forest tribes, hill tribes, primitive tribes etc. up to 1919, the tribes were included under the head of "Depressed Classes". The Indian Franchise Committee in India accorded a separate nomenclature for the Census Reports. In 1931, it was named as "Primitive tribes", in 1941 as Tribes and after Independence it was renamed as "Scheduled Tribes". The term "Scheduled Tribes" was inserted in the Constitution vide Article 342 (1) which empowered the President of India to specify the tribes of tribal communities by public notification. In pursuance of this power, the president has issued eight Presidential Orders: The Constitution (S.T.) Order 1950, The Constitution (S.T.) Part 'C' States Order 1956, The Constitution (S.T.) Order, 1959, 1961, 1967 and 1968.

The term "Scheduled Area" is successor of the term "Scheduled Tracts", backward tracts, and backward areas, excluded and partially excluded area which were used in the Pre-Constitution era in the Government of India Act, 1919, 1935 and even prior to that. Articles 244 and 244 A read with 5th and 6th Schedules give the detailed provisions as to the administration and responsibility of the President, Union Government and Governors regarding the scheduled areas. The purpose of the creating the scheduled areas is to provide for special safeguards for the areas in which Scheduled Tribes are in preponderance. Thus, Article 46, 244, 275 and the 5th Schedule to the Constitution prescribe the whole framework for regulatory and development functions of the state relating to that the tenets of the Constitution cannot be regarded as mere rhetoric. Article 46 in fact, is a "Directive Principles of State Policy". The Central and State Governments regard advancement of the weaker sections as an important trust and obligation to discharge.

In this way, the Constitution of India expressed its concern and established the obligation of the state in a Constitutional framework for the all-round development of these tribal people.

On Fifth Schedule, PESA 1996 and Forest Right Act, 2006

Article 244(1) of the Indian Constitution provides for a Fifth Schedule, which can be applied to any state other than those in North-East India. The Governors of the concerned states have been given extensive powers, and may prevent or amend any law enacted by Parliament or the state assembly that could harm the *Adivasis* interest. Furthermore, the Governor can inform State Government's Administration of the area, by ascertaining the views of a Tribal Advisory Council (TAC). A TAC is to be constituted in each state having scheduled areas, and should consist of no more than 20 members, of who up to 15 should be the representatives of the STs in the State's Legislative Assembly. Eight states with scheduled areas, plus Tamil Nadu and West Bengal, have established TACs. The Governor is also empowered to frame new laws and make regulations in consultation with the TACs, in particular to prohibit or restrict the transfer of land by or among members of STs, and to regulate the allotment of land to STs.

However, all of these laws and regulations must be submitted to the President for agreement. This makes the procedure very circuitous and centralized. Furthermore, if the Governor chooses not to take the TAC's advice, the TAC can do little. Many feel that the Fifth Schedule is vague and inadequate, and that it has not been used constructively. In many states, the TACs hardly meet. Governor could have brought appropriate modifications to Acts like the Indian Forest Act, 1927 the Indian Penal Code and the Criminal Procedure Code, and other mining and land acquisition laws for the benefits of *Adivasis*, extending these to the scheduled areas; but this has not happened. Instead, all laws have been routinely extended to the scheduled areas. All Governors of States with scheduled areas are required to make an annual report to the President regarding their administration. In the case of Bihar, Gujarat, Himachal Pradesh, Maharashtra, Orissa and Rajasthan, no report has been received by the President since 1992, in Andhra Pradesh since 1986 and in Madhya Pradesh which has the highest ST population since 1990. Some *Adivasi* areas were omitted by the President while scheduling. In 1976, Parliament amended the Fifth Schedule to enable the President to increase the scheduled areas. Central Government directed the State Governments to send proposals for scheduling. However, *Adivasi* areas in Karnataka, Kerala, Tamil Nadu, Uttar Pradesh and West Bengal remain unscheduled, and the eight states with scheduled areas. Andhra Pradesh, Bihar, Gujarat, Himachal Pradesh, Madhya Pradesh, Maharashtra, Orissa and Rajasthan have still not been fully covered. (*http://ourtimes-yoursandmine.blogspot.com/2009/12/36grh-or-chhattisgarh-part-4-tribals.html*)

Regarding the function of Tribal Advisory Committee in Chhattisgarh, it may be mentioned that the TAC was formed on 26-07-2006. However, as per the information available from the Assistant Commissioner, Tribal Welfare and Development, Jagdalpur so far two meetings were held by TAC, one on 5th September, 2008 and the other on 28th July, 2009. From the agenda of the meeting held on the later meeting it is evident that a discussion was held for the approval of report of the Governor for the year 2007-2008 which was expected to be sent to the President of India.

Panchayats Extension to Scheduled Areas Act, 1996

The sustained campaign for Rights of the tribal over local resources led first to the 73rd Amendment of the Constitution to give recognition to decentralize governance in rural areas and then the constitution of the Bhuria Committee to look at tribal rights over resources through extension of the provisions of this Amendment to the Schedule V areas. Based on the recommendations of the committee, Parliament passed a separate legislation in 1996 as an annexure to the 73rd Amendment specifying special provisions for Panchayats in Schedule V areas. Known as the Panchayats Extension to Schedule Areas, 1996, it decentralized existing approaches to forest governance by bringing the Gram Sabha centre stage and recognized the traditional rights of tribals over "community resources"—meaning land, water, and forests. PESA was important not just because it provided for a wide range of rights and privileges, but also because it provided a principle as well as a basis for future law making concerning the tribals. According to the Central Government law, the states promulgated their own laws supposedly giving rights to tribals over local resources (Patnaik, 2007).

According to PESA, Gram Sabhas are empowered to preserve their cultural identities, community resources, modes of dispute resolution and equally importantly the right to approve Government plans, programmes and projects within their jurisdiction (Mukul, 1997).

Menon (1997) went a step ahead when he analyses that the presence of STA and PESA, if implemented, legitimizes *Adivasi* claims to land or their own systems of governance. Non-engagement in these legal battles would simply make it easier for the state to do as it sees fit, regardless of prior claims to land. He mentioned about Right to Place and explained these struggles over the law, however, is more than just a livelihood struggle. They are struggle over cultural territories as well. The state claim of eminent domain through the Land Acquisition Act denies the existence of customary claims to homeland by *Adivasi* communities. Hence, the struggle for "good" law is also very much about the right to remain in places which are considered home. Resettlement and rehabilitation, even if implemented properly, deny *Adivasis* these rights to place.

Keesing (1990) too emphasizes about the incorporation of villagers into the process of planning, changes in their own lives. Locally elected bodies—Panchayats in India or Area Councils in the Solomons—may ostensibly provide mechanisms for incorporating local communities into planning and decision-making. But in reality they are likely to represent local economic and power interests in ways that, once more, reinforce local vested interests and inequities, incorporating the poorest villager into the planning process is in the long run more important than incorporating the Panchayat president, who is likely to be the biggest local merchant, landlord, or orchard owner.

The Scheduled Tribes and Other Traditional Forest Dwellers (Recognition of Forest Rights) Act, 2006

The Supreme Court of India in an important case held that the tribals have definite right over the forests and any sort of forest diversion or eviction should have their informed consent. Following suit, in an affidavit to the Apex Court, in June 2004, the Government of India made a significant admission by holding that "historical injustice" had been done to the tribal forest dwellers of the country, which needed to be immediately addressed by recognizing their traditional rights over forests and forest land. What made this admission particularly crucial was its acceptance that colonial perspective on forest management had failed and alienated a large chunk of the forest dwellers, especially tribals from forests and forest-based livelihood options. Patnaik (2007) has explained the Act has defined forest land as land of any description falling within any forest area and includes most types of forests. The law provides for recognition and vesting of forest rights to Scheduled Tribes in occupation of forest land prior to 13 December, 2005 and to other traditional forest dwellers who are in occupation of forest land for at least three generations, i.e. 75 years, up to a maximum of 4 hectares. These rights are heritable but no alienable or transferable. Forest rights include among other things, right to hold and live in the forest land under individual or common occupation for habitation, self-civilization for livelihood etc. Besides, the Act recognizes the rights over "community forest resource" that it defines as customary common forest land within the traditional or customary boundaries of the village including protected areas. Moreover, one of the most crucial aspects of the Forest Rights within a protected area is through declaration and demarcation of the "Critical Wildlife Habitat" (CWLH).

Regarding implementation of this Act in Chhattisgarh, Sharma (2010) revealed that the Act, legislated in 2006 to provide tribals legal access to forest land and resources, was meant to be a crucial antidote to tribal alienation and unrest. Chhattisgarh Government has claimed the four-year-old law was fully implemented by March 2010. Data submitted to the Ministry of Tribal Affairs showed it had settled "100 per cent of individual claims" made by tribals, making it the best performing state in the country. Maharashtra next door had settled just 46 per cent claims, West Bengal 66 per cent and Orissa 87 per cent. Large scale "wrongful rejections" and "blatant irregularities" at the level of *Gram Sabha* not verified by block and district level officials.

However, when we have inquired about the reasons for rejection of application it has been revealed by Forest Department, Jagdalpur that—

1. That a Survey has been done in 1949 for reserve Forest in Chhattisgarh state. The inhabitable area was not included in Reserve Forest. The chance is rather less for omission of such forest dwellers.
2. That question of occupation of the area prior to 13th December, 2006 has been scrutinized by the *Gram Sabha* and thereby the application of the non-occupant was rejected.
3. That in some cases, the villagers who had encroachment of the forest land of nearby villagers were rejected in the *Gram Sabha* of the later villages. For example, in Bastar in Bakawand Block, the villagers of Khomar had an encroachment of land in nearby Satosa village, whose Right to land was rejected by the Gram Sabha of later village.

Regarding follow-up action for the suggestions of the Report of N.C. Sexena, Forest Department, Jagdalpur revealed that they had sought permission from the State Government of Chhattisgarh in order to provide *pattas* to the forest dwellers in Critical Wild Life Area as per the provision of Forest Right Act, 2006. They had got the clarification from the State Government and the process has initiated in this regard. Also steps have taken to keep the record of application, verification and scrutiny etc. in village level.

Regarding Saxsena's suggestion to intimate the reasons of rejection to *Gram Sabha* the Forest Department had taken the steps and one month time period was given to *Gram Sabha* for the appeal of Land Right.

The Case Studies of Lahandiguda and Koida Blocks of Chhattisgarh and Orissa Respectively

The Case of Lahandiguda

Chhattisgarh, a predominantly tribal State, has about 32 big and small tribes and is endowed with rich mineral and forest resources. The Scheduled Tribes are concentrated in the southern, northern and the north-eastern districts of the State. The highest concentration is in the erstwhile Bastar district. The new district of Dantewara has 79 per cent tribals followed by Bastar (67%), Jashpur (65%), Surguja (57%) and Kanker (56%). However, during the past few decades, the demographic profile of tribal dominated areas has undergone several changes. Large scale intrusion of non-tribals in tribal areas is mostly responsible for the creation of a faulty developmental model where tribals are denied their share in development. As observed by the People's Union for Civil Liberties, in one of its reports title Bastar. An investigation into an Encounter, June 1985, A lopsided socio-economic development of the district caused by indirect exploitation through environmental destruction and direct exploitation through cheating and duping has provided an ideal setting for the Naxalities to take root in the area (Kujur, 2006).

Ganguli and Choudhry (2003) through their research has explained how the forest of Bastar have for long been a vital source of sustenance for the many tribal groups who live there. Yet lack of organization and overt dependence on local traders has often led to their exploitation, with most profits of trade accruing to the latter. The onus lies on NGOs and government-designated procurement groups to help them not merely to form effective organization to market their produce, but to ensure foolproof implementation of relevant legislation.

Before explaining the displacement and rehabilitation issue of

Lahandiguda, which is 30 km away from the west of district Headquarter Jagdalpur, in the State of Chhattisgarh, it would be pertinent to cite here the historical importance of the block which has seen violence and bloodshed known as "Lahandiguda firing" and has occurred not very long back in the year 1961.

On market day, Friday, 31 March, 1961, in protest against the arrest of popular king Raja Pravir Chandra Bhanja Deo there was a large meeting at Lohandiguda attended by over 10,000 people. Vijay Chandra was brought to try and disperse the crowd but they refused to leave. The police burst tear gas shells and when the crowd still continued to advance, they opened fire. Thirteen people were killed as several others were injured. The people had been told that the bullets would turn to water but once the firing started and they saw men and women falling, they began running away. Those who stayed were *lathi*-charged by the police (Sundar, 1999).

For this chapter few pertinent observations were made regarding the affected tribal communities of Lahandiguda block of Bastar whose land was supposed to be acquired by a private company. The observations were made during the reconnoiter tour to said Block of Bastar during the implementation of the project "coping strategies of a displaced communities" which took place during 19th to 29th October, 2008 and subsequently during 5th to 14th December, 2008.

The Rs. 10,000 crore TATA Steel Project proposed to acquire 5339 hectares of land in 10 villages, i.e., Belar, Bandaji, Baliapal, Debpal, Bodeparoda, Kumli, Takraguda, Chhindgaon, Bade Dharaur and Sirisguda where village Baliapal is an abandoned village. All the villages come under Lahandiguda block, whereas village Sirisguda comes under Tokapal block.

The field is extraordinary and most challenging for any of the anthropologist for the reason that the inhabitants of these 10 villages which is multi-ethnic, multi-tribal and multi-castes have been fighting since 2005 with tooth and nail with the State Administration and since last two years no administrative vehicles has ventured into some villages like Bade Paroda, Dabpal, Sirisguda, Takaraguda and Bellar etc.

Since the proposed community for the study is Bison Horn Maria, it is interesting to note that administrative vehicles have not ventured into those *paras* (hamlets) of those villages where major Bison-Horn Maria community inhabits.

During the first phase of reconnoiter tour with the help of the traditional tribal leaders (*Majhis* who have been attending the *Majhi Chalki* workshop in Zonal Anthropological Museum since last five years), we could communicate with the Sarpanch and the Ex-Sarpanches and other informants who had played an important role for the rapport establishment in the studied area. The other key persons are Anganwadi Workers who had played a vital role for our access to the villages. It was really very tough to make clear to the villagers that it was a research work and the researcher was not a Tata's agent.

Each and every village has many paras. For example village Sirisguda of Tokapal Block is having seven *paras* like Schoolpara, Kundipara, Meriguda, Deyguda, Dutipara, Nayapara and Bazarpara having multi-religious population, i.e. Hindu, Christian and tribal religion etc.

The villages are multi-ethnic in the sense that they belong to different tribal group, caste group, language group, religious group and above all region like that marthi migrants who have been settled here since three generations. The inhabitants speak Halbi, Gondi, Bhatri, Hindi and Chhattisgarhi etc. the multi-caste of the villager reflected in the fact that they belong to Brahmin, Dhakad, Raut and Mahara caste.

Though Bison Horn Marias is the major tribe of these villages, other tribal groups like Muria, Bhatra and Halba also inhabit. In the second phase of reconnoiter field-work from 5th to 14th December, 2008 total number of households and total population of the affected 10 villages are collected. Thus, data from the block office revealed that the affected villages of Lohandiguda block have 2,762 total households with a total population of 14,242. Village Sirishguda has 350 total households with a total population of 2095 where ST population is 1713 (81.76%). The affected villages have a total land of 14,745 hectares. Of the 45,745 hectares of land, 5,339 hectares of land would be affected for the private company.

Intercommunity tension became evident during the second phase of reconnoiter tour. Extensive photographs were carried on regarding the settlement pattern, physical characteristics of the inhabitants occupation structure, CPR (Common Property Resources like ponds, wells, religious places, sacred groves, Devgudi grazing field and burial grounds) and above all the nature of the agricultural land. It becomes evident that the lands of all the villages are fertile and double crop land except one village i.e., Bade Paroda. Existence of sacred groves in many villages came to light. Archaeological site of village Kumli was photographically documented.

Instances of seasonal migration of the 10 villages to other states came to light. The villages are surrounded by hills of lime stone. The study area comes under 5th Schedule. *Gram Sabha* has approved the land acquisition. People had road blocked. Villagers were put behind the bars for protection of land acquisition in the plea that they are the Naxalites (as stated by one of the informants). Majority of the Sarpanches marched to Delhi to meet the Scheduled Tribe Commission and noted social worker Dr. B.D. Sharma.

With an effort to know the situation more explicitly, the researcher analysed the news of print media in connection to the land acquisition of tribal communities in Lahandiguda.The news of TATA Steel knocking the door of tribal Bastar for its Rs. 10,000 crore Project came in 2005. The news is like this—to set up its plants. TATA needs land in Bastar (*Navbharat*, 27-09-05), TATA offers attractive package to Bastar (*Amrit Sandesh*, 10-11-05), information provided to the villagers along with the survey (*Navbharat*, 03-12-05). The protest of the villagers in Lohandiguda Block was constantly flashed in different newspapers. Around 6015 villagers will be displaced for the plant (*Navbharat*, 11-11-05).

However, different newspapers covered the news of protest as follows—

> Against TATA Steel Memorandum was given to Hon'ble Governor (*Highway Channel*, 13-11-05), protest against survey in Belar (*Dainik Bhaskar*, 28-11-08), villagers are united against TATA Steel plant (*Hindsat*, 08-12-05), villagers wouldn't give land to TATA (*Dainik Bhaskar*, 08-12-05), Tent of the protesters in front Collectorate was removed (*Dainik Bhaskar*, 28-05-06), Tribals are against steel plant. M.L.A., Lachu Kashyap (*Jansatta*, 14-4-06), protest against TATA Steel (*Jansatta*, 12.5.10) and this news came just before approval of land acquisition in *Gram Sabha* on dated: 20th July, 2006. Tension brewing in Balar and Badanjee (*Highway Channel*, 5-6-06), once again protest against TATA (*Nav Bharat* and *Hindsat*, 16-5-08), Bastar winessed the biggest ever tribal rally (*Hindsat*, 2-6-2009), one of the purposes of the rally was to protest against TATA Steel.

Amidst these protests, there was also news of support in favour of TATA Steel. The news was as follows—Huge rally in support of TATA Steel (*Jansatta*, 14-4-06), this rally was backed by all major political parties. Government of Chhattisgarh and TATA Steel celebrate completion of one year MOU (*Highway Channel*, 5-6-06).

News was also coming regarding organization of *Gram Sabha* etc. The news was as follows—

> "Eight villages agreed for TATA Steel (*Nav Bharat*, 20-7-2006). During this *Gram Sabha* there was heavy deployment of police force and more over the boundaries of the villages were heavily cordoned. The place of *Gram Sabha* was declared prohibited area".

Other related news on *Gram Sabha* was as follows—

> "The last obstacles of TATA Steel is removed (*Navbharat*, 4-8-2006), Chhattisgarh Panchayat called special *Gram Sabha* (*Highway Channel*, 21st February, 2007) the Register of Takraguda, Belar, Dabpal, Bade Paroda, Dhuragaon and Badanjee were captured (*Highway Channel*, 21-2-2007)".

Though the news of Better rehabilitation of TATA affected people came on the year 2006 (*Nav Bharat*, 8-4-2006). The compensation of land for land news came two years after (*Nai Dunia*, *Dainik Bhaskar*, *Pratha India*, *Highway Channel*, 30-05-2008). No one will be landless Collector, Bastar (*Channel India*, 20-5-2008) compensating land would be free of tax (*Bastar Sambhag*, 31-05-2008, P.S.).

Not only the rehabilitation package, but also the compensation money was not without controversy. Thus, the related news on compensation money was like this:

> "Even dead person got compensation money (*Highway Channel*, (16-4-2008). Road blockade for compensation money (*Highway Channel*, 10-05-2008). Demand to make public the compensation money (*Highway Channel*, 15-05-2006). Compensation money of Rs. 15 lakh was grabbed (*Highway Channel*, 2-05-2008)".

The Case Study of Koida

The researcher had an exposure to the Paudi Bhuiyan belt of Koida block of district Sundargarh in the State of Orissa during the fieldwork in connection to 11th plan project "the study of folk narratives of Human Origin."

The journey from Kaleipasi to Koida was one of the most dangerous journey the researcher had during her 25 years of fieldwork experience. The 57 km road from Kaleipasi to Koida seems to be a death trap with incessant running of thousand overloaded trucks, roughness of the road with the dry trees on both the sides unable to carry on photosynthesis, because of the layers of dust on their leaves, the speediness of the vehicle that always haunts one for a fatal accident. The "Tensa Ghat" seemed to be a real danger for its many unsafe curves and the reckless driving by the trucks and dumper drivers where a moment of distraction of attention would throw you and your vehicle into a death trap 150 ft. below the *ghat*.

We were narrowly saved by hair point from fatal accident from ramming of a truck in front and from dashing of a truck behind. For 57 km road it took eight hours to reach our destination Koida. However, the government officials and local people at Koida revealed you reached Koida at the earliest. They opined it takes 24 hours or even two to three days to cover the road when road is obstructed because of an accident. Thousands of standard vehicles do not have any other options but to starve without water and food. But the lure of the mining never stops.

Block Development Officer Sri Parikhit Sethi revealed once they had rescued two drivers from three days of fever and starvation when the road was blocked because of an accident. Also the block officials are exempted from reaching the meeting at collectorate in Sundergarh in time due to unpredictable road. However, road that goes through K. Bolang has improved a lot, except the initial 9 km. road from Koida.

On its main road the small town Koida, which is also the block Head-quarter witnesses thousands of trucks blowing dust that percolates to the houses, shops which include hotels etc. The school dresses put on by the students including their hairs while reaching their schools turned into red.

While the researcher carried on fieldwork in Mithida, Kedalia, Kadakala, Kalamanga and Tintoo, Badepatuli, the Paudi Bhuiyan villagers of Koida block an interaction with the Sarpanches of Patta Munda and Dengula Panchayats Sri Sriram Munda and Sri Chakradhar Dehuri respectively revealed their woes who seem be unaware about the power of *Gram Sabha* and PESA.

Sriram Munda explained how they are helpless on the face of incessant mining. The more the area of mining is expanded the more the tribesmen moved away towards the hills. Even, they do not know how to protect *'sasan'*, their burial place. Needless to say mining has not changed the economic conditions of the people. Chakradhar Dehuri Sarpanch of Dengula with his graduate education revealed to get NOC for the road in a village is difficult than to get NOC for mining in a reserved forest area by a private company.

The two Sarpanches also mentioned about 22 crushers working day and night at village Kentarkela has changed the whole atmosphere. Yudhishthir Nayak, a retired school teacher from village Bada Patuli who is also the General Secretary of Panchasahakhanda Bhuyan Samaj, Koida Mandal has awareness about the power of the *Gram Sabha*, the full village assembly. He revealed that once in a *Gram Sabha* we noticed the presence of the outsiders and raised a protest against it that in a *Gram Sabha* only the presence of the villagers is required.

While our journey from Kaleipasi to Koida we had noticed at village Tinkoo sprinkling of water was carried on by Zindel Company to prevent dust pollution. We also observed the primary Sebashram school having a total strength of 174 students out of which 140 were hostel inmates along with its three teachers were in constant threat to their health and safety. However, the lady teacher revealed her trauma with a request not to reveal her name that the only means to cover the road was either the two alternate buses or the dumpers. In urgent case when a hostel inmate falls ill they approach a dumper to take them to the hospital at Lahunipara which is 18 km away from Tinkoo and they have to travel on the same road.

We also noticed sprinkling of water on the main road of Koida. However, a local person revealed the water of our spring has turned into red for thousand trucks use to clean their vehicle. Now, our water is used for sprinkling purpose. Village Tintoo which is 27 km. away from the block Headquarter Koida having 42 households consisting of both Paudi Bhuiyan and Munda down the hills and a river and waterfall nearby is facing the brunt of the mining and the life and livelihood of the people is at a stake. Of the 42 households, 11 households belong to Munda community.

While we had an interaction with the villagers we observed the dust layers are coming down the hills and slowly the verandah of the house, street, paddy field and *Kaman* (hills that are used for shifting cultivation) are coated with layers of dust. They revealed they had stopped the practice of shifting cultivation because of the mining of the hills. Once a big boulder like stone rushed down to the village because of careless explosion of dynamite. Fortunately, there was no causalty and the matter was hushed up.

Tintoo would always haunt the researcher along with its lush green forest and hills, its waterfall, river and the inhabitants of Paudi Bhuiyans who are in the clutches of both legal and illegal mining and whose situation is just like “a leaf in the strong tide”.

Thus, both the cases of Lohandiguda and Koida reveal some common features which are as follows:

1. Both the blocks are rich in mineral resources as well as have fertile land and inhabited by majority of tribal community.
2. Both the region exhibit rich cultural diversity having multi-tribal, multi-caste and multi-religious population.
3. The tribes of mining ravaged Koida and the tribes of “still to be lands acquiesce” Lohandiguda block have expressed their anguish and anger respectively against land acquisition. In case of Koida, the protest in the form of road blocked has gone futile since the tribe could not muster the courage to face thousand trucks and other external threat.

In Lohandiguda—the *Gram Sabha* on 28th July, 2006 and 3rd August, 2010 respectively has approved the land acquisition of private company. However, the print media reveal a different story of constant opposition and protest to land acquisition.The Sarpanches of affected villages of both the blocks are aware of the plight of their villagers. However, in case of Lohandiguda Sarpanches of 10 affected villagers marched to Delhi to meet the Scheduled Tribe Commission whereas the Sarpanches of Koida are still in a dilemma as to whom to look at for protection of their rights. The latest data is that Saha Commission has given some respite to the mining

Conclusion

Thus, both the States of Chhattisgarh and Orissa come under 5th Schedule area where tribal land and cultural rights can be protected only if the provisions of PESA 1996 are properly implemented. In case of land acquisition, the Bison Horn Maria tribe of Lohandiguda would lose their burial place where they have erected their memorial pillars in the memory of their dead ancestors, the Munda tribe of Koida would lose their burial place ‘*sasan*’. If Cultural Diversity is as basic as Bio-Diversity, the question again arises how to protect the culture of the tribes. We need to think seriously how Article 29(1) would be implemented in its true spirit in order to protect the language, script and culture of the tribes. The time has come for Anthropologists and other Social scientists, Administrators, Policy-makers and Planners to find out and trace the lacunas for which the *Gram Sabhas* are nullified, to find out the reasons that stand as a barrier for proper implementation of the spirits of the Constitutional safeguards for protection of the tribal rights.

However, amidst the grim situation the decision of MoFF (Ministry of Forest and Environment for rejection of environmental clearance accorded to state owned Orissa Mining Corporation (OMC) to mine bauxite in Niyamgiri Hills on December 11, 2008 for supply to Anil Agrawal promoted Vedanta Aluminium Ltd.'s refinery in Lanjigarh has come as a respite. The rejection is based on the Saxena Committee and Forest Advisory Committee (FAC) which had concluded that both Vedanta and OMC had violated three central laws: Forest Right Act, Forest Conservation Act and Environment Protection Act while implementing the in principle approval granted in December, 2008 (*Indian Express*, 25th August, 2010:1). It is also heartening to know that The Baiga community is one of the 75 particularly vulnerable tribal groups, or PVTGs, who are eligible to get habitat rights under the Scheduled Tribes and other Traditional Forest Dwellers (Recognition of Forest Rights) Act, also known as the Forest Rights Act (FRA). Over the years, increasing state control over forests and diversion of forest land for development and conservation have seriously threatened these forest communities. The definition of the habitat rights was incorporated through an amendment in the FRA in 2012. As per the amendment, the district level committee under the Act shall ensure that all PVTGs receive habitat rights, in consultation with the concerned traditional institutions of these groups, after filing claims before the *Gram Sabha*.

Seven Baiga villages namely—Dhaba, Rajani Sarai, Dhurkuta, Limau, Jilang, Silpidi, Ajgar, in Samnapur block of the district of Dindori in Madhya Pradesh have received habitat rights. After three years of research, consultation and mapping, it was in November 2015 that the authorities began handing over legal titles. District Collector Chhavi Bhardwaj told Down To Earth that the right has been granted over 9,300 hectares to about 900 families in seven villages (Down to Earth, 2016). We need to take such type of more and stringent steps for the implementation of Constitutional safeguards, so that, the promise and delivery of tribal development would strike a similar chord.

References

Anderson, Robert S., 1988. *The Hour of the Fox, Tropical Forests, the World Bank, and Indigenous People in Central India*, New Delhi: Vistar Publications.

Agrawal, Ashish, 2008. "Indigenous Institutions for National Resources Management: Potential and Threats", *Economic and Political Weekly* XLIII (23):23.

Bhowmick, P.K., 1981. "Forestry, Tribe and the Forest Policy in India", in *Tribal Development and its Administration.* L.P. Vidyarthi (ed.), New Delhi: Concept Publishing Company".

Das, Nityananda. 1972. The Tribal Situations. In *Orissa the Tribal Situation in India.* by K. Suresh Singh (ed.), Shimla: Indian Institute of Advanced Study, Delhi: Motilal Banarasidass.

Elwin, Verrier. 1958. *Leaves from the Jungle Life in a Gond Village.* London: Oxford University Press.

Elwin, Verrier.1963. *A New Deal for Tribal India,* Government of India, Ministry of Tribal Affairs.

Verrier Elwin, 2007. *The Baiga*, Gyan Books, New Delhi.

Forsyth, J., 1889. The Highlands of Central India: Notes on their Forest and Wild Tribes Natural History and Sports. London.

Ganguli, B.K., Kalpana Choudhuri, 2003. "Forest Products of Bastar: A Study of Tribal Exploitation", *Economic and Political Weekly,* XXXVIII (28):2985-2989.

Grigson, Sir Wilfrid. 1949. *The Maria Gonds of Bastar*. Delhi: Vanya Prakashan.

Guha, Ramchandra. 1983. "Forestry in British and Post-British in India: An Historical Analysis", *Economic and Political Weekly,* XVII:1882-96.

Guha, Ramchandra. 1989. *The Uniquiet Woods: Ecological Change and Peasant Resistance in the Western Himalaya*, Delhi, p. 29.

Guha, Ramchandra, M. Gadgil. 1989. *State Forestry and Social Conflict in British India: Past and Present,* CXXIII: 145.

Joshi, G.M., 1990. *Tribal Bastar and The British Administration.* New Delhi: Indus Publishing Company.

Jones, Steve. 1978. "Tribal Underdevelopment in India", *Development and Change*, 9: 47-50. Citing the 1973 *Annual Report, Commission for Scheduled Castes and Scheduled Tribes*: 395.

Keesing, Roger M., 1990. Development Planning: An Anthropologist's Perspective *the Human Dimension of Development Perspectives from Anthropology.* Hari Mohan Mathurs, (ed.), New Delhi: Concept Publishing Company.

Kujur, Rajat Kumar. 2006. Left Extremism in India, Naxal Movement in Chhattisgarh and Orissa, *PCS Special Report*, 25, June: 2-3.

Loomis, Terrence. 1999. *Indigenous Populations and Sustainable Development Building and Indigenous Approaches to Holistic Self Determined Development,* 28(5): 893-910.

Menon, Ajit. 2007. "Engaging with the Law on Adivasi Rights. *Economic and Political Weekly*, XLLII (24): 2240-2241.

Mukul. 1997. "Tribal Areas: Transition to Self-Governance", *Economic and Political Weekly*, 32(18):928-929.

Navalakha, Goutam. "Savage way for Development", *Economic and Political Weekly,* XLIII (16):16-19.

Patnaik, Sanjay. 2007. PESA, The Forest Rights Act and Tribal Rights in India Proceedings: International Conference on Poverty Reduction and Forests. Bangkok September. In *www.rewftc.org/fileadmin.doc*

Rangarajan, Mahesh. 1996. *Fencing the Forest Conservation and Ecological Changes in India's Central Provinces*. Delhi: Oxford University Press.

Ratha, S.N., 1986. *Tribal Development Programme: An Appraisal in Tribal Development and Its Administration.* L.P. Vidyarthi, (ed.) New Delhi: Concept Publishing Company, pp. 86-87.

Rooke, E.A. 1906. Letter to Panda Bajinath, Diwan, B.S., 14 March Summarizing Fisher's Proposal, XXIII (18). Jagdalpur Record Room Collectorate Bastar.

Rosencranz Amin, Sharachandra Lele. 2008. "Supreme Court and India's Forests", *Economic and Political Weekly,* XLIII (5):11-14.

Schneider, Harold K., 1975. "Economic Development and Anthropology", *Annual Review of Anthropology.* B.J. Siegel (ed.), 271-292. Palo Alto: Annual Review Inc.

Sharma, Supriya. 2010. *Times of India*, June 18.

Singh, C.P., 1994. *Tribal Development Administration—A Case Study*. New Delhi: Mittal Publications.

Singh, K.S., 1987. "Anthropology Development and Culture", *Anthropology, Development and Nation Building.* A.K. Kalla and K.S. Singh (eds.), New Delhi: Concept Publishing Company.

Shukla, Hiralal. 1992. *History of People of Bastar.* Delhi: Sharada Publishing House, pp. 69-70.

Sundar, Nandini. 1997. *Subalterns and Sovereigns: An Anthropological History of Bastar (1854-1996).* New Delhi: Oxford University Press.

Vatsyayan, Kapila. 2003. "Strengthening Efforts to Assess the Interconnection between Culture and Development in the Elimination of Poverty". *Kalakalpa* 1(1): 69-77.

THIRTEEN

IRONING OUT THE CREASES

Leprosy Stigma among *Dalit* Women of Sambalpur City of Western Odisha, India

RASHMI PRAMANIK

Leprosy is a disease, which still strikes fear in the societies as a mutilating, disfiguring, contagious and incurable disease. Because of the horrifying nature of the enigmatic physical disfigurement and since no cure was discovered until the 20th century, leprosy has, for centuries, been a highly stigmatizing disease. Though leprosy is not a disease of the poor, yet it affects poor to a much greater extent because of their social and economic vulnerability. The stigma attached to leprosy leads to loss of employment even before manual labour becomes more difficult due to disability, which often results from late or no treatment. It also leads to exclusion from society, causing physical and emotional distress.

Even to this day, when leprosy is completely curable with MDT (multi-drug therapy), some parts of India uphold the belief that leprosy is a divine curse, a punishment of the past sins, and a result of immoral sexual behaviour. These beliefs reinforce the image of the '*leper*' as being physically and morally unclean, to be blamed for contracting the disease and therefore to be ostracized. The repulsive physical image, the fear of infection and the belief that it is incurable are the root causes of the inhuman treatment that is often meted out to those who have leprosy. Leprosy is a complex condition that not only affects patients physically; it has social and psychological implications that must be considered if cure is ever to be complete. The World Health Organization describes health as not merely the absence of disease, but "a state of complete physical, mental and social well-being" (Collier, J. Longmore and M. Brown, 2001). As researchers, it is difficult for us to deal with the issues very sensitive as stigma and ostracism; they are less comprehensible than cellular and biochemical processes. But, as human beings, we need to sensible what leprosy means to our patients and their communities. For holistic care, we must never forget the impact leprosy can have on a patient's psychological and social well-being.

More than any other disease [except perhaps ACQUIRED IMMUNE DEFICIENCY SYNDROME (AIDS)], leprosy has a very negative image. In literature, outcastes are treated like lepers; leprosy and stigma have been almost synonymous. For centuries it was a feared disease, the very word invoking shame and disgust. Stigma is hard to define and measure, being a "complex reality made up as it is from a mixture of belief, attitudes and behaviours" (Romero-Salazar, A. Parra, M.C., Moya-Hernandez, C. *et al.*,1995). For many sufferers, however, it is the hardest part of the burden to bear.

Historically, oppression has been and continues to be a serious issue of concern worldwide in both developed and underdeveloped countries. The structure of Indian society, with its hierarchies and power structures, is an ideal place to better understand the experience of oppression. The *dalits,* are the people so low in social status that they were not included in the caste system. *Dalits* are considered to be unclean from birth and are perpetually filthy and can never escape their status. The form of untouchability is forbidden by law in the Constitution of India, but the social stigma, discrimination and social exclusion of *Dalits* remains both on an institutional and personal level even today. In addition to economic hardships, *Dalits* endure relentless social bigotry. They are viewed as existing beneath the lowest classification of the collective caste structure in India (Vincentnathan, 1996). The *Dalits* are dissuaded from living near or marrying those born into high-caste families, although this does infrequently transpire (Deshpande, 2001).

Vulnerably positioned at the bottom of India's caste, class and gender hierarchies, *Dalit* women experience endemic gender-and-caste discrimination and violence as the outcome of severely imbalanced social, economic and political power equations. Their socio-economic vulnerability and lack of political voice, when combined with the dominant risk factors of being *Dalit* and female, increase their exposure to potentially violent situations while simultaneously reducing their ability to escape. The overall picture of women with leprosy is worrying. Women with leprosy face inequalities due to their sex and their disease. Leprosy increases women's vulnerability due to misconceptions and stigma about the disease within society. The female with leprosy does indeed face a double jeopardy; her socially inferior status and her highly stigmatized disease result in greater social and mental problems, even if the disease is often less severe (physically) in women than in men. In order to understand, therefore, the reality of Indian society in general, and the *Dalit* community and *Dalit* women in particular, a focused analysis of caste-class-gender-leprosy dynamics is imperative. This four-fold lens focusing on the cultural and material dimensions will give a true comprehension on the social relations and social inequalities in India.

Different Categories of Stigma

Stigma is a universal phenomenon. Although stigmatizing is common, not all individuals attach a stigma to their disease or disability (Goffman, 1963) distinguishes the three categories of stigma. Stigma is typically a social process, experienced or anticipated, characterized by rejection, blame or devaluation those results from experience, perception or reasonable anticipation of an adverse social judgement about a person or group. Stigma is not just a matter of using the wrong word or action. Stigma is about disrespect. It is the use of negative labels to identify a person living with physical and mental illness. Stigma is a barrier. Fear of stigma, and the resulting discrimination, discourages individuals and their families from getting the help they need. Leprosy affects many problems like avoidance, negligence, separation, torture and less respect in society etc. because of which they hide their disease.

The distressing prospect of having a stigmatized condition, which is further associated with stigmatized status in society, may be an inducement to ignore or conceal it and forego the kind of help that one might readily acknowledge as useful if the condition were affecting someone else.

- **Felt stigma** refers in particular to the negative attitudes the community felt or perceived by those with a stigmatized condition internalized (or self-) stigma refers the way people who are (or perceive themselves to be) at the receiving end of stigma. This usually includes reduced self-esteem ("I am no good"; "no one will want to marry a person affected by leprosy like myself"), hopelessness ("I can no longer do anything") and sometimes feelings of guilt or self-blame related to the stigmatized condition ("it is probably my own fault that I have developed leprosy").

- **Enacted stigma** denotes actual occurrences discrimination *(e.g.* divorce, denying someone access to public transport) or negative behaviour (*e.g.* gossiping).
- **Institutional stigma** is stigma or discrimination which part of institutional arrangements or policies. This would include separate clinic arrangements for people affected by leprosy, mental illness or HIV/AIDS, insufficient arrangements for confidentiality, laws sanctioning divorce or social exclusion on the basis of a health condition.

Impact of Stigmatization

In one study, Leerapun *et al*. (1989) concluded that visibility of deformity correlates with the level of stigmatization in the community. Some patients perceived rejection by their families and communities and voluntarily left their homes for treatment at hospitals or colonies. Some patients were treated at home but shunned contact with the community. Spouses and children were more likely to accept and take care of patients, although they too feared contagion. Some couples separated permanently. Community members reacted to leprosy patients with fear and disgust, but their condemnation was not overt. Leerapun *et al*. (1989) also mentioned that for most people with leprosy, self-stigmatization precedes negative societal reaction. After the diagnosis, all patients and their families felt anxiety, and patients experienced fear of becoming ostracized and deformed. The level of anxiety differed according to the perceived severity of symptoms, people's familiarity with the disease, and the degree of social support from relatives. Following treatment and cure, people with visible deformities faced difficulty in adapting. They were ostracized, socially isolated, and become poor and emotionally disturbed. Even those without deformities felt uneasy in their communities and withdraw from some social activities permanently (Leerapun *et al*.,1989).

Becker and Arnold (1986) stated that the major origins of the experience of stigma for individuals come from social attitudes that are both discriminating and widespread in the society. The ideology of stigma is produced and reproduced processes of socialization *via* family, school, and the mass media. For example, children are socialized by their parents to internalized negative attitudes about certain stigma. When children went to school, they were taught not to go near a person with '*Khi thut*'[1] because they would contract the disease. Some parents had seriously threatened their children, saying that *khi thut* germs were highly contagious and that the children should avoid the patients as much as possible (Boonmongkon, 1994).

Leprosy Stigma in Various Contexts

Various writers have implicated historical events and practices in leprosy stigma. Firstly, biblical teachings perpetuated by missionaries associated leprosy with sin and uncleanliness; and people with leprosy came to be considered outcastes as a consequence. Secondly, the related concepts of contagion and aesthetic features of leprosy induced fear. Finally, twentieth century Western policies advocating incarceration of people affected by leprosy at various leprosaria due to the social constructions of the disease; also induced fear and ultimately stigma. Social constructions of leprosy are commonly guided by cultural, traditional and religious beliefs or myths about disease and illness, and many African countries, not least in low resource settings like India.

Too often, leprosy infected people are thought of as cursed or as blameworthy/immoral; and their disease well deserved. The social constructs and myths of leprosy are knotted with high rates of illiteracy and misinformation about the disease. Leprosy stigma is not only produced by local beliefs about the disease, however. The wider social, political and economic contexts are also significant. In many previously colonised countries, Government policies and laws on leprosy have lagged behind scientific breakthroughs. An example worth mentioning is the slow pace of changes in Indian leprosy legislation, despite the rapid decline in leprosy prevalence rate from 50.2 per 10,000 in 1994 to 6.2 per 10,000 in 1996.

For *Dalit* women, the situation is even worse, as they suffer from the triple oppressions of being poor, being female and being female *Dalits*. Leprosy is regarded as a chronic and progressive bacterial infection. It is a disease that has been characterized for centuries by immense social stigma. It is not the problem of an individual patient alone, but that of the society at large. Given the fact that stigmatization occurs for both males and females affected by leprosy, the lower social status of females, typical of many cultures, result in greater suffering for women. Both men and women were negatively affected in terms of their family and marital lives, women suffered more isolation and rejection. Psychologically, women appeared more vulnerable because they were deprived of personal contact with others in the domestic environment where they were accustomed to receiving their greatest emotional rewards. The study discusses about the negative social image of *dalit* women affected from leprosy: a lower social status on one hand and the chronic disease on the other hand.

Area of Study and Methods Used in Data Collection

The present study was undertaken in a leprosy colony situated at the outskirts of Sambalpur city. At the initial stage, the respondents were briefed the reason as to why and what sort of information would be collected from them. The basic objectives of our study were told to the respondents. They were also encouraged to ask questions to clarify their doubts. Data was collected from 72 dehabilitated[2] patients both male and female. Relevant information was gathered through interview and observation methods. Besides this group discussion was also conducted among the women residing in the colony. The research is more qualitative than of a quantitative type.

Objectives

Against this backdrop the study tries:

1. To examine the extent of how far does stigmatization with those affected with leprosy bring in differences in the social status between men and women.
2. To discuss that though the *Dalits* are socially excluded from the mainstream society—what makes the women to be more vulnerable than men.

Major Findings

Dalits experience violence, discrimination, and social exclusion on a daily basis. The situation of *Dalit* women in India needs special attention. The traditional taboos are the same for both *Dalit* men and women. However, *Dalit* women have to deal with them more often. *Dalit* women are discriminated against not only by people of higher castes, but also within their own communities. Men are dominant in *Dalit* communities. *Dalit* women also have less power within the *Dalit* movement itself. Women are active in large numbers in the movement, but most leadership positions in the organisations of local bodies and associations have until now been held by men. The women have independence in the decision-making process within the family and also with the matters affecting their own lives.

No disease has been more closely associated with stigma than leprosy, and it has become a metaphor for stigma. When the family or community knows that a person has leprosy s/he suffers economic and social losses as well as participation restrictions in the community. The impact of leprosy stigma explains some paradoxical preferences in the utilization of health services. Although, the availability of nearby health facilities is usually considered an indication of their accessibility and responsiveness to needs, concerns about disclosure of the condition may make nearby health services for leprosy too close for comfort. It is high time that we look beyond the integration of leprosy in the general health care, access to health care and the fundamental right to health etc. It is imperative that we focus specifically on the scourge of discrimination.

Discrimination against leprosy affected people has certain distinctive features—the misunderstanding of the nature of the disease or the psychological, emotional responses towards it that are often described as stigma and which result in discrimination. Many people still think that leprosy is a disease easily transmitted through touching, that if you are affected, the treatment is not perfect and the deformities will follow. This image of leprosy has been around for centuries, and it persists even today, even among well educated people.

Stigmatization occurs for both males and females affected by leprosy. The study reveals the degree to which leprosy patients in the dehabilitated sample area were isolated from family activities. While isolation was not widely admitted by either males or females, women were isolated more often from all activities. Women said that when they were restrained from their roles of cooking and caring for children they felt redundant in the family and decided to leave. Negative reactions such as fear, shame and blame prevailed among the people residing here, but these reactions were more frequent with respect to females rather than males. It is observed that females are extremely shy and initially seem to keep a deliberate physical and emotional distance between themselves and people they do not know. They initially kept an obvious distance from outsiders until a certain level of comfort was accomplished. Oppression often promotes emotional distance from others (Freire, 1994). Due to their repressive situation, they stated that they are frightened of candor and approachable contact with others in their life. This behaviour, in itself, generates a semblance of aloofness. Alternatively, this physical and emotional barrier can be eradicated if they allow establishing a trusting bond.

For leprosy patients, one of the most telling signs of rejection was indifference of others towards them. Patients who remained in their families frequently complained of this failure to acknowledge their presence, symbolizing their loss of significance to others. One of my respondents said, she was being served food in a dog's dish. Yet some women said that their husbands entered into extra marital relationships after learning of their wives' illness, but said nothing about it, their indifference sufficing to keep their partners silent and subdued. When they finally announced that they wanted a divorce, the wives had neither energy nor power to protest.

It is puzzling, yet captivating, to observe the women in the midst of the turmoil for existence. Their outwardly feminine facade has a fervent and unyielding approach to life that is not initially apparent to others when viewing them for the first time. As *Dalit* female, they understand their role within the home, community and the traditional Indian society. These women are mindful of the fact that, although they reside in an area that is less restrictive than others, they still must be careful not to overstep the social boundaries dictated by their non-caste, *Dalit* status. They are fully aware of the unwritten laws that preside over their life and are willing to act in accordance with the prospects of the community composition and the conditions of the system. Furthermore, as *Dalit* female they have experienced the hardships of being at the lowest extremity of their economic, as well as caste, layer. Kathleen Gough (1981) underscores how caste and class, as authority configurations, unite to hinder societal advancements for female *Dalits*.

Many respondents had developed severe deformities at the time of leaving home. Women's work tends to involve the hands, and if they lose sensation, things slip from their hands, they cannot lift heavy articles, and their fingers are burnt easily while cooking. Women play a vital domestic role, and even the thought of being useless in housework and cooking was associated with the unbearable idea of becoming a parasite. For women, the most difficult adjustment was refraining from touching others, especially their children. Women are accustomed to receiving reinforcement for their caring role by the freedom to touch and be touched. When afflicted by leprosy, patients were frequently forbidden, or themselves declined, from touching others, for fear of contaminating them. The loss of this intimate female right symbolized isolation and rejection.

Stigmatization and Marital Relations

Marriage is affected by the stigmatization of leprosy. These include chances of marrying, problems during marriage and ability to stay married, and possibilities of remarriage if the first marriage fails. The study indicates that girls with leprosy found it more difficult to marry than boys, and that they made more compromises in the choice of partners. Children of leprosy patients also had difficulty marrying and again, girls seemed to suffer more. In fact, 35 per cent of the respondents said that one of the reasons they left home was worry about the marriage prospects of their daughters. Among the 40 married couples in the sample leprosy colony, 29 households had both male and female leprosy patients. In the remaining households, 16 leprosy affected men were married to non-leprosy affected and able-bodied women. Four of whom were brought from an orphanage situated just outside the city. Only one female leprosy patient was married to a non-leprosy affected man who was physically handicapped due to a road accident. Male leprosy patients in the colonies thus made fewer compromises than women in the choice of spouse or companion.

It was surprising to note that the only male respondent whose wife left him, described in-depth the time when his marriage broke up. In this case, much pressure was put upon the wife to leave her husband. His leprosy was used to justify her decision, which was further strengthened by the fact that they did not have any children. It is even sad to note, that it was not only the wife's family, but also members of his own family that were persuading her to leave him. Her parents clearly preferred their daughter to divorce rather than stay married to her leprosy-affected husband, this in a society that regards divorce as a harsh fate for a woman.

More than 50 per cent of the respondents reported that they were married. The term "married", in the context of this population, is misleading. Those who reported that they were married were not necessarily with their original spouses. On rechecking, many respondents admitted that they were previously married and had left their first spouses when they became noticeably disfigured. In fact, most of the leprosy affected couples living in colonies were in common-law unions. More women than men reported that they were married. Data reveals that many women continued to say that they were "married" even though they were not residing together with their husbands and sometimes had not seen their spouses for many years. They did so as a security mechanism, both because it was psychologically comforting and as it protected them from the possible advances of male patients in leprosy colony towards them.

It is undesirable to marry someone who has been or is affected by leprosy. The gender implications of these findings are significant, especially in terms of marital relations. The dependence of a wife upon her husband is demonstrated in the case of a woman whose husband left her when he found out she had leprosy. She returned and stayed at her parent's house for the following ten years. She then decided that it was her husband's duty to care for her, so asked him to take her back despite him having remarried. She now lives as a house-worker with her husband, his second wife, their children and in-laws. She wants to stay with him because she wants him to take care of her. This woman realises her dependence on her husband and her status within society as a single woman, so would rather endure the verbal and physical abuse of her current situation than return as a disgrace to her parents' house.

The situation of girls in the colony is really worse. At least boys go out and spend time on the main road, listening to songs and watching televisions that are displayed in the shops in the market. But these girls do not go out. Boys brew and sell liquor and all sorts of people come there. If any of these girls is found to be freely outside the colony, the men would not leave them alone. Girl's mobility is restricted. Their world remains very small within the bounds of this colony. As a result, the young boys find them very boring as partners. In general, the girl's life is extremely complex, with multiple levels of oppression interacting simultaneously to determine their opportunities. While interacting with them some statements revealed their attitude of accepting life as it is (i.e. statements like, "This is the way my life is, I do not know what else there is."), these expressions are not due to ignorance or laziness, but it is their outwardly indifferent stance with regard to hardships caused by class, caste, and patriarchical power structures. It is an endurance strategy utilized by them to manage oppression.

Goldberger's conjectures on *silence* fit perfectly into this venue. Silence, in this regards, could be viewed as a positive response to daily obstacles. Their submissive approach to survival deflects from them rather extreme, yet subtle, methods of endurance. This development of silent 'knowing' according to Goldberger, seems to occur through life's challenges. Certainly, their progression in addressing daily survival strategies falls within this realm of 'knowing.' They have learned, directly, about using their instincts to uncover ways of silently thwarting the system that poses its dictates on a population that does not overtly question their fate (Goldberger, 1997). Experience and know-how have taught them to rely on their own abilities and not to expect anything to come devoid of problems.

Mee Lian Wong (2004) found that the mediating or direct factors leading to stigma were those related to people's attitude of fear and their rejection of people with leprosy. All the following four category of mediating, namely: (i) visible deformities; (ii) perceived incurability and chronic course of disease; and (iii) perceived infectiousness and perceived bad origin of disease have led to people's fear, rejection and hence stigmatization of leprosy patients. Waxler (1981) notes that leprosy has been used as a metaphor for "dread" including a mystical component representing social or moral wrongfulness.

One young boy in the leprosy colony narrates:

> "We do not mind that our parents are deformed and disfigured: we have accepted that fact. But do you have an answer to why I should suffer from a disfigured future? We have a literally hopeless and dark future. It is branded not by our potential, skills and dreams, but by stigma that our parents own and that is all that we inherit. Nobody wants to give us jobs when they take our address, but if we do not give our address we get no job. We will marry one day to one of the girls in this colony itself. So, there is no curiosity, no excitement. We know who the probable matches are and they are few".

Stigmatization has lowered down the social image of the children whose parents are affected from leprosy. The distinctive problems and needs of children of leprosy patients have received very little attention. Even though most of these children are not infected, they suffer from exclusion and severe deprivation in their daily experience thus having few chances for a better life. Special attention should be given to this category, in terms of assuring equal access to education, jobs and health care.

The transfer of stigma to those associated with a stigmatised individual, labelled, "inherited stigma" was found. Threats against the safety of a family were used to force the family to expel the leprosy-affected individual from the village itself. One of the respondents narrated his experience—"Then my villagers forced my uncle", they said "Your nephew is leprosy affected, so what will you do either you kick him out or you have to leave this village. That time my uncle requested me that I should leave this village otherwise he will be in trouble".

Courtesy stigma was also found to be detrimental for the prospects of marriage of unmarried family members. One woman believes as well as causing the end of her own marriage, her leprosy will affect her siblings' prospects of marriage. She also explains the actions, which are proposed to avoid any problems for the weddings. It was quite disappointing to listen to the narration of a woman—

> "They also said that if I remain with their family no one would come to marry them, if I am around, no body will be ready to offer his son or daughter to my sisters and brother. I had been to my parents' home a short while ago. During that time negotiation for the marriage of my younger sister was in progress. The family members were discussing over the problem as to what to be done with me, because if I am there, it could create some problem in the marriage. So, I should be kept in Lalgadh (secluded place) during the marriage so that the groom side will not know about me. They will not invite me to attend the marriage. They did say that I am married somewhere and because of some problem, I could not attend the marriage. My parents think that there will be some problem if they called me."

This reveals that courtesy stigma is also causing secrecy about leprosy to protect the future of family members. Finding of the study show no evidence of courtesy stigma leading to the break up of a marriage, but it was found to have prevented marriages from being arranged. When one couple was searching for a bride for their son, many proposals were offered, but nothing ever materialised. As the community had told the prospective families that she and her husband were leprosy-affected.

Another respondent was told to leave the village "...because it might cause problem in the marriage of [his] brothers and sisters. Evidently, pressure is placed on both the affected individual and his/her family.

Managing Leprosy Stigma: A Way Forward

Leprosy stigma is rooted in various contexts, and therefore, effective and sustainable interventions should have sound theoretical underpinnings with attention to these contexts. Interventions to reduce leprosy stigma are likely to be more effective if they are rapidly adaptable to the prevailing socio-cultural, economic, and political contexts; and are multi-strategic. According to (Floyd Richard and Gurungu, 2000) holistic multi-strategy programmes are more effective in tackling stigmatising attitudes than are single interventions and are therefore needed to address leprosy stigma in broad contexts. Interventions must be participatory, targeting individual, community and policy levels. Comprehensive needs assessment must precede programme planning which in turn must use appropriate planning models that encompass the community's concerns.

At the individual level, educational programmes must be targeted at health care professionals to address their prejudiced attitudes, and at people with leprosy and their family members. This is essential as there is evidence that when the family members of a person with the stigmatised condition are misinformed about the disease, it hampers the coping and adjustment abilities of the infected person.

Likewise, the powerful effect of counselling people with leprosy is important. Group counselling of people with leprosy has been shown to be time-efficient and productive in tackling leprosy stigma. Further, inducing empathy, according to Batson *et al.* (1997) for a stigmatised group member—in this case is a leprosy affected person—can ultimately help to improve attitudes towards the whole group. The impacts of the bodily disfigurement of leprosy on leprosy stigma have been widely documented, so development of leprosy control programmes that specifically target disability prevention will be a critical response to a widely appreciated need of reducing the effects of leprosy stigma.

In addition, interventions that involve socio-economic rehabilitation of leprosy patients are very important. At community level, health education campaigns must shed light on leprosy through messages that sensitively deal with the local community's beliefs and misconceptions while driving home the right information about leprosy to the people. The messages must be structured to make sense within the logic of the peoples' worldviews whilst they tackle leprosy stigma in broad contexts. At policy level, advocacy efforts must centre on a supportive, enabling environment that favours legislative and policy change. To ensure organisation of various information into a logical structure advocacy efforts must use a target-specific stigma-change framework. There is also a need to pay greater attention to the human rights violations faced by people affected by leprosy. Finally, implementation of leprosy stigma intervention programmes does not only require diverse and joint skills, but must also be commensurable with access to health care.

Concluding Reflections

The stigma of leprosy remains an ingrained element of society, with family and community based stigma excluding individuals from activities and interaction. There are clear gender divisions in these restrictions which conform to traditional gender roles. In India, women are considered as *Shakti,* since mythological times. Goddesses are being worshipped in the major religions of India, but still they are considered as weaker section of the society in India. This raises a lot of question about the attitude and our thinking of our society. Women, usually looked as a weaker sex and forced to play secondary role in the society and are often neglected, discriminated and oppressed. These discrimination and oppression have adversely affected the development process. And the worst hits are the *Dalit* women, who are oppressed among the oppressed. Their life has world of difference between theory and practice.

Government of India abolished untouchibilty, but the practice is followed in some parts of India. The practice of untouchability had virtually dehumanized a significant section of Indian society, that they lost their persona and all the basic human rights and fundamental rights. *Dalit* women are dominated by both *Dalit* men and upper caste men also. She has to fight against all kind of atrocities and poverty. Because of this weakness, physical and financial, she has to face two-way struggle—one in house and one outside world—which have both hierarchic and patriarchal system in India.

The struggle for the liberation of *Dalits* right ought to be treated as equal to the struggle for the independence of the nation. National independence cannot be complete unless all the segments of the society are free. The society has to change its attitude towards *Dalit* community. Celebrating "International Women's Year" and "The Year of Girl Child" will not solve any issues. Attitudinal change of the society especially the men and upper caste people is vital in ensuring a respectable status for *Dalit* women. The traditional caste system is disappearing, but is emerging in a newer and modern form, which is more dangerous like honour killing. The dominant and powerful will keep inventing newer means and mechanisms to justify their wrongs.

The situation of *Dalit* women in India needs special attention. Certain kinds of violence are traditionally reserved for *Dalit* women: extreme filthy verbal abuse and sexual epithets, violence including murder after proclaiming witchcraft are experienced by *Dalit* women. Since the late 1980s, therefore, *Dalit* women have increasingly felt and articulated the need for a separate platform—created, developed and controlled by themselves—through which they could forge their own identity, fight for their rights and find solutions to their particular problems as *Dalits* and as women.

This study offers a snapshot of the conceptualisation and dynamics of leprosy stigma in various contexts. For people affected with leprosy, stigma remains a persistent predicament and control efforts so far have not adequately controlled the pervasiveness of the problem. The study investigates a wide range of gender differences in the impact of leprosy. While both men and women were negatively affected in terms of their family and marital lives, women suffered more isolation and rejection. Psychologically, women appeared more vulnerable because they were deprived of personal contact with others in the domestic environment where they were accustomed to receive their greatest emotional rewards. The study highlights the importance of analysing leprosy from a gender perspective.

A gender-aware approach is essential for the consideration of the problems specifically suffered by leprosy-affected women and men, in understanding how local culture can influence local perceptions and attitudes and therefore an individual's experiences of leprosy. It is the institutionalized inequality of the caste system that underpins and reinforces gender inequality in India, rendering marginalized *Dalit* women particularly vulnerable to violence with impunity. Therefore, an understanding of the intersection of gender and caste discrimination incorporated into government policies is vital to ensuring that *Dalit* women's rights to life and security of life are respected and protected. The key to success in all these efforts will be a coordinated intersectoral approach matched by massive commitments by those affected by leprosy, along with Governmental and Non-Governmental Organisations. The involvement of these organisations will be a function of the economic, political, and cultural contexts.

Notes

1. It is a disease in which its germs are very contagious and spreads quickly.
2. Those who had to leave their family, community or job due to leprosy.

References

Batson, C.D., Polycarpou, M.P., Harmon-Jones, E., *et al.*, 1997. Empathy and Attitudes: Can feeling for a member of a stigmatized group improve feelings towards the group? *J. Pers. Soc. Psychol.,* 72: 105-118.

Becker, G., Arnold, R., 1986. Stigma as a social and cultural construct. In: Ainlay, S.C., Becker, G. Coleman, L.M., (eds.), *The Dilemma of Difference—A Multidisciplinary View of Stigma.* New York: Plenum, 39-57.

Boonmongkon, P.,1994. *Khithut*, "The Disease of Social Loathing"; *Anthropological Study of the Stigma of Leprosy in Rural North-East Thailand.* Faculty of Social Science and Humanities, Mahidol University, Salaya, Nakornpathom, Thailand.

Collier, J. Longmore, M., Brown. 2001. *Oxford Handbook of Clinical Specialities.* Oxford: Oxford University Press.

Deshpande, A., 2001. Casting off servitude: Assessing caste and gender inequality in India. In K.M. B.F. Winddance (Ed.), *Feminism and Antiracism: International Struggles for Justice* (pp. 328-348). New York: New York University Press.

Floyd Richard, M., Gurungu, S., 2000. Stigma reduction through group counselling of persons affected by leprosy—a pilot study. *Lepr. Rev.,* 71: 49-504.

Freire, P., 1994. *Pedagogy of Hope: Reliving Pedagogy of the Oppressed.* New York: Continuum.

Goffman, E., 1963. *Stigma: Notes on Management of Spoiled Identity.* Englewood *Cliffs,* NJ: Prentice-Hall.

Goldberger, N.R., 1997. *Ways of knowing: Does gender matter?* In M.R. Walsh (Ed.), *Women, Men, and Gender* (pp. 252-260). London: Yale University Press.

Gough, K., 1981. *Rural Society in South-east India.* Cambridge: Cambridge University Press.

Leerapun, P., *et al.*, 1989. *Health-seeking Behaviour of Leprosy Patients in Northern Thailand.* Bangkok: Mahidol University, Faculty of Social Sciences and Humanities. (In Thai)

Mee Lian Wong. 2004. Designing programme to address stigma in leprosy: issues and challenges. *Asia Pacific Disability Rehabilitation Journal*, 15(2).

Vincentnathan, S.G., 1996. Caste politics, violence, and the Panchayat in a South Indian community. *Comparative Studies in Society and History, 38*(3): 484-509.

Waxler, N.E., 1981. Learning to be a leper—A case study in the social construction of illness. In: Mishler, E.G., *et al.*, (eds.), *Social Concepts of Health and Patient Care.* Cambridge: Cambridge University Press.

FOURTEEN

INDIGENOUS KNOWLEDGE ON FOREST MANAGEMENT

An Approach towards Sustainable Development

SURESH CHANDRA MURMU AND SHREYASI BHATTACHARYA

> "Forests are the world's air-conditioning system
> The lungs of the planet, And we are on the verge of
> Switching it off."
>
> — ***Prince Charles***

Introduction

Sustainable forest management is understood to be a forest system which aims for sustainable yields of various products from the forest and is secondary to complete protection (Peace *et al.*, 2001). Sustainable forest management may be the only viable option of sustaining forests for bio-diversity (Whitmore, 1999). Indigenous knowledge is defined by Gadgil *et al.* (1993) as "a cumulative body of knowledge and beliefs handed down through generations by cultural transmission about the relationship of living beings (including humans) with one another and with their environment." Indigenous knowledge may often contribute to the conservation and the enhancement of bio-diversity (Gadgil, 1993). However, indigenous communities tend to be left out of the conservation management process, even though many indigenous groups not only live in the forest, but also rely on the forest ecosystem for subsistence. Indigenous communities may be best suited for conservation management as they depend on the resources of the forest, and therefore have a clear incentive to manage the forest sustainably (Ascher, 1995). Humans have been dependent on forests from time immemorial, but in the last two centuries there has been extensive degradation of forested land, which has produced a mosaic of natural and managed ecosystems in the Indian landscape.

Forest degradation can be a serious environmental, social and economic problem with the potential to adversely affect millions of people who depend on forest goods and services. Food and Agriculture Organization FAO of the United Nations (2002) defines forest degradation as: The reduction of the capacity of a forest to provide goods and services, though the perceptions of forest degradation are many and varied, depending on the driver of degradation and the goods or services of most interest. For example, a manager who replaces a natural forest with a plantation to supply desired wood products is unlikely to perceive his forest as degraded. On the other hand, his plantation is less capable of providing many of the goods and services that a fully functioning natural forest would provide on the same site, partly because of the reduced bio-diversity generally associated with plantations, which to others would constitute a degraded state. In a recent survey, Lund (2009) found more than 50 definitions of forest degradation, formulated for various purposes. FAO (2009) shows that many such definitions are either very general or their focus is on the reduction of productivity, biomass or biological diversity. Definitions that refer to multiple-use forests or multiple forest benefits may consider forest values comprehensively, but are more difficult to apply universally in a consistent and transparent way.

Forest degradation involves a change process that negatively affects the characteristics of a forest such that the value and production of its goods and services decline. This change process is caused by disturbance (although not all disturbance causes degradation), which may vary in extent, severity, quality, origin and frequency. Disturbance may be natural (*e.g.* that caused by fire, storm or drought), human-induced (*e.g.* through harvesting, road construction, shifting cultivation, hunting or grazing) or a combination of the two. Human-induced disturbance may be intentional (direct), such as that caused by logging or grazing, or it may be unintentional (indirect), such as that caused by the spread of an invasive alien species (FAO, 2009). The International Tropical Timber Organization (ITTO, 2002) estimated that up to 850 million hectares of tropical forest and forest lands could be degraded. The Global Partnership on Forest Landscape Restoration (GPFLR, undated) suggested that more than one billion hectares of deforested and degraded forest land worldwide are suitable and available for restoration. Forests provide a wide range of ecosystem services. For example, they protect soils from erosion; regulate the water regime; capture and store carbon; produce oxygen; provide freshwater and habitat; help to reduce fire risk (in the tropics); and produce wood and non-wood forest products (ITTO, 2002). Forest degradation, therefore, has the potential to adversely affect millions of people who depend, wholly or in part, on forest goods and services at a local scale, and billions of people who benefit from forest services at a regional or global scale. To bring to a standstill of such degradation, a sustainable forest management system is needed which can improve our national forestry condition.

The intense global debate on sustainable development and sustainable management of natural resources can be traced back to 1970s, when there was a growing concern regarding their depletion and degradation. Sustainable development is commonly defined as development that meets the needs of the present without compromising the ability of future generations to meet their own needs. Sustainable Forest Management encompasses all the three components of sustainability, *viz.* ecological, economic and social-cultural well-being. It has been defined by the International Tropical Timber Organization (ITTO) as the "process of managing permanent forest land to achieve one or more clearly specified objectives of forest management with regard to production of a continuous flow of desirable forest products and services without undue reduction of its inherent values and future productivity and without undue undesirable effects on the physical and social environment."

Increased pressure on the forest resources of the country over the last few decades has threatened the livelihoods of millions of forest dwellers and other poor people living in the vicinity of the forests. Indigenous people and communities living in forests and depending on them for subsistence number some 60 million people worldwide (Salim and Ulisten, 1999). Forests are their habitat, and provide their principle means of survival. For most forest-dwelling indigenous people, forests also have aesthetic and spiritual importance. These people see themselves as connected and attached to land, water areas and forest resources which form an integral part of their world, religious and cosmic vision and have multiple uses. Therefore, their notion of forests is quite different from the one, commonly held in national forestry department. As a consequence, reforestation areas or monocultures for example are not regarded as 'forests' by the indigenous people while with few trees are. Similarly, indigenous people do not identify with terms like 'management' to refer to the mechanisms that guide their relationship with the environment. Rather, their traditional knowledge which is acquired over centuries of interaction with forests and trees, generally leads such communities to relate their forest habitat in ways that protect and sustain the forest as a socio-eco-spiritual system. The forest is an extension of their spiritual lives. Their cultural security is bound up with the security of forestlands. Likewise, cultural and spiritual values of forests often determine the extent to which people are dependent on them (Van Rijsoort, 2000). Against such backdrop, the present study tries to find out the major causes those lead to forest based environmental degradation and tries to explore how the indigenous knowledge supports sustainable forest management.

Area and People

The present empirical study is conducted in a tribal village named *Pahadpur* in the Kusumi Block of Mayurbhanj district in Odisha. The village is also known as *Ichahghutu* (Literally *'Ichah'* signifies a plant and *'Ghutu'* stands for upland) by the local inhabitants. According to the villagers, the area is usually covered with *'Ichah'* plants for which the nomenclature *'Ichahghutu'* was bestowed. The ethnic composition of the village consists of three tribal communities namely Santal, Munda and Kolha where the Santals are numerically dominant. Total population of the village is 572 (male-302 and female-270) as per 2011 Census of India. Most of the households in the village are settled agriculturists but, forest plays a significant role in the day-to-day socio-economic and magico-religious life of the tribals inhabiting in the village. Other than *Pahadpur,* the two adjacent villages namely: *Angarpada* and *Dighiabeda* also utilize the forest and its products to some extent.

Objectives

Keeping in view the above perspective, the present study makes a humble attempt:

- To find out different types of Indigenous forest related knowledge.

- To analyse the major causes leading to forest degradation.
- To discuss the process of sustainable forest management and level of community participation.
- To highlight the threats/barriers to the preservation of traditional knowledge.
- To lay emphasis on the transmission of the indigenous knowledge to the subsequent generations.

Methodology

The present study is purely qualitative by nature and basically focuses on an in-depth understanding of the intricate Man-Nature relationship. Primary data has been collected through random sampling technique from 60 households among which 30 are *Santal* households, 15 are *Munda* and rest 15 *Kolha* households. Semi-structured interview schedule with open-ended questions were asked to both elderly and young generation to obtain the emic outlook on the forest related indigenous knowledge and its sustainable management. Focused group discussion was conducted among the village committee members to understand the entire forest management process. Few voices have been recorded to supplement to the findings. Information has also been gathered from the key informants for a comprehensive understanding. The study has taken support from existing relevant literatures as secondary source of data.

Discussion and Results

Traditional Forest Related Knowledge

Forests in Indian context are a part of cultural landscape linked to livelihood concern of rural and traditional societies. Most forest inhabitants and more specifically indigenous people see themselves as connected and attached to forest land and recourses which form an integral part of their world. In the present day context, where forest resources are rapidly degrading, traditional forest related knowledge has emerged and seen as an issue which involves all stakeholders in forestry management strategies, to ensure sustainability. For sustainable forest management, there is a need to understand how a human culture interacts with landscapes and shape them into cultural landscapes. The traditional management systems and indigenous use of non-timber forest products

(NTFPs) in forest management can be studied in cultural landscapes (Berkes and Davidson-Hunt, 2006; ICSU, 2002).

Mayurbhanj district is the largest district in terms of geographical area (10,418 sq.km.). Area under forest cover in the district is 4,392.13 sq. km. which is 42.16 per cent of the total geographical area (*http://oddistricts.nic.in/district_profile/dist_glance.php*). Interrelationship between the tribes and forest is reflected in the underlying structure of tribal social system in the district. In the study area tribal communities have classified the forest into three different categories on the basis of size and structure:

(a) **Buru:** High Mountains are called '*Buru*' in Santali term where big trees are available along with big wild animals like elephant, tiger, lion, bear etc. *Badham Buru*, *Ukam Buru* and *Ghusuria* are the three nearby *Burus* found near the village where the village people used to go for hunting. But now it has reduced as government has banned hunting of the wild animals. Villagers of Pahadpur go to *Burus* (usually Badham Buru) for the collection of *Saru Alah* (type of edible leaves) and *Hutar Baha* (edible flowers). Sometimes *Shal* leaves and branches (used as tooth brush) are collected from the high mountains collectively for a particular family especially during marriage ceremony or death rituals in the village. In the *Burus* while hunting and gathering people take precautionary measures with them as there is always a chance of encounter with wild animals.

(b) **Dumha:** The village forest is locally known as '*Dumha*' which is generally medium in size and its height is less than the '*Buru*'. Regarding the composition of plants; difference is not very much observed as all varieties of plants are available which are found in the Buru. Village forest is the pasture land not only for the studied village but also for neighbouring villagers. Wild animals like elephant and bear also occasionally visit *Dumha* in search of food, but do not stay for more than one or two days.

(c) **Dungri:** *Dungri* is a sub-section of *Dumha* which is generally covered with stone and very small numbers of trees. *Dungris* are believed to be the abode of Gods and Goddesses. Villagers usually do not cut trees from these small forest areas due to such supernatural existence. For instance, "Tuar Dungri" one sub-section of the village forest is believed to be the abode of forest God. When there is delay in rain especially in the month of June-July, villagers worship in the Tuar Dungri and request supernatural power to bring rain.

Since tribal people have been living in and with the forest from time immemorial, they have very clear and in-depth knowledge on it. By using trial and error methods they have identified different usefulness of forest and transmit it to their next generations. By making scientific analysis of their forest related knowledge, they use specific categories of plants for specific purposes. Trees locally known as *Saal, Arjun, Kauha, Atnah* are used for making agricultural implements, construction and repair of houses by the village people. Different types of leaves, fruits, flowers, underground nuts are being used for edible purpose. Some medicinal piants have also been identified by the local people. Names of some forest products which are used by the village people in the studied area are show in Table 14.1.

Table 14.1: Edible Forest Products Available in the Village Forest:

Fruits (Jo)	*Leaves (Arah)*	*Mushrooms (Ud)*	*Flowers (Baha)*
Ul (mango)	Hesah	Torman	Hutar
Amda	Kidu	Patkasagah	Matkom
Jojo (Tamarind)	Saru	Motam	Neem
Tiril	Miru Chupi	Kadhan	
Tarob (Char)	Hudhuda	Gitil	
Mandar	Neem	Bunum	
Meral	Muj	Satpuhti	
Soso	Sirgitij	Sim Ud	
Lupung	Rotepan	Murum	
Baru (Kusum)	Chaurij	Gede	
Bale (Banyan)	Hat	Tumba	
Role	Dhrup	Muchichanda	
Tiril (Kendu)	Khodam	Kud poga	
Loa	Kana	Bale poga	
Bhurudu	Kundri	Sarjom poga	
Merlej	Sinj	Mad poga	
Kud	Garudi	Putka	
Hesah	Hasa	Seta Putka	
Didhauli	Munga		
Podo			
Sahar			

Ethno-medicinal Knowledge and Practices

Forest of any kind is the store house of medicinal plants though knowledge on ethno-medicine is usually limited to the village Shaman locally known as *Ojha*. The common tribal inhabitants of *Pahadpur* possess minimum knowledge of it. Medicine men or *Ojha* play the role of traditional healer and spiritual leader in the village. Therefore, collection of medicinal plants from village forest as well from the Buru and its administration to cure different ailments is the primary duty of the shaman. The names and usage of the ethno-medicinal plants are given Table 14.2.

Table 14.2: Medicinal Plants Used for Curing Different Diseases

Local Names	*Odia Names*	*Botanical Names*	*Ailments*	*Parts Used*
Karibahu	Bhuin Nimba	*Andrographis paniculata*	Malaria, Itching and wound	Whole plant, leaf, root
Saparum sakam	Gangashiuli	*Nyctanthes arbor-tritis*	Stomach pain, fever & malaria	Leaf
Munga	Sajana	*Moringa oleifera*	Cold & cough	Leaf, bark
Neem	Nimba	*Azadirachta indica*	Malaria, headache and wound	Leaf, flower, bark
Karanj	Karanja	*Pongamia glabra*	Tooth problem, Wound and Leg injuries	Branch, seed oil
Baru	Kusum	*Schleiche Oleosa*	Rheumatism and skin itching	Seed oil
Suitam	Pijuli	*Psidium guajava*	Dysentery	Leaf, fruit
Wool	Amba	*Msngifera indica*	Sickling, gastric & *dhatu*	Tender leaves, bark, gum
Jada	Amruta Bhanda	*Carica papaya*	Purification of blood	Juice
Kahua	Asan	*Terminalia Clliptick*	Toothache	Bark and branches
Didhauli	Barakoli	*Prunus Domestick*	Throat ache	Bark
Kud	Jamu Koli	*Syzygium Cumini*	Dysentery	Fruit
Jojo	Tentuli	*Tamarindus indica*	Fever, dysentery and injuries	Bark
Murud	Palasi	*Butea monosperma*	Goiter, Stomach pain	Seed, Juice
Sinduari	Begunia	*Vitex negundo*	Rheumatism and believed to bring fertility	Leaf
Tandi meral	Anla	*Emblica officinalis*	purification of blood and better eye vision	Fruit, Juice
Akaona	Apamaranga	*Achyranthes aspera*	Rheumatism	Bark
Jojo Bandaa	Tentuli	*Tamarindus* indica	Diarrhoea	Bark
Bel	Bela	*Aegle marmelos*	Pneumonia, Loss of Appetite, Indigestion and Diarrhoea	Leaf, young fruit
Agnijhal	Agnijhal	*Clausena excavate*	Loss of Appetite	Root
Sengelsing	Bichuati	*Laportea interrupta*	Headache	Fruit

Forest and the Supernatural World

Village forest is believed to be the abode of benevolent as well as malevolent supernatural entity. They worship forest deities in the sacred groove (*Jaher Thaan*) along with supreme deities of the society during village level rituals and festivals. For example: Dilli Jharna, Ghantal Gada and Tuar Dungri are the places in the forest are believed to be the abode of the gods and goddesses. As mentioned earlier, majority of the villagers are settled agriculturists and studied area does not have the irrigation facility. Therefore, they have to depend on the rainwater for cultivation. When there is delay in rain or insufficient rain, it is believed to be due to dissatisfaction of the forest gods and goddesses. Village priest along with all the tribes in the village with musical instruments go to the places mentioned in the forest and propitiate the deities by offering (sacrifice of animals). They beat the drums day and night with songs (*Bir Serenj*) in the forest and many people are possessed by the forest deities which is very interesting to watch. This process in the forest is called "*Dah Sendra*", which literally means "Rain Hunting" or "In Search of Rain".

Besides worshipping the deities of village forest, they also worship the gods and goddesses of mountains (*Buru*) in the *Jaher Thaan*. For example, Ukam Halam (mountain Ukam), Badham Halam (Badam mountain), Athara Diuli (somewhere in Similipal national forest) and Lugu Halam–Lugu Budhi (mountain in Bokaro district of Jharkhand). The purposes of worshipping forest deities are timely rain, success and safety while hunting, collection of forest products and safety of the cattle population while grazing in the forest.

Traditional Ecological Knowledge (TEK)

Besides the knowledge on flora, the tribal people in *Pahadpur* have also expertise in studying behaviour of animals and birds in the forest. Though hunting is reduced due to the numerical decline of wild animals and birds, still then the people in the village use different indigenous techniques for it with the help of proper understanding of their behaviour. An interesting instance is found in case of *Gunduri* birds which are usually caught by the people in the village by using a trap (*Gundri Pasi*) in a cloudy weather. They are generally available in areas where there are small bushes. They do not stay in dense forest.

Inhabitants of *Pahadpur* have also expertise to understand the behaviour of a bird locally identified as ***Lipi***. This bird generally makes nest on the ground. This natural tendency helps to forecast the direction from which rain would fall. Her nest is like a small hut with an open door. People in that area believe that rain will never fall from the direction on which the door of the nest is facing. Such kind of knowledge helps them to repair their house when it is damaged.

Forest Degradation and Its Major Causes

Deforestation often leads to the degradation of forest land, by converting it to an alternative permanent non-forested land use such as agriculture, grazing or urban development (Van Kooten and Bulte, 2000). It is primarily a concern for the developing countries of the tropics (Myers, 1994) as it is shrinking the areas of the tropical forests (Barraclough and Ghimire, 2000) causing loss of biodiversity and enhancing the greenhouse effect (Angelsen *et al*., 1999). According to the older generation in the village, the same happens in the foregoing time when total area was covered with dense forest. But after the establishment of the village, the inhabitants gradually started converting the forest area into agricultural fields and the total process got accelerated with the migration-induced population increase. With the passage of time, the forest area which was once covered with big trees was gradually converted into the field for paddy and other crops cultivation. Growing settlement and expansion of agricultural lands are the key causes of deforestation. The findings reveals that mining, forest fire and *mafias* attack as the prime causes of forest degradation in the sample area.

(A) Mining and Forest Degradation

Mining is very intensive and as well as a very destructive process. Though it is not seen as a major cause of forest degradation always, it proved to be a lucrative activity promoting development boons which may attract population growth with consequent deforestation and degradation of forest resources. Mining is not only a direct, but also an underlying cause of forest loss and degradation. The area where the present study has been conducted is full with iron ore. *Badam Pahad* iron mine which is famous for iron ore production is situated 6 kms. away from the forest area. Illegal mining which takes place on a frequent basis leads to rigorous deforestation which is predominantly done by the local non-tribal people residing in the area. At present continuous intervention of local forest authority at a meticulous interval and vigilant behaviour on the part of the tribal inhabitants of *Pahadpur* have somehow managed to check such illegal mining in the village forest. As a matter of fact before five years a serious dispute took place among the villagers and people involved in illegal mining. It was observed that some people were trying to dig out the iron ore from the village forest. The people in the village made a combined effort to strongly protest such kind of illegal activity and seriously warned them never to take such an attempt.

(B) Degradation Induced by Forest Fire

In India one of the major causes of forest degradation is the forest fire and 90 per cent of them are initiated by humans. It is estimated that the proportion of forest areas prone to forest fires annually ranges from 33 per cent in some states to over 90 per cent in others. Repercussions of the forest fires have *Adverse Ecological, Economic and Social Impacts* (P.S. Roy, 2003: 362). In the studied area, surface fire is found to be the major reason causing deforestation in the village forest which usually takes place in the summer season. This is sometimes natural and quite often man-made. But big trees usually are not affected by this fire rather the small bushes and shrubs.

(C) Mafia Attack and the Villagers

Another cause of forest degradation in the sample area is found to be the disturbances caused by the local forest *mafias* who cut down the valuable trees during late hours in dark night and smuggle the logs fell from the trees. As soon as the villagers took notice of these activities they immediately took up some precautionary measures to protect the forest. They quickly formed several groups constituting of ten members each. They decided to watch over the forest as night guards on rotation basis so as to resist such kind of unwanted indulgence by these local *mafias*.

Forest Management and Community Participation

A noteworthy example on sustainable forest management is observed in *Pahadpur* village. The forest management committee in the village is found to consist of few elderly people in the village that belong to *Santal, Munda* and *Kolha* communities. The committee members are selected by a simple public opinion. The committee members always prefer to take opinion of all villagers before taking any decisions regarding dispute related to the village forest. If anyone needs a big tree for repairing or constructing house, he has to take permission from the committee members. It is the responsibility of the committee members to enquire whether the demand is genuine or not. Usually, the villagers are permitted to cut big trees (only one or two) when there is a damage of existing house. For the construction of new house they have to bring trees from the nearby mountain (*Buru*). Any dispute or conflict in the village related to the forest is solved at the village level meeting which is presided over by the ward members. If people from the other village caught while cutting trees, they are fined by the village council and not by the forest department. It is interesting to note that, when there is any instance of cutting of trees by the local *mafias* at night, villagers try to protect their forest by rigorous effort.

One of the informants Narsingh Hansda narrated the indigenous process of management:

> "We villagers always try to protect our forest as we find ourselves intensely fastened with it. One member of each family in the village is compulsorily expected to participate all through the day and night. Groups are formed comprising of ten members and their duty is to guard the forest on rotational basis. If any member does not participate without informing the head of the village, he is penalised with a heavy fine by the village council."
>
> *Narsingh Hansda, Age 55, Santal*

The above narration of Narsingh Hansda clearly reveals his deep sense of concern towards the protection of forest. While explaining the indigenous method of guarding the forest he also lays heavy emphasis on the punishment pattern regarding any negligence towards that duty. Thus, strong village unity plays a very crucial role in the successful management and sustainability of the forest. The strong feelings of Narsingh bring to light his involvement and initiatives for stopping forest degradation and natural resource conservation. He does not agree to any sort of compromise when it comes to the question of protecting their forest.

Forest related in-depth knowledge and its association with the socio-cultural practices have furthermore enhanced the relationship between man and nature. The tribal inhabitants of *Pahadpur* know sustainable use of forest very well. Various forest produces they use for consumption and selling purpose. *Tarob* is one type of berry which is found in the village forest. The seed of *Tarob* is very expensive. While collecting it from the trees they do not break the branches as they know that if it happens, that tree will stop producing the seed for one year. Same treatment is done in the case of *Baru* (Kusum) plant as the indigenous village people know it very well that if they also collect the fruit by breaking the branch, usually it will be unproductive for one year. Another example of such intensive knowledge and sustainable management is found with the plants called *Putus* and *Shirhi*. Tribal inhabitants of *Pahadpur* use these plant to fence their kitchen garden. As *putus* grow very rapidly and prevents other valuable tree to grow, the village committee put no restriction in cutting it.

The date and time of cutting *Shirhi* is always fixed in village meetings. Only two members from each family are allowed to participate in such gathering. Other than *Shirhi*, no other plants are allowed to be cut from the village forest in the stipulated time period. Any violation if reported leads to cash fine by the village council. Now, this practice has been stopped because of conflict occurred on the day of cutting these plants in the recent past. Dry small branches of trees from the forest are collected for fuel wood not only by the people of *Pahadpur*, but the adjacent villages. But only people of Pahadpur can participate when the naturally dried up logs of the valuable big trees are auctioned in the village at a very reasonable price. The received auctioned money is used to meet different village level requirements such as purchasing or repairing of musical instruments etc. During *Sohrae* festival each and every family is allowed to cut a medium size tree which is used as fixed pole to bind the cattle in the village street.

Threats to Preservation of Traditional Knowledge

Several issues arise when the question with regards to the threats to the preservation of indigenous knowledge in *Pahadpur* village is discussed. Earlier the strong unity and community sentiment among the village members are found to be the key reasons behind their success in preserving the traditional knowledge and forest management. In spite of being a multi-tribal village, the members always are found to stand together regarding any of the village issues especially during the crisis situations. Because of a strong network of kinship, the village people are found to share a feeling of unity and solidarity. But the advents of industrial and post-industrial era have now bred different economic classes in the village society of *Pahadpur* and widen the difference between them. In addition to that, influence of modern politics in the village is found to be another prime factor for the declination of the unity between its members. Statistical data discloses the very fact that, in the district of Mayurbhanj, most of the tribal villages have been divided into two/three groups as a result of political disputes. *Pahadpur* is not out of many of them where such division can be observed at rituals, festivals and other village level activities. This has also affected in the preservation of traditional knowledge and managing the forest successfully.

Growing accessibility of modern medical facilities and availability of non-traditional medicines are gradually decreasing use of ethno-medicines among the villagers in present days. The tribal inhabitants of *Pahadpur* are slowly getting inclined to the modern health care facilities available at the newly construct health centres at *Badam Pahad* which is only 4 km away from the village. Such growing practices among the villagers also putting latent threats in the preservation and use of their ethno-medicinal knowledge.

Transmission of Indigenous Knowledge

The Director General of United Nations Educational, Scientific and Cultural Organization (Mayor, 1994) defines traditional knowledge:

> "The indigenous people of the world possess an immense knowledge of their environments, based on centuries of living close to nature. Living in and from the richness and variety of complex ecosystems, they have an understanding of the properties of plants and animals, the functioning of ecosystems and the techniques for using and managing them that is particular and often detailed. In rural communities in developing countries, locally occurring species are relied on for many—sometimes all—foods, medicines, fuel, building materials and other products. Equally, people have knowledge and perceptions of the environment, and their relationships with it, are often important elements of cultural identity".

The indigenous knowledge in *Pahadpur* village passes on from one generation to another orally. There is no formal training or instructions given to the present generation regarding that as these are considered to be the integral part of the socialization process. Family, peer group and older generation play crucial role in the process of transmission. Such knowledge is considered by the tribal inhabitant of the village as their social capital or main asset which they can invest in the struggle for survival, food production, and getting shelter or to achieve control of their own lives. In a nutshell it can be inferred that indigenous knowledge for the tribal people of *Pahadpur* can be considered as an integral part of their daily lives as their livelihood solely rests on such specific skills and knowledge which are eventually essential for their survival. It is same in case of the inter-generational transmission of forest-related knowledge between the village members where again socialization plays a crucial role regarding the forest related knowledge.

A Santal inhabitant by the name Chatray Soren of Pahadpur narrates:

> "Our next generation are only able to know about different types of plants, animals, birds, mushrooms from us. They have developed both the forest and ecological based local knowledge from the present generation and also from their previous generation. Our forest gets very much intertwined with our day to day activities and identity since time immemorial. Such knowledge as a social capital has become a part of our survival."
>
> *Chatray Soren Age 50, Santal*

The above statement given by Chatray unearths how the traditional forest based knowledge is transmitted to the next younger generation. It reflects that the local knowledge on flora, fauna and all the different types of forest products are well known to the inhabitants in this area. This flows on to the next generation as they are closely associated and also involved in different activities with the elderly people of the present generation. Thus, it shows how indigenous knowledge is an important asset as it transfers specific skills which are very essential for survival.

Shamans of *Pahadpur* also play the role of medicine-men in the village and in case of identifying medicinal plants, their disciples are taken to the forest occasionally on an expedition. But it has been found while conducting the present study that, the administration of ethno-medicines by the shaman is gradually declining due to increasing and easy accessibility of modern health care services in the area. So, the knowledge on medicinal plants is found to be limited to the existing shaman and its transmission to next generation is also declining.

Concluding Remarks

Indigenous knowledge is the unique knowledge confined to a particular culture or society. This knowledge is generated and transmitted by communities, over time, in an effort to cope with their own agro-ecological and socio-economic environments (Fernandez, 1994). Indigenous knowledge is considered as the social capital of the poor. It is their main asset to invest in the struggle for survival, to produce food, to provide for shelter and to achieve control of their own lives. Most of the indigenous knowledge disappears due to the intrusion of foreign technologies and development concepts that promise short-term gains or solutions to problems without being capable of sustaining them. The tragedy of the disappearance of this knowledge system is most obvious to those who have developed it and make a living through it. But the implication for others can be detrimental as well, when skills, technologies, artefacts, problem solving strategies and expertise are lost. Forest in any indigenous society throughout the globe is found to be a part of their cultural landscape and linked to livelihood concern. In the present day context when forest products are rapidly being depleted and degraded, Traditional Forest related Knowledge (TFK) can only help in doing sustainable forestry providing larger economic benefit to the society.

Innovative forest management practices can help the tribal inhabitants of *Pahadpur* to protect their '*Dumha*' from various outer disturbances along with contributing in the maintenance of its outstanding beauty. It is very clear that there is much to be learned from the indigenous knowledge systems of local people. All the academics, policy-makers, planners should pay greater attention to this invaluable treasure of knowledge that is threatened by extinction. If we are to move towards interactive technology development from the conventional transfer of technology approach we all may have to learn many things from our village level experts, the *gurus* of indigenous knowledge.

Preserving and safeguarding traditional knowledge has assumed great significance in the recent era and a variety of initiatives are being made across the globe towards achieving it. However, urgent measures are required to preserve valuable oral or folk knowledge of the natives of

Pahadpur as it is facing a greater risk of loss and misappropriation. All these knowledge needs to be preserved carefully in order to achieve inclusive development. Thus, traditional knowledge and associated practices are recognised as having an essential role to play in sustainable forest management among the *Pahadpur* aborigines which also helps in their community empowerment.

References

Angelsen, A., 1999. Agricultural expansion and deforestation: modelling the impact of population, market forces and property rights. *Journal of Development Economics,* 58: 185-218.

Ascher, W., 1995. *Communities and Sustainable Forestry in Developing Countries.* Oakland CA.: Institute for Contemporary Studies.

Barraclough, S. and Ghimire, K.B., 2000. *Agricultural Expansion and Tropical Deforestation.* Earthscan.

Berkes, F., and I.J. Davidson-Hunt. 2006. Biodiversity, traditional management systems, and cultural landscapes: examples from the Boreal Forest of Canada. *International Social Science Journal*, 58:35-47.

FAO. 2002. *Proceedings: second expert meeting on harmonizing forest-related definitions for use by various stakeholders.* Rome.

FAO. 2009. *Towards defining degradation*, by Markku Simula. FRA Working Paper 154. Rome.

FAO. 2009. Sustainable Management of Forests and REDD+: Negotiations Need Clear Terminology, Information.

Fernandez, M.E., 1994. Gender and indigenous knowledge. *Indigenous Knowledge and Development Monitor,* 2: 6-7.

Food and Agricultural Organization. 2007. *State of the World's Forests 2007.* Rome: FAO.

Gadgil, M., Berkes, F. and Folke, C., 1993. Indigenous knowledge for biodiversity conservation. *Ambio.,* 22: 151-156.

GPFLR. Map and analyze restoration potential. Global Partnership on Forest Landscape Restoration (*www.ideastransformlandscapes.org/what-we-do/map-and-analyze/*).

http://oddistricts.nic.in/district_profile/dist_glance.php; Accessed on 10th August, 2016.

International Union for the Conservation of Nature. 2004. IUCN red list of threatened species: A global species assessment. IUCN: Gland, Switzerland and Cambridge, UK.

ITTO. 2002. *ITTO guidelines for the restoration, management and rehabilitation of degraded and secondary tropical forests.* ITTO Policy Development Series No. 13. Yokohama, Japan.

Lund, H.G., 2009. *What is a degraded forest?* Forest Information Services, Gainesville, USA.

Mayor, Federico (1994). Director General of United Nations Educational, Scientific and Cultural Organization (UNESCO). Retrieved August 18, 2009, from*http://www.unesco.org/education/tlsf/TLSF/theme_c/mod11/uncom11t01bod.html*

Millennium Ecosystem Assessment (MEA). 2005. *Ecosystems and Human Well-Being: Policy Responses*. Volume 3, Ch. 8. Island Press, Washington, DC.

Myers, N. and Mittermeier, R.A., 2000. Biodiversity hotspots for conservation priorities. *Nature,* 403: 853-854.

Nasi, R., D. Brown, D. Wilkie, E. Bennett, C. Tutin, G. van Tol, and T. Christophersen. 2008. Conservation and use of wildlife-based resources: the bushmeat crisis. Secretariat of the Convention on Biological Diversity, Montreal, and Centre for International Forestry Research (CIFOR), Bogor. Technical Series no. 33, 50 pages.

Pearce, David; Putz, Francis E.; Vanclay, Jerome, K., 2001. Sustainable forestry in the tropics: panacea or folly? *Forest Ecology and Management*. (172): 229-247.

Roy, P.S. 2003. Forest Fire and Degradation Assessment Using Satellite Remote Sensing and Geographic Information System, Proceedings of a Training Workshop on *"Satellite Remote Sensing and GIS Applications in Agricultural Meteorology"* held 7-11th July, 2003 in Dehra Dun, India Edited by M.V.K. Sivakumar, P.S. Roy, K. Harmsen, and S.K. Saha.

Salim, E. and Ullsten, O., 1999. *Our Forests, Our future,* World Commission on Forests and Sustainable Development, Cambridge.

SCBD. 2008. Subsidiary Body on Scientific, Technical and Technological Advice (13/3). In-depth review of the expanded programme of work for forest biological diversity. Accessed at:*http://www.cbd.int/doc/meetings/sbstta/sbstta-13/official/sbstta-13-03 en.pdf.*

UNCED.1992. *Indegenous Peoples Traditional Knowledge and Management Practices,* International Indegenous Commission Report.

United Nations [UN]. 2004. Traditional forest-related knowledge: report of the Secretary-General, United Nations Forum on Forests 4th session. DocumentE/CN.18/2004/7. Available via *http://daccessddsny.un.org/doc/*UNDOC/GEN/N04/261/74/PDF/N0426174.pdf?OpenElement. Cited 5 March, 2011.

Van Kooten, G.C. and Bulte, E. H. 2000. *The Economics of Nature: Managing Biological Assets*. Blackwells.

Van Rijsoort, J., 2002. *NTFPs: Their Role in Sustainable Forest Management in the Tropics,* Theme Studies Series 1, Forests, Forestry and Biological Diversity Support Group Wageningen, The Netherlands.

Whitmore, T.C., 1999. Arguments on the forest frontier. *Biodiversity Conservation*. (8) 865-868.

World Health Organisation (WHO), The WHO Congress on Traditional Medicine *http://www.who.int/medicines/areas/traditional/congress/congress _background_info/en/index.html*

FIFTEEN

COCKFIGHT AND CHAMPA-BIRDFIGHT

Adivasis, Farmers and Popular Pastimes in North-Western Odisha

UWE SKODA

Introduction

Travelling around in the winter months in the former princely state of Bonai one may encounter forms of animal fights such as cockfight or Champa-birdfights, sometimes also referred to as bulbulfight.[1] While participation is not restricted to particular communities, the former is relatively more popular with *Adivasis* and lower castes and the latter is a preferred pastime among farmer castes (*e.g.* Kultas) coming and migrating in the region in 19th century. Among the two, the bulbulfight is clearly less known and has not been mentioned in the literature so far, is certainly less widespread in Odisha and perhaps not as popular these days as it used to be if the impression of my interview partners is correct.

Talking about cockfights, one might immediately think of the Balinese tradition of cockfighting documented by Mead and Bateson [2012 (1942)] and analysed in Geertz's pioneering work, in which he unearthed various layers of meanings of an event, discovering the specific "intimacy of men with their cocks" [1995 (1983): 418] and considering it a kind of "sentimental education" about the "culture's ethos" (*ibid.*: 449). Geertz argued:

"What sets the cockfight apart from the ordinary course of life,

> lifts it from the realm of everyday practical affairs, and surrounds it with an aura of enlarged importance is not [...], that it reinforces status discriminations (...), but that it provides a metasocial commentary upon the whole matter of assorting human beings into fixed hierarchical ranks and then organizing the major part of collective existence around that assortment. Its function [...] is interpretative: it is a Balinese reading of Balinese experience, a story they tell themselves about themselves." (448)

Like Geertz's famous example cock-/bird-fighting in Odisha reveals a nexus between animal fights and the male domain in terms of participants and audiences, which is, however, not the main focus here.[2] Unlike Geertz, I compare two different types of fights preferred by certain communities and seen as a distinguishing marker on the community-level. I argue that the contrast between these fights taking place in close proximity sheds light on differences among communities particularly with references to three dimensions: (a) historically as a situation of a multiple cultural encounter in western Odisha that has shaped the local society since the princely state era, had repercussions on historically conditioned forms of societal integration, somehow persists despite later changes and is possibly reflected in terms of pastimes favoured; (b) in terms of caste values particularly impurity combined with social and spatial hierarchies; and (c) concerning the legality of such animal fights and the relatively ambivalent role of the state which is being ignored or challenged if required. Thus, the (displeasure of cockfighting and birdfighting is intimately tied to an enduring chasm between predominantly farmer castes on the one hand and an indigenous "tribal"/*Adivasi* population (*e.g.* Bhuiyans) and lower castes on the other, though this rift has occasionally been bridged by royal families such as the one in Bonai patronising and indulging in both activities. As Geertz poignantly argued: "Every people [...] loves its own form of violence" (*ibid.*: 449). Juxtaposing the two ways of fighting, which are more or less violent, offer collective reflections on "others" within a relatively remote society or even some Geertzian "metasocial commentaries" on such a chasm and its transformation.

The Cockfight (*ganjaa ladhei/kukraa ladhei*[3])

The day of Char Khai, first day of the month of *Margosiro*, usually marks the breaking of the fasting, which many observe during the preceding month of *Kartik* (roughly November) and particularly during the final five days of this month known as *Panchaka*. On this day in front of the Bonai palace an arena has been demarcated and fenced by the organising committee that also included members of the royal family. Around noon time the place is crowded with hundreds of people, their bicycles, because most of them have come from nearby villages, and, most importantly, their cocks—preferably slim and bigger in size. Importantly, they have not been fed—or if at all with very little rice—in order to make them more aggressive.

In the crowd some people are sitting displaying the sharp blades (*kati*) which they bind to one leg of the cock before fights—also known as "slasher fights" elsewhere. A fight is arranged by the owners of the cocks, who look at each other's cock and try to evaluate their chances. Or as the late Rajasahib of Bonai, K.K.C. Deo said: "you go round if you are interested in a fight. You look, which size and what size, height and then who wins, wins." All fights are equally important—there is no final, semi-final, main fight whatsoever. If a fight is agreed upon there are a few rules: 1. The owner of the winning cock gets the other cock, which might be dead or severely injured by then. 2. If the cocks do not fight at all—a very rare case indeed—it is counted as a draw. 3. If one cock manages to push the other out of the arena or one cock tries to abscond, the other cock is declared to be the winner. 4. The owner of the winning cock pays Rs. 10 to the organising committee—a rather nominal amount compared to the monetary value of a cock.

A fight usually starts by the owners holding their cocks respectively in their hands and moving the cock closer to the enemy. The speed of this movement increases with the aim to arouse the aggressiveness. Then, both cocks are put on the ground at a distance of half a metre and they are finally pushed by their owners into the enemy's direction. The cocks are prancing their feathers to impress their adversary, before they attack them. Some run straight to the other cock, sometimes they jump into fray. If they manage to pounce at the enemy they quickly injure the other with the help of the blade and the fight turns into a bloody affair. The fight may go on for quite some time until one finally collapses and a winner is declared. The winning cock is taken back by the owner while the losing one, if dead or almost dead, is just thrown to a side, where the blades can be removed again and where it can be picked up—almost like a trophy—by the new owner later.

The almost completely male crowd densely surrounding the arena is not only excited by the fight itself, but also by the betting accompanying the spectacle. Banknotes are held order to show one's willingness to bet on one or the other cock. There is a permanent shouting—partly to announce the intention to bet and in a rush money is placed just before the fight is about to begin, partly to push forward one's own fighter, partly out of sheer excitement and joy and partly related to the concurring alcohol consumption. Unlike the Balinese cockfights, betting itself is rather simple, both parties fix an amount of money and the winner takes it all. No complicated or sophisticated quota.

The atmosphere around the arena is charged and not all participants always agree with the declaration of the organising committee standing on the side of the arena. As Stefano Fulvio (personal communication) noted in 2008 while observing cockfights next to a cattle market in the neighbouring district and former princely state of Keonjhar: "*There is always a very tense atmosphere and often I found myself in trouble. A time when the competition-judge allowed me to enter the enclosure to take better photographs, the loser then had a fight with me.*" However, unlike the relatively improvised cockfights close to markets without proper organizing committees, on Char Khai in Bonaigarh the police patrolled openly and prevented an overlap of the fighting spirit from cocks to men. The event used to be patronised by the Raja earlier, is still performed in front of the palace and considered part of the tradition of the area with the police nolens volens accepting or tolerating the event. Yet, the later the day the more likely a fight is contested by owners and bettors alike, who have often consumed more alcohol by then and by 4 p.m. the gathering was finally dissolved.

The Birdfight (*champa ladhei*)

The picture of the bulbulfight, popular among farmer castes such as the Kultas, could hardly be more different. The day of *Makar Sankranti*, the 14th of January, linked to games in various places in India (Armstrong/Bates 2001: 192), is considered to be the traditional day for birdfights in villages near Bonaigarh dominated by Kultas, where around 10 a.m. a little ritual (*puja*) is performed by a village Brahmin at the *mandap* or village altar for ceremonial occasions and *prasad*, leftovers of the gods, is distributed afterwards. Slowly men with their small birds, known as *champa,* gather next to the *mandap*. The birds have been caught a few weeks before the fights in the fruit trees close to the villages or kept in cages. Around one leg of each bird (male and female birds are engaged) there is a small thread with which the bird is tied to the forefinger of the owner or a bamboo stick. To the thread a specifically coloured bunch (*kala bhaunri*) is tied—for the balance of the bird and for the recognition of ownership.

As in cockfights birds are not fed before the fight and the rule regarding the leaving of the demarcated arena by one of the birds – then immediately declared to be the loser—is the same. In fact, flying away is the most common way to decide the fight and in any case no bird is killed. In other cases, however, also the sitting of one bird on another bird, which does not move anymore, is considered to be a victory. The overall system is more complicated than the one-to-one cockfight. As a Kulta explained:

> "Prizes are given; only 1st, 2nd and 3rd prizes are given.... Here 100 birds will come, 50 pairs of birds. Two birds will fight and the winning bird will stay and the other will be left to go. Here is "ticket system". For one bird one ticket is necessary. See, there are total 100 birds; all will be kept in one place. Only two will be brought for fighting. The winning bird will be kept in a separate place and the other will be left. To the 2nd round there will be only 25 pairs. To the next round there will be 12 pairs and to the next round six pairs then three pairs will remain and at last three birds will remain. Out of three one will be called '*baya*' [mad] bird who will wait till the fighting of the other two will be decided. The winning bird will fight with that '*Baya*' bird. Those who will win will be declared as first, then the second and third. We have done this "prize system" only for the sake of "enjoyment"; the fighting of *champa* birds are organized for that."[4]

In this well-organized manner the names of all owners are written on small papers and afterwards the matches are determined by a lottery, which means that a "chief guest" has the honour to pick the first two sheets of paper from an earthen pot. Unlike the cockfights, the owner cannot influence the match. The rather nominal prizes includes a blanket, *dhoti* (traditional loincloth) and *gamja* (armless shirt) and used to be sponsored by village headmen (Gauntia), while now-a-days, an organising committee is responsible.

Compared to the cockfight the event is not only very well-planned, but also much less emotional. Alcohol is forbidden and so is betting. There is hardly any shouting and the men joke about birds escaping from the arena. However, all birds remain with their respective owners—even the losers. They are far too small for eating anyway. Generally, the atmosphere is rather joyful than tense and the absence of blades prevents any bloody birdfight.

Historical Encounters, Princely State and Societal Integration

In order to understand the different fights and perhaps even some of their structural features I follow a historical approach. Considering the farmer castes' history under and involvement in princely state/colonial rule brings up parallels to the fights' organising principle which is worth-considering. At present a Sub-Division of Sundargarh District in north-western Odisha, Bonai came finally under British control in 1818 and was officially ceded to them in 1826. Though relations with the British slowly intensified, Bonai remained fairly remote—a hardly accessible and sparsely kingdom surrounded by hills and tiger-infested jungles as W.R. Gilbert, A.G.G. Hazaribagh, reported in 1825 to G. Swinton, Secretary to the Government after travelling through the neighbouring princely state of Gangpur (now also part of Sundargarh District).[5] Gilbert did not just mention the want for cultivators and the way peasants were actually encouraged by rulers of these states to migrate offering not just land, but tax reductions as additional incentives. As Gilbert continues to report a military road from Calcutta to Sambalpur was already under construction, which, passing Gangpur, would make the area more accessible. Railway projects, particularly the Bengal-Nagpur Railway passing through Gangpur slightly north of Bonai, followed soon and farmer castes such as the Aghrias, Kultas, Kurmis/Mahantos or Chosas migrating into the region from various directions and now-a-days, settling in a high concentration in Sundargarh District as well as in neighbouring Sambalpur District seem to have made use of these new opportunities.

Thus, the combined efforts of British colonizers and local princes resulted in a constant influx of settlers increasing considerably the density of the population of the feudatory states of Western Odisha which almost doubled between the Censuses of 1881 and 1931 (Schwerin, 1977: 48). However, those migrants did not just occupy land but took up the headmanship of villages becoming revenue collectors for the petty Rajas.

As such, the search of farmers like the Kultas, Aghrias and others was not only instrumental for transforming a landscape—notably by clearing the forests and spreading plough-related intensive wet-rice cultivation—but also the state, here an emerging princely state, that could intensify its grip on certain areas with the help of the newcomer-farmers generating and collecting revenue.

The area Gilbert passed through was, as he noticed, sparsely populated by "aborigines"—*Adivasi* or relatively more autochthonous groups who had often settled prior to the arrival of these peasants. Thus, a situation of a multiple cultural encounters emerged including British colonial administrators and an older elite including the Rajas, rather industrious migrant-farmers brought in to raise the revenue and relatively autochthonous communities such as the Bhuiyans. The latter, literally "earth people" and first settlers, were considered powerful communities with their own militia and only loosely linked to certain Rajas, *e.g.* by offering tokens of allegiance to "jungle kings" [*see* also Roy, 1970 (1912): 199; Gell, 1992: 4] instead of paying substantial revenue or tax—occasionally rather "rebelled" against attempts to raise tax. Thus, their degrees of outside involvement or better integration into state structures differed considerably from the often wealthy and hardly rebellious migrant headmen and may still differ to a certain degree, for example, if one considers communities in relatively remote hill areas such as the Paudi Bhuiyans—classified by the Indian administration until recently as one of the Primitive Tribal Groups (PTGs)[6] (now renamed as Particularly Vulnerable Tribal Group).

The contrast between (Paudi) Bhuiyans and Kultas is rather striking and resembles ideal types in a Weberian sense [2002 (1922)], but the empirical situation is more complex with other communities such as the Kandhs, Gands, Bhuiyans etc.—considered *Adivasi*/Scheduled Tribes (ST), though not PTGs—in the plains and living historically in closer proximity to and were relatively more influenced by migrants like the Aghrias or Kultas. To complicate the picture further there also communities such as the Mundas, Orams etc., claiming *Adivasi* status and regarded as ST by the administration, but having their own history of migration under colonial rule too and thus, cannot claim an autochthonous status like the Bhuiyans (and to a lesser extent Gonds and Kondhs).

However, though the societal situation is complex in practise with significant differences between hills and plains, in terms of participation in the two fights considered here one finds a more clear-cut distinction.

Though everyone is free to participate in any fight—Aghrias or Kultas in cockfights, Bhuiyans or Mundas in bulbulfights etc. – and that itself may be seen as a sign of convergence in the north-western 'hinterland' of Odisha—migrant-farmers such as the Kultas, but also Brahmins etc. or more generally higher castes (classified as General Castes and Other Backward Classes) tend to participate in or patronize bulbul-fights, while Bhuiyans, but also Kondhs or Mundas (i.e. *Adivasis* or Scheduled Tribes), but often also communities classified as Scheduled Castes (SC) tend to enjoy cockfights more. This close connection might partly be explained by the fact that these communities classified as SC by the state have often lived for a long time in close proximity to *Adivasis* and in fact may be considered as integral parts of a larger tribal society (*e.g.* in Koraput), in which so-called *Harijans* (Pano, Dombo) have acted as clients and outside-mediators for *Adivasis* for centuries (Pfeffer, 2002).

Considering this history of migration and evolving princely state structures and the rather "ideal typical" cases of the Paudi Bhuiyans and Kultas it is tempting to relate it to the different organising principles of the fights, i.e. the contrast between the order of the bulbulfights as a very systematic arrangement with an unambiguous winner and less centralised cockfights. Such a contrast would be even stronger if one considers all cockfights in the region, i.e. Char Khai with its organising committee and patrolling police as a special, slightly more institutionalised and legalized version of what is going on otherwise during market days. Thus, one could actually imagine cockfights around the markets and the bulbulfight of the Kultas as two poles of a continuum with Char Khai was in-between, though closer to the more spontaneous cockfights near local markets.

Considering the ends of such a continuum one would find the cockfight pairs on one side, i.e. A is fighting against B in a way, which could be seen following Sahlins (1965: 144) as a form of "negative reciprocity", which he linked to social distance and also occasionally to violence. As Sahlins (1965: 148) writes:

> "Negative Reciprocity is the attempt to get something for nothing with impunity, the several forms of appropriation, transactions opened and conducted toward net utilitarian advantage. Indicative ethnographic terms include "haggling" or … "gambling" … and other varieties of seizure. Negative reciprocity is the most impersonal sort of exchange."

Cockfight for which people of different villages around Bonaigarh had gathered could fall into this category. Significantly, Sahlins (*ibid.*, 144) also quotes Oliver (1955) and Pospisil (1958) in this regard who mention that the negative reciprocity concerns often far-off people, those socially most distant, and particularly traders, believed to cheat anyway, figure in the list of those distant "creatures". Cockfights understood as a form of negative reciprocity may thus also offer a clue about the common link between the fights and local markets—often held at the periphery of villages rather than at a sacred centre like the Champa birdfight.

Looking at the typology of exchange Sahlins (1965: 141) developed one finds one the one hand reciprocity (direct or indirect, negative or otherwise) as a *between-relation*, which is contrasted with forms of pooling or redistributions termed by Sahlins a *within-relation*, i.e. a collective group action rather than an exchange between two parties. This group dimension comes to the fore during the bulbulfight when every participant is and agrees to be part of a pyramidal structure—or a redistributive system. The Gauntias or presently the organising committee redistribute pooled resources in form of prizes (*see* Fig. 15.1).

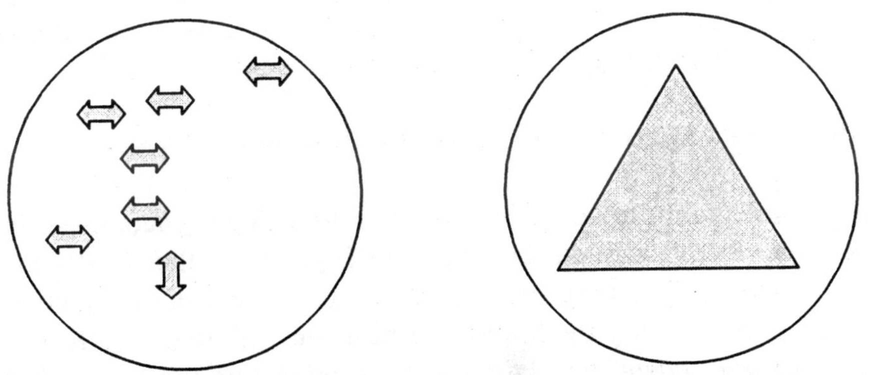

Fig. 15.1: "Atomistic" Structure of the Cockfights *Versus* Pyramidal Structure of the Birdfights.

Without denying that all communities are more or less integrated into structures of the modern state and "little kingdom"/princely state structures have largely been transformed, the kinds of fights preferred as pastime may well reflect historically conditioned forms of societal integration and mirror somewhat enduring ideas about societal structures. They may be seen as a kind of resilient metasocial commentary in the sense that the pyramidal structure of the Kulta bulbulfights indirectly correspond to the involvement of the Kultas into the princely state, i.e.

the Kulta farmers used to pay tax to the headman, the Gauntia, who then forwarded a share of it to the Raja, who in turn paid tribute to the British, but redistributed it at least partly in festivals patronized by ruler etc. Farmers like Kultas or Aghrias, and particularly their headmen as revenue collectors, but also village justices of peace, were directly involved in and part of pyramidal, redistributive power structures of "little kingdoms" and contributed to their transformation into princely states.

The cockfight with—to use Geertz's [1995 (1983): 248] phrase here—"radically atomistic structure" in turn corresponds to Sahlins (1968: 5) notion of 'tribe' being characterized by an absence of a central authority and a Hobbesian state of "warre"— that is, as the absence of an institutionally guaranteed peace and a lack of "a sovereign political and moral authority; the right to use force and do "battell", is held by the people in severalty". Cockfights around markets where everyone can let his cock fight against another cock, if the owner does not back down and without or with relatively weak umpires (or without organising committees or police to settle disputes) come close to such an idea of "tribe" or "warre", while (Paudi) Bhuiyans at least pledged allegiance to the Raja of Bonai and offered nominal tributes and thus, show some forms of relatively centralised authority which progressively increased historically with an expanding (princely) state.

"Small People", Spatial Hierarchies and Brahmanical Values

While the integration of different parties into a larger encompassing competition clearly distinguishes the bulbulfight from the one-to-one cockfights another feature seems to be of equal importance: a distinction in status, i.e. particularly the farmers despise cockfighting. As a Kultas argued: "*In our 'caste' we do not require wine (mod) and chicken (kukuraa). So, we never do the cockfights. In former times there was no play for enjoyment (manakhusi). So, they were catching the champa birds*..." While alcohol might be avoidable during cockfights poultry is obviously a must and here lies the crux as one Kulta-participant told:

> "We never touch chicken. …we do not eat chicken… It is our 'custom' that if we touch chicken then we have to change our cloths. If we eat chicken meat then we are driven out from the caste (*jati*) and only after observing due formalities, i.e., only if the hair of the head are cleanly shaven and sugarcane juice drink is given etc., only then we are again included in the caste."

It is impossible to say, whether the avoidance of chicken is indeed a strictly observed rule as claimed here or perhaps rather an exaggerated self-image of the community, but I think there are certain clear indicators hinting at the link between purity or rather impurity and poultry. Among Aghrias it is quite common to keep chicken in the house and also to consume them, but it was often mentioned that this was a recent development and in fact it was accepted as characteristic of their community lowering its status. Instead, *Malis,* considered to be a caste of gardeners, follow— according to the Aghrias (and my own somewhat superficial observation)—such strict rules of chicken avoidance and Aghrias accept it as a marker of their relatively higher status. In fact, Aghrias claim to have observed similarly strict rules regarding the avoidance of poultry farming but argue that in an age of general degeneration, the present *Kali yug* or "age of vice", caste members hardly follow the tradition. Similarly, many Kultas claim that they avoid chicken completely and link this feature to their status. This was clearly expressed in a group interview in which Kultas were asked about their participation in cockfights on the day of Charkhai and the answer was "no":

Ans. The "low caste" people are going there, because they are eating chicken.

Q. Lower caste means? Are they Kultas? [*as my Brahmanical assistant provocatively asked.*]

Ans. No. No. Those who are below the Kulta samaj [society—US], they were going: *Adibasi* and *Harijans.*

The statement exemplifies processes of othering and the role of cockfights as medium of distinction between "self" and "other". Not only the Kultas, but also Aghrias or members of royal families consider the bulbulfights as "well-cultured" and a "civilised" alternative or substitute, while cockfights in this perspective are something for lower communities, for so-called *chhot lok* or "small people", i.e. *Harijans* (*Dalits*) or so-called Scheduled Castes (SC) are presumed as "low castes" in the same or at least in a very similar way *Adivasis* are. However, the Kulta-interviews stand in stark contrast to the perception of the cockfight among *Adivasis*, among whom I never heard any excuses or any pejorative comments about cockfighting. On the contrary, in a press statement Golak Bihari Naik, Odisha's Fisheries and Animal Resource Development Minister, representing a reserved ST-constituency argued that:

> "the fighter cocks were the 'life and pride' of a tribal family. … a family possessing a number of fighter cocks were considered as 'affluent' and 'powerful' in the tribal community."[7]

While he stresses power and wealth linked to cockfights, what seems to be at stake here for the farmer castes is something very different: the underlying notion of potential impurity. Chicken are despised because of their diet, i.e. they are running around in villages and picking whatever food is available to them and thus being in contact with polluting food remains or even excrements. As a newspaper praising the fighter cocks noted: *The chicken are allowed to* scavenge *[my emphasis] for their food in the backyard—to build up that 'fighting' spirit.* [8] Free ranging chicken are linked to scavenging—a term otherwise used with reference to so-called "Untouchables" and their work.

Champa birds, in contrast, are believed to survive exclusively on a vegetarian diet consisting basically of fruits. Thus, a differentiation of animals and fights is ultimately linked to a hierarchy of food as a pillar of the caste system. However, the risk of pollution and contamination is also closely associated to blood and death. A royal family member who experimented with fighter cocks out of curiosity made this point explicit:

> US: Some of the Aghria told me, they were criticized when they joined cockfights, but fights with bulbul were quite alright…
> KGD: … because they never died. No blood.

The link between caste status and purity is also manifested in terms of locality and spatial hierarchies—at least from the perspective of the farmer castes. While the cockfight in front of the Bonaigarh palace, a multipurpose place, was somewhat exceptionally, most commonly they are held on the fringe of local markets. This link between *Adivasi* communities, cockfighting and markets has been frequently mentioned in the literature on Middle India with weekly markets being "well-known venues" [Grigson, 1991 (1938): 162], also Ghosh, 2006: 26; Hahn 1907, S.69).

In contrast, the bulbulfight is often organized inside a *mandap* or pavilion, i.e. a locality explicitly demarcated for temporary religious purposes and in one case I had accompanied the Bonai Raja a few weeks earlier to observe a festival for Krishna taking place in the very same *mandap*. And the locations of these two events are certainly not coincidental. The late Bonai Raja also narrated that his grandfather, Raja Nilamdar, being very fond of bulbulfights, had ordered to hold these fights inside the premises of the Jagannath temple, i.e. inside the walled temple compound and not far away from the open square, where the cockfight was organized. However, for the Raja it was unthinkable to perform a bloody cockfight in a sacred temple space.

However, while the fighting animals and the locations are hierarchized into pure and impure, it is important to keep in mind that everyone is free to participate in the all events and the collective norms and stigmata among farmer castes linked to cockfights, even the risk of being expelled from the community as the Kulta mentioned, may be overruled by personal considerations and the attraction of the fights. For example, occasionally Non-Kulta villagers from surrounding villages bring their birds for a relatively unproblematic fight, but Kultas usually dominate the occasions. *Vice versa* everyone is welcome to join the cockfights, but I found relatively few farmers among the participants. For example during the cockfight in Bonaigarh there were about ten people known as *katidar* renting out the blades (*kati*) to be bound on the cocks' claws. Out of them there were one Chosa, a retired teacher, and one Mahanto/Kurmi working for a bank. The others were Kisan, Gand, Munda and Bhuiyan—all communities listed as Scheduled Tribes. The Mahanto told that his son and daughter-in-law criticized him for his presence and charged him: "Why are you in this business? You are earning enough money, why are you indulging in this work of low prestige?" These words again indicate the social stigma associated with the event among farmers, but apparently did not prevent him from enjoying this pastime.

In case of the Kultas, I did not hear of any case in which the aforementioned sanctions after touching chicken were actually enacted—provided of course that the caste brethren come to know about any participation. This is also mirrored by a statement of the old Bonai Raja:

> "The bulbulfight is for those who are interested, that might be Brahmins etc., there is no blood. No bloodshed. And cockfights the Brahmins may also do, but through somebody".

That means that status-conscious Brahmins, paradigmatically linked to the value of purity, central to the caste hierarchy [Dumont 1980 (1966)], to which the status-conscious farmer castes subscribe as well, would rather not like to turn up with their cocks for a fight and would not like to be seen, but may ask their servants etc. to arrange the fight for them. Or it might be something which can be excused in case of youngsters only. As the son of last Rajguru of Bonai, the Brahmin family highest in status and also former headman (Gauntia) of a village, told me that as an adolescent boy he used to go to a nearby market to watch the cockfights, but as he added immediately: "Now, I feel ashamed about it." Such statements hinting at ideas of shame are reminiscent of Elias' (1976) work on processes of civilisation linked to varying degrees of affect-control, embarrassment etc. In fact, as shown in the earlier quote, the Kultas claim to be "civilised"—in contrast to the *Adivasi/Harijan*—by linking themselves to this bloodless fight of fruit-eating birds staged in sacred spaces and in this way claim a higher status according to brahmanical values.

The Ambivalent State: Fights, The Law and Contestation

Apart from the question of the fights' potential to integrate parties and apart from the just analysed distinctive caste dimension there is a third element coming to the fore: the (il)legal dimension. The aura of illegality surrounding cockfights— particularly next to local markets, rather than in front of the palace in Bonaigarh—is well-known to the participants as well as those staying away from it. Technically, it is primarily linked to the Prevention of Cruelty to Animal (PCA) Act of 1960[9] under which, as newspapers[10] also widely report, cockfights are banned. However, as I argue the "state" as a multi-layered institution appears in often contradictory *avatars* and is not just banning cockfights and promoting animal welfare, but is also valuing and protecting customs and promoting tourism. But let me start with the provisions in the PCA as the most important law in this context.[11] In the law in Chapter III titled "Cruelty to Animals Generally" forbids that any person:

(a) Beats, kicks, over, ever-drives, overloads, tortures or otherwise treats any animals so as to subject it to unnecessary pain or suffering or causes or; being the owner permits, any animal to be so treated; or...

(o) For the purpose of his business, organize, keeps uses or acts in the management of any place for animal fighting or for the purpose of biting any animal or permits or offers any place to be so used or received money for the admission of any other reason to any place kept or used for any such purposes; ... [12]

Furthermore, there are provisions to protect "performing animals" stating that: "*No person shall exhibit or train ... any performance animals unless he is registered in accordance with the provisions of this Chapter...*[13] Violations can be punished with a fine of Rs. 100 or even a jail term of up to three months.

Looking at the fights again from this legal angle, it is clear that cockfights violate a number of provisions of this law e.g., slasher fights could be interpreted as torture (a). And indeed, for outsiders the treatment particularly of the losing cocks may be rather shocking. Sometimes, they are just thrown to the side or as Stefano Fulvio (personal communication) noted:

> "I have seen a lot of drunk people [and] if the cocks were losing the fight, sometimes the drunk owners killed them [by] kicking against [them]"—*all aspects the law is trying to prevent.*

It is debatable whether any "unnecessary pain" might be also inflicted on *champa*-birds, even if the fight is usually neither bloody nor fatal. One may also wonder if the birdfights would require any registration as "performance animal", but in none of the cases I observed I heard anything whatsoever about registrations and people were hardly aware of any such law applicable to birdfights.

Irrespective of legal provisions, it is only cockfighting that has an aura of an illegal or at least semi-legal activity, which may not be limited to the PCA. Interlocutors among Aghrias told me with reference to cockfights at a nearby local market that part of the money earned during cockfights by a "contractor" who organised it was utilised as a bribe for the local police. However, despite that there were also eyewitnesses telling me about occasional police-raids and sometimes villagers lost their cocks which were tied somewhere on the ground before the fight, but had to be left behind in order to escape quickly, when the police suddenly rushed in.

Such incidents or raids, when the state tried to uphold the ban on cockfighting and particularly betting going along with it, have also been reported in newspapers when and an example from January 2013 may suffice here:

> "A special police team that raided the village arrested 20 people for betting over cock-fights involving roosters in a violent fight for entertainment in a village in Odisha's Ganjam district. Around

160 people had gathered in the ground to participate and witness the scene. The police team also seized 26 roosters, some with injuries, knives, 22 motor-cycles, two four-wheelers and Rs. 9000 cash from Alipur village in Aska area yesterday. The arrests followed a tussle between those involved in betting and police personnel, said Sub-Divisional Police Officer – [SDPO – US], Sarah Sharma. A constable was injured when the gathering started attacking the police party, Sharma said. "We managed to nab 20 of persons, while others fled from the ground", Sharma added. *And Sharma was further quoted saying*: "It's nothing but a high-stake gambling and cruelty to the animal. We have booked them on charges of practising of gambling and meted cruelty to the birds."[14]

In the same article it is also mentioned that "*Cockfights are a popular way of celeberating festive occassions in many parts of India. In Mayurbhanj, another district of the state, Christians observed Christmas betting over cock-fights last month*" and "*The sport prevails, even though it is illegal under the Prevention of Cruelty to Animals Act, 1960. But animal rights activists point to the lack of enforcement of the law.*"

The police may or may not enforce the ban on cock fights depending on the situation and on the people involved e.g., the participation of legislators as representatives of the state may have an impact here. If they are present and enjoy the fights the police may prefer to look "the other way".[15] Moreover, courts may even officially sanction such events and various such court orders have been reported from Tamil Nadu so that "Cock fight [were – US] held after court nod"[16] because they were considered by the court as "traditional games". Yet, certain restrictions were imposed *e.g.*, a check-up of all birds by a veterinary doctor.[17] While I am not aware of any such court order for Odisha, the non-interference of the state in the staging of the cockfights on the day of Char Khai in front of the palace was motivated in a similar way. It was seen, as also the Raja argued, as a customary event and police guards patrolled openly in order to prevent any fights between participants or spectators rather than raiding the scene.

In passing, one should note that not only the state tries to uphold a ban on cockfights —at least occasionally—, but other actors as well. If newspapers are to be believed, such a ban is also imposed by the Maoist guerrilla in Odisha, but with relatively little impact as the paper noted:

"despite the ban, cockfighting continues to flourish in public places of tribal Odisha and is the most popular rural sport."[18] And apart from Maoist groups animal rights activists such as *People For Animals* (PFA—*www.peopleforanimalsindia.org/*) championed by the politician and activist Maneka Gandhi[19] try to uphold the ban by staging demonstrations. Discussing the issue with the late Bonai Raja and mentioning the PFA chairperson, the Raja said: "Oh yes, [that is] honourable, but you see, still in the whole *Adivasi* areas it is going on. That is their sports." Thus, as the Raja pointed out, it had rather little impact on locals considering it to be a sport rather than a criminal affair and even many animal rights activists seemed to focus more on animal sacrifices rather than cockfights.

However, cockfights are not only tolerated occasionally by the state, but certain state agencies even seem to actively promote or indirectly patronise cockfights. On the official webpage of the Odisha Government one can read in a section of "Other Activities" of the "People" of Odisha that—

> "On festivals like *Raja*, *Dasahara*, *Malrar*, etc. wrestling, stick play and athletics are organised. Kite flying and cockfight are common pastimes on the day of *Makar Sankranti* [sic]. The people of Odisha in general are lovers and connoisseurs of art."[20]

Here cockfighting is neither morally condemned nor outlawed, but rather presented as an art or at least an indigenous pastime attracting and meant to attract tourists. And indeed, the possibility to "witness [a] cock fight at the market" is a central part of many "tribal tours" offered by travel agents in Odisha and neighbouring Chhattisgarh. They advertise not only visits to Dongria and Desia Kondhs, Gadaba Tribe, but also to Bondas as "the most interesting tribes [sic] of Orissa" but include cockfights into the tour schedules[21], while animal rights activists such as the PFA lobby for being "a responsible eco-friendly tourist", which includes rules like "Do not go [to] animal fights."[22]

Debates around the culling of chicken due to the outbreak of bird flu in Odisha in 2008 also exemplify an ambivalence on the side of the state. While the Government of Odisha decided to cull birds, locals were worried that due to the culling "unique fighter breed cocks"—locally known as *'hansli'* in Mayurbhanj—would perish. And it was the Fisheries and Animal Resource Development Minister Golak Bihari Naik, hailing from Mayurbhanj District and an *Adivasi* himself who opposed the Government decision by arguing that the fighter cocks were the "life and pride" of a tribal family.[23]

The ambivalent attitude of the state towards cockfights, however, is not a recent phenomenon, but dates back at least to the princely state time. Late Kesri Gang Deb (henceforth also KGD), then the senior-most member of the Bamra royal family (bordering Bonai) explained the policy in Bamra state prior to the merger with the Indian Union in 1948 starting probably under his grandfather Raja Satchidanand.

KGD: At one point of time cockfight was strictly prohibited in Bamra.
US: When was that?
KGD: During State-time it was strictly prohibited.
US: For which reason?
KGD: Cruel. It is a cruel sport.
US: Like in the Prevention of Cruelty Act…
KGD: …no, no, that was much before. Let's say in the 30s. 20s or 30s, since then cockfights were strictly prohibited. And after the state merged cockfight restarted and all that. But the bulbul fight was never prevented.

In this interview he then went on describing how progressive Bamra state was having the first hydroelectric power plant in Odisha, the first printing press etc. and I tend to believe that he wanted to present his family in the light of these "progressive" innovations and considered the cockfight "cruel" or indirectly as "backward", though he also mentioned his own experiments with and curiosity for cockfights.

Thus, the legal status of cockfights in princely Odisha seems to have differed from state to state, but also from ruler to ruler. Contrary to Bamra, the Raja in Bonai—as neighbouring state very close-by—did, according to his son, the late Raja K.K.C. Deo, enjoy cockfights and encouraged his relatives to participate with his own cocks and their own cocks. At the same time his grandfather was apparently fond of bulbulfights and held them on many occasions. Thus, in Bonai the royal family seems to have indulged in and participated in both kinds of event and as such may have rather bridged an apparent gap between indigenous population and newcomer-farmers here.

In rejecting cockfights many Aghria and Kulta farmers have a lot in common and it might be linked to their already mentioned role as revenue collectors in these princely states, i.e. they also despise cockfights simply because they are not fully legal. Adherence to the law or not coming into conflict with law agencies seems to be a value as such specifically for village headmen or Gauntias who were historically appointed by the ruler and part of the—though not very elaborate—bureaucratic structures of the former princely states. As Gauntia they also acted—and in many cases still act—as justices of peace in village matters. As some told me, for them as Gauntia it was a shame to call the police or outside forces if they were unable to control their own village affairs—in fact calling the police from outside was coming close to admit that one was unable to fulfil the role of village headman properly. Aghrias, Kultas and others were implicated into state structures in a way *Adivasi* communities were usually not and this ethos might have a persisting effect.

In contrast, rather than subscribing to the law and staying away from cockfights as most member of farmer tend to do, *Adivasis* may rather contest the law, stressing their own customs and complaining about forms of discrimination and economic disparities as an incident or rather anecdote indicates narrated by the late Raja of Bonai. According to him—and I am paraphrasing his account here—the cockfight has a long tradition in the former princely states of western Odisha, but was prohibited after merger. There were many accidents because of the sharp blades bound to the cocks' claws and because of the simultaneous consumption of alcohol. It was simple considered as being too dangerous. The new law prohibiting the fights was strongly disapproved by the *Adivasi*, the main participants of the cockfights. Therefore, they decided to send a delegation of four Majhi to Delhi to meet Pundit Nehru. He offered biscuits and asked: "Anything I can do for you?" The speaker of the group, an eloquent matriculate—an exception among *Adivasi* as the Raja emphasized—replied:

> "We were all happy about the Indian independence, the freedom of the country and the unity of the country under one flag. However, he added, did we really become free, if we are not allowed to follow our traditional customs such as the cockfight? Our ancestors and these Rajas and their ancestors, always we had cockfights for one month or something and suddenly the new government has stopped it. Of course, these fights are dangerous, but what in life is totally safe?

Even while taking a walk, one can have an accident. And alcohol simply belongs to our culture. To every new-born baby out of joy the mother gives a drop of *mahuli* (liqueur made of *mahua*-flowers) on the lips and then we celebrate and dance. Is the new freedom only holding true for the rich, who are allowed to enjoy dog racing and horse racing, who may bet on these occasions as they wish, who may play cards etc. What about us, the *Adivasi*? You should not interfere. Rich people, who have money and power, everything is excused in their case, but we poor *Adivasi* people, we are proud *Adivasi* people, why shall we be deprived of our rights?" And they said: "In the eyes of law everybody should be the same." And Nehru: "I agree. I am a barrister myself." "Sir, in the clubs how people get drunk. If we, the *Adivasi* drink, what is the harm? We canot afford to drink foreign liqueur in the hotel. So, if we drink in our own ways is there any harm? That's number one. And what about greyhound races and horse racing? There is a lot of gambling there and there is no bar to it. Why our sports? Why there is a bar? And security? Everywhere is insecurity." Nehru listened and agreed and sent an order to the Odishan Chief Minister Mahtab: "Do not stop *Adivasi*, do not stop cockfights. Legalize the cockfights again." This account, whether true or not, certainly portrays Nehru as benign but distant representative of the state and interestingly illustrates a perceived nexus between cockfights, alcohol and betting on the one hand and tradition, custom or what Orans (1965: 7ff) once called an *Adivasi* "pleasure complex" on the other, but also a certain assertiveness and willingness to challenge the state—whether by sending a delegation or by simply continuing to stage fights despite a ban.

Conclusion

While an individual might be passionate about a particular type of animal fight and may therefore disregard norms there are clear collective preferences. Farmer castes tend to indulge in the birdfights, while *Adivasis* rather prefer cockfights. Despite legal ambiguities especially around cockfights these animal fights continue to flourish in western Odisha. Thus, the two types of fights introduced here differ to a great extent in performance, but also participants and audiences, though generally predominantly male. The cockfight having characteristics of a "real", a bloody fight, a battle over life and death without centricity in Polanyi's terms, stands in contrast to the bulbulfight, which—though also considered to be fight (*ladhei*)—may be rather seen as a match, a competition of sportsmen comparing their power and strength without killing each other. Compared to the cockfight the bulbulfight appears to be a kind of domesticated or tamed variant of the former.

The collective preferences for either of them could be explained through a combination of three overlapping dimensions: a historical, a caste and a legal one. Firstly, the historically conditioned different position of the communities differ significantly, i.e. a relatively more autochthonous population nominally acknowledging a Raja *versus* farmers migrating into the area. The preferences for the fights and their integrative potential, especially the pyramidal structure of the bulbulfight, shows interesting parallels to the societal position of the farmers and their headmen being strongly involved in emerging princely state structures with similar forms. Secondly, particularly in the perspective of the farmers the fights are hierarchized and bulbulfights are preferred because they are in line with Brahmanical ideas, i.e. potentially polluted chicken are avoided, purified spaces are chosen and people engaging in cockfights are generally considered "small" or "low", while *Adivasi* not following this logic see ownership of roosters rather as a sign of wealth and pride. The farmers' migration seems to have led not only to an expansion of the state, but also to an endorsement of caste values thereby turning the way of fighting into a game of status. Thirdly, the legal side and the ambivalent involvement of the modern state, banning it through the Prevention of Cruelty to Animals Act, but also partially protecting or tolerating it as customary, has an impact on the fights, influences the preferences and distinguishes the involvement of the communities with *Adivasis* ignoring bans or even challenging the state's right to impose it in the first place. Thus, the animal fights may well be understood as "dramatizations of social structure" (Guggenheim, 1994: 159) and particularly by juxtaposing these co-existing fights seem to reveal even a "metasocial commentary" on a societal chasm and transformations in a relatively remote area.

Notes

1. I also heard about, but never witnessed other fights such as *titer ladhei* or partridge fight. Generally, animal fights as pastime have a long tradition in India and are known from the courts of the Moghuls.
2. *See* also Dundes 1994 on this nexus.
3. *Kukraa* signifies "chicken" referring to cocks and hens alike. However, in the context of fighting it only refers to cocks, for which the term *ganjaa* is used more specifically.

4. The names have been omitted.
5. Miscellaneous Despatch Book from 26th September, 1822 to 4th May, 1826.
6. *http://tribal.nic.in/index1.html*—accessed on 22/03/05.
7. *See The Tribune, http://www.tribuneindia.com/2008/20080208/nation.htm#8*, accessed on 15-04-2008. His comments were made in the wake of a bird flu epidemic and in order to avoid the culling of chicken.
8. *See The Telegraph, http://www.telegraphindia.com/1080211/jsp/nation/story_8885973.jsp*, accessed on 14-04-2008, *see* also *The Hindu, http://www.hindu.com/2008/02/08/stories/2008020857250300.htm*, accessed on 14/04/08.
9. See *www.mp.gov.in/veterinaryanddairy/12crueltyact.doc*—accessed 14-04-08.
10. For example, *Sunday Times of India,* Bhubaneshwar-National, 21-12-03, p. 12.
11. The NGO "People For Animals" lists on its webpage other laws protecting animals, but the PCA seems to be the most relevant in this context. *See* also *http://www.peopleforanimalsindia.org/animal-protection-laws-a-judgments/65-animal-protection-laws-in-india.html*—accessed 07-11-2013.
12. See *www.mp.gov.in/veterinaryanddairy/12crueltyact.doc*—accessed 14.04.08.
13. *Ibid.*
14. *http://southasia.oneworld.net/news/twenty-arrested-in-cock-fight-betting-case#.Uni7vOKr8SU* – accessed 05-11-2013.
15. Such an incident was reported in the following way: "In neighbouring Andhra Pradesh, for instance, several legislators cheered on as cock-fights took place. The police looked the other way."—*http://southasia.oneworld.net/news/twenty-arrested-in-cock-fight-betting-case#.Uni7vOKr8SU* – accessed 05-11-2013.
16. *http://articles.timesofindia.indiatimes.com/2013-07-23/madurai/40747745_1_court-nod-court-orders-birds*—accessed 05-11-2013.
17. *Ibid.*
18. Interestingly, the cockfights are not only condemned by the state, but also banned by the Maoist guerrilla very active in the region and controlling various tracts in Middle India. *See Indian Express*, BBSR edition, 09-11-06, p. 5 and *http://www.rediff.com/news/2006/nov/09Odisha.htm*, accessed 14-04-08.
19. Second, in later years enstranged daughter-in-law of Indira Gandhi and wife of Sanjay Gandhi, grandson of Nehru.
20. *http://Odishagov.nic.in/people/other.htm*—accessed on 14-04-2008.
21. Watching cockfights is part of the itinerary of various travel agents offering trips to Middle India, *see* e.g. *http://www.aetravel.com/india_tribal_tours/Odisha_tribal_tour.html*, accessed 14/04/08.
22. *http://www.peopleforanimalsindia.org/articles-by-maneka-gandhi/1269-how-to-be-a-responsible-eco-friendly-tourist.html*—accessed 05-11-2013.
23. Another case in point for an ambiguity on the side of the state was the recent discussion whether all chicken in northern Odisha bordering West Bengal should be culled or whether the unique species of fighter cocks so valued among certain tribal communities should be spared because of a tradition. *See* e.g. *The Telegraph, http://www.telegraphindia.com/1080211/jsp/nation/story_8885973*.jsp, accessed on 14.04.2008, *see* also *The Hindu, http://www.hindu.com/2008/02/08/stories/2008020857250300.htm*, accessed on 14-04-08.

References

Bates, C. and G. Armstrong, 2001. Selves and others: reflections on sport in South Asia, In: *Contemporary South Asia*, Vol. 10, No. 2: 191-205.

Bateson, G. and M. Mead, 2012 [1942]. Balinese Character: A Photographic Analysis, in antonius C.G.M. Bobben and Jeffrey A. Sluka (eds.), *Ethnographic Fieldwork: An Anthropological Reader,* pp. 450-64. Oxford: Wiley-Blackwell.

Dumont, L., 1980 [1966]. *Homo Hierarchicus. The Caste System and Its Implications,* Chicago: Chicago University Press.

Dundes, A. (ed.) 1994. *The Cockfight—A Casebook,* Madison: University of Wisconsin Press.

Elias, N., 1976. *Uber den Prozeb der Zivilisation: soziogenetische und psychogenetische Untersuchungen*, Frankfurt/M.: Suhrkamp.

Geertz, C., 1995 [1983]. "Deep Play": Bemerkungen zum balinesischen Hahnenkampf, In: *Ibid.* Dichte Beschreipung, Frankfurt/M.: Suhrkamp.

Ghosh, Abjik (2006). *The World of the Oraon: Their Symbols in Time and Space.* Delhi: Manohar Publishers.

Grigosn, W., 1991 [1938]. *The Maria Gonds of Bastar,* Delhi: Vanya Prakashan.

Guggenheim, S. (1994). Cock or Bull: Cockfighting, Social Structure, and Political Commentary in the Philippines, In: Dundes, A. (ed.). *The Cockfight—A Casebook,* Madison: University of Wisconsin Press.

Han, F., 1907. *Einfuhrung in das Gebiet der Kol-Mission*, Gutersloh: Bertelsmann.

Orans, M., 1965. *The Santal: A Tribe in Search of a Great Tradition,* Detroit: Wayne State University Press.

Pfeffer, G., 2002. The Structure of Middle Indian Tribal Society Compared, In: Preffer, G./Behera, D. "Contemporary Society: Tribal Studies", Vol. 5, *Concept of Tribal Society*, New Delhi: Concept Publishing Company.

Polanyi, K., 1968 [1957]. The Economy as Instituted Process, In: LeClair Jr. E.E./ Scheider, H.K. (ed.) "*Economic Anthropology, Reading in Theory and Analysis*", New York: Holt Rinehart and Winston.

Sahlins, M.D., 1965. On the Sociology of Primitive Exchange, In: *The Relevance of Models for Social Anthropology*, ASA Monographs, Vol. 1, London: Tavistock.

Sahlins, M.D., 1968. *Tribesmen, Englewood Cliffs: Foundations of Modern Anthropology Series.*

Weber, M., 2002 [1922]. *Wirtschaft und Gesellschaft: Grundriss der verstehenden Soziologie*, Tubingen: Mohr Siebeck.

AFTERWORD

To Deepak with blessings

In 1996 and 1997, on the verge of superannuation, when Deepak Kumar Behera, a former student and latter a colleague in the Department of Anthropology, Sambalpur University, and my esteemed friend Professor Georg Pfeffer of the Free University of Berlin, brought out three volumes of research papers contributed by scholars from all-over the globe in my honour; I hardly imagined that I would be alive this long to associate myself with their Felicitation volumes, two decades later, I am grateful to God Almighty for keeping in working condition for this honour and auspicious task.

When I joined Sambalpur University in 1976, as the Professor and Head of the newly established Department of Sociology and Social Anthropology, I had already taught at the University of Gauhati for about a decade and a half. My students, in sixties and early seventies, were from my age group. They were like friends. From the late seventies, eighties and nineties, with the exit of old students and the entry of new, they were increasingly from the age group of my children.

Deepak, his classmates and the following batches were not old enough to be treated as friends, or young enough to be looked upon as children. In the resultant situation, depending on the situation, sometimes I treated them as friends and sometimes as children. This resilience in inter-personal relationship, I had learnt from two of my unforgettable Father-like teachers; Professor S.V. Ramayya, in the college and Professor A. Aiyappan in the University. Deepak was found to be equally resilient in playing the dual role.

In the best tradition of the Indian teaching-learning process, a teacher's desire is to be overtaken by his students in the achievement index. I am not fortunate enough to give this honour to my teachers; but fortunate enough to be overtaken by some of my students. Deepak tops the list. May he live long to be associated with the felicitation of his superannuated students.

S.N. Ratha

INDEX